CARLYLE
TO " THE FRENCH REVOLUTION "

This is the best likeness of Carlyle before he let his beard grow in 1854. The original drawing by Samuel Laurence is in the Carlyle House, 24, Cheyne Row, Chelsea. The grand-daughter of John Sterling presented it, and said that her grand-father had been so delighted with it that he would not let it stay in the studio for the artist's finishing touches, lest these might diminish the likeness, and so he carried the picture home himself: which was quite in the style of John Sterling.

CARLYLE

TO

"THE FRENCH REVOLUTION"

(1826—1837)

BY

DAVID ALEC WILSON

LONDON
KEGAN PAUL, TRENCH, TRUBNER & CO., LTD.
NEW YORK : E. P. DUTTON & CO.

1924

[*Printed in Great Britain*]

Fox, Jones & Co., Kemp Hall Press, High Street, Oxford.

PREFACE

NO apology is needed for the spacious quotations here from the letters of Francis Jeffrey. He was one of the most amiable public men in our history and greatly influenced Carlyle. He was like a spiritual father or elder brother, and it would be difficult to match the candour with which he laboured to deliver Carlyle from conceit, which is the besetting sin of " successful " students, and from priggishness, caught from rustic pharisees. At the same time he taught by example more than precept the best of the gospel of silence, tabooing ill-natured gossip.

There was a three years' break in their friendship because of a misunderstanding here explained, but never cleared up while they lived. Then their mutual goodwill drew them together again ; and in the nineties of the last century there were still old men alive in Edinburgh who had seen them together, and assured me they never saw two men more plainly devoted to each other. Jeffrey deserved well of his country in many ways, as a pioneer in criticism and political reform ; but none of his works of merit deserves more honour than what he did for Carlyle, for the pleasure of helping his friend.

His grand-daughter, Miss Empson, to whom we owe permission to quote these letters, which was refused to Mr. Froude, was one of many who have helped this work, but died before it began to appear. Another was Laurence Anderson of Ayr, who indicated for revision anything written or quoted which might pain the pious. He died on 23.8.1923, in his ninetieth year, by which time this volume had long been in its final form, and most of the rest of the work, in a less finished condition, had received his criticism.

To Mr. Lumsden, the Secretary of the Carlyle's House
Trust, and to the other trustees and to Mrs. Strong, the
good old caretaker, I must without delay express my
thanks for their help through the last 27 years. The original
of the likeness of Carlyle in this volume is at the House,
24 Cheyne Row. It was purchased from the artist,
Samuel Laurence, by John Sterling, and was in possession
of his daughter Julia till her death in 1910, and then his
grand-daughter Frances Sterling presented it. It shows
the face of Carlyle as people saw it for the first twenty years
or more after he went to live in London. In 1843 Carlyle
was solicited to give sittings to some other but answered :—
" If anyone wants a likeness of me let him apply to
Laurence and arrange with him for it : for Laurence is
the only man living who has any of the elements of my face
within him—and is besides a very fine little fellow " :
which seems to imply,—he can make you a likeness
quickly, without consuming my time. Laurence had had
many sittings and made several portraits. This is the
best I have seen.

For courteous acquiescence in fair quotation the usual
thanks are due to many. The foremost is Alexander
Carlyle, who as owner of the manuscripts has the copyright
of the nine volumes Prof. Norton edited, as well as of the
eight volumes and of the magazine articles which bear his
own name. Thanks are also due to his publishers, Macmillan and Co., John Lane, and Fisher Unwin, and the
editors of the *Nineteenth Century and After* and *Cornhill* ;
and in respect of many other books our thanks are due to
Longmans, Green and Co., Allen and Unwin, Cassell and
Co., Hodder and Stoughton, Chatto and Windus, and
many more—too many to mention.

For the comfort of readers, the dots of omission . . .
are omitted wherever possible, and to minimize foot-notes
the writings of Carlyle and the journals and letters of
himself and his wife are generally taken as read, especially
so far as published by Messrs. Froude, Norton, and A.

Carlyle. The *Guide to Carlyle*, by A. Ralli, makes it needless to give footnotes to these.

A fine collection of Letters by Mrs. Carlyle came to light after the appearance of *Carlyle Till Marriage*, and is about to be published by John Murray, edited by Mr. Leonard Huxley. From one of these letters it appears that the portrait of Mrs. Carlyle which was in *Carlyle Till Marriage* had been painted by Gambardella in 1843. Another copy of it is given here now, and also a copy of an earlier portrait. Both pictures belong to Miss Chrystal, the daughter of Mrs. Carlyle's cousin, who gives permission to reproduce them. At the time she first showed them to me, the letters now being published had been mislaid, and in the absence of letters, I had to depend upon an artist's advice as to which was the younger. My adviser cannot be blamed, for in 1843 Mrs. Carlyle wrote to her cousin,— " Gambardella's own criticism " of the portrait he painted " was (with a look of ineffable complacency), ' it looks too young ! I must put in some wrinkles.' " Which of course he never did.

DAVID ALEC WILSON.

Ayr, 1924.

BOOKS "TAKEN AS READ"

i.e. generally not mentioned in footnotes.

By J. A. FROUDE :—
Thomas Carlyle, 4 volumes.
Letters and Memorials of J. W. Carlyle, 3 volumes.
Reminiscences. By T. Carlyle, 2 volumes.
My Relations with Carlyle.

By PROF. C. E. NORTON :—
Reminiscences by T. Carlyle, 2 volumes.
Early Letters of T.C., 2 volumes.
Letters of T. C., 2 volumes.
Correspondence of T.C. and R. W. Emerson, 2 volumes.
Correspondence between Goethe and Carlyle.

By ALEXANDER CARLYLE :—
New Letters of T.C., 2 volumes.
New Letters and Memorials of J. W. Carlyle, 2 volumes.
Love-Letters of T.C. and Jane Welsh, 2 volumes.
Letters of T. Carlyle to J. S. Mill, J. Sterling and R. Browning.
The Nemesis of Froude by A. Carlyle and Sir James Crichton-Browne.

Also :
Guide to Carlyle. By A. Ralli, 2 volumes.

CONTENTS

ix

CONTENTS

BOOK VIII

SARTOR (1830–31)

CONTENTS

BOOK IX

LONDON AND BACK (1831-32)

BOOK X

WRITING HISTORY (1832-37)

CONTENTS

LIST OF ILLUSTRATIONS

BOOK VI

IN EDINBURGH
1826–28

I

PROSPECTING

(1826)

THOUGH strangers to their neighbours on arrival, the newly-married pair were rich in friends in Edinburgh. They made a rule to give no dinner-parties and go to none ; but were " at home " on Wednesday evenings. It is a proverb in China—

> " However poor a man may be,
> He entertains his friends to tea ; "

and tea and trimmings were the usual limit of Mrs. Carlyle's hospitality.

By and bye she allowed tobacco, but not at once. Her husband made another trial of life without tobacco when they came to Comely Bank ; but he did not continue it more than three weeks, as he had to swallow extra castor oil and salts.

She was a passable housekeeper from the beginning. Her husband gladly reported to his mother that she made two pounds a week suffice, assisted by supplies from the farm. It was an old story.

> " John Gilpin kissed his loving wife ;
> O'erjoyed was he to find,
> That, though on pleasure she was bent,
> She had a frugal mind."

The tales she told in old age about her housework bear the same proportion to reality that a tree bears to a seed. She did not invent but magnified her doings. Carlyle had given more than half his savings to his father and brothers, but still had more than £300 in hand, and they had no immediate anxiety.

He was hoping for regular employment which would leave him free to write or not as he might feel " the spirit move

3

him." To live by writing books was a novelty in Scotland, tho the gains of Scott had made many think of it. Yet even he was an official by trade, and said he meant to make "literature my staff, not my crutch," a proper way of talking for a man with a salary ; but to many an unemployed divine or lawyer "literature" was a welcome makeshift, pleasanter than teaching. Thus Thomas Murray on failing to get a church had cheerfully betaken himself to magazine work, and was proud to boast that "every sixpence he possessed was drawn from literature."[1] This was said in 1841, and shows how he would be talking now when calling as he often did at Comely Bank. By praise, precept and example he did as much as anyone to lead Carlyle into the trade of literature, and was always proud of it. In 1841 he himself desisted from thinking of making money by writing and went into printing, and it was as a printer that he prospered enough to become a "much respected citizen." Many of their best contemporaries did likewise. Thus Thomas Galloway now teaching at Sandhurst and great in astronomy became Registrar of an Assurance Company and grew rich by business ; and Robert Chambers depended on his shop from the start and wrote for pleasure first and profit after. Meanwhile this very summer, 1826, Murray had been urging Carlyle to buy the *Scots Magazine*, which the trustees in bankruptcy of Constable were ready to sell cheap. So sure was he of his friend's capacity that he was ready to advance "a hundred pounds or so." Brewster too continued eager to see Carlyle take hold of his project of a literary newspaper. But Carlyle recoiled from both proposals, though eager for regular employment. "Let the booksellers attend to buying and selling" was his reply, and he would fling himself with all his heart into the work of an editor, "should their highest estimate of editorial dues and my lowest be found capable of stretching until they meet."

Nothing happened. He drafted a proposal of an *Annual* which would have been a wonderful contrast to any of those that for a generation longer were a profit to the trade. Instead of pretty pictures and poems and tales and fun, as much as possible by famous favourites, his *Literary Annual Register* was to provide :—

---

[1] *Autobiographical Notes*, etc., by Thomas Murray, Dumfries, 1911, pp. 27–30.

1.—Picturesque biographies of persons lately deceased (Byron, Parr, Jean Paul, Talma, etc.).
2.—Essays of all sorts to show the "shortcomings and perversions" as well as the "merits" of current literature, morals and manners !
3.—Books of the year, and 4.—Art, and 5.—Science.
6.—Preserving in form the usual taboo of politics, the *Annual* was nevertheless to reproduce whatever in that line seemed to illustrate "the spiritual condition of man in our time." Thus Prince Hohenlohe, a miracle-worker, the Genevese persecution, the Commercial Joint Stock mania, the Catholic Association, etc.—"provided correct information could be obtained regarding them—were well worth a few words."

Nothing happened.

Now was the time for the long-intended masterpiece, the "valuable book" he had been talking of writing for the last five years at least,—as if he only needed leisure. There was abundant leisure now, but the impulse was lacking. His working hours were filled with reading at large not only German—Werner, Tieck, Mendelssohn, etc.—but also in deference to Coleridge and Co., old English writers. He had previously read Browne's *Vulgar Errors*, and nothing else of his ; but now he found that Lamb was right in saying his *Urne-Burial* was better, and his *Religio Medici* seemed best of all—" only he gives himself far too good and orthodox a character," such as makes the reader despair or envy him, or disbelieve him as a moral *dandy*.

"I should like to know more of him," he concluded, uncertain whether "the *spirit* of that age" was better than ours.—"Sir W. Raleigh's advice to his son ; worldly-wise, solid, sharp, far-seeing—The motto : 'Nothing like *getting on* !' Of Burleigh's advice, the motto is the same ; the execution gentler. These men are like so many Romans or Greeks. There in that old age, lies the *only* true *poetical* literature of England. The poets of the last age took to pedagogy—see Pope—those of the present age to ground and lofty tumbling"

He was disappointed by Shaftesbury's writings and Sir William Temple's, but considered Temple himself a "wise and benignant man of action ; almost the beau ideal of an English gentleman."

He found Burton, whose *Anatomy of Melancholy* Johnson praised, a "thinking, observing man ; but of no

admirable gifts—except memory, and of little or no wisdom,"—about the level of " English country parsons
As a scientific treatise his book is worth absolutely nothing."
The quotations in short were readable, but would have
been worth more by themselves, which illuminates the
opinion of Fitzgerald in 1842 [1] that part of the " foundation
of Carlyle's style " was " in Burton : one passage quite
like *Sartor*." No doubt ! The difference was that Burton
was in earnest with his pedantry, Carlyle was making fun
of it.

Some of the most striking thoughts in *Sartor* appear in
his note-book now for the first time. For example :—
"The fraction of life will increase equally by diminishing
the denominator as by augmenting the numerator."
Another note shows him above the theories of " rewards
and punishments " :—" Virtue *is* its own reward—because
it *needs no reward*."

Another sign of maturity was a note added in brackets
to some bad couplets of his own—Dryden's saying about
Swift, " Our cousin Swift has no turn for poetry."

Admitting with reluctance that literature was to be
his trade, he was looking round for any work of that
kind likely to bring wages. About the end of the year
there is a significant note.—

' What a fine thing a *Life of Cromwell*, like the *Vie de
Charles XII* (by Voltaire), would be ! The wily fanatic
himself, in his own most singular features, at once a hero and
a blackguard pettifogging scrub ; and the wild image of his
times reflected from his accompaniment ! I would travel
ten miles on foot to see his *soul* represented as I once saw
his body in the Castle of Warwick.'

It was merely a passing thought. No publisher would
look at such a thing. Cromwell seemed a problem solved
—defunct at any rate, as dead as Charlemagne or the
Pharaohs of Egypt. Carlyle himself did not even turn
back to the notes he made in 1822.

---

[1] *Letters of Edward Fitzgerald*, MacMillan, 1894 ; Vol. I. p. 139.

II

SIR WILLIAM HAMILTON

ONE of the pleasures of life to Carlyle in Edinburgh was walking and talking with the Professor and philosopher Sir William Hamilton—another man of metaphysics besides Kant for whom it can be claimed that he was one of the models of Teufelsdröckh. Erasmus, Ruhnken, Ulrich von Hutten, and many more were favourite topics. With beautiful politeness Sir William tabooed metaphysicians " when not expressly called upon. He was finely social and human in these walks," reported Carlyle. The party was usually of three or four.

' His talk was forcible, copious, discursive, careless rather than otherwise ; and on abstruse topics, apt to become embroiled and ravelly, much less perspicuous and elucidative than with a little deliberation he could have made it. " The fact is," he would often say ; and then plunging into new circuitous depths and distinctions, again on a new grand, " The Fact is," and still again, —till what the essential " fact " might be was not a little obscure. He evidently had not been engaged in *speaking* these things, but only in thinking them, for his own behoof, not yours. By lucid questioning you could get lucidity from him on any topic. I can still remember animal magnetism and the German revival of it, not yet known in England.'

Sir William's investigations of the brains of men and animals had been extensive. He had " weighed by a delicate balance above 1,000 brains of above 50 species of animals " ; and " phrenology," then the " prevalent rage," he had studied with care, and come to look on " as a mischievous humbug."

When Dr. Spurzheim, its champion, came to Edinburgh, and challenged Hamilton to " a public oral discussion " to be decided by a popular vote, he " very decidedly declined both the discussion and the tribunal "—the matter

was settled : for in private and before a competent audience, he had already demolished it, and was always ready
to do so again.   Carlyle reports :—

' One evening I recollect listening to a paper *on Phrenology*, read by him in the Royal Society.   The meeting was
very much larger than usual ; and sat in the deepest silence
and attention, and, as it gradually appeared, approval and
assent.   My own assent was complete ; I only wished the
subject had been more important or more dubious to me.
The argument, grounded on cerebral anatomy, philosophy
and human sense, I remember, went on in the true style of
vires acquirit (stronger and stronger) ; and the crowning
finish of it was this :—" Here are two skulls.   One is the
skull of a Malay robber and cut-throat, who ended by mur-
dering his mistress and getting hanged ; skull sent by
some official at Penang ; the other is George Buchanan's
preserved here.   One is probably among the best of mankind, the other among the worst.   Let us take our callipers
and measure.   Bump of benevolence is so and so, adding
all, your callipers declare the Malay to transcend in goodness
the Buchanan, by such and such inches."
' I said to Sir William next time we met : " Were I
in your place, I would decline to say another word on that
subject.   Malay cut-throats *versus* Buchanan ; explain me
that ; till then I say nothing." ' [1]

The advice was sound, for even " Society " was shaking
in its faith in Dr. Spurzheim, calling him " Douster-
swivel," and turning to some other folly.   The popular
view was expressed by Hogg, the " Ettrick shepherd,"
when the learned doctor had felt his bumps and claimed
they showed his genius.   " My dear fellow," said Hogg,
" if a few knots and swells make a skull of genius, I've seen
mony a saft chiel get a swapping organization in five
minutes at Selkirk Tryst."
Carlyle and Hamilton had convictions in common about
much more than phrenology.   Both felt with Kant that
time and space are merely ways of thinking or perceiving,
and that of all outside us we can never know more than
appearances, and even of appearances know infinitely
little.   Hamilton used to quote the Athenian inscription—
" To the Unknown God "—as the last word of religious
philosophy.

[1] *Memoir of Sir William Hamilton*, by John Veitch, pp. 113-126.

III

SOCIAL AMENITIES, WALTER SCOTT, &c.

THE destined husband of Bess Stodart, the Rev. David Aitken, had been introduced to Carlyle in November, and received from him a certificate [1] (17.2.1827), which helped to persuade the Earl of Minto to " present " him to the parish of Minto.—

' Of Mr. Aitken's talent in the pulpit I can speak only by report.   In knowledge of Art, of Literature ancient and modern he has made distinguished acquirements : in German Literature especially, for which his long and varied residence in that country gave him peculiar opportunities, his knowledge, I believe, could be rivalled by few in Scotland, perhaps in Britain.   His tastes also are still intellectual and his habits regular and studious.

' I have known Mr. A. only three months.   As a clergyman, especially in an intellectual neighbourhood, he promises to be peculiarly suitable : for his religious persuasions seem to be at once earnest, unostentatious and tolerant ; and in point of culture, and polish of mind, I can say without reserve that I have found few men in any profession, and certainly in his no one, that deserved to be compared with him.'

Some time about then this Rev. David Aitken and Carlyle were walking in Princes Street together and turned aside into Hanover Street to the shop of Tait in an upper floor there.   It was Tait who published *German Romance* and was now the most urgent in pressing Carlyle to undertake a literary newspaper.   While he and Aitken and Carlyle were talking together Sir Walter Scott came in and said : " Mr. Tait, have you got a copy of *Horace* at hand ? I want to make a quotation."   Tait gave him a handsome quarto.   He sat down with it in his lap within hearing. Carlyle continued to talk to Tait, and Scott, who would be

[1] *Early Letters of Jane Welsh Carlyle*, by D. G. Ritchie, pp. 120–123.

interested in any "literary newspaper" project, was presently noticed by Aitken to be looking up repeatedly and watching Carlyle with an expression on his face as if he were saying to himself, "He's a ken-speckle looking chiel that ; I wonder who he is."[1] Here is what Scott had been writing in his private note-book about Goethe (20.2.1827)[2] :—

' I have a letter from Baron von Goethe which I must have read to me ; for though I know German, I have forgot their written hand. I make it a rule seldom to read, and never to answer foreign letters from literary folks. It leads to nothing but the battledore and shuttlecock intercourse of compliments, as light as cork and feathers. But Goethe is different and a wonderful fellow—the Ariosto at once and almost the Voltaire of Germany. Who could have told me thirty years ago I should correspond and be on something like an equal footing with the author of Goetz ? ' (This was Goethe's work which Scott translated).

Aitken did not make any immediate record of the conversation of Carlyle, but he has given a general description of it.[3]

' He combined extraordinary frankness, a habit of speaking out most strikingly and picturesquely whatever was in his mind, with the most perfect command of temper in meeting objections, evading attempted slights or provocations to anger, or changing the subject when the opposition was becoming noisy or the opponent was evidently a fool. Again and again I observed this and wondered at his tact and suavity, especially when he had propounded something startling to commonplace people, and the expression on (their) faces was—" Who are *you* that dare thus advance notions discomposing to your seniors ? " '

Scott speedily sent what Goethe called " a cheering and warm-hearted " answer, which delighted Goethe ; and in a few months the kind old man sent Carlyle six medals, requesting him to present two of them " to Sir Walter

[1] Scotch for "remarkable-looking fellow." *Edinburgh Sketches and Memories*, by David Masson, pp. 344-352, and footnote, p. 352.
[2] Lockhart's *Scott*, Vol. IX., pp. 91-98, and 98 footnote.
[3] *Edinburgh Sketches and Memories*, by David Masson, pp. 330-1.

Scott with my best regards."[1] But when they came,
Scott was in London being "lionized," and overlooked a
letter from Carlyle about them. By the time he came home,
Carlyle was away. Receiving the medals from the hand of
Jeffrey,[2] Scott sent his thanks by word of mouth, and never
suspected the kind purpose of the gift, which was to make
him acquainted with Carlyle. It may be added at once
that both he and Lockhart by-and-bye gave their names
and subscriptions to a birthday present of a seal to Goethe
from "fifteen English friends," at the instance of Carlyle,[3]
and that the entries about Scott in Carlyle's note-book
show that his valuation of Sir Walter's work was not affected
by the inadvertent discourtesy.

Mrs. Carlyle's capacity for listening made her a popular
hostess, and their callers were of many kinds. Her
"Wednesday-nights" were all the more attractive because
informal. One of the "habituals" was Madame Viaris,
an "honest Pomeranian" lady, who by teaching German
was supporting her husband, "an ex-Napoleon-officer,"
and their boy. She is audible one night, denouncing a bad
translation of Werner, and to ratify her censure reading the
original "in a high shrieky tone." Another frequenter
was a "blusterous" Welsh Archdeacon Williams, head of
the Edinburgh "Academy", who deserves to be remembered for this.—He told a sympathizing circle the thrilling
tale of a dreadful illness he had had, at the crisis of which
the medico had to be stern as Fate and say,—"You
shall die, unless you can dine for three weeks without wine."
"And I did it, Sir," concluded "blusterous" Williams,
looking at Carlyle, and enjoying in simplicity his laughter
and applause.

Here is Carlyle's report to Mrs. Montagu a few months
after his marriage, in sending her two sets of his *German
Romance*, one for herself, and one for Badams.[4]—

'Indeed, indeed, I am not mad enough to forget I have
found but *one* Mrs. Montagu. My good wife exceeds all
my hopes. She is sitting by me, knitting you a purse :
you must not cease to love her, for she deserves it, and few

[1] *Correspondence Between Goethe and Carlyle*, p. 43 : and see 53–6, 82–4,
and 121.
[2] *Ditto*, and unpublished letter from Jeffrey to T.C.
[3] *Corr. Goethe and Carlyle*, pp. 291–8.
[4] *Thomas Carlyle*, by Moncure D. Conway, pp. 233–240.

love you better. Of society, in this modern Athens, we
have no want, but rather a superabundance, which we are
reducing. True it is, one meets with many a Turk in grain ;
but a better class too, sober, discreet, logic-loving, moderately well-informed : with these I talk and enjoy myself ;
but only talk as from an upper window to people in the
street ; into the house—of my spirit—I cannot admit
them ; and the unwise wonderment they exhibit when I
do but show them the lobby warns me to lose no time in
again slamming-to the door. But what of society ? Round
our own hearth is society enough, with a blessing. I read
books, or like the Roman poet and so many British ones,
" disport on paper " ; and many a still evening when I
stand in our little flower-garden—it is fully larger than two
bedquilts—and smoke my pipe in peace, and look at the
reflection of the distant city lamps, and hear the faint
murmur of its tumult, I feel no little pleasure in the thought
of " my own four walls," and what they hold.

   ' On the whole, what I chiefly want is occupation ; which
will not fail I suppose, to present itself. To dig in the
mines of Plutus, and sell the gift of God—and such is every
man's small fraction of intellectual talent—for a piece of
money is a measure I am not inclined to ; and for *invention*,
for Art of any sort, I feel myself too helpless and undeter-
mined. Some day—Oh that the day were here !—I shall
surely speak out these things that are lying in me, and
giving me no sleep till they are spoken ! Or else if the Fates
would be so kind as show me—that I had nothing to say !
This, perhaps, is the real secret of it, after all ; a hard result,
yet not intolerable, were it once clear and certain. Literature, it seems, is to be my trade ; but the present aspects
of it among us seem to me peculiarly perplexed and unin-
viting. I love it not : in fact I have almost quitted modern
reading : lower down than the Restoration I rarely venture
in English. These Hookers, Bacons, Brownes, were *men* ;
but for our present " men of letters," our dandy wits, our
utilitarian philosophers, our novel, play, sonnet, and song
manufacturers, I shall only say, May the Lord pity us and
them ! But enough of this ! For, what am I that I should
censure ? Less than the least in Israel.'

   Then he enquired about her health, and discussed her
son Charles, whose " history at Cambridge " she had been
giving him, and as a transfer of " the wayward youth "

to Edinburgh was contemplated Carlyle assured her,—
" Again and again I say, if I can be of *any* services, command me," concluding :—

' I have finished my sheet, and more I must deny myself
at present. Will you get these tomes conveyed to Badams,
my own good Badams, whom I swear I had rather see than
any ten men in England ? I have begged of him to write,
but I know he will not : my good wishes are always with
him. From you I expect better things, being minded to
become a better correspondent myself.'

IV

FRANCIS JEFFREY

IT was not till January, 1827, that the volumes of *German Romance* were published, and before the end of that month, "ill off for something to do," he began a "didactic novel," *Wotton Reinfred*, to fill his working hours, and seemed to his wife more contented in consequence. Then a happy thought occurred to Procter, Mrs. Montagu's son-in-law, as he reflected on the letter just read. He knew Carlyle's opinions, and had also known Jeffrey for years, and knew that Jeffrey was in want of good articles.[1] So in congratulating Carlyle on *German Romance*, he enclosed an introduction to Jeffrey, "a very fine fellow," and one evening in February Carlyle went to Jeffrey's house in George Street to deliver it. Being ushered into the study, he found there the nimble and shapely little man, whose figure had long been familiar to him, busy at a big baize-covered table loaded with books and bundles of papers. There were two candles and a cheerful fire—to show the uncommonly bright black eyes that were raised to see him. Jeffrey laid his work aside, and received the stranger most kindly. He "talked with me," wrote Carlyle to his mother,[2] "for an hour, though very busy, on all possible things : and really proved himself by much the most agreeable citizen of Edinburgh that I had ever met with. I am sorry the man is so immersed in Law ; otherwise we might become friends."

In spite of "Law," they fell into an instantaneous friendship,—liked each other from the first. "Repeatedly" during this first hour together Jeffrey said : "Come to the Court any morning and I'll introduce you to " several including "Sir Walter Scott." He spoke of employing him on the *Edinburgh Review*, declaring : "We must give you a lift."

"Read the *German Romance* first," was the modest

---

[1] B. W. Procter, *Barry Cornwall, An Autobiographical Fragment*, etc., (1877), pp. 255–261 for Jeffrey letters before this date.

[2] On February 16th, 1827, and therefore more likely to be correct than "perhaps 20 minutes " in *Reminiscences* II., 236, dated January, 1867.

answer, " to see what manner of man I am, and whether I can suit you." They parted in the friendliest style. Jeffrey returned the call. He brought his wife to make acquaintance with Mrs. Carlyle ; and the women were able to tolerate each other.

Disesteem for fiction was the best of the Bible-Religion now fading away. Carlyle was to return to that part of his earliest creed ; and as long as he lived in Scotland, he would find it in " the air." The " prodigious " profits of Sir Walter Scott were impressive mainly as a revelation of ignorant English gullibility. Contempt for looseness in stating events was common to serious men of every shade, to " New Lights " and " Old " inside the Church, and all sorts outside it. So when Carlyle was sending *German Romance* to his father last month, he confided to his brother, " He will not read it, I know " ; and the most that would now be expected of Jeffrey was that he might look at the Preface and Biographies to confirm the result of their interview, and perhaps ask some article on similar lines.

Which was what happened. Jeffrey knew little and cared less about Goethe ; but would note with satisfaction what Carlyle honoured most in him. Goethe ' is king of himself and of his world ; nor does he rule it by Will or Passion but Reason. This is the true Rest of man. Goethe's inward home has been reared by slow and laborious efforts ; but his peace is not from blindness, but from clear vision. The grand characteristic of his writings (is) not knowledge, but wisdom. There is no whining over human woes ; it is understood that we must simply all strive to alleviate or remove them. There is no noisy battling for opinions.' In short he is like Shakespeare, and nothing was more natural than the hope excited in Jeffrey's mind that the fervid admirer of such a sage would soon be a trenchant Whig.

By 1827 Jeffrey's increasing practice was making literary work every day more difficult, so that not very long ago he had been writing to John Allen, his old friend and contributor, the " prototype of Major Dobbin," it is said, and long the resident doctor of Holland House : " Can you not lay your hands on some clever young man who would write for us ? The original supporters of the work are getting old, and here the young men are mostly Tories." [1] In Carlyle

---

[1] *Life of Lord Jeffrey* by Lord Cockburn, I., p. 279.

he could easily see at once the literary ability he wanted and superiority to the common craving for a job, and many years had to pass before he relinquished the hope of seeing him a partisan : which shows at least the sincerity of Jeffrey's Whiggery.

Till after 1820 Scotland seemed to Cockburn, Jeffrey's colleague and biographer, like " a village at a rich man's gate." The lawyers and parsons and teachers of Edinburgh were like the flunkies of the house. The Whigs themselves were flunkies in revolt, but flunkies all the time. The new contributor Jeffrey had caught had never truckled and felt no call to be impudent, and was averse to taking sides. He was minded to live by writing and to tell the truth, and he had developed so far that he knew as well as any man in Edinburgh the absurdity of the current creeds. He differed from the able men of the world in his greater devotion to truth, and seemed to them a fanatic or a Don Quixote. They were not altogether wrong. He was like Epictetus and many another of the right sort ; but he did not realize till after he was tied to the trade of words the difficulty of telling the truth while writing for a living.

The " daring originality " of the *Edinburgh Review* was limited by the rules of the drawing-room. It was really little less conventional than the Tories, which enhances Jeffrey's merit in admitting Carlyle. " Poetry has this much in common with religion," wrote Jeffrey, " that its standards were fixed long ago by certain inspired writers, whose authority it is no longer lawful to call in question."

This was meant as written, in the matter of poetry, and tho there was a humorous sneer at religion, it was not intended to be obtruded on the common reader. Jeffrey and Wilson had quarrelled because Wilson had let Lockhart impute " infidel principles " to the competing periodical. None of the men in either set cared a fig for priest or prophet : but Wilson was engineering *Blackwood* and Jeffrey the *Edinburgh Review*, and business was business.[1] Gentlemen tabooed religion in private to minimize the mischief of fanaticism and make the best of it. The women wanted it, occasionally. At funerals it seemed to fill a gap, and it helped to keep the common crowds content.

[1] *Christopher North, A Memoir of John Wilson*, by Mrs. Gordon, I., pp. 280–295.

FRANCIS JEFFREY.

[face p. 16

As yet Carlyle was ready to go as far as David Hume or Professor Leslie in toleration. He "took seats" in a church, and especial pains to let his mother know it. He read a chapter every Sunday to wife and maid—when they would allow him, and it must be confessed, for his mother's benefit.

V

JOHN WILSON AND OTHERS

(1827)

PERHAPS the most prominent man in Edinburgh after Scott was John Wilson, Professor of Moral Philosophy, and efflorescing in a magazine as Christopher North, exhaling his soul in floods of words with a flavour of whisky punch—though his daughter is careful to mention he was teetotal when writing.[1] He owed his " chair " to the Tories, but by 1827 his eminence as a lecturer was denied by nobody. Carlyle had known him by sight since 1814, and on coming to live in town he went three or four times to hear him lecture.[2] Wilson " stood erect like a tower, the wish to be sincere looking out from every feature," wrote Carlyle, who noticed he was not at home in metaphysics, and generally dealt with human life in the concrete.—Picturesque description was his favourite way of teaching :—

' Snatches of human portraiture—savage men careering free and far in their savage deserts, under a silent law of nature ; or again the civilized man, the civilized criminal, in the heart of an earth and a heaven become articulate, fancy him at last resolved on the atrocity of murder, finger on the pistol-trigger, trigger not yet drawn tho fully intended to be, and what an awful never-alterable infinitude of difference to him when once it *is* drawn ; ' etc., etc., ' the Professor's eyes flashing in certain high passages, and his brow knitting itself. I could well conceive his effect on raw young minds of the better sort,' to say nothing of a mature reporter like Carlyle, only ten years junior to the lecturer, and fated to imitate and improve on this

---

[1] *Christopher North*: *A Memoir of John Wilson*, by Mrs. Gordon, II. pp. 149, 265, etc.

[2] *Nineteenth Century Magazine*, " Christopher North," January, 1920, by Alexander Carlyle, pp. 103–117, and contemporary letters, etc.

method, in *Sartor*, though now devoting every morning
at home till the end of May to making himself write a novel
—in vain. *Wotton Reinfred* was never finished. After
many years the manuscript was stolen,[1] and it was printed
after his death ;[2] but it is a faint reflection of Wilhelm
Meister, and like Rasselas, uneventful. A mind awake
enough to think of things as they are cannot grow back-
wards and play with events like a story-teller or a child
with toys.

Besides, his interest was in superior men and women,
and such are not the affair of the fictioneer, which is to hold
the mirror up to common life. It is hard enough to believe
in superior qualities, however documented. In fiction
they are out of place. The novel without a hero is the best ;
and the maxim of Aristotle would apply to it—there is
more room for earnest truth in a *typical* story than in a
report. The stage has been sanctified by Shakespeare,
as Buddha made begging beautiful ; but times are changed.
A prince like Buddha would not beg to-day—he would
behave like Prince Kropotkin ; and a very small share of
such learning as Carlyle's handicaps a man of sense in
fictioneering. Carlyle tried hard but could not do it.

John Gordon is the best authority for his habits now.
Replying to Masson,[3] he said Carlyle was "not a bit "
morose or gloomy, sarcastic or bitter—he was " the pleasantest and heartiest fellow in the world, and most excellent
company. He was most methodic in the arrangement of
his time, reserving the solid hours," till 1 or 2 p.m., " for
his literary work in Comely Bank, but very accessible and
sociable in the afternoons and evenings." About two he
generally went out for a walk, returning for dinner at four.[4]

As Gordon had been a favourite pupil and was now a
friend of John Wilson, he introduced Carlyle to " the
Professor," who liked him well and never missed a chance
of a chat when they met, according to the custom there and
then, but quietly tabooed the theology and kindred
speculation in which Carlyle was interested still. He
looked down upon all that without an effort, as Carlyle
also was able to do in time. Meanwhile—" he will not be

---

[1] 1856–7, which see in later volume.
[2] *Last Words of T.C.*, Longmans, 1892.
[3] *Edinburgh Sketches and Memories*, by David Masson, pp. 330–331 ;
and *Carlyle Personally and in His Writings*, by D.M., p. 44.
[4] Contemporary letters.

really serious and sincere with me," thought Carlyle to himself, admiring Wilson's freedom from hypocrisy, and not realizing how that required silence from a professor of moral philosophy among fanatics and fools. When he tried to give the conversation a " serious " turn, he discovered Wilson was quizzing him, and did not like it, tho' he could not help enjoying the good-humoured fun with which Wilson was brimming over—" the very tones of his voice testified of it," wrote Carlyle after forty years, recalling a sample.

He and Brewster were strolling in the sunshine up towards Princes Street, discussing the literary newspaper which Brewster was eager to persuade Carlyle to start, when Wilson joined them in the quiet part of their road where the gardens are to-day, between Heriot Row and Queen Street, and announced to Carlyle : " Young Mr. Bell is meditating literary enterprises, and thinking an *Edinburgh Literary Gazette* might do considerable things if you would embark along with him."

Brewster knew the man but not so Carlyle, who never saw him and objected—" I ? But he doesn't know me at all."

Wilson explained in his satirically polished way : " Has heard ; has read ; your German faculty, etc."

" Dear me, is that a son of old James Bell ? " cried Brewster, in surprise.

" The same," replied Wilson, " and is quite bent on going into literature and doing exploits in that line."

" And ready to co-operate with any man," said Carlyle.

" With *any* man ! " answered Wilson, in such a tone of broad recognition as seemed to picture the truth completely and sent the other two into a peal of laughter, while on Wilson's big face mantled a multitudinous smile, like the many-twinkling motion of sunshine on the sea.

VI

HOW A RAT GOT THE HEART OF NAPOLEON, &c.

BOTH Carlyle and his wife continued bilious, which made them think of Craigenputtock when an offer of an engagement to translate Goethe's autobiography came to him in the spring from a London publisher. He wrote about it to Mrs. Welsh, who was getting no rent from the tenant she had accepted in a hurry and had bad news of the state of the farm. She was eager now to see the Carlyles there. The difficulty was the lack of housing,— the ancestral home was a small farmhouse. But the Carlyles were masons and stone was cheap. His uncle John was still in that business. His brother Alexander was still seeking a farm, and Mrs. Welsh so anxious now to see him at Craigenputtock that she offered an advance of the money needed for a start. It is mainly moorland pasture with little arable ground and needed " capital."

The London offer was indefinitely postponed by the publishers ; but Mrs. Welsh came to Edinburgh and pressed her views upon her son-in-law. He stopped work on his novel and took Alexander to see the place, while Mrs. Welsh kept her daughter company at Comely Bank.

On Saturday night (14.4.1827), he wrote to his wife reporting the neglected condition of the farm and received instructions by return of post in what seems to have been her first letter after their marriage. The opening sentences were typical of what she used to write to him whenever separated. Their married life was one long honeymoon of forty years, with hardly enough of a breeze to vary the monotony, so that in general her letters after marriage may be left out of his history. But here is the beginning of the first (Monday, 16.4.1827) [1] :

' Dear, dear, Cheap, Cheap,—I met the postman . . . yesterday morning, and something bade me ask if there

---

[1] *New Letters of Jane Welsh Carlyle*, edited by A. Carlyle, *Nineteenth Century Magazine*, August, 1914, pp. 327-8.

were any letters.   Imagine my agitation when he gave me
yours, four-and-twenty hours before the appointed time !
I was so glad and so frightened ! so eager to know the
whole contents, that I could hardly make out any *part*.
In the little Tobacconist's, where I was fain to seek a quiet
place, I did at length however, with much heart-beating,
get through the precious paper, and find that my Darling
still loved me pretty well, and that the Craig o' Putta was
still a hope ; as also that if you come not back to poor Goody
on Saturday, it will not be for want of will.   Ah ! Nor yet
will it be for want of the most fervent prayers to Heaven
that a longing Goody can put up ; for I am sick, sick to the
heart of this absence, which, indeed, I can only *bear* in the
faith of its being brief.   Oh, Dearest, I *do* love you in my
very innermost being, far better than words can tell or even
kisses ; though *these* (when not the *experimental* sort)
are rather eloquent in their way ; and, to me at least, have
often told such things ! and they shall tell the same story
over again, shall they not, yet a thousand and a thousand
times ?   " I expect but I doubt not."

'Alas the poor Craig o' Putta ! what a way it is in, with
these good-for-nothing sluggards ! I need not recommend
you to do all that is possible, nay, to " *do the impossible,*"
to get them out.   Even suppose we did not wish the place
for ourselves, it would be miserable to consign it to such
hands.   You will use all fair means then to recover it from
them ; that is all honest means ; for, as to the tenderness
and delicacy, which would have been becoming towards
a worthy tenant, it were here out of place.   I shall be very
anxious till I hear from you again.'   (And more to the
same effect and so on.)

Accordingly Carlyle and his brother met the Craigenputtock tenant and his brother, drovers both, at Dumfries
on Wednesday, April 18th, 1827, about two o'clock ; and by
dint of " eight or nine hours of incessant discussion, varying
from ' An' please your honour ' to ' Damn it, Sir,' " they
settled amicably that Alexander was to enter into possession next month.   The value of some corn was the only
difficulty left to arbitration, and Carlyle advised Mrs.
Welsh : " I think if the judges do *not* give it against us, we
ought almost to give it *against ourselves*, that is, in case the
drovers behave themselves, for really they have had a poor
year."

Mrs. Welsh's health was drunk in fiery punch, and
Carlyle upbraided as a " Whig " for swallowing no more
than teaspoonfuls of it. Not till near eleven at night,
when the papers were signed and moneys paid, did the
Carlyle brothers separate from the drovers, all " in fair
spirits and fine fellowship, with cordial shaking of hands."
They had " nineteen rough miles " to ride to Scotsbrig,
with a large sum of money in pocket and no pistols. So
the drovers let them go, and another man from Closeburn
sat down to get " fu' " in their stead. " I was fu' when I
got it," said one of the two brothers who had had Craigenputtock, " and by God I'se be as fu' when I *quut* it."

Next afternoon, Thursday, 19.4.1827, Carlyle and
his brother Dr. John were drinking tea at Ecclefechan
with Dr. Arnott, the only English physician who had been
acceptable to Napoleon in his last illness at St. Helena,
and nominated by him as the only one to attend the post-
mortem, at which accordingly Dr. Arnott presided.

The good doctor had liked his patient and been well paid
by him—not less than 500 guineas. So there is nothing
wonderful in his best story, which has never yet been
printed, tho he was fond of telling it to Carlyle and other
friends.

Napoleon wanted his heart to be taken by Dr. Antommarchi to his widow, and at the post-mortem it was put in
spirits in a silver vase for that purpose. But Governor
Hudson Lowe ordered Antommarchi to bury the heart with
the body. So the silver vase had to be put in the coffin
and was buried—only not the heart, at least not the heart
of Napoleon. It passed into an insignificant-looking glass
jar, *and was in Dr. Arnott's cabin on his voyage home.* One
stormy night a smashing sound awakened the doctor. He
rose to make sure of the most precious of his possessions,
and found the glass jar broken. Hastily lighting a candle,
he was in time to see the heart of Napoleon in the jaws of
a rat ; but whether he was able to retrieve it remains
unknown. The story was—never finished, like " Wotton
Reinfred," [1] and in its simplicity surpasses Hamlet.

When Carlyle resumed his " didactic novel " after this

---

[1] First heard by D.A.W. in Ecclefechan in 1890 from several ; but not
thinking of repeating it, he did not then write the names of those who had
heard it from Dr. Arnott. J. T. Wells confirmed it ; and all the details
that can be corroborated are found correct. See e.g. *Life of Napoleon*,
by J. H. Rose, II., p. 571 ; and Hazlitt's *Napoleon*, IV., pp. 558–567, etc.

interruption of a week or two, it was like metal grown cold on the anvil, and was laid aside for ever about the end of May.

The occasion was this. Neither *Schiller* nor *German Romance* seemed likely to come to a second edition, which ratified the admonition of Irving that the way to live by writing was to write for periodicals. A book is like a lottery ticket ! So he went to Parliament House to see Jeffrey. " The little Jewel of Advocates," as he described him, did not need to be reminded of his kind offer to give Carlyle a lift. " The Article ? Where is the Article ? " was the gist of his talk as Carlyle walked home with him, and was encouraged to begin Germanizing the public— " provided you do not treat the whole of the earth which is not yet Germanized as a parcel of blockheads." The next number of the *Edinburgh Review* being about to go to press, he was to write for it what they called a short article —longer than the average to-day—on Richter. He began in the first week of June and the printer had it before the end of the month. It is the first of the " Miscellanies " in his " works."

VII

AN AMBROSIAL SUMMER NIGHT WITH
JOHN WILSON

(1827)

IN July the Richter essay was noticed in Edinburgh, where it seemed to some like sacrilege towards Scott,— and to others like party spite of the Whigs—to glorify so much a foreign fictioneer. The sincerity of it if seen at all would only make it the more disturbing to common Tories, but the contrary to the like of Wilson, who about this time agreed to spend a night at Gordon's rooms and sample the new specimen of Whiggery. A Whig Carlyle would never think himself, but many besides the drovers in Dumfries called him one and thought him a Puritan or prig with a smack of sanctity, preoccupied about his own affairs.

Wilson was willing to think him better than this. He liked John Gordon well and was persuaded by him, and so foregathered at his supper-table soon after nine in the dusk of a fine summer evening, with Carlyle on his left and a lawyer Roy on his right and Gordon opposite. They were like the merry-makers in the song—" We arena fu'." Wilson said he had come from calling on Lockhart, whose Life of Burns was just out. As Editor of the *Quarterly*, Lockhart had to live in London, but he did not like it, and when questioned had answered Wilson : " Oh, don't ask me ; don't bid me speak a word of that—I have run away to forget all that delirious stuff for a week or two among you." [1]

Over the supper and the whisky-punch that followed, Wilson drinking steadily, Roy and Gordon following far behind, and Carlyle taking merely water coloured by port- negus, Wilson let himself go in a " blaze " of talk,—a flow of spiritual lava. He was not fuddled though drinking freely and was not a " soliloquy talker," pumping into you, like Coleridge or Humboldt, " so unendurable, were they

---

[1] " Christopher North," *Nineteenth Century Magazine*, January, 1920, by Alexander Carlyle, pp. 103–117.

eloquent as seraphs.   On the contrary he rather seemed to
wait for your enquiry and gave you, with careless abundance,
whatever lay in him on the topic going, and never failed to
pause at once, when his quick glance told him you nearly
had enough."

" The landlord's laugh was ready chorus," Roy's delighted
attention never flagged, and as fast as Carlyle suggested
names of distinguished contemporaries, Wordsworth and
Coleridge, De Quincey and Dugald Stewart, Brougham and
Jeffrey, Wilson would launch into vivid matter-of-fact
descriptions of them, mixing praise and satire and producing
brilliant caricatures that made a lasting impression on his
docile junior, who drank in all he said with delight, and
remembered it and profited by the example of his method
all the better because not drinking whisky-punch but only
sipping wine and water.

In the course of five or six hours many topics arose, but
they always gravitated back to personalities.   There
were plentiful cigars and snuff, and sometimes spacious
silences, one of which ended in a brilliant flash, as of lightning in the dark.   It was towards two o'clock.   Wilson
appeared to be sunk in a brown study.   His ruddy complexion had a gray-blue tinge and the snuffy nose and
upper lip had an off-hand defiant look.   Suddenly he
enquired of John Gordon with an irresistible air : " I hope,
Mr. Gordon, *you* don't believe in *Universal* Damnation ? "[1]
A sally rewarded by roars of laughter.   This was the only
sort of theology that was then " good form " in Edinburgh.

About three o'clock the sunshine streaming through the
windows made them rise, tho' all were loth to go.   Wilson
and Carlyle sauntered homewards together, their ways being
the same.   Carlyle was smoking.   They parted in Gloucester Place at Wilson's door,[2] intending and promising to
see more of each other.

On reaching home Carlyle was surprised to see his wife
" quietly reading and waiting "[3] for him, sitting up in
short—a womanly way of minimizing the risk that he
might drop into the habits of the Professor of Moral
Philosophy and keep such hours on every night but Sunday.

Deep drinking was the fashion ; and the Professor of

[1] From a contemporary letter.   Italics added.
[2] *Christopher North, a Memoir of John Wilson*, by Mrs. Gordon, II., p. 82.
[3] " Christopher North," *Nineteenth Century Magazine*, January, 1920,
by Alexander Carlyle, pp. 103–117.

Moral Philosophy was never " as drunk as a Lord ", say witnesses. Only, he could stand a lot, and a bottle of whisky spread over 9 or 10 tumblers and five or six hours was easy to bear. He became teetotal when his health required it ; but at present in his prime resembled the Highland captain who was able to drink brandy and water with Sir Walter Scott, disposing of all the brandy and leaving Scott the water.[1]

[1] *Reminiscences of C. MacFarlane*, p. 24.

VIII

STATE OF GERMAN LITERATURE, &c.

(1827)

HERE is a note from Jeffrey dated only Thursday evening which cannot be later than the beginning of July :—

'My dear sir, I will not let you wait till Saturday to learn that I am not at all frightened at your Teutonic fire, and shall receive your larger exposition of the faith that is in you, with all respect and thankfulness. I feel at once that you are a man of genius, and of original character and right heart, and shall be proud and happy to know more of you. I fairly tell you that I think your taste vicious in some points, and your opinions of your German idols erroneous. But (we will talk them over, in short) by and bye.'

The Carlyles spent most of July in the country, and from Thornhill rode one day to Craigenputtock, where Alexander Carlyle was farmer now, and uncle John the mason was waiting by appointment. It was decided to have everything ready for them to live there from May 1828. A story was to be added to the original house for them, and a new house built for the farmer,—who was soon to need married quarters. They were home by the beginning of August, and most of the month was given to reading for his article.

A letter came with a necklace for Mrs. Carlyle and other presents from Goethe, to whom he had sent *German Romance*, and in his letter of joyful acknowledgement (20.8.1827) Carlyle wrote :—

'You are kind enough to enquire about my bygone life. How often have I longed to pour out the whole history before you ! As it is, your Works have been a mirror to me ; unasked and unhoped-for, your wisdom has counselled me ; and so peace and health of soul have visited me from afar. For I was once an Unbeliever, not in Religion only, but in

28

all the Mercy and Beauty of which it is the Symbol ; storm tossed in my own imaginations ; a man divided from men ; exasperated, wretched, driven almost to despair ; so that Faust's wild *curse* seemed the only fit greeting for human life ; and his passionate *Fluch vor allen der Geduld* ! (cursed be Patience most of all !) was spoken from my very inmost heart. But now, thank Heaven, all this is altered : without change of external circumstances, solely by the new light which rose upon me, I attained to new thoughts, and composure, and look forward with cheerfulness to a life spent in literature, hoping little and fearing little from the world ; having learned that what I once called Happiness is not only not to be attained on Earth, but not even to be desired. No wonder I should love the wise and worthy men by whose instructions so blessed a result has been brought about.'

The new London University was reported to be in need of a Professor of Literature or Moral Philosophy. So he wrote to Edward Irving and to Henry Duncan, who was a friend of Brougham, who bossed it, to know whether and how he could try to get such a post, and doubtless mentioned it to Jeffrey when he went out to see him at his suburban house, Craigcrook, and found him friendlier than ever. There was nothing in this inconsistent with what he had written to Goethe about " hoping little from the world." As he said in the *State of German Literature* which he now wrote for the *Edinburgh Review* (October) :—

' The German authors are not poor, (but) better situated than our own. Their booksellers cannot pay as ours do ; yet Chattertons are much rarer in German than in English history. What is far more important : From the number of universities and other institutions we question whether the chance which a meritorious man of letters has before him, of obtaining some permanent appointment, some independent civic existence, is not a hundred to one in favour of the German, compared with the Englishman. For the votary of literature, the relation of entire dependence on the merchants of literature is highly questionable. It tempts him daily and hourly to sink from an artist into a manufacturer '—(and so on).

Jeffrey wrote to him (6.9.1827) :—

' My Dear Sir,—I hope you do not think I require a day's deliberation to say that I shall be ready at all times to recommend you as a man of genius and learning. But still it requires some deliberation to answer your letter, and would require still more, if I did not think so highly both of your candour and your temper, as to feel quite secure that whatever opinion I form on the subject, I may safely and explicitly express.

' I tell you therefore at once that I see difficulties in the way of your appointment. You are, to say it in one word, a *sectary* in taste and literature, and inspired by some of the zeal by which sectaries are distinguished—a zeal, that is, to magnify the distinguishing doctrines of your sect, and rather to aggravate than reconcile the differences which divide them from the votaries of the Establishment, and I confess I doubt whether the patrons of the new University either *will* or *ought* to appoint such a person to such a charge. The very frankness and sincerity of your character tend to make this objection more formidable. If your admiration of the German models were a mere air or singularity adopted capriciously or to create a sensation it would be easy for you conscientiously to disguise or qualify it, so as not to let it very conspicuously affect your academic instructions. But I very greatly mistake you if this be the case, and indeed can fancy that I see you, as you read the surmise, swelling with all the virtuous indignation of one who would rather submit to martyrdom than renounce any article of his philosophical and critical creed. Now I suppose you are aware that there is scarcely one of the patrons of the L.U. who adopts that creed, and probably but few of them who do not regard it as damnable heresy—and, without supposing that they are as zealous in the opposite faith as you are in yours, do you think it likely that they will put it in the way of being impressed on the academic youths for whose instruction they are providing ?

' This however is *the* question for your consideration. In all *other* respects I have no doubt that you are fully qualified for the situation to which you aspire, and likely to do great honour both to yourself and the Establishment by the manner in which you would discharge its duties. As a man of virtue, temper, genius, and learning, I shall most readily and warmly recommend you—but I know you would not wish me to disguise those singularities of opinion on which (though I think erroneously) I believe you most value yourself, and from which I foresee the obstructions to your success at which I have now hinted.'

Then with a frankness which was safe because Carlyle could be trusted to keep a secret he let him know the chair he wanted would be offered to Thomas Campbell, " if the disagreements which I am aware have arisen between him and some of the Directors are healed." As he might himself have to go soon to Harrogate, he suggested that Carlyle might fetch his wife out to Craigcrook and dine there on Monday (10.9.1828) ; which being done gave them five hours together. In consequence of the letter just read, Carlyle would be sure to turn the unsectarian side of himself uppermost, so to speak, perhaps without knowing it. He certainly did so in the treatise on hand, which delighted Jeffrey alike as Editor and as friend of the writer.

Carlyle wrote to his brother at Craigenputtock the next day (11.9.1827) :—

' If I go to London, Craigenputtock (is) like to see much less of us ; only two months yearly. On this, however, it were very rash to calculate at present ; for that I shall *not* go is likelier. I feel that the thing which lies in me *will* be spoken out, go whither I may. Meanwhile you do well to get forward with that house on the Moor.'

He wanted his brother John, who had been staying with them in Edinburgh and was a " fully qualified " doctor, to start practice at Dumfries, the town nearest to Craigenputtock ; but John would not. A mere student's life is apt to be demoralizing, making duty seem dull ; and John was also conceited, or afflicted by " the old devil's disease, haughtiness of heart," as his elder brother Tom said to their mother, and was only with difficulty held back from abandoning his trade and trying to live by hack-writing. In the meantime, on the invitation of an acquaintance, Eichthal, he was off to Munich, to " study " there and at Vienna, his brother advancing funds with obvious reluctance, consoling himself by the thought that it would keep him at his trade.

This made Craigenputtock less attractive ; and tho the relatives of both husband and wife were eager to have them living there beside them, their Edinburgh acquaintances remonstrated, the loudest of all being Jeffrey, who wrote from Harrogate (October 17th, 1827) :—

' I am a little startled at the notion of your Nithsdale retreat, and my impressions—perhaps somewhat selfish —are certainly against it. I think it has been your misfortune not to have mixed sufficiently with intelligent men of various opinions, and open and intrepid minds. . . . Think better of this scheme then, my very good friend, before you let it sink into your fancy. Give my love to my dear cousin (Mrs. Carlyle [1]), and ask her if she does not in her heart think my plan a wiser and safer one than yours ?

' We shall be at Craigcrook Sunday and the sooner I hear of you after that the better. I hope for ten days' or a fortnight's quiet there before my professional work begins.'

So for a week or two Jeffrey and Carlyle strolled in the woods together, or paused to look at beautiful views of land and sea. Their talk went at random over time and space, for both were interested more in the drama of life in general than in their own little parts ; and many a time—in particular one Thursday morning, 25.10.1827, from Craigcrook to Edinburgh—they were seen conversing as they moved together along the country roads, Carlyle ot and Jeffrey on a small pony, but their heads almost on a level as the man afoot was longer and the rider shorter than the average. So far as anything was said about economics, it would be an expansion of what Jeffrey wrote to him from Harrogate about the London " chair." He had then advised Carlyle to send direct to Brougham an advance copy of the October *Edinburgh Review*, and would now be told that had been done, and would be telling in more detail what he had written :—

' I find Mr. Brougham singularly shy on the subject, and though I introduced it half a dozen times during the day I spent with him on my way here, he contrived always to evade it in a way that showed me that he had not at all made up his mind with regard to it, and did not wish to be pressed for an explicit answer even by an intimate friend. He said that this being a chair on which the eyes of all the enemies of the Institution would be very keenly fastened, either for censure or ridicule, it is particularly necessary

[1] Cousinship was counted in Scotland to many generations.

to be cautious about it, and that he himself had an impression that it might be most prudent not to fill it up at all in the first instance, but he promised to read your paper, and to think afterwards of what I had said to him.'

On reaching home that day (October 25th, 1827), Carlyle wrote to his brother John, who could best sympathize with what Jeffrey called his " views of ambition," poking fun at his self-conscious superiority to material considerations.

' No appointment whatever to that Chair will take place for some time, perhaps for some considerable time ; and in the meanwhile Brougham will keep his eye on me, and if he finds that I prosper, may apply to me ; if not, will leave me standing.'

As Thomas Campbell never reconciled himself to Brougham and Co., the chair that Carlyle coveted lay vacant long, and Montagu kindly wrote to him to suggest that he should apply for it. But it was not needful. He knew that thanks to Jeffrey he was before the Directors, if they wanted him, and he lived to think it providential they never did.

Brougham was not a bad man. The would-be winners of the Woolsack cannot afford to be nice ; and he was better than the ruck of them, tho he had not the conscience of Jeffrey and detested the candour which Jeffrey liked. His besetting sin was the itch to domineer. An Edinburgh editor and writer, McCulloch, an intimate of Thomas Murray, was presently proceeding to London in consequence of a letter from Brougham, rejoicing to be his Professor of Political Economy ; but soon discovered that he was serving men who wanted Professors to be common " Yes-sirs," so that a man of self-respect might have to resign. The grateful McCulloch became the most " virulent " and " uncompromising " assailant in the press of the " arch-quack " Brougham.[1] Which shows that though Mephistopheles Brougham made many mistakes, he was doing the safe thing in his own interests when he resisted the solicitations of Jeffrey and kept out of contact with Carlyle. He felt an instinctive aversion, like that of evil spirits to the daylight.

[1] *Autobiographical Notes*, etc., by Thomas Murray, edited by J. A. Fairley, Dumfries, 1911, pp. 86–87.

D

IX

"A MYSTIC HIMSELF"

(1827)

THE best excuse for Brougham was that he had never seen Carlyle. He had to go on what he heard from Jeffrey and saw in the *State of German Literature*. Defending his German clients there from the reproach of "mysticism," Carlyle defined it as either having no meaning or being unable to express any ; and to show how obscurity might be blameless, he dwelt on the existence of objects which had no shape and could not be pictured in any. Instead of Heat or Light or Electricity, he instanced "the Soul" and "God." This was bad writing, darkening his drift, and really nothing worse ; but it must have seemed to Brougham deliberate humbug, as if parading a belief in the Christian God and immortality.

Those who knew Carlyle made no such mistake. His utter honesty was transparent. Sir William Hamilton said to him his essay was "capital" ; and Wilson told John Gordon, "It has done him a deal of good."

Carlyle's success in demonstrating that the best of the Germans were no "mystics," in any objectionable sense of the word, led a friendly journalist with a sense of humour, maybe Murray or McCulloch, to declare he was "a mystic himself." This was a happy hit, as the word was understood then and there, and pleased him well. He was fond of quoting it, and if better known he might have been labelled a leader of "mystics." Edinburgh was aware how Hume had used the word in his Dialogues concerning natural religion, where it was applied to both the religious Demea and the free-thinking Philo. They were "mystics" because they maintained against the philosophic Cleanthes that the Cause of Causes, God or Nature, remained infinite and incomprehensible, while they scornfully reprobated as a delusive nightmare the philosophic formula wherein Hume wished to rest, that the Universe was a machine,

34

indifferent to right and wrong. So it was as sure as any demonstration in Euclid that according to the use of the word by Hume, Carlyle was " a mystic himself."   He would be called an Agnostic to-day, and not confounded with any Bible-believer ; but there are Agnostics and Agnostics. He was of the kind that cultivate the conscience and have faith in Nature, or what the Chinese call the Justice of Heaven and Christians the " Providence of God."   Jeffrey appears to have been the only acquaintance who heeded his liking for the label of " mystic " ; and Jeffrey used it in fun, affecting to suppose a mystic must be confused and mysterious, and applying to Mrs. Carlyle, the most rational of women, the honourable appellation of " the Master Mystic."

To be thus chaffed instead of taken seriously was one of many lessons Carlyle was learning. Like Confucius he was fearless, as men go, and full of self-satisfaction. Perhaps they both needed their many disappointments. At any rate they both became remarkable for modesty, by precept and practice diligent to correct themselves and taboo fault-finding and self-assertion.

Confucius carried this farther than his modern counterpart. He called himself a transmitter and not a maker, who had learned all he knew. Carlyle might have said the same, and Jeffrey often told him so, but he never could believe it. Their differences of opinion rather enhanced than diminished their friendship. Carlyle himself said they were like a new Pylades and Orestes, and in a letter to Procter this winter exclaimed [1] :—

' What do I not owe you already for one of the kindest and most pleasant friends I ever had ! Francis Jeffrey is a man meant by Nature to be an intellectual Ariel, with a light etherealness of spirit which the weight of whole Courts of Session resting on it for quarter-centuries has not been able utterly to suppress. There is a glance in the eye of the man which almost prompts you to take him in your arms. Alas that Mammon should be able to hire such servants, even tho' they continue to despise him.'

[1] *Thomas Carlyle* by Moncure Conway, p. 243.

X

WERNER AND TASSO, &c.

(1827-8)

CARLYLE gave Jeffrey one of Goethe's medals, and reported to Goethe that by publishing his articles Jeffrey was "thought to have virtually recanted" his previous disesteem of German literature ; but he soon discovered he was mistaken. The *Edinburgh Review* had no room for more of it.[1] Alluding to an article in a new foreign quarterly, Jeffrey said :—" I agree with the critic on what he calls the fantastic style of the Germans, and that it is nothing better than fantastic, and has not a deep moral meaning as you suppose."

Observing that Carlyle himself had admitted German poetry " as a whole " was inferior to Italian as well as English, he suggested an article on Tasso. Carlyle already knew Tasso's epic, and started to study his critical writings ; but on Friday, 26.10.1827, began an article on Werner, applied for by London booksellers interested in a new foreign review and eager for German stuff which he could supply at once. He was feeling as he did it :—" I will get my mind spoken out, and have a trade to follow in this earth like others."

He finished and sent off within a month a racy but charitable history of the popular playwright, who had been fantastic in more than style. Beginning life in the Prussian civil service, Werner became famous for religious dramas and decided to be a prophet as well as a poet, with a new religion of his own, complete with creed and clergy. " Art, Religion and Love " was to be the new Trinity. Common Protestantism he detested, and agreed with Schleiermacher that the hope of immortality " perverted " Religion, and " impaired its sacredness." Not so his own performances. Not counting occasional concubines, he had three wives in succession, who each in turn divorced him, apparently for incontinence. He lost his official job when the French came to Berlin in 1807, and going on his travels, peram-

---

[1] Unpublished letter of Jeffrey.

bulated the best society as a " human goat of genius,"
to use the phrase of a German admirer. Werner was
familiar with de Staël and Goethe, to say nothing of
common royalties and people of fashion ; and biographers
have lately discovered it was he who led Goethe back into
flirtation at Jena with Minna Herzlieb, the original of
Ottilie in *Elective Affinities*. Werner ended in a course of
spiritual vapour baths at Rome, prayer-meetings and
fastings and so on, which decided him to turn papist and
plump for celibacy. He became a priest and preached his
new belief in Vienna pulpits for the rest of his life, with all
the fervour of a proselyte and a wealth of experience few
priests could boast.—Which would make Jeffrey more sure
than ever of his own opinion. We are left to imagine the
" Ha, ha's ! " of Wilson. Goethe felt uncomfortable—as
if Werner had come to life again.

Carlyle re-read some of Tasso next ; but the result of his
reading was left in his journal :—

' Tasso was a serious man, and *had* high views of Epic
poetry.' (Then comes what helps to show why he liked
to be called a mystic himself.) ' Tasso was a mystic.
Must not every true poet be so ? That is to say, must he
not have a sense of the Invisible Existences of Nature, and
be enabled as it were to read the symbols of these in the
visible ? Can any man delineate with *life* the figure even
of a Trinculo or Caliban otherwise ? For is not the poorest
nature a *mystery*, the most grovelling street porter ? . . .
Not one of Scott's *Fairservices* or *Deanses* etc., is *alive*.
As far as prose could go, he has gone ; and we have fair
outsides ; but within all is rather hollow, *nicht wahr* (is
it not so ?)—Alas, I do not see into this, and must talk
rather falsely of it, or " altogether hold my peace," which
perhaps were better.' (8.1.1828).

Which explains why Jeffrey never got an article on Tasso.
The London booksellers were delighted to order at once an
article on Goethe's Helena, the second part of *Faust*, and
another on Goethe himself to follow it, so that there was
work in sight on topics for which he was ready. Such
was his devotion to Goethe this winter that he was discussing with his wife an " excursion " they would soon make
together, spending six months with Goethe at Weimar
" for the study of music and painting ! "

XI

DE QUINCEY, &c.

BEFORE the end of 1827 his mother came from Scots-brig with one of her daughters, Jane, whose black hair made them call her " Craw Jean." He took them to see the Castle, John Knox's house, the Martyr's Grave, and the other wonders of Edinburgh. His mother went and stood upon the pier of Leith from which the ship had departed with her son John in it, and gazed wistfully seawards. One Sunday Tom took her to a " braw kirk " where she beheld and heard the famous Andrew Thomson without the usual admiration. She would not be so un-charitable as to say he read his sermon, but she suspected it and did remark : " He had to light four candles before ever he could strike," as if he could not preach well without light to read.

She saw Jeffrey once when he called ; and shook hands with a true German doctor, Becker, who could not only reassure her about the dangers surrounding the absent John, but was also curing now the suppurating throat of Tom in a miraculous way. He seems to have been the first medico to diagnose correctly that familiar affliction of his as due to liver and not to cold. But as the days passed she grew rapidly restless, being used to work, and was with difficulty persuaded to complete four weeks with them. Then she departed, leaving " Craw Jean " behind.

Perhaps the most curious of their callers was De Quincey, the opium-eater, whom Wilson had introduced and taught Carlyle to like. De Quincey was not easy to know. " The time when he was *most brilliant*," said Wilson's daughter, who knew him well,[1] " was generally towards the early morning." Her father and he were a comical contrast. Both were blue-eyed blonds, but Wilson far above the average size, and De Quincey " one of the very smallest " men Carlyle ever saw, " hardly above five feet " and most

[1] *Christopher North, a Memoir of John Wilson*, by Mrs. Gordon, II., pp. 156–8.

of that legs, so that he was like a pair of tongs. When sitting in candle-light he might have passed for a child. He has "a most gentle and sensible face," wrote Carlyle in 1827, " only that the teeth are destroyed by opium and the little bit of an underlip projects like a shelf. He speaks with a slow, sad, and soft voice in the politest manner I have almost ever witnessed "—avoiding contradiction, but leaving you in no doubt of his opinion all the same, if he differs—" and with great gracefulness and sense, were it not that he seems decidedly given to prosing." The tradition in Edinburgh was that he talked as he wrote, only better.

" What wouldn't one give," said Mrs. Carlyle, " to have him in a box, and take him out to talk." He was ten years older than her husband. It had been his praise of Richter that started Carlyle's admiration of him ; but De Quincey considered Goethe a tedious and immoral old imposter in comparison with Richter, and was aware how much Carlyle was handicapped by a female hearer in debating Goethe's ways with the women.

When his children were in Edinburgh, he would fetch them to pass the evening at the Carlyles' ; and when he had no such reason as their presence for early departure, would sit and talk till midnight. One winter day the Carlyles discovered, perhaps by some hint from Wilson whose wife was ill, that De Quincey was not only alone in his lodgings but sick. They brought him to their house, and there he stayed till he was better. Mrs. Carlyle was his nurse ; and " many many times " he used afterwards to speak " with touching earnestness " of her kindness. Her mother's example had given her skill, and skilful nursing was exactly what he needed. Besides the bad effects of too much laudanum, he had to endure the chronic ailment which had made him take to the drug—" gnawing pains in the stomach," due to slow ulceration.[1]

When he was at Wilson's, a daughter of the house who waited upon him said she used to " find him in his room lying upon the rug in front of the fire, his head resting upon a book with his arms crossed over his breast, plunged in profound slumber," after taking his morning dose. " For several hours he would lie " thus ; and if he had taken no more than she said, an ounce a day, it might have done little harm. But he has been seen to rise from among his

[1] *De Quincey*, by David Masson, p. 39, and for quantity, etc., p. 55.

friends, walk to the sideboard, pour out a wine-glassful of laudanum, toss it off like sherry and resume his seat.[1] A truthful biographer has to tell how he would let himself go to seven such ordinary wine-glasses in a day. Depression and death were the sure result of such excess, if continued ; but time after time he pulled himself together and diminished the drug, which he might not have been able to do but for female tenderness. Speaking in old age of Mrs. Carlyle's nursing on this occasion, he roundly declared :— "She was, indeed, the most angelic woman I ever met upon this God's earth." [2]

Without the friendship of big Wilson, however, the women might have failed. The sudden success of his *Confessions of an English Opium-Eater* might have spoiled him if Wilson had not befriended him in public and private, calling him in *Blackwood* "a man of a million," [3] and confirming him in his good resolutions. When he came home to Grasmere from London squalor, Wilson congratulated him thus :—" Thank God you are not now domineered over by circumstances, and may your noble nature never more be disturbed but by its own workings! " [4] He coaxed him to Edinburgh where he could help him best ; found him work, and made him feel his house a safe refuge in distress.

The readiness of Carlyle to forget that De Quincey had fiercely attacked his *Wilhelm Meister* would reveal him to Wilson as a man of the right sort, and Wilson's own demeanour to the disreputable waif who was yet a man of genius reveals himself as " a man of a million " among Professors of Moral Philosophy. Dr. Chalmers was another big man in academic cloisters. He was now professing " Moral Philosophy " at St. Andrews, and in Edinburgh used to notice " the curious creature " De Quincey," creeping along Great King Street like a separated shadow, or a man going about apologizing to all men for the unpardonable liberty of being in the world."

[1] Seen by a credible man who told David Masson, who gave leave to tell it here.

[2] *Nights and Days with De Quincey*, by James Hogg, in *Harper's New Monthly Magazine*, January, 1890 ; and A. H. Japp's *True and Noble Women* ; both quoted and a misdating neatly and rightly corrected in Mrs. Ireland's *Life of Jane Welsh Carlyle*, pp. 313–4, Appendix, IV.

[3] *De Quincey*, by David Masson, p. 76.

[4] *Ditto*, p. 81.

XII

THE PRINCIPAL AND PROFESSORS OF ST. ANDREWS PROMISE TO MEND THEIR WAYS

(1827-8)

WHEN Thomas Chalmers, the great divine of the day, departed from his pulpit-throne in Glasgow to become the Professor of Moral Philosophy in the smallest university in Scotland, St. Andrews, the world had wondered at a new event in history. A Diocletian might doff the purple, or a David Garrick take leave of the stage, but did a Pope of any colour ever retire before ? A preacher Scotland was so proud of, and in the prime of life ! Great was the excitement in December, 1827, when he agreed to come to Edinburgh as Professor of Divinity, and thus emerge again. The Principal and Professors whom he had been honouring with his company determined to seize their opportunity, when the eyes of Scotland were upon them, to show themselves public-spirited and superior to jobbery, and announced they would elect as his successor at St. Andrews the best man available. They never doubted he would be a divine. The salary was between three and four hundred,[1] above the average stipend and worth keeping in the church, but not expected to draw any formidable competitor, so that the ostentation of impartiality would redound to the greater glory of the clergy, and they would feel like the man in an old play :—

> " That happiness is well-deserved
>   Which now is mine who speak to you,
> Who feel that I've my country served,
>   And done a stroke of business too."

Intellectual Edinburgh laughed aloud, incredulous, and instigated Carlyle to apply ; some like Jeffrey from mere goodwill to him, and some for the fun of the thing. Jeffrey wrote (24.12.1827) :—

---

[1] Lawson's *Gazetteer of Scotland*, 1841, p. 919.

'MY DEAR SIR,

Though my holidays have not yet begun—
for I am just returned from a jury trial—I have not been
quite idle in making enquiries about the probability of
your success at St. Andrews, though I am afraid I have
nothing very encouraging to report. The nomination I
find is understood to be in substance with Dr. Nicol, the
Principal, an active, jobbing, popular man, who has placed
most of the present professors, and conferred obligations
on all, and who, from having great influence with Lord
Melville in his day of power, has acquired an absolute
ascendancy over these grateful and obsequious sages. If
you can secure Nicol therefore, you may command their
votes, and if he is against you, there is no hope in them.
I do not well know through what channel you can approach
him, and to say the truth I have but little hope of your
finding favour in his eyes. He is a good-natured, sensible,
worldly man, and not without some sense of the propriety
of bringing known talents and reputation to the aid of his
declining college. But he is a cautious, prudent person,
without genius or learning, and without reverence for them,
very zealous for moderation in matters ecclesiastical, and
having a great contempt and distrust for all sorts of enthusiasm. It is not unlikely that he has already cast his eyes
on some decent, manageable and judicious priest for this
office, though I have not yet heard of any candidate but a
young man . . . who is said to be given to study.

'Think over what sort of recommendations you could
muster, and from what quarters? Your high religionists,
like E. Irving, will do you no good, but harm. Men of rank
and high titles I take it will weigh most in the scale, and
after them men of repute for learning. I shall think of
something to be done and pray tell me how you suppose I
can be useful.

'But do not run away to Dumfriesshire, though this
Temple of Glory and Science should for the present be shut
to you. You can be as quiet here as there, when the reading or the studious fit is on you, and you surely may divert
yourself as well, and certainly give more pleasure, when
you can condescend to be social. And so God bless you.

Ever very truly yours,

F. JEFFREY.'

Nicol had made his choice, an " old stager," the Rev. Dr. Cook ; but of course he did not say so.   In showing Carlyle the answer received from him, Jeffrey remarked :— " You see (it) amounts to nothing, sincere as he boasts it to be.   My own notion is that he reckons on Cook, and will support him if he appears—the roll of other candidates is not very frightful.   Think what you will do, and command any service of mine."

When he heard Carlyle was to apply, he sent him a testimonial that delighted even Mrs. Carlyle ; and so did Prof. Leslie, and Edward Irving at great length, and his namesake, Dr. Irving, an author famous then, and Brewster and Buller and Procter and others.   He wrote to Goethe himself for a certificate, but sent in his application in the last week of January, without waiting for Goethe's reply. What must have given pause to Nicol and his flock was that the intellectual leaders of the Tories agreed for once with the Whigs, and in particular the man who more than any other was *Blackwood* then, the Professor of Moral Philosophy in Edinburgh, John Wilson.

XIII

WHAT WILSON AND GOETHE THOUGHT OF CARLYLE

(1828)

CONTEMPORARY letters show Wilson breakfasting at Carlyle's one Sunday, perhaps when De Quincey was there. Sunday was Wilson's quiet day, as Edinburgh did not approve of Sunday convivialities. Carlyle and he were mutually attracted, but their women did not coalesce, Mrs. Carlyle being already too much in Mrs. Jeffrey's circle, and Mrs. Wilson " far from well " [1]; while Carlyle never entered the tavern where Wilson reigned—he had neither the leisure nor the money to frequent it. Their intercourse was therefore mainly of the accidental meeting kind, but that meant more then than now, and they made the most of it.

If both were alone when they met, they would " join up " and walk together—when one is out for a walk, the direction matters little. To Carlyle the sound sense and discernment of his senior were always apparent, though the shape of his talk was apt to be witty or merry, and he loved to put things concretely, as when in telling of the trouble he had in shaping testimonials, he named a man and said—" You cannot write, ' I certify Mr.——— is an ass ! ' "

The one he gave Carlyle himself in January, 1828, must have been pleasanter to write.

' From my acquaintance with your various writings and with yourself, I have formed a very high estimate of your moral and intellectual character ; nor do I know a man better qualified than you are for the chair to which you now aspire. On such an occasion there can be no indelicacy

---

[1] *Christopher North, a Memoir of John Wilson*, II., by Mrs. Gordon, p. 125.

in declaring my belief that you are a man of distinguished abilities, and of great erudition—of abilities and
erudition that could be brought to bear, with uncommon
effect. . . . I have no doubt that you would, if elected to
this chair, discharge its duties conscientiously, ably, and
eloquently, and prove an admirable teacher. . . .

Your very sincere friend,
JOHN WILSON.' [1]

Goethe had never seen his disciple, but had materials
for an opinion in his writings and wrote :—

' True conviction proceeds from the heart ; the Soul, the
real seat of the Conscience, judges concerning what may be
permitted and what may not be permitted far more surely
than the Understanding, which will see into and determine
many things without hitting the right mark.

' German literature has effected much for humanity in
this respect, introducing not ascetic timidity, but a free
culture in accordance with nature, and in cheerful obedience
to law, and therefore I have observed with pleasure Mr.
Carlyle's profound study of this literature, and I have
noticed with sympathy how he has not only been able to
discover the beautiful and human, the good and great in us,
but has also contributed what was his own, and has endowed us with the treasures of his genius. It must be
granted that he has a clear judgment as to our Æsthetic
and Ethic writers and, at the same time, his own way of
looking at them, which proves that he rests on an original
foundation and has the power to develop in himself the
essentials of what is good and beautiful.

' In this sense, I may well regard him as a man who would
fill a Chair of Moral Philosophy, with single-heartedness,
with purity, effect and influence ; enlightening the youth
entrusted to him as to their real duties, leading their minds
to moral activity, and thereby steadily guiding them towards a religious completeness.'

Goethe's praise of his originality went to Carlyle's heart.
He quoted it proudly to his brother John, and all his life
was conscious of his originality. Yet Jeffrey was also right

[1] "Christopher North," *Nineteenth Century Magazine*, January, 1920, by
Alexander Carlyle, p. 109.

in telling him he was not nearly so original as he supposed. There was almost nothing new about him, and even the eccentricities of his style were mimicry. He was not endowed by nature with mental wings ; but like an airman, found a way to lift himself. The essence of what he supposed " originality " was sincerity. He needed to see and feel and believe whatever he had to tell—and then, were it nothing more than that two and two make four, he spoke from insight and conviction, not from hearsay and authority. " Seeing once," they say in the East, " is better than hearing a thousand times."

Two of Goethe's phrases bear a double meaning which needs explaining. " Obedience to law " did not refer to the law of the " courts," and Goethe meant something different from the English Bishop who said the people had nothing to do with the law but obey it. In modern words, he spoke of " law " as science does or should, and not in the style of a lawyer or a Bishop ; and the " religious completeness " to which he pointed as the crown of education was behaviour in harmony with good conscience and sense—it had nothing to do with orthodoxy.

It is needless to speculate whether the simple persons at St. Andrews to whom Goethe was a mystery might have been misled by such phrases. They never saw them. Goethe wrote in March ; and Carlyle sent in his testimonials before the end of January.

XIV

PRINCIPAL NICOL SHOWS PRESENCE OF MIND, AND FULFILS HIS FATE

(1828)

INTELLECTUAL Edinburgh, a few score men of sense, were laughing for two or three weeks at the dilemma in front of Nicol and his flock. Surely they would have either to incur derision by doing a job without disguise, or appoint Professor of Moral Philosophy a man from Edinburgh who was not a divine, which was enough to make all the divines in Scotland turn in their beds.

Nicol was disconcerted by the sight of such testimonials as Carlyle sent in, but never faltered in his fidelity to Cook. The first intention had been to solicit that great man— " no candidates that can be compared with you," and so on ; but that could not be said of Carlyle, with Jeffrey and Wilson both at his back.

Nicol had the presence of mind to whisper to Chalmers, who " unaccountably " delayed to send in his resignation. The public were told that nothing would be settled till November, and even Jeffrey believed this—for a day or two.[1] But by the middle of February a man behind the scenes at St. Andrews reported that only the announcement was delayed—Cook was to be appointed. So when Goethe's certificate arrived a few weeks later, Carlyle did not let the electors " smell " it, as he said, describing them as " dogs."

No wonder he began to feel a faint belief in particular providence as he looked back in old age. He had sought this employment for the sake of a livelihood, intending his writing to be a thing apart ; but assuredly his writing in that event would never have been the same.

Even at the time, he was reverent of reality, and accepted what had to be without repining. Thus Nicol and his

[1] Unpublished letter.

followers did him no harm, though they never intended to do him any good. Serving class interests with the single-minded devotion of the Stock Exchange, they were instruments of Fate, and furthered the designs of Providence— unawares.

It is not well to want to justify the ways of Nature, which makes no mistakes in morals any more than in materials. The whole of what humanity can know, though one could learn it all, which is impossible, remains an insignificant snippet of reality. Whoever cannot find the sanction of righteousness in his heart will never discover it in history.

Nevertheless it may be said that Chalmers had not forgotten " that laddie," as he called Carlyle, whom he had tried to convert to Christianity in vain. Perhaps he thought a pocket-Christian like the Rev. Dr. Cook a safer teacher of Morals, if not a better—a much-esteemed divine and maker of Church histories. None can know the motives of another. Chalmers may have been conscious of nothing but obliging Nicol. Only this is history, that in the ten years' hubbub in the Church Assemblies which ended in the Disruption, Cook was the leading opponent of Chalmers.

XV

LAST MONTHS IN TOWN

(1828)

REALITY is funnier than fiction. For many years in London Mrs. Carlyle had to hinder her husband from returning to live at Craigenputtock or somewhere else in the country, as he hankered to do. To help her arguments she invented sacrifices she had made for him, magnifying his illusions about rich offers she had refused and pretending it was entirely on account of *his* health that they ever went to live at Craigenputtock. The longer she lived, the surer she felt of this, and the less he doubted it, though he never forgot as she was fond of doing that the real reason for the change was economy.

So when at last she died he saw nothing in her behaviour as he looked back but self-sacrifice and magnanimity, and lamented her as lovingly as ever man lamented woman ; but the beautiful reality has been pictured as if by a caricaturist, and by the most dangerous of all caricaturists, one who thinks he is making a portrait and has no sense of humour. The hero of Mr. Froude's Thomas Carlyle laments like the Gargantua of Rabelais :—" ' My so good wife is dead, who was the most *this*, the most *that*, that ever was in the world ! ' With these words he did cry like a cow." In place of the litanies of French priests attending Gargantua, Froude was professionally sad, like an undertaker's man, and wrote whatever fictions came into his head.

Let us humbly bend our minds to the facts. It was on her account only that her mother was anxious to see them in the country. Carlyle's sore throat this winter was treated correctly for the first time and quickly disappeared. His wife was always ailing more or less. He nursed her once, she said, " as well as my own mother could have done " ; but naturally her mother wanted to have her near herself. In writing to his brother, Dr. John (1.2.1828), Carlyle reported, after mention of their sister Jane whom their mother had left in Edinburgh—" *My* Jane, I grieve to say, is yet far from well ; but I hope much from summer weather, and a smart pony in the south. She is not by any means an established *valetudinarian*; yet she seldom has a day of true health, and has not *gained* strength certainly since you left her," which means about four months ago. The reference to possible benefit from riding is interesting, as proof of what many a modern doctor can guess, that none of the medical advisers of Mrs. Carlyle suspected then what the best doctors who afterwards knew all her symptoms believed, that from her early teens she had been suffering from an internal trouble peculiar to her sex, and which riding would make worse.

In March there was a literary dinner party at Sir William Hamilton's, which lasted to the small hours though it began in the afternoon. The editors and lawyers and tourists of letters talked without intermission, more than one at a time, and filled the hours if they did not make them fly, but no Boswell reporting, we can only look, not listen, and need hardly name. Sir William's brother, Captain Hamilton, " Peninsular hero " and successful fictioneer, kept Carlyle in countenance by eating and drinking like him— half a glass of claret and one potato sufficing each of them for supper. Sir William watched them with a radiant smile, but rose superior to current conventions and said nothing. De Quincey was there, but quiet, looking worried, " in the *low* stage of his opium regimen." Even Sir William's hospitality did not stretch to a decanter of laudanum on the sideboard.

A " wizened " little Captain Skinner, " lively " and "harmless," called at Comely Bank with a card from Goethe, and at one of Mrs. Carlyle's evening teas he sang to general satisfaction " Kennst du das Land "—Knows't thou the Land—the song in Wilhelm Meister. Then returning to Weimar he gave Goethe " good and pleasant news " of Carlyle and his surroundings.

Before March was out, Mrs. Carlyle had gone to Templand to help her mother to nurse Aunt Jeannie who was dying there, while her husband had finished Goethe's *Helena* and gone to Scotsbrig and Craigenputtock, where he found the plastering and other work so far behind that he saw it would be more comfortable to stay another year in Edinburgh. But the death of Aunt Jeannie delayed them, and their house was let when they returned, so that they had to leave it on Whitsunday, and stick to their first plan. The last thing he wrote in Comely Bank was the essay on Goethe, quoting and expanding the notice of his hero in *German Romance*, and dwelling on his favourite passage in the *Wanderjahre* or *Travelling Years* of Wilhelm Meister. It classifies religions into three kinds, Reverence for what is above us, and around us, and under us. The last was the Christian. The imitation Popes presiding were such perfect gentlemen, however, that they said they " specially adhered to all the three," which may have suggested a good thing Carlyle said to Spedding that the Trinity was like a man in three coaches at once ; but that was long after now. In 1828 he was very much in earnest about his German evangel, and glorified his hero as a poet with the " dignity " of a priest, speaking wisdom and practising it, and in short combining the faith of a saint with the clearness of a sceptic. Which after all is not so difficult for a saint who can have three religions at a time. A little scepticism would sweeten the mixture. A sign of grace in the essay was the frank admission it is special pleading, which may have enhanced the delight with which Jeffrey read it, declaring it made him proud of Carlyle.[1]

In May the town was flooded with elders and divines attending the annual assemblies, while for twelve mornings the biggest church available was overflowing with them, jostling each other for seats at six—an early hour selected for their convenience so as not to clash with other engagements—to hear Edward Irving " preaching like a Boanerges "[2] on the Apocalypse. Many a reverend gentleman confessed to using force, and Dr. Chalmers himself, over from St. Andrews, was one of those who failed to get in at first, in spite of force. Such was the stampede of Bible-believers, appalled by the prospect of the Test Act being repealed, and Catholic disabilities ended—supposing the Last Day in sight.

Henry Inglis reporting said : " The town is quite divided about him, one party thinking that he is quite mad, another that he is an entire humbug." Yet the believers were many and rich enough to give a Public Dinner to their prophet. He called upon the Carlyles that day, though he could hardly have hoped to fetch his friend to such a function. " The Lord bless you ! " was his greeting as he entered their room.

Unknown to Carlyle and his wife, young Jane Carlyle

---

[1] Unpublished letter.
[2] *Life of Edward Irving*, by Mr. Oliphant, Ch. XIII., p. 228, etc. Details not taken from there are from Carlyle, *Reminiscences* and Letters.

who was living with them, " Craw Jean," secreted herself
behind some furniture in the hope of seeing and hearing the
great man unnoticed. His long black hair touched her
with sympathy—it was so like her own still hanging down
her back. When cake and wine came in, she was amazed
to see him rise and waving his hands over the tray deliver
himself with unction of these words—" Lord bless your
basket and your store, and the little maiden who abideth
with you." Which thrilled the little maiden, who never
forgot it ; but whether the others knew she was there
remains a mystery.[1]

He stayed only half-an-hour, no time for more—" very
friendly," but talking in a stilted way in spite of all they
could do to bring him down to common conversation, so
that Carlyle wrote to his brother, after quoting Inglis :
" Positively there does seem a touch of extreme exaltation
in him : I do not think he will go altogether mad, yet what
else he will do I cannot so well conjecture. Cant and
enthusiasm are strangely mingled : he preaches in steam-
boats and all open places, wears clothes of an antique cut
(his waistcoat has flaps or tails midway down the thigh)."

Rising to depart, he proposed to pray, and receiving no
encouragement, did it as he stood, and then—" Farewell,"
said he, " I must go then—and suffer persecution as my
fathers have done ! " And so he went to the Public Dinner,
alone for the moment, but speedily comforted by his swarm
of simpletons. They were little like Christ. " Their
hearts were the stuff would be powder enough, and their
skulls were a storehouse of lead." When Irving was not
expatiating to them on the day of judgment when they would
enjoy the damnation of others, or any other dream that gave
delight, he was articulating their foolish horror of the repeal
of the Test Acts, and writing for them " eloquent " letters
to George Guelph IV. and other " Christians." Carlyle
was ashamed of him. Old Walter Welsh wondered they
did not " lay him up." Jeffrey smiled and Wilson laughed
aloud, but they were too polite to chaff him as a friend of
Irving—it was too much like lunacy. " What think'st a
(thou) he means ? " demanded old James Carlyle of his son,
' our Tom.' " What think'st a he means, gawn (going)
up and down the country tevvelling [2] and screeching like
a wild bear ? "

---

[1] Often told by her to a daughter who repeated it, 28.8.1922.
[2] Scotch for making things confused.

LAST DAYS IN EDINBURGH

(1828)

A DAY or two after Irving's public dinner, the Carlyles left Comely Bank, and stayed two nights with the Jeffreys in their new town house in Moray Place, to let the carts with the furniture get a start on the way to Craigenputtock. Jeffrey enjoyed the two nights of late talking so much that he was ever afterwards ready for more ; but tho Mrs. Jeffrey liked Carlyle, she could barely endure his wife. The women never quite harmonized.[1] They avoided friction. No more was possible ; and that is the key to the courtesies of Jeffrey towards the younger woman. She was young enough to have been his daughter ; and he always called her " My Dear Child," and as soon as they discovered some distant connection called cousinship in Scotland but never heeded in England, it was " My dear child and cousin." [2] Jeffrey's only aim was to prevent any feline amenities interfering with his friendship with Carlyle ; but Mrs. Carlyle imagined he meant a harmless flirtation. Her husband believed whatever she told him with a simplicity almost bucolic, which saved time and bother.

On this occasion Jeffrey seems to have reminded Carlyle that he was ready to accept an article on Tasso, and added— " One on Burns, too—either or both." Nobody Carlyle respected had ever yet spoken of Burns as he could hear Jeffrey doing now. When Jeffrey was a boy of thirteen in Edinburgh, he had stood staring at a man in the High Street who seemed remarkable, and a stranger standing at a shop door tapped him on the shoulder and said—"Ay, laddie, ye may weel look at that man ! That's Robert Burns ! " [3]

---

[1] Told by Miss Roberta Anderson, Barskimming, Ayrshire, reporting the talk of her friend, Miss Empson, Jeffrey's grand-daughter, who repeated her mother's report of what she heard from *her* mother, Mrs. Jeffrey.

[2] Unpublished letters from Jeffrey to Carlyle. There are some to Mrs. Carlyle only ; but in general she gets merely a short note on the sheet whereon he is writing to T.C. at length.

[3] *Life of Lord Jeffrey*, by Cockburn, I., p. 8.

What he now said at length was doubtless to the same effect as what he was presently writing to Carlyle at Craigenputtock : " After what you said about working for booksellers I am half afraid to ask you. But mine is a free service, I hope, and if you like it better you shall command. Lockhart's Burns is but a poor affair, but sensible and honest. And I can never read anything about Burns without a melting and a burning in my blood." Besides, he added in chaff, " You need not do more than *pretend* reviewing."

Carlyle said he was hoping to do both Tasso and Burns, but had first according to promise to do Heyne for the *Foreign Review*. He had given Jeffrey one of the medals Goethe sent. Before leaving Edinburgh he called at Wilson's house to give another to him. He begged Wilson to visit him at Craigenputtock, and doubtless said Jeffrey had promised to do so. " Yes, I will come," said Wilson at last, " and see you, Craigenputtock and you, for certain I will. But you must write specially to ask me," [1] when you are ready for visitors ; and Carlyle said he would.

[1] " Christopher North," *Nineteenth Century Magazine*, January, 1920, by Alexander Carlyle, p. 114.

BOOK VII

AT HOME IN THE COUNTRY

1828–30

I

THE START AT CRAIGENPUTTOCK

(1828)

AT Craigenputtock he did Heyne as soon as possible, in spite of the noise around. It was several months before the workmen ceased from troubling him, and occasionally he called the place a "Devil's Den." But he never repented coming to it. They could not live in Edinburgh for much less than £200 a year, and half as much was enough at Craigenputtock. Now by steadily writing in the best periodicals the most he could reasonably expect to make was two or three hundred.[1] So Craigenputtock was the place to live if they wanted to afford a six months' holiday at Weimar, and if he was to feel free to write something which was not hack-work, something like *Wotton Reinfred*. Life was quieter in the country, but better for work. Both he and his wife were hoping for better health, and found it; and while their friends lamented loudly their departure from Edinburgh, Jeffrey the loudest, the relatives of both rejoiced, Mrs. Welsh the most of all.

One of the carpenters used to tell how Carlyle came and stood watching his work this summer. He criticised what was being done in such a way that the carpenter lost patience, flung down his tools, and said he would go away. The talk went on. Carlyle did not unsay anything; but what he was saying took another turn; and to show him something, the man took up his tools again, and ended by going on in high spirits, and finishing his work with delight. All he could repeat exactly was that when he had finished Carlyle surveyed what he had done and said to him: "I could no more have done that than I could have written Isaiah."[2]

---

[1] Calculated in great detail by David Masson in the hearing of D.A.W. See also his *De Quincey*, p. 80.

[2] Told on 14.12.1896, by Dr. McKenzie, Health Officer, Leith. The carpenter was not named.

'My Dear Carlyle,' wrote Jeffrey, 27.6.1828, 'Why do you not write to me?' (Then, after many details of his own health and work, and his thoughts of them :—) 'You will see there is to be a *new* London University, under the especial patronage of the bishops and the good Duke. Perhaps they may want a Professor of Mysticism there. Shall I speak for you to some of my orthodox friends? We have been burying Dugald Stewart, and if I were a little more at leisure, I should compose a small panegyric upon him : for tho' a bit of a humbug, he was a man of a lofty and pure mind, and could for the most part be understood, for which you of course will despise him. I sometimes ride past your deserted little mansion at Comely Bank, and see vulgar heads at the windows through which your intellectual countenances used to smile on me. And now God bless you and good night, for the morning light is coming in at my shutters, and I must go to bed. Let me know when you think I can do you any service, and believe me always very affectionately yours,—F. JEFFREY.

'Tho' I mean this only to revive and refresh you, I may as well ask whether you have been thinking of doing anything for me in the reviewing way—with Burns, or Tasso or anything else?'

A few weeks later Charles Buller was writing to him about the same Institution, the King's College, and suggesting lectures in London such as he delivered nine years afterwards.

'Suppose you were to propose to give lectures on German literature and philosophy, I should think you would get an innumerable quantity of pupils. It would certainly be a great thing to have one person in that establishment who knows anything beyond that slender and antique lore of Oxford and Cambridge. But I only mention this, for I am utterly ignorant whether this new King's College is to teach anything beyond loyalty and Church of Englandarianism, or to have any teachers except a Greek and Latin lecturer, and perhaps one in Divinity to explain the Catechism. But if you think it worth while I would obtain information from the Bishop of Llandaff, who is the best of the people who have anything to do with it.'

Carlyle did not delay to write to Jeffrey and received a

reply (16.7.1828) overflowing with kind confidences. Jeffrey was overwhelmed with work and said :—

' If my health were quite entire, I should not care at all, but I cannot always get time now to walk out before going to sleep in the dewy dawn, or even to read for half-an-hour in some sweet and soothing poem, after my dull task is over, washing its earthy stains from my brain in these waters of healing. And so I often go to sleep with my fancy defiled, and join toil to toil with a tumbled sleep— and that is irksome, and is a profane dulling of a summer day.'

He promised a visit ' about September,' and said :—
' If there is anything I can do to serve you, in money matters, or anything else, pray tell me frankly, and I shall answer with the same simplicity.' As Jeffrey always paid contributors at the highest rate, the wish to oblige his friend would be blended with his love for Burns in making him press for an article which Carlyle now undertook to write at once, in a long and cordial letter for which Jeffrey thanked him, when advising dispatch of all the books on Burns.

In this connection it is noteworthy that tho' there were many in Dumfries who had known Burns well, and his widow was still there, Carlyle made no attempt at direct research. He had the best of Burns engraved on his memory from boyhood. His earliest pilgrimage had been to the then neglected grave. He knew the widow by sight and at Haddington had been intimate with the poet's brother Gilbert. He felt as if he knew Burns, and without a day's delay sat down to read the books sent to him, and write.

His wife was preoccupied about curtains and such things, making ready to welcome the Jeffrey family soon ; and here is what she wrote to her old confidant, Bess Stodart (29.8.1828) :—[1]

' My Dear, Dear Angel Bessy ! ! ! By this writing you will know that I have survived my astonishing change ; and the talk about tea, etc., will show you that I even look hopefully into life. Indeed, Craigenputtock is no such frightful place. Till lately, indeed, our existence here has been made

---

[1] *Early Letters of Jane Welsh Carlyle*, by D. G. Ritchie, pp. 127-130.

black with smoke ; and confusion unspeakable was nearly turning our heads. But we are beginning to get a settlement made at last, and see a distinct prospect of being more than tolerably comfortable. The solitude is not so irksome as one might think. If we are cut off from good society, we are also delivered from bad ; the roads are less pleasant to walk on than the pavement of Princes Street, but we have horses to ride, and, instead of shopping and making calls, I have bread to bake and chickens to hatch. I read and work, and talk with my husband, and never weary.

'I ride over to Templand occasionally, and my mother and Agnes Ferguson were here last week. They seemed content with the aspect of things.'

After thirty-nine years Carlyle's deliberate verdict was :

'It looks to me now like a kind of humble russet-coated *epic*, that seven years' settlement at Craigenputtock. I incline to think it the poor *best* place that could have been selected for the ripening into fixity and composure, of anything useful which may have been in me, against the years that were coming. And it is certain that for living in, and thinking in, I have never since found in the world a place so favourable. And we were driven and pushed into it, as if by necessity, and its beneficent tho' ugly little shocks and pushes, shock after shock gradually compelling us thither ! " For a Divinity doth shape our ends, rough-hew them how *we* will " ' (and he underlined for emphasis the " we," to the ruin of the rhythm, which was like him). . . . 'We were not unhappy at Craigenputtock ; perhaps these were our happiest days. Useful, continual labour, essentially successful ; that makes even the moon green.'

II

THE CREED OF JEFFREY

JEFFREY had long been the most successful of editors, but many contributors thought he meddled too much with what they wrote, an opinion to which Carlyle inclined, before they were done with Burns. Before he began to write, in the very letter (1.8.1828) wherein Jeffrey " thanked him from his heart for his kindness," he was made to feel the curb :—

' I hope you will be able to do something about Burns. But I really cannot consent to your *déchaînement* upon (depreciating freely) all the harmonists of the age. Felicia Hemans is my delight, and for Moore I have the most profound admiration. What you say of them is thoroughly unjust. Apart from all that is *amatory*, I will show you infinite passages in Moore, to which I defy you to find a match in Goethe and any of his followers. It is mere deadness to music and fancy not to see this. And for Felicia, she is a pearl or rich crystal, and as gentle as a female fairy—a fie on your ungallant, unkind, insensible prejudices. I would as soon tolerate an exclusive admirer of Pope as of your Germans. Do renounce paradox, and outlandish absurdity, and stand on your own feet—a true British man.'

The Jeffreys went to Loch Lomond in August, but came home soon. Writing to Mrs. Carlyle (23.8.1828) to announce their impending visit, Jeffrey asked, " what he is doing ? " and letting his pen run on with news moralized extempore for the benefit of both.—Indeed there was nothing he ever wrote to either which the other might not read.

' We came home by the falls of the Clyde and paid some visits, which I daresay you think was very frivolous. But they diverted us and did no harm. Tell me how you occupy yourself, and what thoughts you cherish, of life and truth, and happiness and duty ? My creed is a very humble and quiescent one on all these matters—it is to think action and effort no otherwise right than as they are necessary or agreeable ; and, seeing in what a vast proportion of things we *must* be *passive*, and submit to be borne on the stream of destiny, to learn to be contented with that lot, and to await patiently for the accidents of enjoyment and illumination which, as well as the contrary, will come to us at any rate, and in spite of our little impatient struggles, in this life or another.   Bad heresy this, in the eyes of your man of energy who expects to make discoveries as to these our notions and to acquire dominion over them, poor things. I am sure my notions are the most natural, and I am persuaded you agree with me in your heart, and so will your husband too, when the fermentation subsides, and the intellectual fluid receives its transparency.'

To Carlyle himself he wrote :—

' You have no mission upon earth, whatever you may fancy, half so important as to be innocently happy, and all that is good for you of poetic feeling, and sympathy with majestic nature, will come of its own accord, without your straining after it.   This is my creed, and right or wrong, I am sure it is both a simpler and a *humbler* one than yours, and so God bless you.'

The reply to this is lost.   The rejoinder is in Jeffrey's finest blend of chaff and earnest :—

' We are all predestinarians in our hearts I fancy, and run our risks patiently, simply because we cannot avoid them. I hope I may be the means of weeding out some of those damnable heresies to which I see you are still devoted.   One is, that our modern songsters in the minor key are worthy of bitter hate and eloquent reprobation, which is much more like the sentiment of some spiteful disappointed brother of the craft, than the judgment of a philanthropic philosopher.   Another is that men are less noble than in the days of Shakespeare or Cervantes.   Do cure yourself of this tendency to exaggeration.   You may talk as long as you like about a false principle of pride or honour, and the necessity of having a right creed as to your relations with

the universe, but you will never persuade anybody that the
regulation of life is such a mighty laborious business as you
would make it, or that it is not better to go lightly through
it, with the first creed that comes to hand, than to spend
the better part of it in an anxious verification of its articles.
If you were only amusing yourself with these paradoxes,
I should have no objection, but you take them so dreadfully
in earnest that it vexes me—for it will neutralise half the
fame and all the use of your talents—and keep aloof from
you most of the men who are fittest for your society. And
so much for my renewed testimony against mysticism, which
I repeat, you see, as Cato did his *delenda est Carthago*—
" Carthage must be destroyed," words Cato was continually
repeating in the Roman Senate—' and I hope with the
same chance of ultimate success as attended his damnable
iteration.'

It is easy to feel why Jeffrey and Carlyle enjoyed each
other's company, with similar sentiments and so many
different opinions. Jeffrey was bourgeois by birth and
breeding, and though he had still a conspicuous " part to
play," his health and strength were ebbing. The hardest
of his life's work was done. The Whig victory he had done
so much to win was impending, and little remained but
the shouting. Carlyle was the cultivated countryman,
delivered from rustic delusions and able to consider before
accepting the shibboleths of the towns. His work was
but beginning. The essay on Burns he was now to write
was the first intimation to serious readers that the " sweet
singer " of Scotland had added to the Bible of the world.
The Whig Jeffrey and the Tory Wilson could agree for once
with him and each other about Burns ; but men like them
were wondering what would happen if he applied to others
the same measure as to Burns. They were surprised at his
simplicity. A young man from the country might expect
a man of letters to mean what he said and act accordingly.
But the like of Carlyle should have seen long ago that in
modern Europe a man could not live by letters at all on
such terms, or " make a career " in the professions. Both
church and state were standing on delusions, and everybody
seemed to agree to act upon the pre-Reformation maxim,
" humbug the people because they like it." Was he going
to start another disturbance ? Was he itching like another
Rousseau for harmony of thought and feeling, word and

action ? So rare was such health of mind that it was becoming a common opinion that it never existed after infancy. To those who saw Carlyle was sincere, he appeared as mad as King Lear objecting to sophistications.

Jeffrey was sorry for him and could sympathize more than Wilson, remembering the dreams of his youth and the days when even his own mild whiggery was dangerous. The difference between him and Carlyle was mainly the result of difference in age. As Carlyle had early read the whole of the *Edinburgh Review* from the beginning, he was like a disciple of Jeffrey, now mature. It may have been Jeffrey as much as Voltaire or Goethe that convinced him of the folly of fighting and made him the most pugnacious of peace-makers. Assuredly Jeffrey felt that Carlyle was one of his spiritual sons, and was both puzzled by him and sometimes proud of him.—" Ofttimes the pupil goes beyond his master."

III

JEFFREY RETRENCHES THE *BURNS*

(1828)

BY the middle of August Carlyle had started the *Burns*. He finished it in a month (16.9.1828). When Jeffrey returned from Glasgow on the night of 22.9. 1828, he found it awaiting him, and wrote next day :—

' My Dear C.,—Though I had packets enough to look into I contrived to *read through* your paper before going to bed— some proof I think that I either liked it, or took an interest in the writer. The truth is I do both. But it is distressingly long. You do not know how much I am abused, and by my best friends and coadjutors, about these long articles —and really you are *diffuse* this time as well as long. I cannot venture to print 6o pages of such matter (and it would go to that) and it is the more provoking, because the article would be far better, more striking, more indicative of genius, and more effectual for your purpose, if it were condensed to half the size. I cannot reduce it so far, for it would require to be written nearly over again, but I *must* make some retrenchments, and I will send you the proofs when that is done. The latter part is far the *best*, the best written and best conceived. I wish there had been less mysticism about it, at least less mystical jargon, less talk and repetition about entireness, and simplicity, and equipments, and such matters. There is also much palpable exaggeration ; and always the most dogmatism where you are either decidedly wrong or very doubtfully right. But there is a noble strain of sentiment, and kind and lofty feeling, and much beauty and felicity of diction. You will treat me as something worse than an ass I suppose when I say that I am firmly persuaded the great source [1] of your

---

[1] Word uncertain in the MS.

extravagance, and of all that makes your writings intolerable to many, and ridiculous to not a few, is not so much any real peculiarity of opinions as an unlucky ambition to appear more original than you are, or the humbler and still more delusive hope of converting our English intellects to the creed of Germany, and being the apostle of another reformation.   I wish to God I could persuade you to fling away these affectations, and be contented to write like your famous countrymen of all ages, as long at least as you write *to* your countrymen and *for* them.   The *nationality* for which you commend Burns so highly might teach you I think that there are nobler tasks for a man like you than to vamp up the vulgar drams [1] of these Dousterswivels you are so anxious to cram down our throats, but which I venture to predict no good judge among us will swallow, and the nation at large speedily reject with loathing.   But we will talk of this by and bye.   I have no time now for it.'

The reply to this is lost, but on receipt of it Jeffrey wrote at once (3.10.1828) :—

' My Dear C.,—I cannot delay a moment letting you know how much I am gratified by the kindness of your letter, and the reasonableness—though I am afraid it is rather resignation than docility—of your remarks on my proposed mutilation of your dissertation on Burns.   That cruel operation is now over—the MS. is at press—and I hope to bring the proofs with me.   But for your relief I hasten to say that I am not without hope that you will think my proceeding merciful, and that I have not struck out much that you were much in earnest about, or would be particularly anxious to retain.   In the first place I have left you as much as, I reckon, will print [1] to 48 pages or more ;   then my retrenchments have been chiefly on the first 20 pages, and include most of your long quotations from the poetry ; and finally I honestly think they are confined, with very little exception, to mere repetitions, having removed scarcely anything that is not still to be found, two or three times over, in the substance of what remains.   All your general reflections, tho I think some of them rash and unsound enough, are retained ;   and tho I have retrenched [1] you of about 10 pages in all, I hope they will not be much

[1] Word uncertain in MS.

missed, even by their author, but we shall see. In the
meantime I cannot but thank you again for the frank and
goodnatured manner in which you submit to this sad
infliction, which, though I could not decline it, I had
some fear would appear very grievous to one who is so
firm in his opinions, and so sincerely impressed with a
belief of their importance as I take you to be. As for
mysticism and Dousterswivels—we shall talk about them
when we meet, only I cannot but think that you have no
right to refuse that honourable appellation so long as you
profess to think lightly of all that can be readily understood,
and to measure the depth of anything by its darkness. As
for *jargon* I shall point out to you what I mean by it, when
we have certain works on the table before us, and in the
meantime I may intimate that I hold the frequent use of
words at once vague and unusual to come fairly within that
definition ; or any use of words at the mere mention of
which everybody at once recognises the writer, and smiles
at the recollection. It is surely desirable to avoid such
badges.'

He praised the " discourse on Goethe as a work of great
eloquence, ingenuity and good feeling. It is indeed the
only good thing in the new number of the *Foreign*, the only
sunny spot—or region rather—in that dull waste." But
he added :—" England *never will* admire your German
divinities. It thinks better of them at this moment than
it ever will again because of your eloquence and ingenuity."

He had mentioned that they would sleep at Thornhill
on the way to Craigenputtock on Monday (6.10.1828),
whereby Mrs. Carlyle would know to expect them early
on the Tuesday ; but he found room for a little note
all to herself in a corner, with a dainty little sentence that
deserves a place in model-letter-books :—

" We are in no fear of anything at Craigenputtock,
but the pain of leaving it again ; and do not care even about
the trouble to which we may put you."

IV

THE JEFFREYS AT CRAIGENPUTTOCK

(7 TO 10.10.1828)

ON Tuesday accordingly (7.10.1828), their carriage was at the gate and was taken into the yard to stay till Friday, while Jeffrey with his two Charlottes, wife and child, and maid and lap-dog, dismounted and reached the door by skirting the mud of the unfinished road. But everything was ready inside. The winds were cold enough to make the roaring fires agreeable, and did not prevent Jeffrey and Carlyle from riding round the spreading hill on which the house was nestled and looking at Loch Urr and the black moors and mountains of Galloway. Craigenputtock is on the watershed of the Nith.

The talk of Jeffrey was like a rippling brook. When he praised the pancakes, Mrs. Carlyle found a tongue and boasted she had made them, to the polite surprise of Jeffrey and the admiration of her husband, who was proud to see she was not ashamed of work. But in general her attraction was that of a good listener.

One day when James Anderson was present, a youngish neighbour who was a distiller but intelligent, they talked about speeches and Jeffrey gave them samples of what he had had to endure—with a perfection of mimicry which astounded Carlyle, who never saw anything to equal it :—

' The little man strutted about (in the) cosy little drawing-room full of electric fire, with attitudes, with gesticulations, still more with winged words, oftener *broken*-winged, amid our admiring laughter ; gave us the windy-grandiloquent specimen, the ponderous-stupid, the airy-ditto, a little preparatory talk between each. His very body became the specimen's, his face filled with the expression represented, and his little figure seeming to grow gigantic if the personage required it ; at length he gave us the abstruse-

68

costive specimen, which had a meaning and no utterance for it and ended in total downbreak, amid peals of the heartiest laughter. This of the aerial little sprite, standing there in fatal collapse, with the brightest of eyes sternly gazing into nothing, was one of the most tickling things I ever saw ; and winded up our drama.' [1]

It made Carlyle delight him by calling him " a God-like Ariel." The treat was no surprise to Mrs. Jeffrey. As Cockburn his biographer has said [2] :—

' Speaking seemed necessary for his existence. The intellectual fountains were always bubbling over. Everybody else was encouraged ; and he himself was never long at a time. The listener's pleasure was enhanced by the littleness of the speaker. A large man could scarcely have thrown off Jeffrey's conversational flowers without exposing himself to ridicule. But the liveliness of the deep thoughts, and the flow of the bright expressions, that animated his talk, seemed so natural and appropriate to the figure that uttered them, that they were heard with something of the delight with which the slenderness of the trembling throat, and the quivering of the wings, make us enjoy the strength and clearness of the notes of a little bird.'

Describing his private talk, Carlyle said afterwards :—

' I used to find in him a finer talent than any he has evidenced in writing when he got to speak Scotch, and gave me anecdotes of old Scotch Braxfields and curiosities. Which he did with a greatness of gusto, with real comic mirth, much beyond what was noticeable in him otherwise. The perfection of the mimicry itself was something.'

What most delighted Jeffrey now was to debate with Carlyle about things in general. They spent many hours together when the rest were in bed. Jeffrey was old enough to have noticed sadly, as he said once, " the years seem shorter and shorter as there are fewer and fewer of them

---

[1] Erroneously dated 1830 in *Reminiscences*, II., pp. 248–9. J. Anderson died in October or November, 1828 ; so it must have been 1828, not 1830. See *T.C. Letters*, I., pp. 178–9. The death of Anderson is also mentioned in an unpublished Jeffrey to T.C. letter, 4.1.1829.

[2] *Life of Jeffrey*, by Cockburn, I., pp. 362–4.

remaining." But like the Egyptian king in Herodotus, he " lengthened his days " by taking some hours from the night.

On Friday morning (10.10.1828), they " carried off our little temporary paradise " as Carlyle expressed it, while shutting their coach door in the back yard, to which Jeffrey answered by bantering laughter as they rolled away.

V

LESSONS IN PATIENCE AND PROOF-READING

(1828)

A S soon as Jeffrey departed Carlyle read the proofs of *Burns* left behind. He could not deny the changes were such as he had agreed to—before he saw them.[1] "There are three sheets in all, and the last two were not meddled with," he told his brother ; but as it now lay before him, it seemed like—" the body of a quadruped with the head of a bird ; a man *shortened* by cutting out his thighs, and fixing the kneepans on the hips." His first impulse was to demand the whole thing back ; but then it might remain unprinted. He decided to " do nothing for three days."

Meanwhile the Jeffreys had reached home on Saturday about dark, and on Sunday morning " the God-like Ariel " was writing (12.10.1828) :—

' MY DEAR CARLYLE,

If we have any true community of feeling, you must be aware that I have a *besoin* (a need) to write to you to-day—first that I might say to you what we have all been continually saying to ourselves since we left you—What will they be doing *now* at Craigenputtock ? Will they miss us a little, or be relieved by our departure ? Will Mrs. C. blame the rough walks we took her for her cold ? Will C. himself be the worse for the late hours and horrid wrangling into which we led him ? You understand all that, without telling—and the sort of flatness that ensues upon such a parting, and the feeling that we did not make enough of the meeting, and did not comport ourselves in a way to do justice to the kindness and esteem that are in our hearts ? And it is to say this, which you would

---

[1] Unpublished letters read with the published *Letters of T.C.*, I., pp. 167–171, a letter dated 10.10.1828, by mistake for 16.10.1828 or some such date in the week after the Jeffrey visit.

understand without saying, that I cannot rest till I have written to you, and that I leave all my *business* neglected, till I have disburdened my soul of it ! There is one thing more, or rather a part of the same thing, which I feel to be equally urgent, and that is to ask your pardon again for the little burst of irritability which came on me by surprise during our last vigil—and also to explain—tho' that I believe is less necessary—why I spoke with so little soften-ing, perhaps with so much asperity, of what I conceived to be the error, or at all events the monstrous [1] exaggeration, of some of your cherished opinions. Sincerity required that I should speak plainly and firmly, but I was anxious to show you also not only some of the reasons for which sensible people would reject your conclusions, but the tone and temper in which even the candid and thoughtful part of them must necessarily regard them. It would have been more polite and agreeable to have veiled this temper a little, and, as I myself really care less than most people about theories and speculative whimsies, I do not think I should have displayed it at all seriously, if you had been confiding yours to me alone—but it seemed to be a necessary part of my warning against your public apostleship—and I have only to add that I feel confident you cannot now misunderstand my motives, nor doubt for an instant that our verbal and metaphysical differences are perfectly consistent with the greatest respect and affection. I will say further that I shall think calmly over all you have said to me, and consider, with every possible desire to come to an affirmative conclusion, whether grounds may not be found upon which those who agree cordially as to fact and feeling and practice may agree in theory also—tho' after all there is no great harm done—and so God prosper the right !

' Tell me again how I am to address the old books I am to send you ' (referring to books on Scottish history, etc., they had been talking about). ' Will you write me another review soon ? And on what ?

Ever very affectionately yours,

Fr. Jeffrey.'

Before he received this Carlyle had replaced a good deal of what had been cut out, and returned the proofs with a

---

[1] Word in MS. doubtful.

letter the contents of which have to be guessed. He told his brother before writing that he meant to send back the proofs to Jeffrey as restored—" with a private persuasion that probably I shall not soon write another for that quarter. Nevertheless, I will keep friends with the man; for he really has extraordinary worth, and likes me, at least heartily wishes me well."

What he wrote may partly be guessed from the reply, which also reveals a genuine literary curiosity, that Jeffrey insisted on excluding from the *Burns* a " well-used joke " which became the leading idea of *Sartor*.

CRAIGCROOK.

Wednesday, 22nd October.

' MY DEAR C.,

How can you be so absurd as to talk of my cancelling that excellent paper of yours on Burns, after it has given both of us so much trouble—or to imagine that I do not set a due value on it, because I was compelled to make it a little shorter—and induced to vary a few phrases that appeared to me to savour of affectation, or at all events of mannerism ? It is really too childish—and I am tempted to give you a sound scolding for your folly. However I shall only say that I do not think I shall let you have any more proof sheets. It only vexes you, and does no good— for you correct them very badly, leaving half the typographical errors unredressed, and exerting yourself only to replace all the words and phrases, which I, for very good reasons, had taken out. I am afraid you are a greater admirer of yourself than becomes a philosopher, if you really think it material to stick to all these odd bits of diction—and to reject my little innocent variations on your inspired text. *How can you dream of restoring such a word as* FRAGMENTARY, *or that very simple and well used joke of the clothes making the man and the tailor being a creator ? It was condescension enough to employ such ornaments at first, but it is inconceivable to me that anybody should stoop to pick them up and stitch them on again, when they had once been stripped off.*[1] You really must not take the pet, because I do my duty. He who comes into a crowd must submit to be squeezed, and at all events must not think himself ill-treated if his skirts are crumpled or the folds of his drapery a little com-

---

[1] Italics added. The only word underlined was fragmentary.

pressed.   You may be assured that I have given you more room that I would have given any other person, and I cannot think you have any reason to feel sore because I have scored out three or four pages of very ordinary quotation, and about as much of the least important of your remarks.   You have still a good portly article of 46 pages, on a subject by no means new—not interesting in itself to readers and now treated in a manner of which many, though I think unjustly, will disapprove.   *If you had my office to fill but for one year,*[1] you would be more indulgent to the apparent errors in my administration of it.   In reference to your particular case you should remember that I have two duties to perform, one certainly to give you a fair field to display your talents and enforce your opinions—but another, to promote the popularity, circulation and effect of the review.

' You would get my Sunday's letter the day you were writing yours.   I am glad I was beforehand with you, and that my modest expressions of kindness could not appear as returns to your magnificent compliments.   I wish I were worthy of them—or rather I wish you would like me without supposing that I am.   But you mystics will not be contented with kindness of heart and reasonable notions in anybody —but you must have gifts and tasks and duties—and relations with the universe, and strugglings to utter forth the truth—God help you and your vain-glorious jargon, which makes angels smile I take it, and sensible men laugh outright.   You have not told me yet how I am to send you the books. . . .

' You will understand that your article is actually printed, and has the honour of standing in the van and yet you think yourself shabbily used—O vainty of vanities !   I enclose a draft on account of it. . . . Write me soon, and tell me whether you have any good matter in your head for another review.

Ever very affectionately yours,

FR. JEFFREY.

' Fanny desires her respects.'

Fanny was the lap-dog.   A remarkable fondness for pets was a feature of Jeffrey.   He used to take his dog about

---

[1] Italics added.

with him, and his parrot too whenever he went with his family to stay in London or elsewhere for more than a few days.   It was often remarked of Carlyle also that dogs and children drew to him by instinct, as Fanny seems to have done.

The passage beginning " If you had my office to fill but for one year . . ." appears to be the only evidence that Jeffrey thought of recommending Carlyle to be his successor as editor of the *Edinburgh Review*.   In a work of fact, not fiction, no such statement can be made on such evidence.

It was a foible of Jeffrey to be proud of his proof-correcting, particularly the punctuation,[1] and some sheets he had done were an eye-opener to Carlyle, who had hitherto been content to consider it mechanical work and never thought of rehashing a composition after sending it to press. The sight of Jeffrey's doings made him confess a fault and promise amendment with an emphasis that drew from Jeffrey a response which may be read at length (11.11.1828).

' MY DEAR CARLYLE,

I have been dreadfully busy. . . . But I *must* write one line—to say that I admire and approve of your letter in all things.   Your candour and sweet blood are indeed admirable, and as somebody makes a dying pagan say in a play, " If these are Christian virtues, I am Christian," so I am ready to exclaim, " If these are mystic virtues, *I am mystic*."   But it is not so.   The virtues are your own, and you possess them not in consequence of your mysticism, but in spite of it.   You shall have proof sheets—and anything you like—I really cannot chaffer with such a man or do anything to vex him—and you shall write mysticism for me too, if it will not be otherwise, and I shall print it too, at all hazards—with few, very few, and temperate corrections.   After all there are many more things I believe as to which we agree, than about which we differ, and the difference is not radical, but formal chiefly.'

[1] *Life of Lord Jeffrey*, by Cockburn, I., p. 402.

VI

MAINLY MRS. CARLYLE

(1828)

"CRAW JEAN" was now eighteen. During the first
months in Craigenputtock she was " a present
help" in time of trouble. Two or three years ago
her brother Tom had seen in her a parallel to " Jane the
Greater," his wife, and indeed both women were called
Jane or " Jean " and both had black hair. He thought
it " a pity that such a mind should be expended on baking
and churning," but does not appear to have abetted Jane
the Greater trying to teach her Latin. Working and
reading and talking together, the two Janes taught each
other a good deal without knowing it. " Jane the Lesser "
was young enough for the other to matronize her, which
did not apply to the older sisters ; and yet she was old enough
to teach the young matron something in return. Both
were expert in housework—there was co-operation and
no teaching there. But tho' " Jane the Greater" had a
nimble pen, her tongue was numb in company, and what
she learned from Jane the Lesser was to talk and hold her
own against " Tom." A sister thinks nothing of contra-
dicting a brother and cuts him short without scruple. The
Carlyle family were all exceedingly articulate.

In pleading with Mrs. Carlyle senior to send her " Jean,"
the young wife had said, " *Alone* we never weary : if I
have not Jean's enviable gift of *talking*, I am at least among
the best listeners in the kingdom. And my husband has
always something to say. (He complains) that I *cannot*
speak ; often when he has talked for an hour without
answer, he will beg for some sign of life on my part ; and
the only sign I can give is a little kiss. Well ! that is better
than nothing, don't you think ? "

When Jane the lesser was in the house, she had plenty to
say—there was no need for him to talk by the hour. She
knew so little that she was giving lessons to Mrs. Carlyle that

she was completely puzzled when one day she was told by her, " Jean,—do you know ?—I'm jealous of you—Tom thinks you so clever." She was so puzzled that when she went home this winter, she begged her mother to explain it, and afterwards repeated it to her own daughters.[1] And of course when she came back, as she often did, it rather helped than hindered the gush of words which the older woman admired and imitated. Her father came for a week or so when harvest was over, and was among the last of many visitors. The Jeffreys were only the most important.

By November Carlyle and his wife were learning Spanish and reading *Don Quixote* together in the evenings, while every morning till dinner he was " writing hard " on " German Playwrights," Müllner and others. He was so candid in showing trash was trash that he was rather remorseful afterwards, when Müllner died. What he never repented was a suggestion which rather tickled Germany to lessen the brawling of its journalists by gathering an annual Congress of them " in the Nürnberg Market Place, if it would hold them all." There " under proper marshals " they might " sufficiently and satisfactorily horsewhip one another, simultaneously, each his neighbour, till the very toughest had enough of whipping and of being whipped." Which at once reminded Edinburgh of how journalist Douglas came from Glasgow and laid his horsewhip across the shoulders of bookseller Blackwood, and Blackwood backed by shepherd Hogg ran after Douglas and struck him with a stick.[2] Which was better than duelling anyhow. As Carlyle said :—

' In general cases when the brains are out the man will die ; but it is a well-known fact in journalistics, that a man may not only live, but support wife and children by his labours in this line, years after the brain—if there ever was any—has been completely abstracted, or reduced by time and hard usage into a state of dry powder.'

Mrs. Carlyle to Miss Stodart (21.11.1828)[3] :—

[1] And they told D.A.W., the Misses Annie and Margaret Aitken, at their house, Dumfries, 24.9.1896.
[2] *Christopher North, A Memoir of John Wilson,* by Mrs. Gordon, I., pp. 278–9.
[3] *Early Letters of Jane Welsh Carlyle,* by D. G. Ritchie, pp. 135–141.

' MY DEAR ELIZA,

You would know what I am doing in these
moors ? Well, I am feeding poultry (at long intervals,
and merely for form's sake), and I am galloping over the
country on a bay horse, and baking bread, and improving
my mind, and eating, and sleeping, and making, and mending, and, in short, wringing whatever good I can from the
ungrateful soil of the world. On the whole, I was never
more contented in my life ; one enjoys such freedom and
quietude here. Nor have we purchased this at the expense
of other accommodations ; for we have a good house to live
in, with all the necessaries of life, and even some touch of
the superfluities. " Do you *attempt* to raise any corn ? "
the people ask us. Bless their hearts ! we are planning
strawberry-banks, and shrubberies, and beds of roses, with
the most perfect assurance that they will grow. As to
the corn, it grows to all lengths, without ever consulting
the public about the matter. Another question that is
asked me, so often as I am abroad, is, how many cows I
keep ; which question, to my eternal shame as a housewife,
I have never yet been enabled to answer, having never
ascertained up to this moment, whether there are seven
cows or eleven. The fact is, I take no delight in cows, and
have happily no concern with them. Carlyle and I are not
playing farmers here, which were a rash and unnatural
attempt. My brother-in-law is the farmer, and fights his
own battle, in his own new house, which one of his sisters
manages for him.

' In the autumn I had enough to mind without counting
cows, the house being often full of visitors. There was
Robert (my uncle) and Ann (my aunt), a Mr. Graham of
Burnswark, Jeffrey, with wife and child and maid and lap-
dog, George (another uncle) and *his* wife, *our dear* Henry
Inglis, and several others whom you do not know. And
how on earth did Mr. Jeffrey get himself amused at Craigenputtock ? Why, in the simplest manner. He talked—
talked from morning till night, nay, till morning again. I
never assisted at such a talking since I came into the world,
either in respect of quantity or quality.

' John Carlyle is still in Germany. We looked for him
home, but he has found that he could neither have peace in
his lifetime nor sleep quiet in his grave, had he missed
studying six months in Vienna. Little Jane is gone back
to Scotsbrig, another sister being here with Alick. So that

Carlyle and I are quite by ourselves at present, moralizing together, and learning Spanish together, and in short, living in the most confidential manner imaginable. You never saw so still a house : we have not even a cat, just one servant (Grace Macdonald), the cleverest servant I ever had occasion to know. My mother dined here ten days ago, and stayed a night. We are pressingly invited to spend some time with the Jeffreys ; and Carlyle has agreed to go, provided he gets three papers, promised to the *Foreign Review*, finished by then.'

In December, when he was rereading *Novalis* for the second of the three essays his wife mentioned, " *our dear* Henry Inglis " ventured back again for a few days, and was all the more welcome because alone. There was time to spare, and tho' not " a clerk in holy orders," he was a " Writer to the Signet." So Mrs. Carlyle's pony was solemnly baptized " Harry " by his godfather, who broke a cigar upon his nose, recalling how a bottle is broken on the bow of a ship that is launched. Inglis returned to Edinburgh (11.12.1828) in time for the New Year festivities there, with a letter to De Quincey in his pocket, which was to be a letter of introduction and something more.

VII

ENDEAVOURING TO SAVE DE QUINCEY

(1828)

D E QUINCEY in Edinburgh was sinking, drowned in laudanum, entangled in debts.[1] His case was common in China, where many a gifted man who started opium for stomach pains continued it for dreams and stumbled down to death too soon. It was well that his money was done. His wife and children in Grasmere supplied a motive for exertion, while his friend John Wilson's house was always open.

With only prigs about him, he might have perished; but when he had tossed off too many glasses of laudanum and was recovering from their effect, " Hang you ! " said Wilson, in kind remonstrance, " Can't you take your whiskey toddy like a Christian man, and leave your damned opium slops to infidel Turks, Persians and Chinamen ? "[2] De Quincey tried, but the change did not agree with him. His friends were asking each other what to do. Westmoreland would do him no good now. He had broken with Wordsworth. So Gordon or Wilson or some other dropped a hint, and Carlyle gave his faithful Inglis a letter to deliver to De Quincey (11.12.1828)[3] :—

' My wife has learned lately that you were inquiring for her of some female friend ; nay, even promising to visit us here. I am to say, therefore, that your presence at this fireside will diffuse no ordinary gladness over all members of the household ; that our warmest welcome, and such solacements as even the desert does not refuse, are at any time and at all times in store for one we love so well. Neither is this expedition so impracticable. We lie but a short way out of your direct route to Westmoreland ;

---

[1] *De Quincey*, by David Masson, pp. 78, 82–85.
[2] *Reminiscences*, by Charles MacFarlane, p. 80. Macmillan (1917).
[3] *Thomas de Quincey*, by A. H. Japp (pseud. Page), I., pp. 278–281. *Cf.*
D. Masson's *De Quincey*, pp. 83–84.

communicate by gravelled roads with Dumfries and other places in the habitable globe. Were you to warn us of your approach it might all be made easy enough. And then such a treat it would be to hear the sound of philosophy and literature in the hitherto quite savage wolds, where since the creation of the world no such music, scarcely even articulate speech, had been uttered or dreamed of ! Come, therefore.

' In idle hours we sometimes project founding a sort of colony here. I reckon this a much fitter site for such an establishment than your lake country.' (The climate is more bracing, he might have said.) ' Would *you* come hither and be king over us ; *then* indeed we had made a fair beginning, and the " Bog School " might snap its fingers at the " Lake School " itself, and hope to be one day recognised of all men.

' So securely sequestered are we, not only would no Catholic rebellion, but even no new Hengist or Horsa invasion, in anywise disturb our tranquility. True, we have no society ; but who has, in the strict sense of that word ? If we have not the *wheat* in great quantity, we are nearly altogether free from *chaff*. My wife and I are busy learning Spanish ; far advanced in *Don Quixote* already. What would the vain worm, man, be at ? Has he not a head, to speak of nothing else—a head (be it *with* a hat or without one) full of far richer things than Windsor Palace ? What are all picture-galleries to the strange painting . . . that goes on under the cranium of a beggar ? What can be added to him or taken from him by the hatred or the love of all men ? The grey paper or the white silk paper in which the gold ingot is wrapped ; the gold is inalienable ; he is the gold. But truce also to this moralizing. I had a thousand things to ask concerning you ; your employments, purposes, sufferings and pleasures. Will you not write to me ? Will you not come to me and tell ? Believe it, you are well loved here, and none feels better than I what a spirit is for the present eclipsed in clouds. Mr. Jeffrey is still anxious to know you ; has he ever succeeded ? We are not to be in Edinburgh till spring, but I will send him a letter to you—with your permission—by the first conveyance. Remember me with best regards to Prof. Wilson and Sir W. Hamilton, neither of whom must forget me ; not omitting the honest Gordon, who I know will not.

G

' The bearer of this letter is Henry Inglis.   Pray let this be an introduction.'

De Quincey was at home but did not receive Inglis calling with this letter, being unable to see anyone at the moment—his mind away in the land of dreams where the laudanum left him, as Carlyle explained, encouraging Inglis to try again.   Inglis was ready to convey the invalid to Craigenputtock, snug as a baby in its mother's lap ; and once there the dainty dwarf of genius was expected to stay long.   When once rain after supper made him remain for the night at Wilson's, his visit " was prolonged without further difficulty for the greater part of a *year*," said Wilson's daughter.[1]   Even with the wisdom that is easy after the event, no likelier way to save De Quincey can be suggested than to coax him to Craigenputtock and leave him there, to be nursed by Mrs. Carlyle who had cured him before.

When that was found impossible, the men felt baffled ; but Dorothy Wordsworth came to the rescue with a woman's wit, and contrived to send his wife and children to be beside him in Edinburgh ; and that was how the nimble spirit was delivered.   Nature never meant any man to live alone, and the better the man, the more he needs a woman, and most of all when hurt or weak or ill.   In the old Chinese writing now going out of use the " ideogram " of love represents a mother and child, the best of all emblems, the same that kindles the hearts of worshippers of Mary and the little Jesus.   So let all agree to congratulate the De Quincey family and not think the worse of Mrs. Welsh for what followed next.

[1] *Christopher North, A Memoir of John Wilson*, by Mrs. Gordon, II., pp. 156–7.

VIII

"NOVALIS" AND "VOLTAIRE"

(1828-9)

ABOUT the time the letter to De Quincey was sent, they received one from Jeffrey inviting them again to Edinburgh.—" You will find your room ready for you here, and all of us on the alert to give you welcome." The answer to which was a promise to go in the spring. The need for cash made Carlyle want to finish three articles before going away. He had to pay for improvements at Craigenputtock and send money to John in Germany, so that the visit to Weimar was postponed. When it seemed likely that De Quincey was not coming, Mrs. Carlyle went to her grandfather's on a visit extended a week as thus explained :—

TEMPLAND,
December 30th, 1828.

' GOODY, GOODY, DEAR GOODY,

You said you would weary, and I do hope in my heart you are wearying. It will be so sweet to make it all up to you in kisses when I return. You will *take me* and hear all my bits of experiences, and your heart will beat when you find how I have longed to return to you. Darling, dearest, loveliest, " the Lord bless you." I think of you every hour, every moment. I love you and admire you like—like anything. My own Good-Good. But to get away on Sunday was not in my power ; my mother argued, entreated, and finally grat (wept). I held out on the ground of having appointed Alick to meet me at Church ; but that was untenable. John Kerr could be sent off at break of day to tell that I could not come. I urged that food was needed, in short. That could be taken care of by sending anything that was wanted from here. Tea, sugar, butcher's meat, everything was at my service. Well, but I wanted, I said, to be your *first-foot* on New Year's day (Thursday). She would hire a postchaise and take me over for that day on condition I returned at night !

' In short, she had a remedy ready for everything but death, and I could not refuse to stay. So I write " with my own hand " that you may prepare to welcome me " in your choicest mood " ' on the first Sunday of 1829 instead of the last of 1828.

The quotations were unctuosities of poor Edward Irving. In telling of an invitation, she quoted him again :—" I am sure the kindness of those people ! The Lord bless them ! "

Before January and its frosts were past, Carlyle had finished *Novalis*, whom he held up to admiration as a mystic of the right sort, such as the Puritan Divines had been, and Tasso and Dante, illustrating his hero's merits by copious quotations. He delighted to dwell on the great general truth that time and space are merely ways of thinking and not realities outside us, a commonplace upon which " Hume and Kant go together " and all who are able to think agree—for indeed it is merely a particular instance of the truth that abstract ideas have not any concrete existence ; but he is like one handling red-hot coals with a pair of tongs when touching Fichte's " I and Not-I " and the other formulas dear to Novalis and to all the rest " uniting Philosophy and Religion."

The best of his essay was a plausible parallel in the style of Plutarch between his hero and Pascal :—" Both are of the purest, most affectionate moral nature ; both of a high, fine discursive intellect ; both are mathematicians and naturalists, yet occupy themselves chiefly with Religion ; nay, the best writings of both are left in the shape of ' thoughts.' "

Novalis had been bred by parents of the " Herrnhuth," or " Methodist-Quaker " complexion, and clung to his creed like a child to the hand of its mother, which explains the fellow-feeling of Carlyle, who wrote in his notebook :— " Novalis is an anti-mechanist ; a deep man ; the most perfect of modern spirit-seers. I thank him for somewhat," meaning "something," but perhaps intended to suggest, " not much." This was one of the tricks of vagueness in using words which Jeffrey used to warn Carlyle against, and call " jargon." It was a common result of polyglot thinking. If it is true that Carlyle is one of the clearest

EDWARD IRVING.

[face p. 84

of writers, let readers remember their debt to the " Godlike Ariel " who was a faithful censor.

When meditating in February on what was to be the third and last item of his winter work, Carlyle remembered Jeffrey's metaphor and felt his mental fermentation working itself clear. So while cautiously abstaining from any promise, he decided to try to do what had been asked by Jeffrey in his last letter, a very long one in which he had let himself go about anything and everything and said :—

' I wish you would write me a review, if it be not very irksome to you. But I am not much captivated by either of your subjects. What can there be to be said new about Voltaire or Johnson ? However if you will have one of them, I would rather give you Voltaire—both because being a little older and a little farther off, the subject is rather less trite—and because any mistakes we may make about him will be more likely to escape detection.'

So early in March he wrote Voltaire at the top of a sheet and sat facing it for three days before he could begin. " Writing is a dreadful Labour," he noted, " yet not so dreadful as Idleness." He did not need to reread Voltaire who had been familiar to him for many years, but the change from Novalis was startling—it was like stepping out from Westminster Abbey or St. Paul's to the roaring streets. He made himself begin, and Voltaire took hold of him ; and when he read what he had written he said to himself :—" Pieces of it breathe afar off the right spirit of composition. When shall I attain to write wholly in that spirit ? " But Jeffrey was thus disappointed of a visit he had hoped the Carlyles would make in March, and Jeffrey did not even get the refusal of the article begun to please him. He seems to have heard nothing of it till he saw it in the *Foreign Review*, but he was wearying and wrote from Glasgow (17.4.1829) :—

' My Dear Carlyle,—Why have you not written to me ? You ought ' (and so should I, in short, with various details of family history). ' But the main thing is this, when are you coming to see us ? We are anxious to have you as soon as possible. We return to Craigcrook to-morrow, and shall be most happy to have you with us. So say you are coming immediately, and let us have some talk in any easier way than this slow long obscure one of writing, for which I have every day less patience."

Part of the letter was to Mrs. Carlyle, who was, of course, included in the invitation.

They could not go,—the visit was a pleasure deferred ; but that made no difference about the Voltaire, which went to the *Foreign Review* as a matter of course. It was impossible in the *Edinburgh*. Carlyle never thought of bothering Jeffrey. The letters are not only silent about it after it was started, they also show that Jeffrey had taken him into his confidence about his collision with Blackwood. The Blackwood writers had tried to spoil the circulation of the *Edinburgh* by saying it favoured infidelity. They would have " given tongue " like a pack of wolves if *Voltaire* had appeared in it. Why ? The reason is not so obvious now as it was then.

To a modern reader Carlyle appears considerate to Christianity ; but he concedes to Voltaire that the Bible is not inspired—abandoning the common foundation of all the professional Christians, Protestant and Papist ; and he concedes it not as a dimly possible thing, but in his downright way, as a truth beyond dispute, like the Multiplication Table. Which was then " bad form," and Jeffrey had to be more particular than Blackwood in letting it be seen that his review was written for gentlemen by none but gentlemen.

Dr. Chalmers " professing " Divinity in Edinburgh now was thankful so rash a writer had not been his successor at St. Andrews. He would feel like the eagle in the fable hit by an arrow feathered from its own wings as he read his own pet argument for Bible-inspiration in the pages of the new Freethinker, extended to " all Revelations and authentic traditions " : and all of them pronounced " a subsidiary matter, the *light* whereby that divine *writing* was to be read," which was " written in mysterious ineffaceable characters,"—or in Chalmers' words, invisible ink—" in the purest nature of man "—which was orthodoxy in China, and among the Quakers perhaps, but heresy to Christians who believed in the depravity of human nature. From this time onwards, the pulpits occasionally echoed the gossips of Ecclefechan who called Carlyle an Atheist ; and some clergymen were chary of being seen in his company ; but when Chalmers mentioned him at the breakfast parties where he liked to see his friends, he only shook his head and spoke in a tone of sorrow and not anger about "that laddie," [1] as if beholding in his mind's eye nothing but the young man sitting in a Glasgow drawing-room, listening respectfully to the argument intended to reconvert him to Christianity.

The merit of the *Voltaire* made its heterodoxy the worse. It was the best Carlyle had done yet. He held the mirror up to Nature, and showed the real Voltaire, not a misty or smoky shade, such as was imagined in old Hades or may be seen in many a modern biography. His Voltaire was not a figure in a wax-work or a picture, but a living man among men, with death behind them all, like the darkness of space behind the stars.

Such a miracle is only possible to a historian describing one on whom many have looked, and to whom many have listened. In criticising Voltaire, the most successful of all whose business was Literature, Carlyle revealed his own ideal—to keep out of parties and aim at nothing but seeing and telling the truth. It was like a sketch for the portrait in his *Frederick*, for the war-conductor and business-man Frederick was at his best a disciple practising the principles of Voltaire, who is sometimes visible in the history and always felt, like the reigning spiritual sovereign or Pope. " He gave the death-stab to modern Superstition ! " wrote Carlyle now.—" It was a most weighty service." That is Voltaire's best epitaph.

[1] David Masson told this, and said he had heard others tell the same.

IX

A PASTORAL EPISTLE

(1829)

HENRY INGLIS kept them posted on the Edinburgh news. While Carlyle was writing *Voltaire*, Dr. Chalmers and Jeffrey were perorating in harmony to a great shilling crowd for the removal of Catholic disabilities ; and Carlyle sent his disciple an epistle in the style of Paul (31.3.1829). In his long life he wrote enough of that sort to fill a library.

' He who loves truth knows it to be priceless, and cleaves to it as to the life of his soul. The first question with regard to any student is this :—Does he really love truth, or only the market-price of truth—the praise and money it will *sell* for ? Is he faithfully striving against his vanity ? If no ; then truth except mere Macculloch and Co.'s Truth (Political Economy), will never disclose herself to him ; if yes,—then all will be well. Every good man is a martyr —a witness.

' Only be sure you avoid Dilletantism in all things ; be sure you do not take up a subject merely because it is singular, and will get you credit, but because you really *love* it, and feel the want of it, and find your own reward in pursuing it.

' As to *writing*, for the present, I will neither advise nor dissuade you. If you *have* any idea that gives you no rest till uttered, commit it to paper, and the Press. Only if you have no such idea, do not in any wise regard it as a misfortune—most probably it is a blessing, for the sweetest fruit is longest in ripening, and for your own private use, keep plentiful note-books.

' Here, too, we are all tearing one another to pieces about that everlasting " Catholic question." Petitions in all churches. Ruling elders go through the country with them. One poor dissenting-minister in Minnyive (Moniaive) and myself and an old Atheist in this parish are the only three that would not put pen to paper. McDiarmid (of the

Dumfries Courier) rushed in with fifty chosen men to an anti-Catholic meeting at Dumfries, and was received with curses, almost with cudgel-strokes. Had I known in time I would have gone down to help him myself. It was the most gallant thing he ever did in his life. It is to be hoped that in some weeks the Catholic question will be settled in 1829, as all have seen it ought to be since the last four generations. Locke's book was written, I think, in 1690 : *Mais il y a de gens* etc.' (But there are some who need three hundred years to begin to see an absurdity.)

The reference was to the essays on Toleration or Civil Government. The essay on the Human Understanding might have been quoted for what went before, that the " love of truth for truth's sake," as Locke expressed it, was essential to right thinking.

In Ruthwell parish on the other side of the Nith, Henry Duncan was colliding with his " flock," by declining to " promote petitions " against the Bill to emancipate the Catholics.[1] When the Bill became an Act with less benefit than was expected, Duncan still maintained that the " disabilities " were wrong as persecution and therefore rightly abolished, whatever the consequences, and a volume might be filled with proof that Carlyle's opinion remained the same, which explains a talk with Lecky at the end of 1877, reported by William Allingham.[2]

' Carlyle praised Sir Robert Peel—" the only tolerably good minister I have known." Catholic Emancipation (was mentioned, and) Lecky said, " Peel resisted that a long time."

' Carlyle : " He could not venture sooner. You have no notion what a feeling there was against it. In our country, at least in the southern part (it was so). I knew of only one other person (in our parish) besides myself who was in favour of it," the nameless " old Atheist " of the letter to Inglis.

' Lecky : " Lord Melbourne said, ' All the wise men in the kingdom were of one opinion on this, and all the damned fools of the other ; and it turned out that all the damned fools were right.' "

' Carlyle : " Quite true." '

[1] *Memoir of Henry Duncan,* by his son, G. J. C. Duncan, pp. 184-6.
[2] William Allingham, *A Diary,* p. 261. Words inserted for clearness are in brackets.

This was not a short-hand report, of course; and it was a habit of Carlyle to say his say and let others do the same without debating. Whatever words of acquiescence he used might either mean that it was true that Melbourne said what Lecky quoted, or that the fears of the " damned fools " had been justified by the result.

X

CRAIGENPUTTOCK CUSTOMS

FROM the beginning at Craigenputtock the Carlyles had two riding ponies. She was fond of riding. In 1830 a bargain of a second-hand gig made riding needless unless for pleasure. In the *Reminiscences* he says she came to him one night at eleven or so to show the first loaf she had baked, and compared herself to Benvenuto Cellini casting the bronze statue of Perseus, which they had been reading about.

' The saving charm of her life at Craigenputtock was the innumerable practical problems which she mastered, dairy, poultry, piggery. Perfection of housekeeping was her clear and speedy attainment in that new scene. Strange how she made the desert blossom for herself and me there ; what a fairy palace she had made of that wild moorland home of the poor man ! In my life I have seen no human intelligence that so . . . ' (so, so, and so on.)

Mrs. Alexander Carlyle in the farm-house adjoining said [1] :—

' She used to do no work at all but read and write for many days. Then she would suddenly wake up to the fact that the household work was in arrears, and have it all done in a spurt in three or four days, half-killing herself with overwork. Then she would spend two or three days writing about it. She seldom did any hard work, and never needed to do any. Anyone who saw her white soft hands would have laughed at the suggestion of her having used them much. The milking, in particular, was both needless and beyond her, except that she may once have tried to milk a cow to show she could do it.'

One of Carlyle's stories was about " a vicious old sow." One day he was smoking in the front of the house and

[1] To her son who repeated it 29.3.1896.

hearing the pig screaming louder than usual went to the back and beheld her in a slippery place, the clay bottom of a deep new drain. Whatever had taken her in, she now wanted to get out ; but the two ponies Harry and Larry were running loose and preferred to see her stay where she was. So as often as she was about to emerge, Harry cuffed her back with a stroke of the fore-hoof, while Larry looking on was nodding approval every time, " with a perfect perception of the situation," said Carlyle, who did nothing but look on, like Larry, because the pig was screaming not from pain but rage.

" After finishing an article," he wrote, " we used to get on horseback or drive away to her mother's (14 miles) or my father and mother's (36 or 37)—the pleasantest journeys I ever made, and the pleasantest visits. Stay perhaps three days ; hardly ever more than four ; then back to work."

On one such occasion when Carlyle was hoeing turnips with his father in a field he entertained him with details about Francis Jeffrey. Another evening was filled with talk about the Turks. The Chinese also had astonished old James, who read Macartney's *Embassy to China* and often spoke of it. These visits were the " chief pleasure " of their happy " moorland years " ; and were oftenest " surprise " or even unpremeditated. Once after seeing the sights at a Dumfries Cattle Show, where Ramsay McCulloch from London was resplendent in a sky-blue coat, and Sir James Grahame seemed a " baddish, proud man," and the news of the day was the death of another politician, Huskisson, by railway accident, at the opening of the first railway, the " young couple " from the moors, getting into their gig to drive home, made for Mrs. Welsh's instead, and were gladly welcomed. From Craigenputtock somebody went to Dumfries at least once a week for letters—they often went themselves ; and when he was busy, she went driving or riding alone as the spirit moved her. Often her mother drove up to see her, or she went to see her mother. With good roads between and horses ready, a mother-in-law 14 miles away is a neighbour—as near as any man can want !

XI

MORE ABOUT CRAIGENPUTTOCK

ONCE they visited Boreland beyond Criffell, the farm of George Welsh, her father's youngest brother. As they passed the New Abbey ruins, Carlyle remarked the grandeur of the old masonry, the " bounty " of Devorgilla, the widow of John Baliol, contrasted with the " despicable cow-house " of a " Presbyterian Kirk " beside it. Which has been criticized as the prejudice of the son of a mason and a Christian, sentimental and historical and partial to any flavour of piety ; and it has to be admitted Confucius would have paid no heed to religious ruins, and praised as wiser the Egyptian people's horror of the Pyramids and hatred of the waste of building them. But on the other hand, a fellow-feeling makes us wondrous kind, and the widow Devorgilla may have been rather a leader of simpletons than a driver of slaves. However it may be with four-feeted sheep, the human flocks are often led by females. At any rate, the hero of this history sympathized with her, and had always a reverence for such ruins, and never concealed it.

He hated to be bored ; but religious blockheads found it easier to afflict him than others did. Thus the farmer of Nether Craigenputtock, their neighbour, had a brother living in his house, William Corson, a young " Divinity," dull but sincere. He was interviewed in 1881[1] because all round Girvan, where he had been a " minister " since 1848, the people were talking about a reference to him in the *Reminiscences*—" very stupid, used to come and bore me at rare intervals."

In 1881 he was old, but still big and heavy, and if digestion could have been taught by example, a fine pattern to Carlyle, retaining an appetite and digestion " equal to two common farmers," said one who had helped him at table.[2]

---

[1] *Places of Interest about Girvan*, by the Rev. R. Lawson, pp. 24–26.
[2] W. Robertson, J.P., Historian and Journalist, Ayr, to D.A.W., 8.10.1920.

The interviewer was astounded to discover that when he began to recall his young days at Craigenputtock he " had a very high estimate of Carlyle. As an instance of his kindliness, he told me that Carlyle had offered to teach him German, and that he was in the habit of laying his disused (clay) pipes in a cranny of the dyke (or dry-stone wall by the roadside) for any passer-by that was needy."

Regarding which a good story has been told " at Carlyle's expense." [1] He used a new pipe every day, and Jeffrey said, perhaps exaggerating, that twelve smokes a day was his average. Now a long clay pipe which has just been smoked so many times was in many smokers' eyes worth more than a new one, and a certain farmer coveting the pipes Carlyle left out for the poor, took special pains to get them, and has been known to drive round that way on the look-out. The interviewer went on :—

" It was Mrs. Carlyle who was Mr. Corson's special favourite. He said—' She was very pretty ' "—nobody else ever said so—and if it was true, as he said, that " she used to be compared to Mary, Queen of Scots," it was probably by William Corson. He added that " when he was about to be licensed as a probationer," she thus advised him :—" ' Now, William, don't be going about seeking for a church, like the rest of them, but go out to the highways and hedges, and preach away like a house on fire.' "

" How did she address her husband ? " asked the interviewer.

" She always called him ' Carlyle.' "

" Did they keep a free table ? " (meaning whisky flowing freely).

" No, I never saw spirits in their house but once, and that was when we had been shovelling away the snow in front of the doorway. She then insisted on each of us taking a dram."

" Were they greatly respected by the people about ? "

" *She* was, and was always called ' the lady.' But the country folks thought he had married her for her money, and looked down on him accordingly."

Which may be easily misunderstood. The clergy of Scotland were credited with the pursuit of wealthy wives, and the common people would never miss a chance of explaining to a budding divine like Corson how much they despised a man who married for money.

[1] Told by a near relative of the farmer.

At the time when Corson was coming about their house at Craigenputtock, Mrs. Carlyle told the other Jane, her sister-in-law,[1] that once, when she was knitting before the fire with him and her husband, her " clod " or ball of yarn with a core of dry peat escaped from her lap and rolled afar, and big Corson before rising to retrieve it solemnly and slowly enquired :—" May I *take the trouble* of lifting your clod, ma'am ? "

The interviewer asked him,—

" Did they attend church ? "

" They went to Dunscore church once together, and I think she went occasionally when they had visitors, but they were always very friendly with the minister at the Manse," Dr. Bryden.

" How were you brought into contact with him ? "

" Our houses were within a short distance of each other and we used to walk together."

" Can you remember any of his remarks ? "

" He used to call the abrupt ending of a certain road through the moor ' the grave of the last sixpence,' and would speak of the Glaister hills as ' great dumb monsters sleeping there since the Creation.' "

" Did he ever write to you ? "

" Yes, I have one letter of his, written when I was missionary at Gilmerton, saying,—' don't be over-anxious about promotion. Promotion if you are faithful will come when most needed and least expected.' " And so it did.

Exit William Corson till 1868.

Some " shepherds and plain country-folk " who were questioned half-a-century afterwards remembered Carlyle as " a strange gentleman of reserved character " with an aspect of " absorbed thought." His " eyes could brighten up " and his " tongue was ever ready " when spoken to, they said, and " Dr. Bryden, a local antiquarian and estimable minister, was a frequent visitor at Craigen-puttock." [2] Dunscore where he lived was the nearest village, and a mile or two from it was the house of a country doctor, Lorimer, perhaps a " Scotch cousin " of the Rev. Robert Lorimer of Haddington parish,[3] whose wife was an intimate friend of Mrs. Welsh.[4] Dr. Lorimer had been in

[1] " Craw Jean " or Mrs. Aitken, who told her daughter, Miss M. Carlyle Aitken, who told D.A.W.
[2] *Thomas Carlyle*, by the Rev. John Wilson, pp. 72–73 ; corroborated by correspondence,   [3] 1796–1843.
[4] *Early Letters of Jane Welsh Carlyle*, edited by D. G. Ritchie, p. 3.

practice there for several years before 1828, and continued for more than half a century. " Every summer," he said, Mrs. Carlyle brought her husband at least once " to visit us. They sat in the drawing-room and conversed on ordinary topics. Carlyle was a little short in his remarks, and *she* did not say much. They seemed on good enough terms with each other. Indeed Mrs. Carlyle was concerned about her husband's welfare,"[1]—dyspepsia belike, on first arrival.

The only other indication of " professional " services rendered was when there was an epidemic among the horses, and disease in the lungs was threatening " Harry " with a premature death. Carlyle discovered the " vet." called in was " an ignorant puppy," and asked Lorimer— " How would you treat a *man* in inflammation of the lungs?"

The answer was, " Bleed him, blister on breast, no food but slops."

So Harry was treated in that way, and recovered as if he had been a man. His mistress was never Lorimer's patient. She was often sick, but not beyond what her mother could treat. Mrs. Welsh had much experience and skill in sickness, and specialists can still admire her way of handling her daughter at this time. There was chronic biliousness, female troubles, and " nerves," the usual consequences of neglecting bodily work and upsetting the natural balance of mind and body. Her mother hoped for pregnancy, and prescribed abundant castor oil and rest, with exercise and life in the open air as much as possible, and diet, of course ; but she was in a dilemma about diet. Her daughter had inherited from the father's side a tendency to tuberculosis, and so she had to be richly nourished. A thin diet would make pregnancy likelier, but might bring on the dreaded consumption. Mrs. Welsh both prescribed for her daughter and nursed her, and seems to have done everything possible under the circumstances. Thanks to her advice and attendance, the six years at Craigenputtock may be said to have given Mrs. Carlyle a stock of health which carried her on to old age.

[1] Letter to D.A.W. from Dr. J. W. Martin, Charterhall, Newbridge, reporting the talk of Dr. Lorimer.

XII

A TRANSIT OF IRVING

(1829)

THE principal occasion when Carlyle and his wife were entertained by Dr. Bryden at the Manse in Dunscore was a Monday in June, 1829,[1] when they had been invited to dine " with certain reverends of the neighbourhood " and meet Edward Irving, whose passing presence was moving Scotland then as John the Baptist moved Judea. Believers were eager to hear him, ministers and congregations coming together. Devout Dumfriesshire was determined to make the most of its luck. It seemed a peculiar blessing that the relatives of such a man were among them. On Sunday, the day before he was to dine at Dunscore, he preached at Dumfries, and his father was among the happy ten thousand in the Academy grounds on the banks of the Nith, where he was three hours in the pulpit. Reporters [2] said it was the biggest crowd they ever saw listening to one man. His voice was " audible a quarter of a mile away." The crowd was excited when the loose sheets of the sermon fluttered to the ground ; and breathlessly they watched a man collect and hand them up, and admired when Irving put the papers into his pocket, and continued with unabated fluency without looking at them.[3]

On the very same day he did four hours more in the pulpit at adjacent Holywood, where six thousand were waiting for him, his happy father again among the hearers, congratulated by acquaintances. At Annan there had been " tens of thousands."

Next day Irving went to Dunscore ; and from there he was taken by the Carlyles to Craigenputtock, and stayed two nights, as happy and frank as ever he had been in the best

---

[1] Details not in the *Rems.*, are in Mrs. Oliphant's *Edward Irving*, Ch. XIV.

[2] According to Mr. Henderson, proprietor of the *Standard*.

[3] According to Mrs. Aitken "looking on"—a sister of T.C., whose words were told by her daughter, Miss M. Carlyle Aitken.

of the days gone by. They sauntered about in the green solitudes through the bright long summer evening, where there was no sound but their own voices and the music of the birds.

The honest apostle had nothing to hide. Mr. Gosse[1] has lately explained how, long after Irving's day, his own father, a man of science and of sense, could still suppose the Bible peculiarly inspired and revel in Revelations and such-like. So Irving seriously told of great " Prophetic Conferences " in London, especially at the house of a certain rich aristocratic Henry Drummond, described as " a great, evangelical, yet courtly, and indeed universal gentleman," whom he would make Carlyle know the next time he came to London.

On Tuesday morning Irving and Carlyle and his brother John were strolling over the fields, and had all sat down on a green knoll when Carlyle enquired his opinion of Methodism.

" Not a good religion, Sir," said Irving shaking his head ; " far too little of spiritual conscience, far too much of temporal appetite. Goes hunting and watching after its own emotions, that is, mainly, its own *nervous-system* ; an essentially sensuous religion, depending on the body, not on the soul ! "

" Fit only for a gross and vulgar-minded people," Carlyle continued ; " a religion so-called, and the essence of it principally *cowardice* and *hunger* ; terror of pain, and appetite for pleasure, both carried to the infinite ? " To which Irving seemed to assent.

That evening at Dunscore there was a congregation the church could not hold. They gathered in the Churchyard, " two or three thousand people tho' it be but a lonely place," wrote Irving to his wife. The sermon flowed along, " like true discourse direct from the inner reservoirs, and everybody seemed to listen with respectful satisfaction," reported Carlyle, who had accompanied his guest. They rode back together in the dusk. Mrs. Carlyle had supper ready. She had remained at home, alleging duties—she never did like sermons.

Next morning there was an early start. They rode together to Auldgirth bridge and hamlet, the nearest point for the Glasgow coach, and Irving thinking aloud was planning a six weeks' tour on the continent with Carlyle

[1] *Father and Son*, by E. Gosse, chapter IV., p. 102.

for the dragoman, which would have been one way of secur-
ing the rest he needed ; but it never came to anything.

He was in the middle of drinking a glass of ale in the
inn when the coach was announced. " No time to be
lost—horses to be changed at Thornhill, not here ! "
Irving hastily sprang to the only vacant seat on the roof
of the coach and rolled away, waving a kind farewell and
vanishing among the woods.

Soon afterwards, Walter Scott was writing in his diary,
describing Irving at a dinner-party [1] :—

' Irving is a fine-looking man—bating a diabolical squint.
I could hardly keep my eyes off him while we were at table.
He put me in mind of the devil disguised as an angel of
light, so ill did that horrible obliquity of vision harmonize
with the dark tranquil features of his face, resembling that
of our Saviour in Italian pictures, with the hair carefully
arranged in the same manner. There was much simplicity
in the manner in which he spoke. He rather *made play*,
spoke much, and seemed to be good-humoured. But he
spoke with that kind of unction which is nearly allied to
cajolerie. He boasted much of the tens of thousands that
attended his ministry at the town of Annan, his native
place.'

The hair of Irving was long and black and wavy. There
was no intentional imitation of Italian Christs. It was
an old fashion. The historian and bishop, Gilbert Burnet,
used to wear his hair the same and longer, down to the
shoulders, and in many a pulpit after Irving and Scott
had passed away the fine long hair of a preacher was
admired by his female flock.

[1] Lockhart's *Scott*, Vol. IX., pp. 329–330.

XIII

GOETHE AND CRAIGENPUTTOCK

(1829)

THE Life of Schiller was now being translated into German, to be published with an introduction by Goethe, who appended a bit of a letter from Carlyle :—

' Our dwelling-place is fifteen miles to the north-west of Dumfries among the granite Mountains and black moors which stretch westward through Galloway almost to the Irish Sea . . . a green oasis in that desert of heath and rock. We have two swift horses, which, with the mountain air, are better than all physicians for sick nerves. This exercise is almost my sole amusement ; for this is one of the most solitary spots in Britain. It might have suited Rousseau almost as well as his island of St. Pierre ; [1] indeed I find that most of my city friends impute to me a motive similar to his in coming hither. But I came for this one reason ; that I might not have to write for bread, might not be tempted to tell lies for money. (Here) we can live and write and think as seems best to us. A mail-coach will any day transport us to Edinburgh, which is our British Weimar. I have a whole horse-load of French, German, American, English reviews and journals, encumbering the tables of my little library. Moreover, from any of our heights I can discern a hill to the eastward, where Romans left a camp ; at the foot of which I was born, where my father and mother still are. Time, therefore, must be left to try ; but if I sink into folly, myself and not my situation will be to blame. Nevertheless I have many doubts about my future literary activity ; on all which, how gladly would I take *your* counsel ! Surely, you will write to me again, and ere long.'

[1] 1764 : in Lake Bienne.

Carlyle was hoping to be able to afford to go to Weimar and see and hear his hero ; but he never could.   The letter he begged came early in July, 1829, on a " beautiful summer evening."   He was lounging out of doors, admiring as he smoked a gorgeous sunset, when the clatter of ponies ambling up made him look round, and he was surprised to see his brother John and his handsome eldest sister, his favourite, Mag.   They delivered a letter from Goethe which had been lying at the Dumfries Post Office when they passed, and leaving him to read it, went inside.

John was now home from Germany, and coming and going a good deal, less willing than ever to drudge as a doctor at Dumfries, and feeling the lure of London.   The letter he now delivered ran :—

' Were an echo to reach you as often as we think and speak of you, you would very often be aware of a friendly presence to whom you would gladly give audience.'   (Then Goethe told of sundry travellers and the death of " Good Skinner," who had sung to them in Comely Bank.)   ' And now I pray you indulge me in a wish I am wont to express to distant friends.   When I visit them in my thoughts, I do not like to let my imagination wander in space.   I therefore beg for myself a drawing, a sketch of their dwelling and its surroundings.   And so I ask of you a drawing of your house, with its immediate surroundings towards the mountains, and another of the view from your windows.   Perhaps an acquaintance may visit you, who will have the kindness to make them ; for it is only a question of sketching.   The mention of Burns in your letter leads me to take up his poems again ' (and so on).

XIV

THE SIGNS OF THE TIMES

(1829)

WRITING *Voltaire* appears to have made Carlyle look round his contemporaries; or maybe it was only because Jeffrey wanted an article, and was willing to let him speak his mind on politics, tho not on religion. He soliloquized :—

'Above all things, I should like *to know England*. But how? I have not even a *history* half precise enough. With Scotland it is little better. To me there is nothing poetical in Scotland, but its Religion. Perhaps because I *know* nothing else so well. England with its old Chivalry, Art and " creature comfort " looks beautiful, but only as a cloud country, the distinctive features of which are all melted into one gay sunny mass of hues.

' The English have never had an Artist, except in Poetry. Purcell and Hogarth are exceptions such as confirm the rule.

' He who would understand England must understand her Church, for that is half of the whole matter. Am I not conscious of a *prejudice* on that side? Does not the very sight of a shovel-hat in some degree indispose me to the wearer thereof? Shut up my heart against him? This must be looked into : without love there is no knowledge.' This may have been suggested by Jeffrey writing to him of a recent Review,—" I do nothing but Bishop Heber, whom I entreat you to love for my sake." The Notes run on.—

' Do I not also partly despise, partly hate the Aristocracy of Scotland? I fear, I do, tho' under cover. This too should be remedied.

' Have the Scottish Gentry *lost* their national character of late years, and become mere danglers in the train of the wealthier English? Scott has seen certain characters among them ; of which I hitherto have not heard of any existing specimen.

' Is the true Scotchman the Peasant and Yeoman ; chiefly the former ?

' Shall we actually go and *ride* thro' England to see it ? Mail coaches are a mere mockery.

' Is the characteristic strength of England its Love of Justice, its sense of Fair Play ? The Scotch have more enthusiasm and more consideration ; more sail and ballast. The old Scottish music, our songs, etc., are distinctive.'

After finishing *Voltaire* he turned to Luther, reading much about him, and boldly coming to an estimate far above any ever current as yet among sensible people. Compare Hume's, for example.—Hume was unable to feel as if in the skin of a Bible-believer, and imputed to Luther the temper and vanity of an ambitious churchman and a jealous monk. Carlyle's conclusion from his reading may seem commonplace now, but was odd when he was writing in 1829.

' Luther's character appears to me the most worth discussing of all modern men's. He is a great man in *every* sense ; a Conqueror and a Poet. His attachment to music is very interesting, it was the channel for many of his finest emotions ; for which words were ineffectual. Is it true that he *did* leave Wittenberg for Worms " with nothing but his Bible and his Flute "? There is no scene in European History so splendid and significant.—I have long had a sort of notion to write some life of Luther. A picture of the public Thought in those days, and of this strong lofty mind over-turning and new-moulding it, would be a fine affair in many senses. It would require immense research. Alas ! Alas ! When are we to have another Luther ? Such men are needed from century to century : there seldom has been more need of one than now.'

After he parted from Irving he turned to the political article Jeffrey was waiting for,—" Signs of the Times." He mentioned nobody in particular ; but the crowds pre-occupied about the end of the world were one of the " Signs." He took for his text a German verse which was lithographed in Goethe's own handwriting below a portrait hanging on his wall.—" If yesterday is lying clear and open behind you, and you are working to-day freely and with vigour, you can also hope for a morrow that may be no less happy."

But the word " happy " was hateful to Carlyle, and he never realized how wooden he was in making verses. So he broke into poetry :—

> ' Know'st thou *Yesterday*, its aim and reason ;
> Work'st thou well *To-day*, for worthy things ?
> Calmly wait the *Morrow's* hidden season,
> Need'st not fear what hap soe'er it brings.'

Jeffrey knew how sore the abbreviating of *Burns* had left him, and sent the " Signs of the Times " to the printer unaltered in its prose. But he had himself been a rhymer in his youth, and stuff like this set his teeth on edge. He had no suspicion of how hard Carlyle had laboured to learn to rhyme, for in a later letter he was advising him to try it a little ; and now he put " then " in front of the third line and rewrote the fourth :—

> " And fear not thou what hap soe'er it brings ! "

Carlyle complained and by-and-by restored his " inspired text ". Here is a simple version for the use of schools.—

> When yesterday's open behind you and clear,
> To-day you are strong, to-day you are free ;
> And doing to-day as you should without fear,
> To-morrow as happy as ever you'll be.

The German was Goethe's paraphrase of a French poem by Canon Maucroix,[1] quoted in Voltaire's *Louis XIV* and said to have been written after the age of eighty. The doctrine had long been familiar in Scotland,—" Do what you should to-day, don't worry about to-morrow," or in the words of Christ,—" Take therefore no thought for the morrow," etc., Matthew, vi. 34. Jeffrey was delighted to see the fanatics rebuked on principles they could not deny. They were now excited by the hope of a Second Coming of Christ, and distracted by the repeal of Catholic disabilities. The earnestness of Carlyle added weight to his argument that Intolerance " could be nothing but a

---

[1] Discovered by Leonard L. Mackall. See the *American Journal of Philology*, XLI, 4, (1920).

Monster," and the public excitement a foolish frenzy and panic.

There was a stroke of humour which pleased the best of the pious as much as Wilson and Jeffrey, but must have made the like of Brougham squirm.

'At such a period, it was to be expected that the rage of prophecy should be more than usually excited. The Fifth-monarchy men prophesy from the Bible, and the Utilitarians from Bentham. The one announces that the last of the seals is to be opened, positively, in 1860; and the other assures us that " the greatest happiness principle " is to make a heaven of earth, in a still shorter time. Time will bring relief and the noises die away in space.'

Another humorous touch was about the Press:—

'The true Church of England lies in the Editors of its Newspapers. These preach to the people daily, weekly; admonishing kings, advising peace or war; inflicting moral censure; imparting moral encouragement, consolation, edification; in all ways diligently " administering the Discipline of the Church." It may be said too, that in private disposition the new Preachers somewhat resemble the Mendicant Friars of old times: outwardly full of holy zeal; inwardly not without stratagem, and hunger for terrestrial things.'

There was more of the like on " every little sect among us, Unitarians, Utilitarians, Anabaptists, Phrenologists," in " this age of ours, the Mechanical Age."—

'A new trade has arisen among us, under the name of " Codification," or code-making in the abstract; whereby any people, for a reasonable consideration, may be accommodated with a patent code;—more easily than curious individuals with patent breeches, for the people does *not* need to be measured first.'

This was a palpable hit, but a fair one. The whole of the essay was sweetness and light, like unexpected daylight shining on the political acrobats. Remarking how " on every hand, the living artisan is driven from his workshop " by machinery, he yet admits the " grateful reflection which forces itself on every one, how much better fed, clothed, lodged, and accommodated men now might be by a given quantity of labour "; and at the same time he dwells on what nobody was noticing, the social changes " increasing the distance between the rich and the poor, a question for Political Economists, and a much more complex and important one than any they have yet engaged with." The question of surplus value had to wait till Karl Marx was older. He was only eleven when this was printed.

It was not merely the artisan who was being turned into an attendant on machinery. Philosophy, Science, Art, Literature, all depend on it. " Men are grown mechanical in head and in heart, as well as in hand. They have lost faith in individual endeavour, and in natural force, of any kind." Carlyle was more of a reformer than any Edinburgh Reviewer, declaring that the whole of civilised Europe was crying for " a reform of Government, a cry which, every one now sees, must and will be answered." Nevertheless he affirmed again what both sides were forgetting, " the great truth " taught by Socrates and Plato, Hooker and Taylor, the " infinite worth " of goodness, and " that our happiness depends on the mind which is within us, and not on the circumstances without us." Like a good-humoured Rhadamanthus he ridiculed the delusion that " were the Government in good order, all were well with us ; the rest would care for itself !" Yet such nonsense was common ground for Whigs and Tories and Radicals. " Widely and angrily as men differ," he said, they agree on this.

The modern economic interpretation of history is merely a continuation of the Utilitarian Gospel of the Mechanical Age, and at best a bit of the truth mistaken for the whole, as if wages were the whole of economics, and economics the whole of history. It is not yet an idle curiosity, tho' nearly a hundred years have passed since Carlyle showed it failed to explain the great events, the Crusades or the Reformation, the English Revolution or the French, or any great achievement. Literature, Science and Art "have, from first to last, been the free gift of Nature", arising by "spontaneous growth" miraculously.

' Mechanism—meaning political, ecclesiastical or other

establishments—can embrace but a limited portion of man's interests. There is a science of *Dynamics* in man as well as of *Mechanics*, a science of primary forces as well as of " motives."

' Their relative importance will vary at different times. Only in the right co-ordination of the two, and the vigourous forwarding of *both* does our true line of action lie. Undue cultivation of the inward or dynamical province leads to visionary courses, Superstition and Fanaticism. Undue cultivation of the outward, again, must, by destroying Moral Force, prove pernicious. This is the grand characteristic of our age.

' We figure Society as a " Machine," and that mind is opposed to mind as body is to body ; whereby two, or at most ten, little minds must be stronger than one great mind. Notable absurdity ! Minds are quite different, and one man that has a higher Wisdom is stronger than *all* men that have it not.

' It is more profitable to reckon up our defects than boast of our attainments. However it may be with individual nations, the happiness and greatness of mankind have been continually progressive. This age also is advancing.

' Great outward changes are in progress. The time is out of joint. Wherever we can gather indications of the public thought, whether from printed books, as in France or Germany, or from Carbonari rebellions and other political tumults, as in Spain, Portugal, Italy and Greece, the voice it utters is the same. The thinking minds of all nations call for change. There is a deep-lying struggle in the whole fabric of Society ; a collision of the New with the Old. The French Revolution was not the parent of this mighty movement, but its offspring. The final issue was not unfolded in France, it is not yet anywhere unfolded. Political freedom is hitherto the object of these efforts ; but they cannot stop there. It is towards a higher freedom than from oppression that man dimly aims,—" man's reasonable service."

' On the whole, as this wondrous planet, Earth, is journeying with its fellows through infinite Space, so are the wondrous destinies embarked on it journeying through infinite Time, under a higher guidance than ours. Go where it will, the deep Heaven will be around it. Therein let us have hope and sure faith. To reform a world, to reform a nation, no wise man will undertake ; the only solid reformation is what each begins and perfects on himself.'

Sensational as this seemed at the time, it is more remarkable now. Prime Minister Wellington and all the politicians were still shuddering at the French Revolution and hoping nothing like it ever would recur. But Carlyle used to say by-and-by, " I should not have known what to make of the world without it " ; and now he was cheerfully looking for more of the same.   The new French Revolution next year, 1830, disagreeably surprised the politicians, and made many of them watch him—askance —as if asking :—" Who is this son of a ploughman that understands politics better than all the gentry and kings of Europe ? "   On finishing the essay, he said to himself, (5.8.1829), it is " bad in general, but the best I could make it."   When his own work was in question, he was always hard to please.

XV

A NIGHT IN DUMFRIES

(1829)

IN the beginning of July 1829, Jeffrey had been unanimously elected Dean of the Advocates or head of the Scottish bar, the Tory Solicitor-General retiring from the contest in his favour. Strange as it may seem in England, where jobbery in judgeships is unashamed, it had for some years been the common expectation that Jeffrey would soon be promoted to the Bench, altho' the Tories were in power when the vacancy arose; and under the circumstances, as the *Edinburgh Review* was a party organ, and a judge should be clear of parties, Jeffrey now retired from the editorship.[1] He took care to accept " The Signs of the Times " for the next number, as his "last speech."

On his way to England with his wife and daughter in August, he stopped one Saturday night (8.8.1829) at Dumfries, where the Carlyles were expecting them in the King's Arms Inn. Jeffrey sat talking things in general with Carlyle till two in the morning, and perhaps because he was pleased with the political article, he was so much more complaisant than usual that Carlyle told his brother that he was "slowly coming over to mysticism." He quoted in proof of this that Jeffrey said to him: "you are paradoxical " yet "right in the main," and "could preach very well, if they would let you make your own religion."

The humour here may need explaining now. The verdict is the recognisable commonplace addressed to apprentice divinities of any colour who outgrow their creed, like " Father Prout," and many another. But there and then it connoted such a thought as was implied in this verse of the *Holy Fair* of Burns :—

[1] Cockburn's *Life of Lord Jeffrey*, I., pp. 278-285.

> Wee Miller next the guard relieves,
>   And orthodoxy raibles,[1]
> Tho in his heart he well believes
>   And thinks it auld wives' fables :
> But, faith ! the birkie [2] wants a manse,[3]
>   So, cannily he hums them ;
> Altho his carnal wit and sense
>   Like hafflins-wise [4] o'ercomes him
>   At times that day.

Carlyle was ever conscious of the duty, not to say the joy, of being a martyr,—it seemed to him the essence of the writing trade, as Jeffrey used to remind him in chaff. What made him peculiar was not so much his opinions as his readiness to speak out. To compare such a one with the timid " moderates " of the Church was a stroke of humour enough to send Jeffrey and Carlyle to bed to laugh themselves asleep. Yet the simplicity of Carlyle, in supposing Jeffrey was coming over to " Mysticism ", shows there was abundant excuse for Jeffrey laughing at him as well as with him. Carlyle did not realize where his plain-dealing would land him. Who ever can ? He was only sure he would have no truck with falsehoods.

Next morning after breakfast Jeffrey was taken by Mrs. Carlyle to call upon a Dumfries widow, Mrs. Richardson, whose poetry he liked,—in parts,—perhaps because she had been " an old flame of his thirty years before." " These old loves don't do," said Mrs. Jeffrey to Carlyle ; and then she began to satisfy his curiosity about Brougham, whom they were on their way to visit, it seems. She spoke of him, wrote Carlyle afterwards, " with candour, not with enthusiasm,"—one can imagine the details !—When they rolled away now from Dumfries, it was settled that the Carlyles were to visit them about October.

---

[1] Rattles nonsensically.   [2] A lively young fellow.
[3] A parsonage.   [4] Nearly half-way.

XVI

JEAN PAUL RICHTER AGAIN

(1829)

FOR the next month or two his work was an article on Richter for the *Foreign Review*. It is a common guess that the style of *Sartor* was shaped by the example of Richter. In matter as well as manner there is a likeness. Neither Schiller nor Goethe had the humour of Richter ; and Carlyle admired his endurance of poverty and perseverance in well-doing and devotion to literature in the spirit of the old-fashioned Lutheran pastor, his father.

Twice already Carlyle had written of him, to say nothing of translations ; but he did not now send a mere rehash of what he had done before. The previous stuff was plainly quoted, and biographical details were added from what had been printed since the death of Richter, who was described as writing his early books in the room where his mother cooked and scoured and washed, and then sat down beside him to spin.

' A lofty indestructible faith in the dignity of man took possession of him, and a disbelief in all other dignities ; and the vulgar world, and what it could give him, or with-hold from him, was, in his eyes, but a small matter.

' There are some whom Misery itself cannot teach, but only exasperate. There have been many Johnsons. But even among the better instances, there is scarcely one who has drawn from poverty and suffering such unmixed advantage as Jean Paul. Diogenes and he would have found much in common : above all, that resolute self-dependence, and quite settled indifference to the " force of public opinion." '

Long before the Peninsular War emboldened Wellington & Co. to make their men happy by letting them cut off their pigtails, Richter had scandalised his neighbours by doing so to save time and money in hair-dressing. To

" Literary England," Carlyle commended him as an example for " daring to believe that he is poor." It needed moral courage then to write as Carlyle did.

' What a wondrous spirit of gentility does animate our British Literature. We have no Men of Letters now, but only Literary Gentlemen. Samuel Johnson was the last, rough old Samuel, the last of all the Romans! ' Then in the pugnacious spirit natural to him when off his guard, he scoffs at the scribes around who make their lives a farce of " High Life below Stairs," declaring the old English fashion to be—" Every Man in his Humour," and the " Literary " Gents no better than Frenchmen asking each other,—" What'll people say ? " and goes on. . .
' Seriously speaking, we must hold it a remarkable thing that every Englishman should be a " gentleman "; that in so democratic a country, our common title which all assert for themselves, should be one which depends on station, on accidents, or as Coleridge interprets it, " on a certain indifference to money matters," which must be wise or mad exactly as one possesses much or little ! We suppose, it must be the commercial genius of the nation, counteracting and suppressing its political genius ; for the Americans are said to be still more notable in this respect than we. Now, what a hollow, windy vacuity of internal character this indicates, all pushing, rushing, elbowing on towards a false aim, a full purse. Fools that we are. But, leaving the money-changers and honour-hunters, has the Poet and Thinker adopted the philosophy of the Grocer and Valet in livery ? '

Then he quoted with contempt nonsensical letters of Lord Byron declaring " all rules for poetry were not worth a damn," as the one thing needful for English poetry was to be familiar with High Life in London ! ! ! This careless nonsense of Byron was as hollow as his ridicule of hereditary rank in his poetry, and Carlyle's caustic contradiction may have made Moore thankful he had burned many of Byron's papers. It may also have prevented MacVey Napier from accepting Carlyle's proposal to review Moore's *Byron*.[1] The essay on Richter was finished when Carlyle and his wife went to stay with the Jeffreys in October.

[1] *Correspondence of MacVey Napier*, p. 96.

XVII

VISITING THE JEFFREYS

(1829)

CRAIGCROOK, the home of Jeffrey when the Courts were not sitting, was three miles west of Edinburgh, and when the day was fine the two men strolled in the woods together, as they used to do on Sundays when the Carlyles were at Comely Bank. Indoors "the God-like Ariel" delighted to quiz Carlyle before the ladies; but the best of their talk was when they were left alone. In a long series of what Mrs Jeffrey called "stormy sittings," which lasted to two or three o'clock, for both were used to late hours, Jeffrey said all he could—in vain—to wean Carlyle from his outspoken rustic downrightness into the ways of Whiggery. An Ariel may have to work with Calibans and Trinculos, but longs for better company.

He never responded as Wilson had done to Carlyle's curiosity about persons. He gave him a practical lesson in the gospel of silence. Regarding Wilson, however, as Carlyle was a friend of both and eager to make peace between them, Jeffrey confided to him more than he ever told anybody else about their quarrel. The nastiness in *Blackwood* which was the apparent cause was known by this time to be Lockhart's writing. For some other reason, revealed as a secret to Carlyle and never known to any other, Jeffrey said, "I should hate above all things to have any going back upon such matters." [1] The peacemaker's pains were not entirely lost,—Wilson and Jeffrey continued strangers, but enemies no longer.

Party passions were running high. The Tories were coming to the end of their tether for a time, and the Whigs likely to come soon into power. Neither Jeffrey nor Carlyle gave a thought to personal interests in shaping their opinions in politics. But "one thing struck me,"

[1] Unpublished letters.

said Carlyle, " he was always as if speaking to a jury,"
heedless of what could not be made plausible. " The
Highest cannot be spoken of in words," said Carlyle
quoting Goethe now and then, but " without the least
acceptance," he complained ; and it is easy to understand
that habit had made Jeffrey too tolerant of the favourite
fallacy of logic and of law-courts, that " whatever does
not appear is all the same as if it did not exist."

In this and other ways he seemed to Carlyle like
Voltaire, and " it is certain," he said, " there has no critic
appeared among us since who was worth naming beside
Jeffrey ; and his influence has been very great. Nothing
in my time has so forwarded ' Democracy ' as Jeffrey and
his *Review*. A Scotch Voltaire," was his final verdict on
Jeffrey, tho' not so big as the Frenchman, he admitted,
adding :—" In the voice too there was a fine, half-plangent,
kind of metallic ringing tone, which used to remind me of
Voltaire's *voix sombre et majestueuse*."

Many who had seen Jeffrey and Carlyle together lived
to read the *Reminiscences* and understood aright the
like of this.—

' He and I had long arguments, far *too* frank and equal
on my side, I can now see with penitence. I was of
thoughtlessly rugged rustic ways, and faultily irreverent
of him.

' I had not acquired in my solitary existence the art
of gently saying strong things, or of insinuating my dissent,
instead of uttering it right out.

' The series of fencing-bouts could decide nothing
except our radical incompatibility in World-Theory.

' Jeffrey seemed bent on converting me from " German
Mysticism," back into dead Edinburgh Whiggism, Scepticism, and Materialism,' which was impossible. " You are
so dreadfully in earnest," said Jeffrey once or oftener to
Carlyle, who reported :—

' We went on in brisk logical exercise, with all the rest
of the house asleep ; and parted usually in good humour.
I found him infinitely witty, ingenious, sharp of fence ;
not deep ; and used without difficulty to hold my own.'

The " penitence " here was the sheer simplicity of old
affection. The two men were extremely fond of each other,
like father and son. The younger had assimilated early the

teaching of the other, and was now like an adult disciple, thinking for himself,—" offence " between them was impossible.[1]

Jeffrey had to listen to much about Luther on this visit, with the indulgent smile befitting a tale that has been told. Carlyle was as full of it as ever Scott had been of chivalry. Of the two extinct volcanoes, Jeffrey liked Luther the better, and by-and-by suggested an article from Carlyle on Luther to his successor, who readily agreed, but only within the limit of 36 pages. So it was never written. Carlyle desired to expatiate on Luther as fully as on Voltaire or Burns.

After leaving the Jeffreys, the Carlyles were some days with Bess Stodart and her uncle in George Square, and then with the Donaldsons in Haddington, old family friends of the Welshes. But by the end of October [2] they were home.

[1] Unpublished letters and David Masson's verbal report of what he was told by contemporaries of T.C. and F.J.

[2] Unpublished letters correct " November " in *Reminiscences*.

XVIII

HOME AGAIN

(1829)

AMONG other Edinburgh acquaintances they had seen was one who by reason of his "very small bodily stature" was called "little Geordie Moir," an Advocate, who cultivated Literature along with law and prospered in both. As yet his chief achievement was a translation of Schiller's *Wallenstein*. He had been in Weimar this summer, but missed Goethe, who was not at home. However he hoped to go again, and when he heard that Goethe wanted sketches of Craigenputtock which none of their visitors had been able to make, he undertook them ; and as soon as the Carlyles were ready for him, came and did all that was wanted. Two of his sketches were reproduced in the German edition of *Schiller*. " In return for his workmanship " and recognition of his other merits, he received the last remaining Goethe medal Carlyle had to give.

As soon as Jeffrey found that Moir had come back without a letter to Craigcrook, he wrote (3.11.1829) :—

' My Dear C., You should have written first. Since you will not, I must, especially as the Session is coming fast on me, when no man can write anything but law arguments and opinions. One thing I want to say too, which, though hinted at, was not properly said when you were here, about the *E. Review*. Napier, though his nose may have a tyrannical expression, is anxious to avail himself of your talents. But he is more alarmed at your mystical propensities even than I am. Apply to me, whenever you are in any perplexity, as freely as if I were still in the chair of the Editor. To you, and for your sake, I will be Editor always. I think too that you should mention to N. or me any subjects that you contemplate before giving yourself much trouble in preparation.

THOMAS CARLYLE

Leben Schillers

AUS DEM ENGLISCHEN

eingeleitet

durch

GOETHE.

Frankfurt am Main 1830

Verlag von Heinrich Wilmans

Craigenputtock, a sketch by George Moir, made for Goethe, and published in 1830 at Frankfurt-on-Main, in the German translation of Carlyle's *Schiller*, with an introduction by Goethe.

[face p. 116

' And so you are back again at Craigenputtock, in full enjoyment of solitude and tobacco, unmolested by those idle socialities you hold in such contempt, and those audacious contradictions which wear out your spirit still more. Well, if you are happier there, I am sure we ought not to repine. But it is impossible not to wish that you were a little more tolerant of this lower world, and difficult to believe that it is really good for you to be so alone. I do not care a farthing for your opinions, and never imagine that either your speculative errors or mine are much worth enquiring into. But the unsocial dispositions which yours lead you to indulge are a matter of regret to me, and I cannot but suspect a source of discomfort to yourself. My main practical quarrel with you is for the unreasonable and really absurd contempt you foster, first for the genius of your country, and next for multitudes of men in all countries whom it would suit you far better to admire. There are so few high intellects in the world that it is pitiful to see them grudging and carping at each other, and then it is so much more agreeable and amiable and useful to admire. But I will not preach any more to you—forgive this—and believe that nothing could give me more pleasure than to see you happy and famous in your own way. . . . . I have a word to say to my fair cousin. . . . I hope you were not too much chilled on your journey, (and so on). . . . I shall have a moon in a night or two, but even stars have been scarce lately.'

This last sentence was very like Jeffrey, he hated the dark. Carlyle was writing to Goethe on the same day (3.11.1829).

' In regard to my employments I am still but an Essayist, and longing more than ever to be a Writer in a far better sense. Meanwhile I do what I may ' (and gives details). ' I have some thoughts of writing a separate book on *Luther*, but whether this winter or not, is undecided.
' I delayed three weeks, writing this letter, till a proposal ' from William Fraser of the *Foreign Quarterly* on behalf of some ' London booksellers ' for a *History of German Literature* were decided, but nothing is yet settled.

A few weeks later, when he was going on with it, he

was modestly altering the title to *Historical View* instead of *History*, and wrote to the same " Respected Sir."—

' Were this *Historical View* once off my hands, I still purpose to try something infinitely greater ! Alas, alas ! the huge formless Chaos is here, but no creative voice to say, " Let there be Light," and make it into a world.

' Some time ago we spent three weeks in Edinburgh ; warmly welcomed by old friends ; and looking on the current of many-coloured life, which here we rather listen to than see. I found the Literary men still active, and to me, kind and courteous : nevertheless, the general tone of their speculation was such as to make me revisit my solitude with little regret. The whole bent of British endeavour, both intellectual and practical, at this time, is towards Utility. Great controversies and misunderstandings are to be expected among us at no distant period.'

When they had been more than a fortnight home, Mrs. Carlyle wrote to Bess Stodart (11.11.1829).[1]

' MY DEAR ELIZA,
    ' Well, it is all over (the visit to Edinburgh I mean), and we are gradually subsiding into our old still-life—no longer " *in the midst of everything that is intellectual and delightful*," but in the midst of a pretty extensive peat-moss. Which mode of living is best ? In the sun or in the shade ? I declare I cannot tell ; my mind seems to have a peculiar knack of adapting itself to either. I liked Edinburgh last time as well as I did at sixteen (you know how well that was), and I cried as much at leaving it ; yet, returned to our desert, it affrighted me only the first day. The next day it became tolerable, and (the) next again positively pleasant.

' I was happy in Edinburgh, because you, and your Uncle, and the Jeffreys, and one or two more were so friendly towards us, so *very* kind ! And now I am happy here also, because Carlyle always likes me best *at home*, wherever that happens to be. . . . Mr. Moir stayed only two days with us, and both were rainy ; but he made his sketches for Goethe nevertheless. . . . And so God bless you, dear. A kiss to your uncle.'

[1] *Early Letters of Jane Welsh Carlyle*, by D. G. Ritchie, pp. 148–153.

XIX

JOHN WILSON

(1829)

AWAITING books for the History, Carlyle wrote an essay on Schiller and at the same time (19.11. 1829) a letter to John Wilson.[1]

' Your kind promise of a Christmas visit has not been forgotten here ; and hope lingers. If we must go unserved, it shall not be for want of asking. Come, then, if you would do us a high *favour*, that warm hearts may welcome in the cold New Year, and the voice of poetry and philosophy for once be heard in these deserts. You shall have a warm fire, and a warm welcome ; and we will talk in all dialects, concerning all things ; climb to hill tops, and at night gather round a clear hearth, and forget that winter and the devil are so busy in our planet. There are seasons when one seems is if emancipated from the " prison called life," as if man might love his brother without fraud or fear ! A few such hours are scattered over our existence, otherwise it were too hard, and would make us too hard.'

Then followed details about coaches and where horses would be waiting for him and Gordon, for of course, ' Gordon will follow you, as Hesperus does the sun.'

Remarks on current news conclude with,—' I have some thoughts of beginning to *prophesy* next year, if I prosper, that seems the best style, could one strike it rightly.' And in reiterating the invitation, he said,— ' My wife sends you her kindest regards, and still hopes against hope that she shall wear her Goethe brooch this Christmas—a thing only done when there is a man of genius in the company.'

[1] *Christopher North* : *A Memoir of John Wilson* . . . by Mrs. Gordon, II., pp. 149-151.

Wilson never came. He liked Carlyle. They agreed in glorifying Burns. But no man, not even Sir John Falstaff, could alone have made Craigenputtock a match for Edinburgh at the jolliest time of the year.

Besides, it has to be confessed, he felt they would be friends more easily if not too much together. Carlyle was puzzled to see himself held at arms' length ; but need not have wondered. He did not drink fair, for one thing. Nobody likes to expose himself in liquor to the eyes of Pure Reason or Pure Reason's wife, and least of all a Professor of Moral Philosophy in a land where fanatics abound. It would feel too much like walking naked in the streets. Wilson's feelings towards Carlyle may have been like Caesar's towards Cassius. Carlyle had never " let himself go " as Wilson continually did, and Wilson could not know he ever would. In years to come, there were many who thought *Teufelsdröckh* a German translation of *Christopher North,* with tobacco and beer for whisky ; but *Teufelsdröckh* had not been written yet.

XX

BURNS AGAIN

WILSON'S essay on Burns and Carlyle's leave little room for additions. Yet Carlyle seemed to feel that a great deal still needed to be said to keep Scotland alive to her greatest blessing. " He was very fond of talking about Burns," said David Masson,[1] " and always did so when discussing his boyhood and his father. If he said anything depreciatory, it was to make you finish it by praising Burns, which was what he liked to hear."

The influence of Burns on the character of Carlyle may be guessed as more than has been supposed. They both were fearless and felt joy in strife, but thought avoidable fighting wrong. Invading Englishmen have made it impossible for any Scot or Irishman to doubt the duty of self-defence, and the history of Scotland is one long lesson in the folly of offensive war. That fighting was wrong was the best of the New Testament, which the Reformation set us reading. So the likeness of Carlyle to Burns in many ways may be due to similarity of origin and circumstances and religion. But there was one important point in issue between Carlyle and the other critics, including Wilson. Even Goethe, who had Carlyle's essay translated and set going a translation of Burns into German, lamented that he lacked the gift of " managing life and making good any adequate position."

" All the poetry, by which he was suddenly made famous, had been written," says Wilson, " without the thought of *money* having so much as flitted across his mind." He hoped for nothing more than a few pounds to pay his fare abroad, when he published his poems. The unexpected hundreds he received did not awaken in him the ambitions of the money-makers. He was not concerned about an " adequate position." He gave some to his mother, and started farming, and for the rest of his life he made his

---

[1] Verbally to D.A.W. on many occasions.

earnings as a farmer and exciseman suffice, declining an offer of £50 a year for a weekly newspaper article. He refused to be paid for the glorious songs he was sending editors in Edinburgh, preferring to borrow £5 at a pinch instead, in time of sickness. But in general he kept out of debt, and maintained his independence by thrift. " As to any remuneration," wrote he, when he had a wife and children to support on £70 a year, " you may think my songs either above or below price, for they shall absolutely be the one or the other. In the honest enthusiasm with which I embark in your undertaking," a Collection of Scottish songs, " to talk of money, wages, fee, hire, etc., would be downright prostitution of soul. A proof of each of the songs that I compose or amend I shall receive as a favour. In rustic phrase,—'Gude speed the wark !'"

" Burns was beguiled by the remembrance of the inspirations of his youthful prime," said Wilson, agreeing with Lockhart and the rest of the world ; but what seemed weakness to Wilson and the world was a natural gesture Carlyle understood and admired.

' Some moments of poetic life were yet appointed him, in the composition of his Songs. We can understand how he grasped at this employment ; and spurned reward. The money was not necessary to him ; he struggled through without it ; long since, these guineas would have gone, and now the high-mindedness of refusing them will plead for him in all hearts for ever.'

To fail to see that Burns was right in refusing money for his songs was Wilson's worst mistake. In many other details he supplements Carlyle's interpretation, so that the two pictures from different points of view complete each other, as stereoscope photos are taken from different angles to make the figures stand out. Wilson saw in Burns a man like himself, and more so, who wrote only from impulse, as Scott remarked, and delighted in the contrasts between reality and appearances, and cheerfully accepted the convivial customs of his time. Carlyle held the mirror up to nature, as if looking at banqueters by morning light ; and wished Burns had concentrated on poetry. No doubt—and it is the surest sign of genius—Burns was growing better and better till he sickened and died. What he wrote just before his last illness was about his best. But the wisdom of Carlyle was largely learned from Burns, and he made the same mistake which many have made about himself, — he underestimated Burns by accepting as faults the self-reproaches which were in truth a creditable sign of real humility.

The web of our life is a mingled yarn, good and ill together. Wilson shows us the poet among his neighbours; Carlyle sets him against the background of eternity, to be compared with none but his peers, the handful of noblemen by nature.

Confucius, who loved a good song above everything, would have welcomed the best song-maker of the world, and praised him if he noticed his private life for being a pious son and a patient husband and father. It is likely Christ would have blessed him. In reviling pharisees and hypocrites the poet was following the example of Christ.

What should not be overlooked is that Burns was one of the most successful men in the history of Scotland and did much to clear the heads and warm the hearts of his readers. He was not to blame for the alcoholic poisoning of which he was the victim. Let us clear our minds of cant and snobbery and remember the customs among which he lived. He was less of a " drinker " than the average of contemporary gentlemen, including professional men and professors, to say nothing of Pitt and the politicians.

The best success of Burns was his influence on Carlyle. Perhaps if he had not written the dirge, *Man was made to mourn*, Carlyle might never have put into words so well as he did the social sphinx-question—the right to work. The spirit of the best of the poetry of Burns suffused the prose of Carlyle, and his hero-worship of Burns as a boy must have strengthened him to walk onwards and upwards into the light on the spiritual mountain-tops, where he was now arriving. Even in politics he learned from Burns. The glorious song, *A Man's a Man for a' that*, made Carlyle as a boy feel to his finger-tips that all men are brothers and should live at peace and work together; and now in a letter to Goethe (22.12.1829) *he said plainly that the object of teaching German Literature in England was to bring into existence " by degrees a harmony of nations, a universal goodwill."*

XXI

THE GREATEST HAPPINESS PRINCIPLE, &c.

(1829)

IN 1828 the *Westminster Review* had had an article by James Mill on Government, which angered Macaulay, who replied to Mill in the *Edinburgh* (March, 1829). Rejoinder and fresh reply succeeded, with vituperation. The Edinburgh bookseller Tait may have been thinking of this battle when he told Carlyle in October that Bowring, the editor of the *Westminster*, had said he would like to publish for him; but Carlyle kept out of the quarrel.

Personalities apart, the question was " the Greatest Happiness Principle," on which Carlyle and Jeffrey seem to have ended in complete agreement in their midnight debates in October. At any rate some sentences in the next thing Carlyle wrote, an essay on Schiller, sent off in December, might have been written by Jeffrey.

' A foolish controversy on Happiness now and then occupies some intellectual dinner-party; speculative gentlemen we have seen more than once almost forget their wine in arguing whether Happiness was the chief end of man. The most cry out, with Pope: " Happiness, our being's end and aim;" and ask whether it is even conceivable that we should follow any other. How comes it, then, cry the Opposition, that the gross are happier than the refined; that even though we know them to be happier, we would not change places with them? Is it not written, Increase of knowledge is increase of sorrow? And yet also written, Pursue Knowledge? Whereupon the others deny that increase of knowledge is increase of sorrow,' and are answered by a quotation from Aristotle, and thus the argument circulates.

' So far as that Happiness-question concerns speculative gentlemen, we leave it. But there are earnest natures for whom Truth is no plaything, but the staff of life; men whom the " solid reality of things " will not carry forward;

who, when the "inward voice" is silent in them, are powerless, nor will the loud huzzaing of millions supply the want of it. To these men, seeking anxiously for guidance ; feeling that did they once clearly see the right, they would follow it cheerfully to weal or to woe, comparatively careless which ; to these men the question, what is the proper aim of man ? has a deep and awful interest.

'For the sake of such, it may be remarked that the origin of this argument, like that of every other argument under the sun, lies in the confusion of language. If Happiness means Welfare, there is no doubt but all men should and must pursue their Welfare, that is to say, pursue what is worthy of their pursuit. But if, on the other hand, Happiness mean, as for most men it does, "agreeable sensations," Enjoyment refined or not, then there *is* a doubt ; or rather a certainty the other way. Strictly considered, this truth, that man has in him something higher than a Love of Pleasure has been the text of all true Teachers and Preachers, since the beginning of the world ; and we may hope, will continue to be preached and taught till the world end.'

Which seems neat enough, but enlightens little those "seeking anxiously for guidance, feeling that did they once clearly see the right, they would follow it cheerfully to weal or to woe, comparatively careless which." "Seek welfare and not happiness" would not lead them far.

The meaning of Carlyle's floods of phrases here and in *Sartor*, etc., is put shortly and well in the Chinese scriptures,—we should go along with our conscience in the same way as we go with our senses, avoiding what is wrong and doing what is right spontaneously, as we dislike a bad smell or enjoy a pleasant taste, in the one case as in the other awake to realities and eager to see right. In short well-doing is an Art and not to be shaped by the dictates of any Legislators. The Universe is infinitely beyond the comprehension of men of sense, to say nothing of politicians. The rules they call laws are like roads, which may be convenient but seldom give any guidance. Welfare or whatever else we call the result of doing right depends on harmony *not* with them but with Nature, the eternal living world; and our best clue when groping in the dark is in our cultivated conscience.

XXII

A STRUGGLE FOR LIFE IN WINTER

(1829-30)

THE storms of December made " Craw Jean " or "Jane the Lesser" stay longer at Craigenputtock than she had intended. She was not home at Scotsbrig till near the end of the year, which was fortunate, as the other Jane had to take to bed with a sore throat. " Craw Jean " stayed till Mrs. Welsh was able to come and nurse her daughter, and the worst of it was only that Mrs. Carlyle had to be in bed on New Year's day, instead of presiding at the dinner for which she had killed her fattest goose. Three days later Mrs. Welsh went home as her daughter needed no more nursing than her husband could do.

In the middle of January, it was "the sharpest black frost for some years." But soon the clouds came down in frosty feathers that made everything white.

MRS. CARLYLE TO MISS STODART, 5.2.1830.[1]

'DEAREST ELIZA,—

'Contrary to my usual practice, " I must plant a remark " or two on the weather. It is well we have meat and fire " *within ourselves* ", otherwise we should live in hourly apprehension of being snowed up, and consequently starved to death without even the mournful alternative of " *eating our own children.*" Oh for a sight of the green fields again, or even the black peat-moss, anything rather than this wide waste of blinding snow ! The only time when I can endure to look out (*going* out is not to be dreamt of) is by moonlight, when the enclosure before the house is literally filled with hares, and then the scene is really very picturesque, the little dark forms skipping and bounding over the white ground so witch-like ! A still

[1] *Early Letters of Jane Welsh Carlyle*, by D. G. Ritchie, pp. 171-2.

more novel spectacle exhibited itself the other day at broad noon. Seven blackcocks, *" as fine as ever stepped the streets of Greenock,"* came running down the wood to within a few yards of the door.'

Her pleasure would have been less if she had reflected that the hares and the blackcocks were starving ; but she did not think of that.

One of her husband's best Boswells was William Knighton, who reports.[1]

' I mentioned a fight between an eagle and a stag in which the stag had succeeded in saving his life by plunging into a forest.

' " I was a witness to a similar encounter when I lived at Craigenputtock," said Carlyle, " but it was a fight between some ravens and a dog. I had a useless little creature, a poodle, Ponto by name. We were walking together, and I had descended into a ravine to look after some ferns. Ponto remained above, and I was lost to sight. Presently I heard him uttering quick yelps of distress. I made my way to the summit as quickly as possible, for I was young and active in those days, and to my amazement I saw half-a-dozen ravens attacking Ponto. We had had just before a long-continued frost, with much snow. The ravens, I fancy, were well-nigh famished. Here was a dainty meal for them—a fat, useless, tender little dog—and so they set on him. Where half-a-dozen of them could have come from all of a sudden I cannot tell. It was strange. But there they were, and I had to use my substantial walking-stick energetically before they gave over. It was a savage attack, an affair of life and death. Ponto was fighting for life, and the ravens half-starved most probably, were fighting to ward off starvation. Audacity and temerity on the one side, self-defence on the other. Ponto was so much injured, we had to destroy him afterwards. His was a useless life. But amongst mankind there are constantly examples of a struggle for existence as keen and as terrible as that between Ponto and the ravens." '

[1] See *Struggles for Life*, by William Knighton, Ch. XIII., pp. 286-7.

XXIII

JEFFREY AGAIN

(1829-30)

JEFFREY was busier than ever this winter, yet writing more and more to the Carlyles. His trade was law, but his heart was in letters, as he frankly confessed.[1] Long afterwards Carlyle said he might have been a Goldoni. Goldoni indeed! Carlyle must have been thinking of his friend's private taste and comfort, and meant that he would have been happier writing literature than the dull law-drudgery which made him rich.

'I am glad to hear you are busy,' he wrote to Carlyle this winter, 'for yours is all willing work, and you are best pleased with yourself when you work it, and we may all profit by it in season, and the more you work now the less you will grudge being idle hereafter with your friends. I have been busy enough too, though not very willingly or proudly, and for no great pride or profit hereafter, but it is the task appointed me, and I try to do it cheerfully. I have been unwell,' and then he gave details, and gossiped, and said :—' I will not be importunate with you about reviewing. But if you *do* review, pray do not give all your custom to the *Foreign*, but let some of your lights shine before those of your own kindred. So Goodnight to you.

'Pity me my dear child,' he goes on, addressing Mrs. Carlyle now, 'for I am sick and sorry, and obliged to work through it all, like an old pauper. I am allowed to take no exercise, and that has made my little sleep less than ever, and if it were not for some kind friends, and loving beasts,' (the pet dog and parrot), 'that are with me in the lonely watches of the night, I should often be low enough. But true affection sustains me, and the entire reliance I have upon those to whom it is directed. Tell

[1] Unpublished letter.

128

me what you are doing. I have had my visions about
Craigenputtock of late, especially since this mild December
moon has risen upon your deserts. I hate dark nights.
I wish you would put me on doing some good or kind action.
I have a great *besoin* (need) of that sort upon me at present,
a sort of deadness of the heart, for which I feel instinctively
that *that* would be the best relief. What is C. working
upon ? That view of German Literature ? Or only things
for his *Foreign Quarterly* ? Does he get books enough
from the libraries near, or does he still indulge in illiberal
moans at their illiberality ? And now Good Night and
God bless you.'

The chaff at the end referred to complaints about not
getting books on loan. Whatever Jeffrey could do he
did to help him in that direction, and sometimes when
himself at his busiest was sending him books. In January
1830 Carlyle was acknowledging to MacVey Napier how
" liberally " that " fine collection," the Library of the
Writers to the Signet, had been " opened " to him, which
is likely to have been Jeffrey's doing. But all the libraries
in Scotland could not supply what he needed now for his
History of German Literature, and the London books that
arrived on 4.1.1830, for which he had been waiting four
weeks, " were scarcely of any value " to him.

Which made it easy to fall in with Jeffrey's suggestion,
and he offered to write an article on Napoleon for the
Edinburgh, but Napier excused himself.[1] He was bent
upon making his maximum size about half of what Carlyle
required for *Burns* or *Voltaire*,[1] and would want for
Napoleon or *Luther*.

One of the compensations of sickness is that it helps
us to sympathize, and Carlyle had had a long training
in suffering. He responded to Jeffrey's sad complaints
in a way that made Jeffrey write again at great length
about things in general, and say (17.1.1830) :—

' For my health, I am I suppose, better, at least I am
more used to my maladies, and think less of them.'
(Gives details.) ' And I practise my philosophies, and
turn away my thoughts all I can from disagreeable con-
summations, that must come but need not be anticipated.

---

[1] *Correspondence of MacVey Napier*, pp. 64, 65, etc. ; and for the Signet
Library, see pp. 77–8.

K

I am much touched and gratified by your kind and genuine sympathy, and feel almost that it is but selfish in me to make such a call on it. But no exercise of kindness can be purely painful, and I will do as much for you perhaps some other day. The rest of my household is well, and talk and think, I will bet you any money, as much of you and yours, in their stirring and half racketty existence, as you can do of us, in the tranquillity of your lonely upland. Tell us a little more of your occupations. How do you come on with the Spanish ? ' (It was stopped.) ' To how many score of pipes do you restrict yourself ? What practical futurity do you look forward to in this life ? What do you most wish for, that can be procured by your own efforts, or those of your friends ? What portion of your time do you pass in talking idly, or do you ever at all indulge that gentle and fair spouse of yours with a measure of gossip ? I will give her a little taste of it myself, and this very moment. So goodnight to you my most magnificent of mystics.' Then, as if turning to Mrs. Carlyle :—' I am very sorry for your sore throat my very dear child ' and, in short, delighted to give amateur medical advice of good quality and chat on paper at length.

Soon after answering this letter, Carlyle appears to have started his new book, which did not much attract him. It was a compilation " done to order." He calculated however, on making enough by it to be able to spend next winter in Weimar, and see Goethe and " prepare all the raw material of a right *Luther*, there at the fountain head." He said to himself :—" It must be more than a biographic chronicle or less."

On 13.2.1830 Jeffrey wrote again to coax them to revisit Edinburgh.

' MY DEAR CARLYLE,

'I am glad you think my regard for you a *Mystery*, as I am aware that must be its highest recommendation. I take it in an humbler sense, and am content to think it natural that one man of a kind heart should feel attracted towards another ; and that a singular purity and loftiness of character, joined to great talents and something of a romantic history, should excite interest and respect. You hermits really must not think all who live in the world mere worldlings, when the truth perhaps is, that there is as much morbid feeling in your distaste for ordinary pursuits, as there is of corruption in our too great devotion to them. It is a great triumph for me to find that your *wishes* at least, are turned towards a more social existence. But you must begin by tolerating the ordinary specimens of our common nature a little more than you now do, which you would certainly do if you were only forced to mix long and intimately with a large assortment of them. It is for this reason I have wished so earnestly that you had betaken yourself to a profession. I have not time however to lecture you to-day. Come straight to us here, where you shall have a warm room and a warmer welcome, and *where the sight of your quiet smile and thoughtful eyes will diffuse general satisfaction.*[1]

Receiving no reply he wrote again (1.3.1830), but it may be said at once that business prevented the visit. He gave some news.

' My friend Macaulay has come into Parliament. I predict that he will make a great figure. He has a paper on Southey which I think admirable, but I fear he will soon be drawn away from literature by all-engrossing Politics. I am thankful that I am old, and provincial, and out of the way of temptation, or Heaven knows what that fatal lure, from all domestic joys and all rational philosophy, might have drawn me to.

' I have not time to say one word more, and you will observe that this is not a letter, but an enquiry, and a notice. Pray do not despise your fellow creatures, and especially your fellow scribblers, who are among the best of them, and at all events as much above your hedgers and ditchers, as *they* are above their *collies*. . . . . God bless you and mend us all.

Ever affectionately yours,
F. JEFFREY.'

A hurried word may be a revelation. The reference to " hedgers " and " ditchers " shows the chasm between the rustic-souled Carlyle and the bourgeois Jeffrey.

---

[1] Italics added.

XXIV

ON HISTORY IN GENERAL

(1830)

IN March, 1830, Carlyle was again hampered in his
History of German Literature by want of books,
but that was not the only difficulty. He told
himself in his note-book.—

' I have now almost done with the Germans. Having
seized their opinions, I must turn me to enquire *how* true
are they ? That truth is in them, no lover of Truth will
doubt : but how much ? And after all, one needs an
intellectual Scheme—or ground plan of the Universe—
drawn with one's own instruments.'

He had made himself begin, and written to several
announcing an early completion of the first volume ; but
at the first start found himself discussing History in
general. The fact was that he was shaping an idea which
he had put into his note-book two years before, and which
had been ripening for utterance ever since. A few months
after he had written it down, Guizot was delivering in
Paris the lectures on Modern History which made him
famous, and Macaulay writing on History in the *Edinburgh*
to the admiration of Jeffrey and the rest of the polite
world. Which made Carlyle, who knew better, impatient
to speak out like another Paul telling the Athenians,—
" I perceive that in all things ye are too superstitious."
He quickly felt that what he was writing would never do
for the work in hand, but he went on with it and finished
it, and it soon appeared in *Fraser's Magazine*.

Between him and the others, the only agreement was
about the importance of history. For the rest he exposed
their nakedness like a Luther handling a College of
Cardinals, but politely, without names.

They had been posing in the usual style of would-be
intellectual Dictators, as if *they* knew everything as well
as a leader-writer, and had been taken into the confidence

of the Recording Angel himself, who not long ago was lamenting in Byron,—

> " That he had stripped off both his wings in quills,
> And yet was in arrear of human ills."

They affected to have no difficulty about knowing things. Their only puzzle was how to tell a pretty tale out of what they knew,—they knew so much ! " Facts," said Macaulay, " are the mere dross of History. No past event has any importance," unless the great historian sees fit to tell it !

Carlyle impeached the infallibility of historians as Luther did that of the Church, insisting on the supreme importance of making sure of facts, scrutinizing evidence and sifting hearsay. He brought to history the matter-of-fact methods of Mathematics and Astronomy, Geology and Chemistry and other sciences. Which naturally led to " Mysticism,"—the discovery of the narrow limits of human knowledge.

' History may be said to be born with us. All men are historians. Most men speak only to narrate. Cut us off from Narrative, how would the stream of conversation, even among the wisest, languish into detached handfuls, and among the foolish utterly evaporate ! Thus, as we do nothing but enact history, we say little but recite it.

' History proper, which treats of remarkable action, (always) among the highest arts, never stood higher. Whereas, of old, the charm of History lay in the wonderful, the unknown, (like) that of a Minstrel and Story-teller, she has become a Schoolmistress, and professes to instruct. Poetry, Divinity, Politics, Physics, have each their adherents. History is a Free Emporium, where all peaceably meet. Sentimentalist and Utilitarian, Sceptic and Theologian, with one voice advise us : Examine History, for it is " Philosophy teaching by Experience."

' Far be it from us to disparage such teaching. Yet difficulties, never wholly surmountable, lie in the way. The inward Life of mankind is the same in no two ages ; neither are the more important outward variations easy to fix on.' Hannibal may be less important than the ' nameless boor who first hammered out for himself an iron spade. In formless oblivion, our chief benefactors lie entombed.

' So imperfect is that same Experience. Nay, even with regard to recorded occurrences, the old story of Sir Walter Raleigh's looking from his prison window, on some street tumult, which afterwards three witnesses reported in three different ways, himself differing from them all, is still a true lesson for us.

' It is not in acted as it is in written History,—every event is the offspring not of one, but of all other events, and will combine with others to give birth to new : it is an ever-living, ever-working Chaos of Being. And this the historian will depict, and scientifically gauge by threading it with single lines of a few ells in length ! Narrative is *linear*, Action is *solid*.'

This is one of the best of Carlyle's sayings, beautiful and true, a perfect blend of poetry and science.

' Truly, if History is Philosophy teaching by Experience, the writer fitted to compose History is hitherto an unknown man. The Experience itself would require Allknowledge to record it, were the All-wisdom needful for such Philosophy as would interpret it, to be had for asking. Better were it that mere earthly Historians should lower such pretensions, more suitable for Omniscience than for human science ; and aiming only at some picture of the things acted, at best a poor approximation, leave the inscrutable purport of them an acknowledged secret.'

He was painfully plain upon current politics, calling ministers " conjurors " out-conjuring 'each other, and describing what they call " the rudder of Government " as " the spigot of Taxation, wherewith, in place of steering, he (that held it) could tap, and the more cunningly the nearer the lees," which seems to mean that the aim of our state-craft is to draw money unawares by indirect taxes and rent from the poorest workers. Even the " Church " received a kick.

' Power—wealth in these days, arms and adherents in old days—is the purchase-money of Good. True Good, however, is never offered for sale (for) that coin. So that, for man's true advantage, not the outward condition of his life, but the inward and spiritual, is of prime influence ; not the Government but the Church and the *moral elevation he can acquire* [1] by means of its in-struction. Church History ' should be ' a sort of continued Holy Writ, a History of the Invisible as well as of the Visible Church ; which latter, if disjoined from the former, is but a vacant edifice ; gilded, it may be, and overhung with old votive gifts, yet useless, nay pestilentially unclean ; to write whose history is less important than to forward its downfall.'

Guizot and Macaulay never doubted that the common history which they made their business was the only kind that mattered, whereas Carlyle foretold and welcomed in advance an " increased division of labour," producing in addition to Political histories not only Ecclesiastical but also Philosophical histories of many kinds, and histories of the Practical Arts, of Medicine and Commerce, of Chivalry and Monkery, Mathematics and many Sciences, and " what might be the most bountiful contribution of all, a History of Inventions."

Wherefore he now the more readily recognised that his conclusions on history in general were out of place in a history of German Literature, his immediate work, and returning to it made a fresh start with Wulfila's Bible and bloody old ballads, and soon was sure his first volume would be ready in May.

[1] Italics added.

XXV

A PRAYER ON PAPER

(1830)

As he buckled to his compilation, he soliloquized in his *Note-book*, (March, 1830)—

'Does it seem hard to thee that thou shouldst toil, in dullness, sickness, isolation ? Whose lot is not not even this ? Toil, then, *et tais toi*,'—and hold your tongue.

'Either I am degenerating and shall never think another reasonable thought ; or some new and deeper view of the world is about to arise in me. Pray Heaven, the latter ! It is dreadful to live without *vision* : where there is no light the people perish.

'With considerable sincerity I can pray at this moment : Grant me, O Father, enough of wisdom to live well ; prosperity to live happily—easily—grant me or not, as Thou seest best !' (The hesitation about "happily" is amusing, it is so like him. He goes on). 'A poor faint *prayer*, as such, yet surely a kind of wish ; as indeed it has generally been with me : and now a kind of comfort to feel it still in my otherwise too withered heart.

'Religion, as Novalis hints, *is* a social thing Without a Church there can be little or no Religion. The derivation of *Schwärmerei* indicates some notion of this in the Germans. To *schwärmen*—to be enthusiastic—means to *swarm*, to crowd together, and excite one another.

'I think I have got rid of Materialism : Matter no longer seems to me so ancient, *certain* and palpable as Mind. *I* am Mind : whether matter or not I know not —and care not.

'Do I really love Poetry ? I sometimes fancy almost, not. Jingle is fatiguing. My greatly most delightful reading is where some Goethe musically *teaches* me. Nay, *any* fact, relating especially to man, is still valuable and pleasing.

' *What we have done* is the only mirror that can show us what we *are*.'

To which it need only be added that the healthy man of the right sort seldom or never hankers to see himself at all, and does what is right with as few words as possible. Many such among Carlyle's contemporaries turned away from Literature for the same reason as from the Church, unable to live by it without lying. But even if Carlyle had done likewise, he would have found it hard to desist from feeling his feelings. He had been bred to piety and the trade of words and the habit of prayer ; and it is all the more to his credit now that he was growing out of his spiritual swaddling-clothes,—better late than never ! It is easier far to be an ascetic than to shun extremes and do what is right, neither overvaluing nor under-valuing things outside us. His present aspiration, call it a prayer or not, is ideal good sense,—to be content to live well, and as for happiness accept what comes.

XXVI

JEFFREY'S OFFER OF £100 A YEAR

(1830)

REPLYING to Jeffrey's letter of 1.3.1830, Carlyle explained that he did not live in the " desert " by choice because he " despised " his fellow-creatures. He wanted to make £100 a year meet current expenses, and had to earn it. Jeffrey answered (9.3.1830) :

' My dear Carlyle, why should there be any ceremony or any awkwardness between people who have an affection and respect for each other ? You would be more comfortable if you had more money, and I would be *much* more comfortable, and more happy, if you would take a little of mine. Why then should you not ? You wrote me lately that one of your objects in life was—for the present, to earn, by work, not always suitable or grateful to you— something about £100 a year. Now that is a sum, which would not be felt out of my income : and I cannot but feel *ashamed* that I should either hoard it up, or squander it in useless vanities, when such a man as you might be spared some irksome and anxious hours, by merely consenting to let me apply it more worthily.

' Now nobody knows—or shall know, of this project of mine—but you and me—not even my wife. So answer me in the simplicity of your heart, and as one man would have done to another before coins and dignities were invented. *Remember that you would have been richer at this moment if you too had not been a giver, and where there was less call, and I suppose you will not insist on monopolising that practice. If you have really a religious heart, you must have done only as you would be done to, and I can only add that I would not have made you this offer if I did not feel that in similar circumstances I should have freely accepted it from you.*[1]

[1] Italics added.

138

' And now God bless you. I feel assured that you will not at all events *resent* this proposal, nor misjudge the spirit in which it is made. To show you how much I trust you, I at once enclose £50, and expect you to keep it, and to tell me quietly that we have both done right, and no more about it.

Ever affectionately yours,
F. Jeffrey.'

In making this offer Jeffrey overlooked or discounted what Carlyle had written in the essay on Burns.

' As to money again, we do not see how any private man could, even presupposing Burns's consent, have bestowed on him an independent fortune, with much prospect of decisive advantage. Two men could hardly be found virtuous enough to give money, and to take it as a necessary gift, without injury to the moral entireness of one or both. " Patronage " is " twice cursed," cursing him that gives and him that takes ! Each shall rest contented with what help he can afford himself. Many a poet has been poorer than Burns ; but no one was ever prouder.'

The letter lay at Craigenputtock till Tuesday, 16.3.1830, when Carlyle and his wife came home from a week's holiday at Scotsbrig ; and then it received at once " the meekest, friendliest, but most emphatic refusal," giving thanks, of course, but setting out that as the settled law of human society at present was " Republican Equality " of economics, it was " dangerous and not possible except through cowardice and folly, to depart from said clear rule at present at any rate."

Jeffrey returned to the charge (25.3.1830).—

' My dear C.,—I am rather disappointed, though not absolutely surprised at your decision. I respect your feelings far too much to think of *doing* anything in opposition to them, and do not care even to *say* a great deal. I think it right however to state that, agreeing as I do in your *premises* I humbly conceive that you err in your *conclusion*. I admit the general rule to be as you put it, and that men must be either above or below the average, to depart from it with safety. But I did venture to suppose that *we* were *above* it, and I assumed this, with the less hesitation, on the understanding that as the transaction was to be entirely private we had to answer only to each other. I am foolish enough to fancy that this makes a great difference, and almost *excludes* the operation of all rules that depend on common opinion. Whatever *would* be right, if all the world were above low suspicions and misconstructions, *is right*, I take it, as to anything that passes exclusively between those who *are* above them, and have no distrust of each other. I say this merely for my own justification, and your farther reflection, and beg you would not imagine that I am capable of importuning or urging you on such a matter. If we once understand each other, all the rest must come of free will, and *will* come, if it ought. *In the meantime, believe that I am gratified, as I ought to be, by your promise of applying to me if you have occasion,*[1] tho I cannot but say that I am mortified by your expressions of surprise at the very simple and natural course I have followed.'

Carlyle replied as before, and in the *Reminiscences* in old age he explained how he made himself, so to speak, feel thankful, concluding :—

' Jeffrey's beneficence was undoubted ; and his gifts to poor people in distress were a known feature of his way of life. I once, some months after this, borrowed £100 from him, my pitiful bits of " Periodical Literature " incomings having gone awry, but was able, I still remember with what satisfaction, to repay punctually within a few weeks : and this was all of pecuniary chivalry *we* two ever had between us.'

There seems to be a slip of memory here. He should perhaps have said " in about a year " and £60, not £100. Writing to his brother John at the time, he said :

' Whenever we think of our Dean of the Faculty (of Advocates) let us conceive him as a *multum in parvo* (much in little) that does credit to Scotland and humanity.'

To himself he said, recording the offer in his Note-book, what reappeared transfigured in *Sartor :*

---

[1] Italics added.

' On the whole, I have been somewhat in the wrong about "independence"; man is *not* independent of his brother.   Twenty men united in love can accomplish much that to two thousand isolated men were impossible.' He added for his own behoof :—' Know this ; and know also that thou *hast* a power of thy own, and so, get to thy work then.'

XXVII

JAMES CARLYLE AT SCOTSBRIG

ONE of the next things Carlyle did out of working hours was to write to his brother John in London, and give the family news. Their father James now farming Scotsbrig was over 70, and had been ill this winter. Tom reported (19.3.1830) :—

' The good people at Scotsbrig seemed all wonderfully well and happy, and on the whole more comfortable than I expected. I think their way of life one of the most desirable. Our Father has now recovered himself ; walks out to see his dikers, and so forth, and is very bright and speculative. Our Mother we expect here shortly.'

She stayed several weeks, and later in the year their Father came for a fortnight. So much was taken for granted by Carlyle in writing to his brother, that his letters are of little use to strangers. James and his family were like the best of their neighbours, if " best " be taken as healthiest in mind and body, and not in the money-men's meaning of richest. To those familiar with country life in Scotland there and then, this might be enough. But for the benefit of others eager to see with their mind's eye the father of " our Tom," a little of the country clatter, which can be condensed into evidence and continues credible, may be worth repeating.

In the evening as the family and servants gathered in the kitchen, doing something or idly chatting or quietly reading, Mrs. Carlyle used to open the Bible and begin to read aloud, lilting in a musical way, in a low tone at first, and raising her voice by degrees as the increasing silence showed that more and more were listening, while James sat smoking in front of the fire, occasionally making remarks on what was read. One night it was the story of Potiphar's wife, and among the listeners was a tailor Garthwaite, brother of the Ecclefechan tailor who for more than a generation made the clothes in which Carlyle appeared in the best society in London.

Garthwaite went on with his sewing, listening, and thus reported what followed. "When she finished, James took his pipe from his mouth, and apostrophized Mrs. Potiphar hotly, as if she were standing in front of him, concluding,—' and thou wast a bitch ! ' "

"The children and servants burst out laughing, and James rigorously sent them off to bed as a punishment for their irreverence," as many as laughed. Mrs. Carlyle resumed her reading, but only the tailor and some of the youngest children and one old woman, who had not laughed, and perhaps had not been heeding, were able to hear the next chapter.[1] Such a living interest in old stories he believed was a habit of James, and helps to explain his son.

One summer evening there was merry-making near. A shower stopped the fun ; and coming into the farm-house the young people who had been dancing in the open air discovered the elders were abed and they had the big kitchen to themselves. They resumed their music and dancing and went on merrily a long time until Mrs. Carlyle sent her man to stop it as she could not sleep. Into the kitchen came old James and told them they were dancing on the brink of Hell, with details that were familiar then.[2] Here are the words of the "genial Ralph Erskine." Listen to the rumble of the departing thunder. "What a bed is there,—not feathers but fire, no friends but furies, no ease but fetters, no daylight but darkness, endless eternity, fire not quenched, the smoke going up for ever and ever, the wicked crowded like bricks in a fiery furnace." [2]

The young men were angry ; but it may be doubted whether they spoke loud enough for James to hear them saying,—" At least there'll be some comfort—the place'll be warm and you'll not be there." " No, damn him, let him keep his Hell to himself." Burns had not lived in vain ! But the women shuddered, and saw at any rate that they would need to desist. Mrs. Carlyle had quiet for the rest of the night, and the only sympathy the

[1] John T. Wells took down Mr. Garthwaite's statement.
[2] According to Wells this sort of thing happened more than once. T. C. alludes to it.

dancers got from neighbours was the scornful question, " What o'clock was it ? "

The daughters of James said that one rainy day they were travelling in a cart he was driving, and the water dripping from one of their umbrellas ran down his neck till he complained and said,—" I would rather sit all night in my sark under a water-spout on the top of Burnswark," [1] an outstanding hill near by.

At one of the last harvests James Carlyle gathered at Scotsbrig, " I was one of the reapers," said Sam Wolls alias Samuel Wells.[2] " James Carlyle was always particular about the shearing—it needed to be clean and well done to please him. One morning he arranged us all, having to go elsewhere himself. He gave us orders not to get in advance of his own daughters, who did shear slowly and thoroughly. As soon as he was out of sight, we heeded not what he had been saying, but cut away merrily far in advance of his daughters, and never looked behind us. He was angry when he came back. He was not the common kind of brute that grinds the poor, and the women should have held their tongues, but of course they were faultless and proved it, till he exploded on us and dismissed us all with words that struck even the women dumb till they were out of hearing of him."

So said " Sam Wolls," preoccupied about the practical outcome, and correct so far as he goes, however incredible it may seem that any words of a man could make a woman dumb. A young man from Nithsdale, son of a sister of Mrs. Carlyle, was among the harvesters and able to enjoy the scene ; and here is what the son of that witness repeats [3] as his report of what James said to a woman : " Thou nasty [4], dirty, creeshie [5], stinkin' tinkler bitch thou—thou cam' [6] to me to shear and thou canst shear none. Thou's baith heigh and laigh and little

---

[1] Confirmed by *Edinburgh Sketches and Memoires*, by David Masson, p. 281, footnote.

[2] Died 1895, very old ; cousin of the father of John T. Wells, who in 1895 heard him telling over again the tales of the Carlyles, which he first took down from his lips in the 'seventies. To repeat one's tales exactly after twenty years is a fair proof of accuracy.

[3] To D.A.W., 13.9.1919.

[4] "a" as in *place*.

[5] = greasy.

[6] = camest : "a" as in *can*.

o't.[1] Shouther [2] thy hook and sklent [3] the bog ! Get off my park,[4] thou trail [5] thou ! "

A distinguished contemporary judge, Lord Kames, was also fond of using the word " bitch." Accepting the report as accurate, it corroborates Wells, who continued : " He named us one by one in bidding us begone. 'Craw-fitted [6] Henderson from the Cleuch Brae, Sam Wolls wi' thee [7] great ass-[8] bucket feet o' thine,'—that was me, of course, and I edged off, but heard him call Mrs. John-stone, the wife of the postman, and once a servant in a laird's house,—' thou Johnstone, puir ——pot-teemer [9] frae the Lord-knows-where.' She was too surprised to speak another word, and the others who were loud enough he called ' Skull-backit ——' (women), and off they went."

" What was discussed on the way to the village ?"

" Whether and when he'd take us back and which of us. We were laughing at each other too. I was ' ass-bucket feet ' in the village ever after, and Henderson was ' craw-fitted ' all his days. Never heard the words before then."

" Skull-backit," skull-backed meant with a convex back, as of one sitting slackly, the spine like the top of the skull familiar then on tomb-stones. " Ash-bucket " meant feet large and flat, and crow-footed was what is called splay-footed, toes turned out and wide apart. They worked bare-foot.

Another day his son heard him say to a man who was shearing badly,—" Moffat ! Thou has every feature of a bad shearer : high and rough and little on't. Thou maun alter thy figure or slant the bog,"—pointing to the man's road home.

Ecclefechan could not recall anyone in the employment of James Carlyle who ever wanted to leave him. He could always " pick and choose " a man or a woman. He

---

[1] You are both high and low and little of it, *i.e.* You cut sometimes too high, sometimes too low, and get too little grain, *i.e.* spoil too much. Level cutting is the first thing in shearing, so that the bundles may be made rightly and little lost.
[2] = shoulder.
[3] = cross.
[4] = field.
[5] = trollop.
[6] = crow-footed.
[7] = these.
[8] = ash.
[9] = pot-emptier.

L

seldom raised his voice to join the chorus of curses on
the politicians ; but his silence was not misunderstood.
He did not differ, only saw no use in merely cursing. His son
reports his private thoughts. " The lot of a poor man,"
he used to say impressively, " is growing worse and
worse. The world cannot and will not last as it is.
Mighty changes of which none can see the end are on the
way."

Changes indeed ! The people of Scotland were being
shoved into slums or emigrant ships by the depopulators,
the big land-owners and their parasite lawyers, who
rackrented the remainder and flung farms together, with
the single-minded selfishness of wolves. However, Nature
makes no mistakes, tho men do little else, and effects
follow causes. James Carlyle was not the only man of
sense beholding then the current of events sweeping by,
as one witnesses a tornado. Walter Scott thus moralized
to Maria Edgeworth of Edgeworthstown, the same who
inspired Turgenief as well as himself by her example[1] :—

' The great number of the lower Irish, which have
come over here since the peace (1815), accommodates
Scotland with a race of hardy and indefatigable labourers.
But most unhappily for all parties they work at far too
low a rate—at a rate, in short, which can but just procure
salt and potatoes ; they become reckless, of course, of all
the comforts and decencies of life, which they have no
means of procuring. Extreme poverty brings ignorance
and vice, and these are the mothers of crime. The high
civilization to which we have arrived is perhaps scarcely
a national blessing, since, while the *few* are improved
to the highest point, the *many* are in proportion tantalized
and degraded. Whether we shall at last eat each other,
as of yore, or whether the earth will get a flap with a
comet's tail first, who but the reverend Mr. Irving will
venture to pronounce ? '

That men would ever cease to prey upon each other like
fishes in the sea, and work together instead, did not occur
to Sir Walter. He could sympathize with Scottish and
English workers being sweated down to the level of
potatoes and salt, but his soul was swathed in conventions

[1] Lockhart's *Life of Sir Walter Scott*, Vol. IX., pp. 295–298.

like a mummy in bandages ; which makes only the more
remarkable the spiritual second sight, as of another
Belshazzar—he saw things could not continue as they
were. His class complacency made him forget that poverty
had no monopoly of vice—superfluity is at least equally
depraving. " Neither poverty nor riches " is the prayer
of the wise ; and that happiest of all conditions for mind
and body was what James Carlyle worked all his life to
procure and spread around him.

" He was the kind of man you looked at," said Sam
Wolls. "I remember watching him at Waterbeck buying
hooks (or sickles) for the harvest—people came to their
doors to see him. I think I see him yet " (after more than
sixty years). "The hooks were on his left arm, and there were
sharping stones sticking out of his pocket, and he was as
straight as a stick, not stiff, but dignified, striding along
altho' he was old, not slouching in the least, walking
as if he had the diameter of creation to cross before night-
fall," tho Scotsbrig was near.

He drove a cart of turnip-shaws one day to where he
used to shoot rubbish, but the glen was dark and the horse
took fright and stopped short when he was " backing "
it. That night his two young men in feeding the horses discovered one was missing—the same last seen in the rubbish
cart the master was driving. They asked him and he told
them the horse refused to move in spite of all he could
do. " So I just let it have its own way," he concluded,
" and left it there." They found it where he left it and
thought this " very like him." He was kind to his cattle.

One night he told them to take two carts in the morning
and fetch coals from a place fifteen miles off. This meant
an early start but an easy day's work. Without a word to
each other, they both went sweet-hearting in different
directions that night, reckoning on making up arrears of
sleep in the cart next day, and each trusting to the other to
get the horses out and ready before anyone was up. They
stared at each other " speechless " when they met in the
morning, and discovered that " old James " had fed and
yoked the horses himself, and driven off alone. They spent
a miserable day, wondering what he would say. One
thought of running off, but was persuaded by the other to
remain. James came home in the evening with the coals,
and said nothing at all.[1]

[1] Notes of John T. Wells for this, and also for what precedes and follows.

About 1829 or 1830 " my father sent me to Scotsbrig,"
said Sam Wolls,—" to buy a cart-load of potatoes.
Times were hard, food scarce. As I entered the farm-
yard the horse had just been taken out of a cart which
was full of potatoes. The shafts were on the ground, the
horse was standing by. James heard my errand and he
looked at me.

" ' What would the price be ? ' I hesitated to offer.
Old James was watching me. He said ' *Take* that load if
you can put the horse back in the shafts.'

"It wasn't easy. I managed it. Then I offered to pay.
' Take them, boy,' said he. I hesitated and he repeated,
' Take them—out of my sight.' "

No wonder Sam Wolls shared the common opinion
in the village that Tom Carlyle might be clever enough,
altho he was an atheist, but neither he nor any of his
brothers was half the man his father had been. Perhaps
they were right.

I

JOGGING ALONG

(1830)

CARLYLE was planning to go to Weimar next winter to see Goethe and learn more about Luther, whose " Life " he meant to write as a labour of love at the risk of getting no wages for it. He counted on immediate cash for the compilation in hand, which was very far from being what Goethe supposed, a thing he would write and rewrite continually to keep up to date. " You have your whole life to work at it," said Goethe ! In fact it never at the best was more to him than hackwork, preferable to the Reviews because promising better pay. He was growing tired of Germany, and its literary men in general were a bore to him, all but a few of its best. Thus in writing now to the Rev. David Aitken to borrow books he alluded to the " Eichhorn fashion " of chronicling as the way not to do it [1]:—

' Eichhorn, whose terrific farrago now lies beside me, is surely *the* most unspeakably stupid man of Learning that has lived in modern centuries ; " like an ass whose back with ingots bows," he is no richer than if he carried potmetal, and cannot bring himself the smallest necessary.'

It seemed safe to reckon on as much work for immediate payment as he wanted. Among his letters this March was one from a Rev. G. R. Gleig, proposing a Life of Goethe for one of Dr. Lardner's series. " I wish much I had heard of it six months ago," he told his brother, and answered Gleig that the only rational plan was a translation of Goethe's *Autobiography*. He mentioned he would next be writing a Life of Luther, and Gleig " wanted greatly to know *when* " he could get *that* ; but Luther was not to be undertaken without local research.

The Dumfries *Courier* had a letter from him, 12.4.1830,

[1] *Early Letters of Jane Welsh Carlyle*, by D. G. Ritchie, p. 164.

about a young man shot dead near Ecclefechan by the butler
of a house there, who found him courting one of the maids.
Unpublished letters show Carlyle explaining the facts to
Jeffrey, and being told the law and procedure. Jeffrey
communicated with the Solicitor-General, and soon was
able to tell Carlyle the butler was to go for trial.

On 13.4.1830 Jeffrey wrote :—

' I start a little at your project of hibernating at Weimar,
and feel as if you were in danger of forgetting to come back
to us—otherwise I am sure I ought not to start at anything
which is so likely to give you pleasure. . . . I have been
reading Moore's *Byron*, or rather Byron's own *Byron*,
for the charm is almost entirely in his own letters and
fragments, with intense interest, pity and delight. I feel
sure we should have been such friends, if we had met !
and can scarcely help gnashing my teeth with spite that
we never did, and alas never can. There are some traits
of mysticism about him, for which you should like him all
the better, and I believe I do not like him less. It is
miserable that he should have perished in the golden prime
of his days ! '

Which may serve to recall the lines that Campbell
esteemed among Byron's best, his adieu to Jeffrey in Don
Juan (X, 14-16).—

> ' The lawyer and the critic but behold
>   The baser sides of literature and life. . . .
>
> ' A legal broom's a moral chimney-sweeper,
>   And that's the reason he himself's so dirty ;
> The endless soot bestows a tint far deeper
>   Than can be hid by altering his shirt ; he
> Retains the . . . stains . . . (but) not so *you*, I own ;
> As Caesar wore his robes you wear your gown.
>
> ' And all our little feuds, at least all *mine*,
>   Dear Jeffrey, once my most redoubted foe. . .
> ' Are over : Here's a health to " Auld Lang Syne ! "
>   I do not know you, and may never know
> Your face—but you have acted on the whole
> Most nobly, and I own it from my soul.'

Which was a common experience of those who had to
do with the " God-like Ariel." In May he was sending

£60 to Carlyle, who had asked for fifty. There was politeness of the heart in the request, not lost on Jeffrey; and
in the letter that went with the money there was some
unprofessional language from the first lawyer in Scotland
(22.5.1830).

'MY DEAR CARLYLE,

'I feel very sensibly the kindness of your application, and am, not *flattered* I hope, but in some better way,
gratified by it. I did not receive your letter till last night.
So I could not send this sooner. I have made it for £60
instead of £50, knowing that a man who supposes he wants
the latter sum, is sure really to want at least £10 more.
You shall pay it back when you please, but not for any convenience of mine. I could do without ten times the
amount for ten years, or for ever, without being aware of
it. But you shall be lord and master of the arrangement,
as may seem best for you. You will get cash for this
upper slip at any bank, by merely writing your name on
it, below mine.'

Writing again a few weeks later, Jeffrey was guilty of
utterly unprofessional sincerity in defining exactly how
far he was " often almost ready to go with Carlyle's creed "
—he would " despise all other happiness " but affectionate goodwill. Wherein most would agree in words, and
loudest of all those who did it least. Jeffrey knew the
difficulty was in practice, and humorously displaying his
knowledge of other people's infirmities, adjured Mrs.
Carlyle to mend her husband—" Make him temperate in
tobacco, and more indulgent to ordinary people. If God
endures them, and cares for them, and has made them,
such as they are, he has no right either to despise or to
draw back from them. It is all sheer vanity and presumption, and he should be chidden out of it." Which
shows how delicately well the " God-like Ariel " could
translate a human meaning into a Christian dialect.

II

DEATH OF HIS FAVOURITE SISTER

(Midsummer Night, 1830)

CARLYLE'S sister Margaret was his favourite. As a child of six she had " burst into tears " on hearing read aloud his first letter home from Edinburgh, because he spoke of looking at Burnswark " for the last time." She was said to have been the only one of the eight brothers and sisters endowed with their father's capacity for silence. At any rate she was now, at the age of 26, her father's " do-all and necessary-of-life," with a would-be husband in sight also.

But in the spring of this year she was prostrated by dangerous disease. They brought her to Dumfries for better medical advice. Her mother and sister Mary were nursing her, and " Tom " was often down. About the middle of June when she was being removed to new lodgings, she was so weak that she was taken in a sedan-chair, on the knees of the young Mrs. Carlyle, with Carlyle walking by their side. He went home then, and on midsummer midnight (21 and 22.6.1830) a messenger from Dumfries knocked at the window with the news that she was worse. His brother Alexander and he rode down together at once, arriving in the early morning about three o'clock, but all was over, and there was nothing to be done but weep with mother and sister. Riding home in the evening, after sending them to Scotsbrig, he found himself alone in the woods of Irongray and burst into loud weeping for about a quarter of an hour. He never did the like again. The death of " dear Mag " was the first bereavement he had ever felt very bitterly. She haunted his thoughts occasionally all his life.

He poured out his feelings to Jeffrey in a week or two, writing in Dumfries, and was comforted as by a father (19.7.1830).

' My Dear Carlyle,

'Still toiling and bustling on, still wasting the sweet summer in hot courts and the gleaming nights in pouring over bundles of chicanery !—and I ought to have written to you too—though I felt that I could say nothing to comfort you, and that it was not necessary to say that I would if I could. I feel that an affliction of this sort must fall more heavily on you than on most people. There are so few you will let yourself love. But it is over now, and your grief I hope is settled only into a more solemn affection with the soothing of having done all that was kind and dutiful, and having ministered to the brief enjoyments of one snatched so early from both sorrow and joy. We must live for those that live. Tell me what you are doing, and how the days and weeks glide away with you, in strenuous labour, or high meditation. Are you not coming to see us ? Or must we come first again to see you ? However it is, we must meet. It does my heart good to think of your *unworldly* and pure course of life, even while I condemn something of it in my reason, and mourn over something of its consequences in my heart. . . .'

In writing to his voluble young sister "Craw Jean," who had now to take the place of Margaret at Scotsbrig, Carlyle had to express his meaning so as not to hurt his old father, who remained a Heaven-hoping and Hell-fearing man, like most of his neighbours.—

' You tell me, my dear Jean, that you are more solitary now. You have to take a kind of *front* rank. From your own judgment and conscience the best help must be sought. For our Margaret we must not mourn. I think of her daily, hourly, not in sorrow so much as in awe and love ; and trust the Almighty may one day restore her to us, and us to her : who knows but she may even now in some inscrutably mysterious way be near to us. *We* are spirits as well as she, and God is round us and in us, Here as well as Yonder ! Let us not weep for her, but try rather to be wise and meek and humble as she was. I shall hardly see her like again. She had a fairness and loving tolerance in judging of her neighbours, which is perhaps of all virtues the rarest among women. Fewer *idle* words were perhaps spoken by scarcely any. Thus she now lies enshrined in all our hearts for ever. God is great, God is good : if it is His will we shall meet again, and part no more.

'In several respects you resemble her—in one great virtue, Truth. I think if one could never *tell a lie* to one's own heart one had mastered the whole secret of virtue. Persist in what you see to be good and your duty ; be patient, gentle, submissive even to *ill*-usage : what are we that we should be *well* used ? Did they use Jesus well ? Above all, avoid vanity, self-conceit, Presumption of all sorts ; want of Humility—which is a deep and glorious feeling, could we see into it—is simply the want of all Religion, of all true moral worth.'

These words are interesting, for to identify Religion with " moral worth " or good character was the key-note of the " moderate " clergy, who used the Bible stories to edify their flocks exactly as a teacher might use fables to children. Carlyle continued :—

'I know this by the best of all teachers, Experience. Humility is no mean feeling, but the highest—the *denial of Self* it is, the beginning of all that is truly generous and noble. Be kind to every one, especially to our Father and Mother ; one never *repents* kindness ; a thousand times one does the want of it—too late.

T. CARLYLE.'

" Craw Jean " treasured this letter all her life, and well she might ; and tho' it must have been a new idea to her that Tom wanted to be humble, she did not, so far as the evidence goes, reply to him as Ophelia did to Laertes in Hamlet :—

> 'Good my brother,
> Do not as some ungracious pastors do,
> Show me the steep and thorny way to Heaven,
> Whilst, like a puffed and reckless libertine,
> Himself the primrose path of dalliance treads,
> And recks not his own rede.'

III

EVENTS TAKE CHARGE

(1830)

IN 1830 Germany seemed to be sunk in idol-worship.
Goethe almost despaired of his countrymen. To make
them straighten themselves appeared as hopeless as to
get swine on their hind legs, and as the United States had
cut themselves loose from Europe, he had addressed to them
an ode which some consider the best he ever wrote.—

> America ! You are surpassing us here :—
> You've no falling castles in your hemisphere ;
> No teaching of murder the young men to mar,
> No memories fuddled by follies of war.
>
> Good luck to America's glorious spring !
> May never your writers name Baron or King !
> And no bloody thieves in their books beautify ;
> Nor with ghosts from old stories disfigure your sky.

To Carlyle announcing a possible Life of Luther Goethe
said nothing about it, tho' his talks with Eckermann show
that he honoured Luther more than Carlyle supposed.[1]
The second volume of the *History of German Literature*
was far advanced ; and the third and fourth would not
take long. The essays already published covered much of
the ground, and left little but a few gaps to fill. As it was
being done " to order " for payment on publication, it was
reasonable to reckon on the money for the winter's expenses
at Weimar, and it was only because he had to work and wait
for that money that Carlyle was not already there,
and deep in the details of Luther's Life. " Providence
had a better use for him," his father would have said, if
he had lived to know the upshot. Jeffrey enquired
(19.7.1830) :—

---

[1] *Conversations of Goethe*, Trans. Oxenford, p. 568.

'And your German Literature book, is it near done yet? And is there any hope that the closer acquaintance into which it must have forced you with those muddyheaded, half crazy, half affected, and uniformly vulgar scribblers, will open your eyes to their true character, or disabuse you at least of your idolatrous admiration? I had some talk with Macintosh about them when I was in London, which I shall tell you about when we meet. He knows them and their lingo perfectly, and knows more of those they should be compared to than any other man, who knows *them* in this country. He places them higher than I think reasonable, but immeasurably below what you do.'

Before the Jeffreys came to Craigenputtock in September, there was exciting news. A few days after this letter from Jeffrey a " packet of Books" was forwarded from the *Review* office along with a letter addressed in French to the Author of the article on the Signs of the Times. They came from Gustave d'Eichthal, a " Father " of a new Saint-Simon Society or Brotherhood in Paris,[1] and told Carlyle the Society rejoiced at his faith in progress, and— " if you have stopped at doubtful hopes and uncertain wishes, they do not blame you, because they are aware that *nobody can foresee exactly the future face to face except those who have been illuminated by the light vouchsafed by God through Saint-Simon* ! ! ! So you are invited," and so on.

On 27.7.1830, while he was yet examining their books, another " Glorious Revolution " began in Paris. The old Bourbon Charles, whom he had watched six years ago simpering through a picture gallery there, had been employing his Vizier Polignac to put down press and parliament, but his soldiers beginning to change sides, he escaped with his family and was thankful to return safely to their old cheap lodgings at Holyrood.

To everybody's surprise, Dan O'Connell was one of the few who was openly sorry for the change ; but Jeffrey was not alone in suspecting—as he told Carlyle he did—that Wellington and others had " a hankering after obsolete tyrannies." But "whatsoe'er they felt, they acted right," and France was left to settle her own affairs. Sir Walter

---

[1] Letters from Thomas Carlyle to the Socialists of 1830, in the *New Quarterly* April, 1909 (Dent), by Eugene d'Eichthal, a son of the Gustave d'Eichthal who wrote to T.C., pp. 277–288. Italics added.

Scott himself was heard saying,—" Confound these French ministers ! I can't forgive them for making a Jacobin of an old Tory like me." What worried the Tories was not war, which was past hoping for, but a general election at an awkward moment.

It upset the plans of Carlyle too. William Fraser abandoned the *Literary Histories*, and nobody else wanted what Carlyle had been writing. Tait, who had published his *German Romance*, was plain spoken when consulted.—

Edinburgh,

29th July, 1830.

' My Dear Sir,

' I am much obliged by your kind recollection of me on the present occasion and would be proud to publish for you again, *upon almost any subject but German Literature*.[1] In that department I know you are very superior to any other author of the day ; but the subject is one seemingly not calculated to interest the British public. Every one of the books on German literature has been a failure ; most of them ruinously losing concerns. The feeling in the public mind is that anything German is most especially to be avoided. . . .

' As to a collection of your pieces in the Reviews, etc., I am quite clear that such a thing should not be attempted. Sir Walter Scott's *Selected Prose Writings* have scarcely sold at all.'

Carlyle put the History into a drawer and liquidated other things, sending William Fraser's brother James for his new *Fraser's Magazine* the *Cruthers and Jonson* story he wrote in 1822, and everything else marketable that he had, including Luther's Psalm. *The Foreign Quarterly* found room next year for a screed from the History— *Early German Literature*—and Bowring of the *Westminster* accepted another bit of salvage, *The Nibelungen Lied*, so that the work was not altogether lost ; and perhaps the most amusing bit of criticism Jeffrey ever wrote was in a letter to Carlyle about it—for of course when he heard of the catastrophe, in spite of the press of legal business and politics, he insisted on reading the manuscript to see if he could not help him to a publisher. Then he wrote :—

---

[1] Italics added.

' I have great doubts whether it will readily find a
purchaser, just because I fear if it were published, it would
not readily find many readers. The radical error, I still
think was in going back so largely into remote periods. . . .
Then you have fits of spleen and peevish scorn which are
altogether unreasonable and unseemly. What for instance
can be much more absurd than your proem on the want of
public patronage for Poetry ? And your complaint that
while other crafts have Deacons, and dignities in town
councils, and corporation privileges, poor poets must fight
their single way to wealth and honor. You know well
enough that those abominable monopolies are mere discouragements to merit and contrivances for jobbing and
injustice. Would you really have a corporation of poets,
out of which no one should be allowed to practise the art,
and into which no man should get except by serving a
7 years' apprenticeship, or marrying a freeman's daughter,
and paying a sum to the Box ? If you do not mean this,
and if you know that genius, and merit of every sort, has the
best possible chance when the field is most open, and there
is neither public patronage nor public prosecution, what
is it that you do mean ? '

The only possible reply was difficult to word politely.
What Jeffrey took so seriously had been meant in fun.
Carlyle was heedless of " abominable monoplies," but
Jeffrey was excited by the great political battle now
beginning, and did all he could to make Carlyle concentrate
his attention on politics. Thus he wrote on 1.8.1830 :—

' MY DEAR CARLYLE,

' Why do you not write to me ? Pray let me hear
from you. It will be an eventful summer for France, and
for more than France. It stirs my blood and sickens my
heart to see another scene of blood and misery opening on
that fair land, and so wantonly and absurdly opened—and
you profess to take no interest in politics ! And to think
it a fit thing for a man with a head and a heart, to occupy
them about the conditioned and the " unconditioned " and
such gibberish. O fie ! Your brother's blood cries up
from the earth against such idleness. Ever affectly. Yours,

F. JEFFREY.'

There was chaff here, tho' the meaning was serious. It was Sir William Hamilton who was then writing about "the conditioned" and "the unconditioned," and it was a favourite joke of Jeffrey to hold him up as an awful warning to Carlyle of what he might become if he continued a "mystic."

In reply to Jeffrey Carlyle confessed he was "living a very idle and good for nothing life at the present," to which the other answered, " I grudge very much the delay in seeing you till the middle of September, " and *if I were you*, I would have a joyous meeting *immediately* here, under the good green woods of Craigcrook. You could do nothing so wise as to wander down from your paradise, hand in hand with your blooming Eve, to seek a peaceful shelter in our lower world."

Carlyle preferred to wait for the Jeffreys' coming, and while waiting wrote to his idle brother Dr. John in London (6.8.1830):—

' I sympathise in your reluctance to enter on the practice of medicine, or indeed of any professional duty. Neither can I be surprised at your hankering after a literary life, so congenial as I have often heard you hint it would be to your tastes. Nevertheless it *would* greatly astonish me if beyond mere preliminary reveries these feelings produced any influence on your conduct. The voice of all experience seems to be in favour of a profession. You sail there as under convoy in the middle of a fleet, and have a thousand-fold chance of reaching port.

' To my mind nothing justifies me for having adopted the trade of literature, except the remembrance that I had no other but these two—that of a schoolmaster or that of a priest : in the one case with the fair prospect of speedy maceration and starvation ; in the other of *perjury*, which is infinitely worse. As it is, I look confidently forward to a life of poverty, toil, and dispiritment, so long as I remain on this earth, and hope only that God will grant me patience and strength to struggle onwards through the midst of it, working out his will as I best can in this lonely clay-pit where I am set to dig. The pitifullest of all resources is complaining, which accordingly I strive not to practise ; only let these things be known for my brother's warning, that he may order his life better than I could do mine.' Then he wrote at large to the effect—' Up and

M

be doing,' and concluded—'Adieu Jack. We are poor men, but nothing worse. Your brother. T. CARLYLE.'

In 1827 he had read about Saint-Simon and thought him a queer fellow for wanting "wonders on wonders" such as "a priesthood of savants," and the chief thing noted down was of a piece with that :—"*Il se maria* etc.*"—He took a wife in order to produce men of genius, but had no children at all. Anguste Comte and others who passed as his pupils seemed to Carlyle "more sensible" men.

This was the Comte who started Positivism. As for Saint-Simon himself, biographers say that after his childless marriage ended in divorce he proposed to the widow De Staël, explaining that the most extraordinary woman in the world would be sure to bear a child still more so, if she married the most extraordinary man. The widow wanted a second husband, but preferred a meeker partner. So Saint-Simon never had a son. After now reading the literature his disciples sent, Carlyle wrote to Gustave d'Eichthal [1] (9.8.1830) :—

'In these Books I find little or nothing to dissent from : the opinions are often such as I cherish. That the last century was a period of Denial, of Irreligion and Destruction; to which a new period of Affirmation, of Religion, must succeed, if Society is to continue in existence: this is' (true, in short ; and also) 'that as Religion is the only bond and life of Societies, so the only real Government were a Hierarchy : nay either a Hierarchy or Heresiarchy it now is, and must ever be : our real Governors in this age are, not the Capets and Guelfs, but Pope Voltaire, Bishop Hume, Bishop (Adam) Smith, Archdeacon Helvetius, and the like, with their thousand newspaper Curates ; to whom Kings and Premiers and Field-Marshals are but the sacristans and pew-openers—hired, indeed, at a quite mad rate of wages, and doing their work ill.'

All this in short, 'I find set forth in your works. The more curious am I to understand how men above superstition and deception use these extraordinary words : "Dieu est revenu, etc."' God has returned to France in Saint-Simon,

---

[1] Letters from Thomas Carlyle to the Socialists of 1830, in the *New Quarterly*, April, 1909 (Dent), by Eugene d'Eichthal, a son of the Gustave d'Eichthal who wrote to T.C., pp. 277–288.

and France shall proclaim to the world the new God—
" le Dieu nouveau." 'I wait instruction. For in Saint-
Simon I find no Inspiration, save what every man of
Genius may be said to feel,' and 'several of his Disciples
manifest in a still more unquestionable form. Doubt not
therefore, but the Book wherein you are to unfold your
Religious principles, will be specially welcome here.'

He concludes a long screed with the assurance, which
must have been all the more disconcerting because plainly
meant to be polite and comforting, that they must be in
' the right direction for you are animated by that martyr
spirit never altogether wrong ; that you are on the right
path I shall rejoice to find, and hope till the contrary is
plain.'

He added a postscript about his other writings, beginning : —' I hear to-day that your foolish old king
has come to England ; between the nations, who now
begin to understand each other, there will be no war ; let
us hope, never more ! '

Saint-Simon himself had not been mad, but original
and headlong. When young he made his flunky wake
him with : " Get up, Sir Count, you have great things to
do," which so tickled Carlyle that he often quoted it.
Saint-Simon crossed to America to fight like La Fayette,
and did not " emigrate " at the Revolution, but in old
age he was poor, and only the charity of friends and relatives saved him from death by starvation. In spite of
cold and hunger and ridicule, he wrote the great thoughts
that were stirring in him, and with as much serenity as
if he were still a man of money, proposed to the Bourbon
Government which the foreigners had set up in France to
reorganize society with captains of industry in place of
feudal good-for-nothings and with men of science as spiritual
directors in place of priests. He thought women should
be emancipated and the right of inheritance abolished.
As distinguished from communism the Utopia of Saint-
Simon was a centralised Hierarchy, graded by merit, men
in power according to their capacity, and rewarded according to their work. Utopia indeed !

His penury seemed punishment enough. The men in
power did not make a martyr of him except by neglect.
He was a poor old man of sixty-four with few to heed him
when Carlyle and Strachey and Kitty Kirkpatrick were

in Paris seeing sights, and hearing nothing of him or his disciples, as Carlyle lamented now. A year before then he had fired a pistol at himself in despair, but missed his life and only destroyed an eye. With the one eye left he wrote the *Nouveau Christianisme* (New Christianity), the best of his books, and then died (19.5.1835). Carlyle translated it this winter, supposing Bowring might print it, which of course he would not. Nobody in England was thinking of social reform as yet, least of all the active politicians. A Prime Minister was saying that things had come to a pretty pass when Christianity was supposed to interfere with men's private lives. There was no serious thought of applying rudimentary righteousness to politics. Even Goethe now admonished Carlyle to hold himself aloof from the Saint-Simonians, and when Jeffrey saw Carlyle in earnest about telling the truth in politics, he became like the hen which beholds the ducks she has hatched taking to water. By-and-by Carlyle used to say he would not have known what to think of things but for the French Revolution. He certainly might have closed his ears to political clamour for years to come but for the events of 1830.

IV

" THE TALE OF TALES " &c.

(1830)

AMONG other trifles Carlyle was now completing was a translation of Goethe's *Das Mährchen* (The Tale of Tales), which he had done in November, 1825, for *German Romance*. He showed tact in omitting it from that book, for tho' short it is as tedious as *The Faerie Queen*; but in Germany it had long been discussed like a new Book of Revelations, which shows a certain lack of humour.

The machinery is more miraculous than the *Arabian Nights*. There are metal statues that talk; a temple underground which comes up at the right moment with all its decorations, like a flower-bed in the spring made speedy on a film; and a snake more absurd than Bottom himself.[1] It talks and sighs and never bites—a Christmas pantomime darling of a snake, compared to which the one in the Hebrew Garden of Eden was a commonplace creature.

The story is of a beautiful lady living with attendant maids on one side of a river which separates her from a young man on the other, a king out of a job. There is more than the lack of a bridge to bother them. Whatever the lady touches dies, even her canary, in spite of which the hero, after going about barefoot on the burning sands—for he had nothing to wear but his royal purple cloak and his " glittering coat of mail," skin-tight, he had not even a shirt, poor fellow !—gets a lift across the river from the obliging snake, which turned itself into a great bridge for the occasion—what can be too much to oblige a friend ?—and then resumed its living shape and followed to the lady's house, to be ready to comfort her. The young man shivering in a royal funk beheld the lady caressing a poodle and overcame his fears and approached her. " She held out her hands to keep him off and touched him only the sooner." Then down he flopped, as dead as the canary.

[1] *Midsummer Night's Dream*, III. and I.

165

Then came the greatest miracle of all. " The snake formed a wide circle round the corpse, and seizing her tail between her teeth, she lay quite still," and easily continued not only to talk—the story could not get on without her—but also to " keep looking round on all sides " and " shake herself for joy " whenever she liked, without once " changing her posture," which was indispensible to keep the body from putrefaction till the inevitable old man came with a lamp and revived both the lover and the canary.

There was a stray giant hitching about, whose shadow was sometimes convenient and occasionally dangerous. " Superstition " says Carlyle; but biographer Bielschowsky divines he is " political delusion, crazy enthusiasm for higher things." To keep the royal minds at ease he is turned into a red stone Colossus, a giant Sun-Dial ! Thus the story ends as a Christmas Pantomime should with everybody happy.

To Goethe this summer Carlyle had written about his wife.—

' She spends many an evening with you, and has done all winter, greatly to her satisfaction. One of her last performances was that glorious *Mährchen*, a true Universe of Imagination ; in regard to the manifold, inexhaustible significance of which—for the female eye guessed a significance under it—I was oftener applied to for exposition than I could give it ; and at last, to quiet importunities, was obliged to promise that I would some day write a commentary on it, as on one of the deepest, most poetical things even Goethe had ever written.'

So said, so done ;[1] but whether and how far the commentary was original is doubtful,[2] and does not matter. Even according to Goethe's best German biographer *The Tale* was one of his many " failures to embody in artistic form " the French Revolution.[3] He wrote in August and September, 1795, soon after Prussia had made peace with Paris ; and told Mrs. Carlyle now (6.6.1830) : —" That famous *Mährchen* is a piece of legerdemain. Imagination demands that reason should extract from it something logical and consistent, which reason never succeeds in doing.

---

[1] *Fraser's Magazine*, No. 33 (1832). In *Miscellanies*, Appendix.
[2] Compare the exposition in Bielschowsky's *Life of Goethe*, II, pp. 128–132.
[3] Bielschowsky's *Life of Goethe*, English transln. II, 128 and 146.

However, I possess two interpretations, which I will send." Whatever they were, he did not commit himself to either of them, and Carlyle told Espinasse by and by that what Goethe wrote was "ambiguous, not to say unsatisfactory." [1]

Mrs. Carlyle was very much in earnest about *The Tale* this Summer ; but when afterwards she heard her husband and Espinasse discussing it and Goethe's love affairs and " pretty complimentary verses " to herself, she said :— " It would have been much better for him if he had been capable of giving a good hearty laugh. I have been told by Mrs Jameson that when she was visiting Goethe at Weimar, she heard his daughter-in-law Ottilie screaming in another room while her husband August, Goethe's only child, was beating her."

Carlyle and Espinasse were silent, wondering how much of this Mrs. Jameson had really said, and how much of what she really said was true. " The custom of the Country " explains a good deal, and also the reverential German patience with *The Tale*. Whatever a man like Goethe wrote in 1795 that seemed to bear on politics would be scanned for its double meanings, in the hope of getting light upon what was passing in the minds of the people's masters. But why should Carlyle bother about it now ? In a year or two (16.10.1832) he was answering Mill's enquiries, saying, " I am all wonder at it."

There was another similar bit of trash, *The Novelle*, of less account, if less be possible. Both are nothing now except an occasion for the question—why did Carlyle allow such stuff to be printed ? His wife wanted it. Germany admired it. Fraser was willing to pay for it. He was short of cash. These may seem reasons enough ; yet it is likely *The Tale of Tales* would have ended in the waste paper basket if his reverence for Goethe had not be-numbed his sense of the ridiculous. That is why his later letter and talk had to be quoted now—to reveal what would otherwise be incredible, that he never realized the inherent absurdity of what even biographer Bielschowsky calls a failure.

[1] *Literary Recollections*, by F. Espinasse, pp. 222–3, for this and for what follows.

V

WHAT NEXT?

(1830)

CARLYLE did not look at the French Revolution by the light of Goethe's allegories. He was reading Mignet in 1828, and was now going into Political Economy with the same earnestness that he had gone into Astronomy or German Literature. He wrote to his brother in London, (21.8.1830) :—

' Pity that poor fellows should hang so much on cash ! But it is the general lot, and whether it be ten pounds or ten thousand that would relieve us, the case is all the same, and the tie that binds us equally mean. If I had money to carry me up and down the world in search of good men and fellow-labourers with whom to hold communion, and heat myself into clearer activity, I should think myself happier ; but in the meantime I have *myself* here for better or worse ; and who knows but my imprisonment in these moors, sulkily as I may sometimes take it, is really for my good ? If I have any right strength it will. If not, then what is the matter whether I sink or swim ? Oh that I had but a little real wisdom ; then would all things work beautifully for the best ends. Meanwhile the Dunscore Patmos is simply the place where of all others in the known world I can live cheapest, which, in the case of a man living by literature, with little saleable talent, is a momentous point.'

Apropos the Literary History he sent a message very " like him " to its projector.—" Assure Fraser that I feel no shadow of spleen against him, but a true sentiment of friendship and regret at all the trouble he has had." (But he added) " I will work no more in compilation. *If my writing cannot be sold, it shall at least have been written out of my own heart."* [1]

He mentioned that their brother Alexander was giving up Craigenputtock farm, and said :—" I often calculate that the land is all let some thirty per cent. too high ; and that before it can be reduced the whole existing race of farmers must be ruined." Which did not happen only because most of them went to America and the colonies. He went on :—" The time is sick and out of joint. The perversities and mismanagements, moral and physical, of this best-of-all stage of society are rising to a head ; and one day, see it who may, the whole concern will be blown up to Heaven, and fall thence to Tartarus, and a new and fairer era will rise in its room. Since the time of Nero and Jesus Christ there is no record of such embarrassments and crying, or, what is still worse, silent, abominations. But the day, as we said, WILL come ; for God is still in Heaven, whether Henry Brougham and Jeremiah Bentham know it or not ; and the gig, and gigmania ' (meaning snobbery) 'must rot or start into a thousand shivers, and bury itself in the ditch, that MAN may have clean roadway towards the goal whither through all ages he is tending. *Fiat, fiat* ! "' (So let it be done !)

A letter to Goethe about this time, (31.8.1830), is full of self-revelation. He was explaining why he was not sorry that his History of German Literature was stopped : —

' For my own part, as my Name was to have stood upon the title-page, I cannot but rejoice, so far as that goes, that my first professed appearance in Literature may now take place under some less questionable character than that of a compiler : *being ambitious, one day, of far higher honours.*[1] It is true, as you say somewhere, and it ought ever to be borne in mind, that " an Artist in doing anything does All : " nevertheless, how few are Artists in this sense ; and *till one knows that he cannot be a Mason, why should he publicly hire himself as a Hodman* ?[1]

' I must forthwith betake me to something more congenial and original : *except writing from the heart and if possible to the heart, Life has no other business for me, no other pleasure.*[1] When I look at the wonderful Chaos within me, full of natural Supernaturalism, and all manner of Antediluvian fragments ; and how the Universe is daily

[1] Italics added.

growing more mysterious as well as more august, and
the influences from without more heterogeneous and per-
plexing ; I see not well what is to come of it all, and only
conjecture from the violence of the fermentation that
something strange may come. As you feel a fatherly
concern in my spiritual progress, which you know well,
for all true disciples of yours, to be the one thing needful,
I lay these details before you with the less reluctance.'

He was strangely moved, as if by a fever which was not
disease, but the restlessness of one moved by " the spirit. "
He tried his hand again on " dactyls " and jingle, without
relief, and without success, tho' there is a scrap dateable
about now which is rather ejaculation than poetry, and
spontaneous like an unpremeditated " Damn ! "

> ' So here hath been dawning
>   Another blue Day :
> Think wilt thou let it
>   Slip useless away.

> ' Out of Eternity
>   This new day is born ;
> Into Eternity
>   At night, will return

> ' Behold it aforetime
>   No eye ever did :
> So soon it forever
>   From all eyes is hid.

> ' Here hath been dawning
>   Another blue day :
> Think wilt thou let it
>   Slip useless away.'

A child might mend the melody of this, but the meaning
of it is the best lesson of the moving world which we live
in—Move on ! In a slumberous palace near the Ganges,
a Buddha might mourn the everlasting change he saw
everywhere, and when sick of self-indulgence, practise and
preach asceticism, which is mitigated suicide ; but where
man has to work if he wants to live at all, the right sort of
man sees that means " keep doing, " reconciles himself
to what has to be and says, " All right! " And never
was there anyone more sincere in saying so than " our hero".

He had to find a vent for his feelings in prose. His memory was now as full of matter as Macaulay's of words. Recalling such knowledge, he was meditating on the recent writings of Economists. Already he had remarked their " considerable . . . error about improving waste lands as compared with manufacturing : the machine dies ; the improved land remains an *addition* to the Earth *forever*." But what had struck him most was their meanness of mind :—

' Their whole Philosophy (!) is an Arithmetical Computation—performed in words. Even if it were right ! Which it scarcely ever is. The question of National Money-making is not a high but a low one : as they treat it, amongst the lowest. Could they tell us how wealth is and should be *distributed*, it were something ; but they do not attempt it. Political Philosophy should be a scientific revelation of the whole secret mechanism whereby men cohere in society ; instead of which it tells us how " flannel jackets " are exchanged for " pork hams." They are the hodmen of the intellectual edifice, who have got upon the wall, and will insist on building, as if they were masons.'

Such thoughts had prepared him to welcome the greeting of the Saint-Simonians. Bringing a fresh mind to bear upon the politics of Europe, he was reaching strange conclusions, which tried the intellectual honesty he had learned from such as Goethe. He proceeded to think out his economic conclusions, feeling like an explorer among the high places of the world, where none can be happy alone. A prophet has to be a pioneer—a place of honour, when all ends well, but seldom merely pleasant. Near the middle of September the Jeffreys came to visit them ; and in the absence of any Boswell to report what Jeffrey called " four days of intimate talking " the soliloquies of Carlyle in his Note-book in the weeks preceding then make it easy to understand how Jeffrey began to abandon hope of ever seeing him among the sleek Macaulays, magnifying the Whigs and their shibboleths.

' Received about four weeks ago a strange letter from some Saint-Simonians at Paris. These people have strange notions, not without a large spicing of truth, and are them-

selves among the *Signs* (*of the Times*).　I shall feel curious
to know what becomes of them.　*La classe la plus pauvre*
(the poorest class) is evidently in the way of rising from its
present deepest abasement : in time, it is likely, the world
will be better divided, and he that has the toil of ploughing
will have the first cut at the reaping.

' A man with £200,000 a year eats the *whole* fruit of
6,666 men's labour through a year ; for you can get a stout
spadesman to work and maintain himself for the sum of
£30.　Thus we have private individuals whose wages are
equal to the wages of seven or eight thousand other
individuals : what do those highly beneficed individuals
do to society for their wages ?　*Kill Partridges.*　CAN this
last ?　No, by the soul that is in man, it cannot and will
not and shall not !

' Our Political Economists should collect statistical *facts* :
such as, What is the lowest sum a man can live on in
various countries ?　What is the highest he gets to live on ?
How many people work with their hands ? how many with
their heads ? how many not at all ?　and innumerable such.
What all want to know is the condition of our fellow men,
and strange to say, it is the thing least of all understood.
The present " Science " of Political Economy requires
far less intellect than successful Bellows-mending ;　and
perhaps does less good, if we deduct all the evil it brings us.'

These notes reveal Carlyle perceiving society to be an
organism, wherein each must do his bit, and believing the
Revolutionary watchword that everyone has to live by working or begging or stealing, whereas the Gospel of Grab and
" the Devil take the rest,"—the " law of the jungle "—was
the working creed of politicians on both sides.　The Whigs
were the middle class and the Tories the gentry and their
servants.　Meditating on the how and the why of customs
and conventions commonly taken for granted as if they
were laws of nature, with a wider outlook than even
Voltaire, Carlyle was inspired by the Bible and Burns,
Rousseau and Goethe, and seeing what was what, he wrote
with the recklessness of a Scotch Covenanter the thoughts
he was soon to transcribe into *Sartor*.　The loss of wages
for nearly a year of hack-work on the *History* made him
more and not less resolved to speak the truth he saw.
To be nothing but a hack, an author of all work, he felt
no " call " whatever.

(1830). ' September 7th. The " Course of Providence "
seems guiding my steps into new regions ; the question
is coming more and more towards a decision : Canst thou,
there as thou art, accomplish aught good and true, or art
thou to die miserably as a vain Pretender ? It is above a
year since I wrote one sentence that came from the right
place ; since I did one action that seemed to be really
worthy. The want of money is a comparatively insignificant affair.' He had written to Dr. John last
month, ' We are very poor at present ; but that is *all*, and
we will get over that.' His pen-soliloquy proceeds.—' Were
I doing well otherwise, I could most readily consent to go
destitute and suffer all sorts of things.

' I have strange glimpses of the power of spiritual
Union, of Association among men. Men work godlike
miracles thereby, and the horridest abominations
Society is a wonder of wonders ; and Politics—in the right
sense, far, very far from the common one—*is* the noblest
Science.

' *Cor ne edito* !' Do not eat your own heart !—a
maxim of Pythagoras, which may have been suggested
by Homer's saying of Bellerophon, the Greek " Joseph,"
that he was " eating his spirit," when he was excommuni-
cated, so to speak, and had to walk alone. Carlyle was
fond of the phrase and meant by it what he now added :—
' Up and be doing ! Life is rusting and wasting, if thou
use it not. Up and be doing ; and pray—if thou but can—
to the Unseen Author of all thy Strength to guide thee and
aid thee ; to give thee if not Victory and Possession, un-
wearied Activity and *Entsagen*.—

' Is not every Thought properly an inspiration ? Or
how is one thing more inspired than another ? Much is
in this.'

Entsagen is defined in German Dictionaries : —" To
renounce, resign, disclaim." The word was reasonably
used by Goethe for self-control which required an effort
of self-denial. Carlyle required to be making a continual
effort to hold on to the humility and other qualities he had
learned to esteem so much that he wanted more of them
than he had received from Nature. Without feeling the
worse of it he could not let himself go as freely as Shakespeare and Goethe did, and Burns and John Wilson. So he
was often saying " *Entsagen* " to himself—it began to

sound ascetic, or sometimes a nasty shibboleth. It was the legend on a favourite seal used both by him and his wife. Occasionally he seemed to imply it was a new discovery, whereas in fact as he had to admit it was as old as the hills. It must have been one of the earliest discoveries of prehistoric man, for this way of thinking and feeling is what best distinguishes human from merely animal life.

He felt he should be doing something, and was always repeating to himself the artist's maxim—Never a day without a line. Which made him on Monday, 6.9.1830, do some dactyls, tho' he had the sense to look at them when done " with detestation and abhorrence." That night he " sat up very late reading Scott's *History of Scotland*," just published in Lardner's Cyclopedia, and his note about it next morning is perhaps the most frequently quoted thing he ever wrote and never published.—

' An amusing Narrative, clear, precise and I suppose accurate ; but no more a *History* of Scotland than I am Pope of Rome.   A series of Palace intrigues, and butcheries and battles little more important than those of Donnybrook Fair ; all the while that *Scotland*, quite unnoticed, is holding on her course in Industry, in Arts, in Culture, as if *Langside* and *Clean the Causeway* had remained unfought. Strange that a man should think he was writing the History of a Nation, while he is chronicling the amours of a wanton young woman called Queen, and a sulky booby recommended to Kingship for his fine limbs, and then blown up with gunpowder for ill-behaviour.   Good Heaven! let them fondle and pout and bicker *ad libitum*' (as much as they like) ; ' what has God's fair Creation, and man's immortal Destiny to do with them and their trade ?'

This was not so absurd as it sounds.   He would probably have made it clearer in anything to be published that what he meant to blame was bothering to-day about the like of Mary and her paramours.   Their importance to their afflicted contemporaries was as palpable as that of mad dogs, and the Nemesis of snobbery like Scott's was to continue interested in such human wasters.

' One inference I have drawn from Scott : that the people in those old days had a singular talent for nicknames. Apparently there was more humour then than now.

'For the rest, the *Scottish History* looks like that of a Gypsy encampment : industry of the rudest, largely broken by sheer indolence ; smoke, sluttishness, hunger, scab and—blood. Happily, as hinted, Scotland herself *was not there*.

'Lastly' (and the earnest Toryism of Scott makes this like an admission) 'it is noteworthy that the Nobles of the country have maintained a quite despicable behaviour, from the times of Wallace downwards. A selfish, ferocious, famishing, unprincipled set of hyaenas, from whom at no time and in no way has the country derived any benefit. The day is coming when these our modern hyaenas—tho' *toothless*, still mischievous, and greedy beyond limit—will— quickly I hope—*be paid off. Canaille faineante, que faites-vous la ?* (Ye do-nothing dogs, what are ye doing there ?). Down with your double barrels ; take spades, if ye can do no better, and work or die ! '

Next evening (8.9.1830), a whole bundle of *Fraser's Magazines* arrived, and were found to contain " such hurly-burly of rhodomontade, punch, loyalty, and Saturnalian Toryism as eye hath not seen. This out-Blackwoods *Blackwood*, a kind of wild popular Lower-Comedy ; of which John Wilson is the Inventor " ; and most of the Magazines were imitating it. " Printing " he reflected, " is now no more the livery of Literature than writing was in Gutenburg's day."

'Nevertheless the thing has its meaning ' he moralized, as he read the magazine rubbish. 'Great actions are sometimes historically barren ; smallest actions have taken root.

'One thing we see : the moral nature of man is deeper than his intellectual. What is Jesus Christ's significance ? *Altogether moral*.

'What is Jeremy Bentham's significance ? Altogether intellectual, logical. I name him as the representative of a class, important only for their numbers. Logic is their sole foundation, wherefore their system is a *Machine*, and cannot *grow* or endure. Alas poor England, stupid, purblind, pudding-eating England! Bentham with his *Mills* grinding thee out Morality,' which is noticeable as one of the few puns in Carlyle ; ' and some Macaulay, also a grinder, testing it and decrying it, because it is not his own Whig-established *Quern*-morality !

'The sin of this age is Dilettantism ; the Whigs, and all " moderate Tories," are the grand Dillettanti : I begin to feel less and less patience for them. This is no world where a man should stand trimming his whiskers, looking on at work, or touching it with the point of a gloved finger. *Man sollte greifen zu !* (One must grip hold!) There is more hope of an Atheist Utilitarian, of a Superstitious Ultra, than of such a lukewarm, withered mongrel. He would not believe tho' one rose from the dead. He is wedded to his idols, let him alone.'

This is the last entry before the Jeffreys came. Talk like this would explain why in later letters Jeffrey used to put in pleas for the game-killers in his dainty Ariel way. It seems to have been just before their arrival near the middle of September that Carlyle suddenly found something better to write than dactyls and rhymes—he was seized by a new idea. The multitudinous conclusions from knowledge so extended in time and space were suddenly crystallized on an ancient metaphor.

VI

HOW "SARTOR" STARTED

(SEPTEMBER, 1830)

WHATEVER the first suggestion of *Sartor* was it would be like the falling apple Newton noticed, which started the reflections which led to the discovery of Gravitation. For about a million years of human existence, till a few thousand years ago at any rate, a visitor from another planet globe-trotting among us would have seen little to distinguish our ancestors from the beasts but the habit of wearing clothes. This makes it needless to produce the proofs from the most ancient scriptures that to liken other things to clothes was familiar therein, and must have been prehistoric. It is by likening one thing to another that men make languages, and clothes supplied many comparisons. Swift caricatured the old figure of speech, and in the essay on Burns, it was cut out as too trite to be tolerable by Jeffrey. Carlyle had written there about the clothes making the man and the tailor being a creator, and Jeffrey cutting that out made him remember it the more,—it was a habit of his to grip the commonplace very tight, for a reason worth explaining. A maxim or metaphor is not the less but the more likely to be true because it is threadbare. He was not endeavouring merely to be an entertaining scribe, he was trying in a single-minded way to see the truth of things. In the *Fraser's Magazines* which came on 8.9.1830, he had read nothing with so much gusto as the attack on Bulwer Lytton and his fashionable novels. *The Dandiacal Household* was there,[1] and the foolish faith in fancy tailoring that filled the popular *Pelham* made caricature superflous.[2] So it is not strange to find him writing in old age:—

[1] *Sartor Resartus*, III and X : compare Fraser's, M., June 1830, p. 515.
[2] *Pelham* has been expurgated to evade such mockery as that Chapter of *S. R.* See McMechan's edn. of *S. R.*, notes, p. 388–390.

'The first genesis (or birth) of *Sartor* I remember well enough, and the very spot—at Templand' (the home of Mrs. Welsh and her father)—'where the notion of astonishment at *clothes* first struck me.'

The likeliest date was August or September, 1830. In September he and his wife were in Dumfries amusing themselves looking at "the huge bullocks" and strange men at the market there. By eight o'clock they had started to drive home. Before arriving where the Dunscore Road turned off the mail road, he said, "Suppose we go on to Templand? The way is shorter, and smoother for a drive in the dark, and you've to be there at any rate before the end of the week." She at once agreed. He drove on and they surprised Mrs. Welsh at ten o'clock. She was "overjoyed to all lengths", and made them porridge for supper "with her own hands."

Next morning she clipped her son-in-law's hair "with her own hands" too. "She always made a dolly of her daughter," people said, and on this day she would do anything for them except let them go home. She brought friends to join them at dinner, to her father's satisfaction. Some weeks before then Carlyle had written down how funny it would be if at some pompous ceremonial the clothes flew off and left the performers naked; and now when listening to talk on the impending visit of the Jeffreys and the one before, he might re-call the mutilation of the proofs of *Burns* which they had brought then. At any rate he did at Templand begin to think again about the despised old figure of speech, and suddenly saw possibilities in it which had escaped both Swift and Jeffrey.

In the Bible clothes were symbols of many meanings: (1) what covers or wraps, (2) what grows old, (3) what needs to be changed, and so on. The texts were familiar to him from childhood as sacred words, and ditto from boyhood the mockery of clothes by Shakespeare's Lear. The Savignys and Schlegels were now under various guises Court Flunkies to the German Kings, and no better than blatherskites explaining the universe to absent-minded men in whatever way seemed likeliest to please the puppets atop. Here is the text they concocted as a foundation stone for "Historical Jurisprudence."—" The state does not exist for purposes of men, and is not governed by laws of their devising, but by the Cosmic Force above."

Sorrier stuff was never spoken in any Egyptian Temple. "The Cosmic Force"—a shabby name for living Nature—assuredly shapes the State *through men*, and therefore the State is *made by men* in exactly the same sense as their ships are, or their houses, or their hats !

Carlyle wrote in his Note-book a year ago, soon after the talk with Jeffrey at Dumfries, what reads like a conclusion they had reached together :

' An Institution—a Law of any kind—may become a *deserted* edifice ; the walls standing, no life going on within, but that of bats, owls, and unclean creatures. It will then be pulled down if it stand interrupting any *thoroughfare* : if it do not so stand, people may leave it alone till a grove of natural wood grow round it, and no eye but that of the adventurous antiquarian may know of its existence, such a tangle of *brush* is to be struggled through before it can be come at and viewed.'

He continues, as if answering the objection—that is too metaphorical. 'All Language but that concerning *sensual* objects is or has been figurative. Prodigious influence of metaphors ! Never saw it till lately. A truly useful and philosophical work would be a good *Essay on Metaphors*. Some day I will write one ! '

And now instead of writing idly about metaphors in general, he was seeing how to use the one about clothes, familiar and yet sacred from of old, in such a way as to let men see what was what—calling obsolete institutions and religions " old clothes."

He could not begin to write for several days, being away from home. Mrs. Welsh did not want to change her tenant ; but Alexander Carlyle was losing money at Craigenputtock and did not want to stay. What he was to do next was uncertain. His brother Tom went to Scotsbrig to talk over everything with their father, and on Sunday evening, 12.9.1830, Tom walked three miles to Burnswark, for a talk with " good old Graham," ex-Glasgow merchant, a farmer now. Returning at ten on a still fine night, he reached his father's door as the family were singing a psalm to his father's favourite tune, *Coleshill*. He stood outside till worship ended, admiring the piety from which he had been parted against his will, and gratefully recognizing the " noble politeness " which kept it remote from him, forgiving him for thinking of it differently. By Monday morning a messenger had come with the news that the Jeffreys were on the way. He hastened home as fast as his pony could carry him, and found the Jeffreys there (13.9.1830). They stayed till Friday ; and if we could only know what was said between the men when the women had retired, we might find some of the good things in *Sartor* taking shape in their conversation.

What seemed an insignificant extraneous detail is almost all we know. A letter came to Jeffrey from Hazlitt :—

" Dear Sir, I am dying : can you send me £100, and so consummate your many kindnesses to me ?—W. Hazlitt."

It was true. He had just finished his four-volume *Life of Napoleon*, and being wearied consulted a doctor, who purged and weakened him too much. So said Dr. John Carlyle, apparently. Jeffrey did not fail his friend. As soon as possible after reaching home on Friday night, 17.9.1830, at " eleven o'clock, under a glorious canopy of Northern lights and soft burning stars," he sent £50 for Hazlitt's immediate needs, and "instructions" for the doctor, "not losing an hour" after his return, and leaving half the letters waiting him unread to be in time at his banker's. But as he was doing so that Saturday, 18.9.1830, Hazlitt died.

Carlyle wrote to Dr. John that day on the same subject, remarking of Jeffrey :—" We all like him better than we did. He is the most sparkling, pleasant little fellow I ever saw." Then Carlyle began an article for Fraser. He needed cash immediately, for one thing ; and it had struck him that the Tories need not have a monopoly of fun. So he decided to write about " clothes." Apparently it was soon after the Jeffreys departed, 18.9.1830, that he soliloquized with the pen :—

' The Jeffreys here. Very good and interesting beyond wont was our worthy Dean. He is growing old, and seems dispirited and partly unhappy. The fairest cloak has its wrong side. Envy no man.' As the natural leader of the party plainly about to come into power, Jeffrey was then the man in Scotland most envied by the ambitious. Carlyle went on :—' Jeffrey is the best mimic—in the lowest and the highest senses—I ever saw. All matters he has taken up in forms chiefly logical and encircled with sparkles of conversational wit or *persiflage* ; yet with deeper study he would have found poetical forms for them, and his persiflage might have incorporated itself gracefully with the Love and pure humane feeling that dwells deeply in him. This last is his highest strength, tho' he himself hardly knows the significance of it : he is one of the most *loving* men alive ; has a true kindness, not of blood and habit only, but of soul and spirit. He cannot *do* without being loved. He is in the highest degree social ; and in defect of this *gregarious* ; which last condition he—in these bad times—has for most part had to content himself withal. Every way indeed he has fallen on evil days : the prose spirit of the world—to which world his kindliness draws him so strongly and closely—has choked up and all but withered the better poetic spirit he derived from nature. Whatever is highest, he entertains—like other Whigs— only as an ornament, as an appendage. The great business of Man he—intellectually—considers as a wordling does : *To be happy*. I have heard him say : " If Folly were the happiest, I would be a fool." Yet his daily Life belies this doctrine, and says :—"Tho' Goodness were the most wretched, I would be good." '

(This is delicious. One can see the God-like Ariel, as he says this in the drawing-room, looking through the corner of his eye to see how Carlyle is taking it.)

' In conversation he is brilliant—or rather sparkling— lively, kind, willing either to speak or to listen, and above all men I have ever seen, ready and copious. On the whole exceedingly pleasant in light talk. Yet alas light, light, too light ! He will talk of nothing *earnestly*, tho' his look sometimes betrays an earnest feeling. He starts contra- diction in such cases, and argues, argues. Neither is his arguing like that of a Thinker, but an Advocate ; Victory not Truth. A right *Terrae Filius* (Son of Earth) would feel irresistibly disposed to " wash him away." He is not a *strong* man in any shape, but *nimble* and *tough*.

' He stands midway between God and Mammon ; and his preaching through Life has been an attempt to reconcile these. Hence his popularity ; a thing easily accountable when one looks at the world and at him ; but little honour-

able to either. Literature ! Poetry ! Except by a dim
indestructible Instinct, which he has never dared to avow,
yet being a true poet—in his way—could never eradicate—
he knows not what they mean. A true Newspaper Critic,
on the great scale ; no Priest, but a Concionator !' (public
speaker).

'Yet on the whole, he is about *the best man* I ever saw.
Sometimes I think he will abjure the Devil—if he live—
and become a pure Light. Already he is a most tricksy
dainty beautiful little Spirit : I have seen gleams on the
face and eyes of the man that let you look into a higher
country. God bless him ! And I will blab no more.
These jottings are as *sincere* as I could write them, yet too
dim and inaccurately compacted. I see the nail, but have
not here hit it on the head. Basta !' (Enough !) There
was modesty as well as truth in the feeling that he was a
" Son of Earth " and the other a " dainty-spirit." He
paused, and then added :—' I am going to write—Nonsense.
It is on " clothes." Heaven be my comforter ! '

He tried to let himself go with more success than ever
before, as if altogether in fun at first, and that was how
Diogenes Teufelsdröckh arose, a fancy figure not unlike
what he imagined the God-like Ariel might have been,
if he had not wasted his wits and grown rich by drudgery
in law-courts, unravelling chicane, but devoted himself to
" Literature " alone,

It is curious that tho' Carlyle growing older himself grew
more like Jeffrey, he wrote in old age about him what
might have almost been transcribed from early notes
and letters. He never suspected that both John Wilson
and Jeffrey, resorting to chaff whenever he tried to get
them to talk " earnestly " on " fundamentals," were
practising the gospel of silence he was groping after as he
watched them, perplexed. He was slow to discover what
is a truism in China but too little known in the west,
that none can be sure of the thoughts or feelings of another.

From about 19.9.1830 to 20.10.1830 he was " writing by
taskwork again," he assured his mother, which meant that
he covered a good amount of paper daily. He told his
brother about it in finishing (19.10.1830) :—" Begun an
article for Fraser ; then found to be too long—except it
were divided into two ; now sometimes looking almost as
if it would swell into a Book." He sent it for publication

as " two articles and the germ of more," with the title
Thoughts on Clothes.

It was substantially the first book of *Sartor*. The re-
semblances Americans remark between Diogenes Teufelsdröckh and Diedrich Knickerbocker may be due to what
both have in common with Addison's *Spectator*. Carlyle's
appreciation of Washington Irving may have accentuated
some points ; but assuredly the work is veiled autobiography. *Diogenes Teufelsdröckh* was Carlyle's ideal
Carlyle, as much as *Christopher North* was John Wilson or
the *Spectator* Joseph Addison. Indeed there seems to be
some truth in the Edinburgh theory that he was taking a
lesson from their " glorious John " and " letting himself go."

" Diogenes," meaning " Born of Jove" or God, was the
name of the Stoic philosopher whom D'Alembert thought
" the greatest man of antiquity," and whom Carlyle liked
and admired the most,—one of the few " philosophers "
he honoured as a man. His own habit of humorous
exaggeration was much in the style of Diogenes, who used
to say he imitated the teachers of choruses, who spoke too
loud in order that the rest might catch the proper tone.
Carlyle was fond of feeling like Diogenes, and saying
" Freedom first " to himself. Old Selden did the same,
it may be remembered. Another lesson he learned from
the greatest of the Greeks was to praise poverty, as the
condition of independence, and not be ashamed of manual
labour, the usual sign of it.[1] He soon was horrifying
the best of the bourgeois then alive by writing to Francis
Jeffrey,—" I do not see that Literature can support an
honest man otherwise than *à la Diogenes'* (in the way of
Diogenes), 'in which fashion too I mean to experiment
if *nothing* else could be found ; " which seems to show
why such a name would suit the " hero " who was himself.
The surname Teufelsdröckh is German for Asafetida,
literally " Devil's dung." The drug so named was then
familiar. It had a stink like garlic and was a nerve tonic
etc. The Scotch like the Germans called it " the Deil's
Dirt."

Dr. John Carlyle told Moncure Conway [2] :—

" I have no doubt that the framework of *Sartor* was
suggested by what I used to tell him of my experiences

[1] See Yonge's translation of Diogenes Laertius' *Lives of the Philosophers*, pp. 224–248.
[2] *Thomas Carlyle*, by Moncure Conway, p. 71.

in Germany.   There was a Schelling Club, which Schelling himself used to visit (at Munich).   It was devoted to beer, tobacco and philosophy.   I used to amuse my brother rehearsing their free and often wild speculative talk ; and *Sartor* recalls his comments and laughter." Norton heard the same thing.

' If I consider it well,' Carlyle confessed to himself in his journal, ' there is hardly any book in the world that has sunk so deep into me as *Reinecke Fuchs* (Reynard the Fox).   It co-operates with other tendencies. Perhaps my whole speculation about "Clothes" arose out of that.   It now absolutely haunts me, often very painfully and in shapes that I will not write even here.   Yet, again, how beautiful, how true, is this other :   "Man is an incarnate word."   Both these I habitually feel.'

The moral of Reinecke Fuchs is as old as the hills. Men are like beasts.   They are mostly fools, or knaves, and use their words as weapons, and seldom even try to tell the truth unless there is profit in it.   The lesson was confirmed to him as a boy by the Bible and the histories he read, Sallust for example, Tacitus and Voltaire ; and there is truth in it, as palpable as the saltness of the sea. Carlyle was saved from martyrdom because he recognised it.   Facts were always sacred to him.   He cherished no delusions about his contemporaries.   And yet, he told the truth.

" Let me know what you are about," wrote Jeffrey, concluding a long letter dated 28.10.1830, " and whether your *genuine* work is begun, and what it is about."

By that time he was resting, and his father arriving on a pleasant fortnight's visit, in the course of which he found time to satisfy Jeffrey's curiosity, to such purpose that the most important and busiest public man in Scotland hastened to write him at length what is worth reading yet.

VII

JEFFREY REMONSTRATES AGAINST HIS RADICALISM

(1830)

JEFFREY began (13.11.1830) by news. His brother was ill. "I do what I can," he said, "to believe the doctors, tho' Faith, you say, is not among my virtues," a fragment of some intimate talk. Then he told of wife and daughter, " both gone to bed with headache, and sitting alone over my midnight fire, I cannot keep visions of infection and desolating fever quite out of my mind—so I turn to warm my old heart at yours, and feel proud that you should know that neither business nor anxiety can make me forget to do a little good on your suggestion—I wish you could show me how to do more." We are left guessing what was the " little good", thus done in secret. Then he told how his voice was standing the strain.—" Our campaign has begun," and how the winds " put me in mind of my last jog at Craigenputtock." And then, as if suddenly reminded of Carlyle's surprising conclusions on politics, he let his pen run free.—

' I wish I had time to explain to you the grounds of my horror of radicalism. It is nothing but the old feud against *property*, more formidable by the greater intelligence and conceit of those who have none, the increase *perhaps* (for I am not sure that there is any increase) of their distresses, and the glimpses they have had of temporary prosperity. But there is no remedy, but the utter destruction of the right of property altogether, and the establishment of a great co-operative system, which no sane man will seriously consider as practicable. Anything short of that—sumptuary laws, maximum of allowable accumulation, compulsory charity, agrarian reparations—obviously tend, not to make the poor better off, but to make *all poor*, of the very lowest description, and that by no long process—besides importing the entire destruction of all luxury, elegance, art, and mental cultivation, and in short reducing the whole race to the wretched condition of savages toiling and scrambling for mere animal subsistence. It is only by protecting and assuring the right of *property* that we have emerged from that condition, and are still kept out of it, and tho' its ultimate establishment produces many evils, and a most revolting spectacle of inequality, I do not see how you can touch it, without bringing in still greater evils. In short I think it is quite plain that the greater portion of all societies *must* be always on the brink of extreme poverty and waging a hard battle with all sorts of fears and sufferings. In a mere worldly and physical point of view *they* gain but little perhaps by the establishment of property, tho' they are more secure from violence and outrage, and even for the most part from actual starvation. But indirectly even they gain a great deal in the share that comes even to them of that mental culture which is consequently diffused thro' society and in the hope and chance of rising to a higher place in it, which is a source of enjoyment even when not realized. But it is their very wants and urgent necessities which first roused the spirit of invention and improvement—and it is only—as it would appear—by their fears and miseries that their multiplication to a still more frightful extent is prevented. If men could have lived merely by breathing, and required neither clothes, house, nor any other accommodation, I take it to be quite certain first that they would very soon have multiplied till they had not room to lie down on the surface of the earth, and second that they would have so lived and propagated in as brutish a state as the very lowest of the animal creation. Your very rich man after all spends almost all his income on the poor, and except a very little *waste* of food among his servants and horses, is a mere distributor of his rents among industrious and frugal workmen. But if you ever touch his overgrown wealth, it is manifest that there is no stopping till *all* private accumulation or property is divided and made common, and with it all the advantages of working by large capitals destroyed. But this is as tiresome as mysticism, and perhaps as unintelligible—I should like much better to *talk* it to you—. only pray, if you are about to be a politician, set about it modestly and patiently, and submit to study a little, under

those who have studied it much longer and quite as honestly.
Well, tell me about your books, and what you are doing.
Good-night.   I must go to bed now.

Ever affectionately yours,

F. JEFFREY.'

(Tho' he had finished the letter, his pen ran on.—)
' If you are a radical, why do you keep the horses that
produce nothing ?   Why should you waste on the brutes
the food of six starving human creatures, that your feet
may be kept out of the dirt, or your diaphragm healthfully
agitated ?   Riding horses, which you patronise, interfere
with the subsistence of men 500 times more than partridges
which you abominate.   Do you adopt the radical doctrine
about *machinery* too—which is the true parent of the whole ?
And do you not see that, upon that principle, we should
burn our ploughs and carts—aye, and our spades too—and
end by only allowing men to work with *one hand*, or perhaps
with their feet only, in order that the necessary work
may give longer employment to more persons ?   All this
I think may be strictly demonstrated.   Yet you seem to
think a radical insurrection very justifiable, and its success
to be desired—tho' that is their great practical maxim and
would be their first enactment.   Do you really think it
desirable that machinery should be proscribed or that the
overseers of the poor should be obliged to give 12s. or
20s. a week to anyone who cannot—or says he cannot—
earn so much by the labour he has been used to ?   Yet it
is avowedly and expressly for *these objects* that insurrection is threatened or begun—radical reform of Parliament
is now sought only as a means to these ends—and indeed
is now very generally disregarded by the true radicals who
have other and quicker means in contemplation—and
on their principles, they are right.'

Then was then.   The truism that was the only truth
in Malthus was familiar to Carlyle, who wrote in his journal
about this time :—

' Were the landlords all hanged, and their estates given
to the poor, we should be—economically—much happier
perhaps for the space of thirty years ;   but the Population
would be doubled then, and again the Hunger of the un-
thrifty would burn the granary of the industrious.   Never-

theless the divine right of squires is' (ridiculous, in short).
'"The earth is the Lord's." The labourer is worthy of his
Hire ; and the Idler of his also—namely of Starvation.'

It is interesting to see with what simplicity Jeffrey
believed in the wages fund theory now exploded, and laid
the foolish formula of his friend Malthus like a poultice
to his uneasy conscience, while in *Sartor* (III and IV,
"Helotage") Carlyle refuted Malthus in the best style of the
original Diogenes. Instead of imagining facts to fit the
current nonsense, a Diogenes of the right sort sticks to
reality ; and so Carlyle gave all that was new in Malthus
a knock on the head by pointing to the emptiness of the
world. Since then it has been better ascertained that
humanity began to rise above the beasts, not by fighting or grabbing each for himself, like cats in the jungle,
or pigs in a pen, or fishes in the sea, but by helping each
other and working together, living in tribes and villages.
Our foolish idolatry of fighting bosses and our delusions
of "dominion" over fellow-men are a late and, let us
hope, a passing phase of humanity's emergence. There
never was a time in history when "the World" could
not have fed more than double its human population.
The God-like Ariel's next letter (18.12.1830) reveals the
new political "Boss" of Scotland as an uncommon kind
of politician, one who really put the public interest
first and was a man of conscience like Cromwell.—

' O yes, alas, I am Lord Advocate !—and about to be
M.P.—and to be plunged into a vortex from which my soul
recoils, and upon which nothing but a sense of duty, could
have induced me to venture. I have yielded to the judgment of friends. My motives in taking up this heavy
burden have not been tainted with any mixture that I can
detect of wordly ambition or self-interest. I may safely
refer to time for the redemption of any pledges.
' God help me—why do I write all this to you ? I have
written 23 letters since I came home from court, and
it is a relief to say a word to those I love and trust in—
without the intervention of a Secretary or the necessity
of any politic reserve, and to refresh my jaded spirits
with even an ideal gasp of the pure still air of your desert.'
(Then came family news and an appeal for a letter.)
' Can I do anything for you, or for any cause or person

in whom you take interest, in my new vocation ? Nothing vexes and disturbs me so much as the kind of patronage that belongs to it, which I would gladly give all its honours to be rid of. Nothing could reconcile me to London life but the prospect of returning. In the meantine, pray for me, my dear Friends and love me. This is the balm and cordial of my existence, and I think it is not in your natures to grudge or withhold it from me. When shall we meet again ? And now God Bless you. Do not be so long of writing again, and tell me all you are doing. Not much cold yet, but a plentiful lack of daylight. Good-night.

Ever affectionately yours,

F. Jeffrey.'

INTERLUDES TO *SARTOR*

(1830–31)

AFTER finishing *Thoughts on Clothes*, Carlyle returned to the best book of Saint-Simon, the John the Baptist of Socialism, which was a stimulant to the expansion of *Sartor*. It laid down " the cause of the poor " as the ground-work of religion, and their physical and moral improvement as the single end for which the whole of society should be at once re-organized.

" I see in last *Fraser* nothing of mine," Carlyle wrote to his brother in London (19.12.1830). " They may print up what they have got, before I send more. Hang them ! *I have a book in me that will cause ears to tingle : and one day out it must and will issue*.[1] In the valley of the shadow of Magazine Editors we shall not always linger. Courage ! Not Hope, for she was always a liar, but Courage ! Courage ! —For myself I am to write Napier a shortish Paper on Taylor's *Survey* of *German Poetry*,"—a safe and easy pot-boiler, which was done and sent away in a month (20.1.1831), and gave more satisfaction to readers than usual.

Taylor was unexpectedly delighted too. There were some sentences he could have wished to see otherwise, but on the whole he was pleased, recognising the style of— Sir Walter Scott at first, but nevertheless content when he knew better. The conclusion is what interests a reader now :—

' A new era in the spiritual intercourse of Europe is approaching—a World-Literature. The true Pope of Christendom is not that feeble old man at Rome ; nor is its autocrat the Napoleon, the Nicholas. The true Autocrat and Pope is the real seeming Wisest of the past age ; crowned after death ; who finds his Hierarchy of

---

[1] Italics added.

gifted Authors, his Clergy of assiduous Journalists ; whose Decretals, written not on parchment, but on the living souls of men, it were an inversion of the laws of Nature to disobey. All Intellect has fused itself into Literature : Literature, Printed Thought, is the molten sea and wonder-bearing chaos, into which mind after mind casts forth its opinion. Interest after Interest is engulfed in it. The power exists not that can say to that sea, Roll back.

' What form so omnipotent an element will assume is conjecture. One thing we do see and know : that its tendency is to a universal European Commonweal ; that the wisest in all nations will communicate and co-operate ; whereby Europe will again have its true Sacred College, and Council of Amphictyons [1] (or Neighbours) ; *wars will become rarer, less inhuman, and in the course of centuries such delirious ferocity in nations, as in individuals it already is, may be proscribed, and become obsolete for ever.'*

In a letter to Goethe, January 1831, he quoted in advance the hopeful conclusion of this essay, to comfort the sage, distressed in private by the death of his only son and in public affairs by the bloody depravity of princes and politicians. Carlyle was a better comforter than perhaps he knew, for visitors found there was nobody the old man liked so much to speak and hear about. Among other things to please his hero, Carlyle said he had " as good as determined to " try to make a fit translation of *Faust*, which Eckermann had suggested last month (December, 1830).—"In the meanwhile, I am working at another curious enterprise of my own which is yet too amorphous to be prophesied of." Which means *Sartor*, of course.

All his faith in the worth of the written and printed word was needed. His instinctive distrust of MacVey Napier who was now editing the *Edinburgh Review* was right,—the long-nosed fellow had sent Taylor's book for review in reply to an offer of an essay on Byron or Napoleon ! Carlyle wrote to him (20.1.1830) [2] :—

' And now I will pray that the next subject you give me may be an English one—at least no German one. On that I have said enough for a year or two.

[1] An ancient Greek League or Loose Federation. Italics added.
[2] *Correspondence of MacVey Napier*, pp. 102–3.

' I once proposed to Mr. Jeffrey to make a sort of sally on *Fashionable Novels*, but he misunderstood me—thought I meant to *criticise* them ; and so the matter dropt. The Pelham-and-Devereux manufacture is a sort of thing which ought to be extinguished. Perhaps the better method of attack were not to batter but to undermine. *The English aristocracy have as much need of instruction as Swing himself* [1].' (Swing was the genteel nickname of agricultural fire-raisers, then a nuisance).

' A far finer essay were a faithful, loving, and yet critical, and in part condemnatory, delineation of Jeremy Bentham. Bentham will not be put down by logic, and should not be put down, for we need him greatly as a backwoodsman : neither can reconciliation be effected till one party understands and is just to the other. Bentham is a denyer : he denies with a loud and universally convincing voice : his fault is that he can *affirm* nothing, except that money is pleasant in the purse, and food in the stomach, and that by this simplest of all beliefs he can reorganise Society. He can shatter it to pieces—no thanks to him, for its old fastenings are quite rotten—but he cannot reorganise it ; this is work for quite others than he. Hoping to hear from you.—THOMAS CARLYLE.'

Napier had no need for the truth about Bentham,— it might have clashed with what Macaulay had been writing against the Utilitarians. Still less did he want to depreciate " fashionable novels." It is amusing to notice that the next important letter he received after this [2] was from the dandy Bulwer Lytton himself, the happy author of the popular *Pelham* and now M.P. for St. Ives and a conspicuous " Reformer " too. Irresistible to Napier was the courtesy of such an esteemed contributor, enquiring with flattering deference on what subject he would like him next to write. Shall it be on " Public Opinion " or " Taxes on Knowledge," meaning newspapers, or a eulogy of William of Orange or the great and good Lord Bacon ? —" On any of these subjects I should be very happy to treat, to the best of my ability, should you feel disposed to employ me."

So the *Edinburgh Review* wanted nothing more from Carlyle at present, which was awkward when he was short

[1] Italics added.
[2] *Correspondence of MacVey Napier*, pp. 103–4.

of cash ; but what he got from the *Westminster Review* for the " Nibelungen Lied " and from Fraser for papers lying by, supplied immediate needs and left him free to concentrate on making a book out of the " Thoughts on Clothes," which he had recalled in January. He felt it to be a " genuine work," and growing still in his mind. " I can devise some more biography for Teufelsdröckh," he wrote to his brother in London (21.1.1831) ; " give a second deeper part, in the same vein, leading through Religion and the nature of Society, and Lord knows what. Swear every one to secrecy, for I mean to speak fearlessly if at all."

By 4.3.1831 he was working with gusto " night and day " at *Sartor*, declaring to his brother,—it " is not the *right* thing yet, but there is a kind of life in it, and I *will* finish it." Which shows how hard he was to please with his own work. *Sartor* kept him busy and happy till the end of July, and was his nearest approach to pure nature. It was " the book " he had been feeling impelled to write for more than ten years—the truth of things as he saw it. If not all molten lava, at least it is metamorphic rock. It was more spontaneous and pleasanter and less laborious than anything else he ever did, and he could not make himself feel miserable after it, do what he would. It was one of the bad habits of religion which clung to him that he was always trying to worry himself as if he had been under a covenant like Faust—never to feel content. But after finishing *Sartor*, he behaved for once like— " Tam o' Shanter."

In a letter to John (4.3.1831) he announced that their brother Alexander was to vacate the farm in May, and that they hoped to spend next winter in London.

' Surely we shall find a Publisher for Devilsdreck, and look round also, spying all outlooks whether there is absolutely Nothing in God's creation that will unite with me, in the way of work and well-doing. Nay, I have half a mind—but this in deepest secrecy '—it was a suggestion of Charles Buller—' to deliver a Dozen of Lectures on some section or aspect of this strange Life in this strange Era ; on which my soul, like Eliphaz the Temanite's ' (a friend of Job), 'is getting fuller and fuller. Does there seem to thee any propriety in a man that has organs of speech and even some semblance of understanding and sincerity, sitting forever, mute as milestone, while Quacks of every

colour are quacking as with lungs of brass ?   True, I have
no Pulpit :   but as I once said, cannot any man make him
a pulpit, simply by inverting the nearest Tub ?   And what
are your Whigs, and Lord Advocates, and Lord Chancellors,
and the whole host of unspeakably gabbling Parliamenteers
and Pulpiteers and Pamphleteers,—if a man suspect that
" there is fire enough in his belly to burn up " the entire
creation of such ! '   The quotation is a Hindu prophet's
rejoinder to some missionary.   Carlyle went on.—' These
all build on Mechanism : one spark of Dynamism, of
Inspiration, were it in the poorest soul, is stronger than
they all.   As for the Whig Ministry, with whom Jeffrey
might appear to connect me, I partly see that they will
have nothing in any shape to do with me, did I show them
the virtue of a Paul, nay, the more virtue the less chance,
for Virtue is Freewill to choose the Good, not Tool-
usefulness to forge at the Expedient.'

Carlyle was right.   The better he was, the more he tried
to see and speak the truth, the less the politicians would
want him.   Their problem was to humbug the populace.
They were like Thackeray's typical Englishman of title—
truth-telling made them pale.

The " long-nosed " Napier was puffing unashamed the
speeches of Brougham in the *Edinburgh Review*, and ready
to do the same for Macaulay if Macaulay had not warned
him he did not want it ; [1] but as for Carlyle ! To avoid
displeasing Jeffrey, he fell upon a very " longnosed "
method, disguised by false pretences,—he froze him
out by paying him as little and as late as possible, making
him " dun " for payment.

[1] *Correspondence of MacVey Napier*, p. 110.

IX

THE UNPUBLISHED HISTORY

FOR several years Carlyle continued hoping to find a publisher for his *History of German Literature* ; but he never did. It was among the heaps of old papers he gave in the seventies to the niece who kept house for him. She let Mr. Froude take away on loan whatever he liked, and he showed the unpublished History to Max Müller, who returned it with this letter, (26.3.1880).—

'My DEAR FROUDE,

'I have been so very busy all this time that I have only to-day finished Carlyle's MS. It is very pleasant reading—here and there I feel sure there are pages which I had read elsewhere—in his *Miscellanies*, I think. What a pity he did not finish it and publish at the time. Now you could only publish it as a curious fragment showing the state of knowledge of German Literature at the time :—but it was a time *before* Grimm and Lachman and others, and therefore much of it has a historical interest only. It is all strong and sound—much better than thousands of books that are printed every day—yet I doubt whether you could publish it as coming from Carlyle. However you know best. *I* should like to have it in print, but I should not print it myself—except for private circulation.

Ever Yours,

F. MAX MÜLLER.'

The cream of it was in the two essays salvaged from it, the *Nibelungen Lied* and *Early German Literature* ; wherein he used the phrase made famous by-and-by—the *Unspeakable Turk*.

X

A HISTORICAL LEVEE

(1831)

A LETTER from Jeffrey in diary form gave his London news. The "God-like Ariel" was now in the Commons, wife and daughter beside him in London, yet feeling like a man in exile, and clinging to his friends on the moors.

(Wednesday, 23 February, 1831).—' I have been at the Levee to-day and after at a great Cabinet dinner. The last delighted me greatly—so much frankness, simplicity, mutual confidence, and entire absence of all distrust, eagerness or self-assurance. I do not believe there ever was so honest a ministry—so unambitious—so truly anxious to do good. If they fall, *which is likely enough*, it will be a great public calamity, and the inlet to greater calamities. I wish C. could have seen the brotherly gentleness and mutual forbearance with which everything was discussed, and the brevity and clearness with which all opinions were proposed, and opposed, and yet the farthest from indifference, or want of due estimates of the hazards that are impending. Well —but would you rather hear of the Levee ? 1500 fine-looking men, mostly in gorgeous uniforms, and I in the midst of them with my damask gown and lace cravat—kissing kings' hands, and whirled away in the Lord Chancellor's state carriage with his mace and three train bearers !— a vanity of vanities ! But this same Chancellor is no mere pageant, but a master spirit, and a prodigy, to whom all these things are but as the flushing clouds that glare round the rushing course of the naked sun. God bless you.

' 24th. This is the Queen's birthday, but I had not the courage for the Drawing-room, and worked all day at my Reform Bill, till just before dinner when I took a lovely run in the park, and communed with the setting sun. Then I went to a great Dinner at Lord Melbourne's, with all the Judges and the King's Counsels, etc., rather a dull dinner, with plenty of guzzling and gossip, and all in full dress. The Chancellor took me afterwards to Devonshire House—a vast assembly—and perhaps the finest *spectacle* in London, and now I am at home, weary and giddy, and must look over law cases to be argued in the Lords to-morrow. What can you do for me ? There is nothing for it, but on and on—like a squirrel in his cage.'

Then ' an oppressive cold ' kept him awake at nights, and on Monday, 28.2.1831, he had to tinker his reform bill 'to suit the foolish fancy of the English artists, who know nothing of the business.'

It is certain that this letter was fresh in Carlyle's mind when reshaping " Thoughts on Clothes " ; and it is likely enough that it may have suggested to him to expand a sentence or two about supposing the clothes were to fly off, into the pleasant paragraphs concluding " Adamitism," in *Sartor* (I and IX) : as witty as anything in Cervantes or Rabelais, Molière or Dickens or Mark Twain, yet as wise as the best of the Bible, contrasting appearances and reality.   Levees in general signify as little as Lord Mayors' shows ; but for the sake of Jeffrey and *Sartor* the Levee of 23.2.1831 may be mentioned in history. Absurdities of that sort are best handled by humour, which does more to make life bearable than all the Heavenly hopes of all the Egyptians.

XI

WHEN "SARTOR" WAS ON THE ANVIL

(1831)

EVEN at Craigenputtock one could not escape unless by stupidity the all-prevailing excitement, like a fever: for the country was on fire with politics, and in most parts of England and Scotland men were talking of fighting, and they were swarming together, like some migratory birds at the end of a summer. The " middle classes " were coming into power, backed by the populace, who broke Wellington's windows in London while Carlyle was quietly completing *Sartor* on the borders of the desert moors, now lonelier than ever.

Every morning after breakfast, Mrs. Carlyle used to follow him into a little room where he shaved, and sitting on a chair behind him, her face " mirrored in the glass " beside his soapy one, continued to talk. His answers had to be short,—a woman had a man at discretion when he was shaving with an old fashioned razor. When he finished he went to his desk, and was left alone till early dinner. Mrs. Carlyle was giving tongue at last, and his sister Jean who set her the example was much about the house this year, for indeed it has to be told that a baby was twice at least expected, and the two Janes made clothes for it.

One morning as the days were lengthening Carlyle and his wife were sitting at breakfast, sipping a favourite mixture of weak tea and "whipt eggs," prescribed by Badams, and were interrupted by the sound of approaching wheels. As Mrs. Carlyle wrote to Bess Stodart [1] :—

'I thought it could be no one else but Miss Anderson of Sanquhar, and ran to receive her "in my choicest mood ! " But, Lord have mercy, what was I come out for to see [2] ? Seated in an open gig, muffled curiously in Indian shawls, my astonished eyes rested on the large muscular

[1] *Early Letters of Jane Welsh Carlyle*, by D. G. Ritchie : pp. 185–192.
[2] Implied quotation from the Bible.

figure of Miss X. [1]!   Yes, Mary X, of Haddington.   " Hee,
hee, hee !   Mrs. Caarlile !   Hee, hee, hee ! "   She was
obliged to be off the same evening.   But we made the best
use of our time.   I took nothing in hand the whole day
but *milking* news from her, which she with unabated
copiousness supplied ;   and could I tell you but a tenth
of the facts wherewith I in this way stored my mind,
you would wonder.'

Her most " amusing " item was that Dr. Fyffe punished
a lady patient for a practical joke by sending her an " impertinent poem " instead of his further medical attendance.
Both Bess and her uncle were warmly invited to visit them
in the summer.

The only thing like bother when *Sartor* was on the anvil
came from his brother John in London, who was still
eager to drop the trade of medicine and live by writing.
Happily he was a dry mortal and little tempted.   He
was saved from the fate of his unlucky cousin Waugh by
the abundant good advice his brother Tom showered upon
him.   Thus (27.3.1831.) :—

' I am clear for your straining every sinew simply to get
medical employment, whether as assistant surgeon or in
any other honest capacity.   Without any doubt as the
world now stands your safety lies there.

   ' Think and scheme and inquire, or rather continue to do
so :   once foiled is nothing like final defeat.   So long as
life is in a man there is strength in him.   *Ein anderes Mal
wollen wir unsere Sache besser machen*——(another time we
will do better)—this was Fritz's *Wahlspruch*, (maxim of
Frederick the Great) ;   and in this place of hope, where
indeed there is nothing for us but hope, every brave man
in reverses says the like.

   ' For your success with the *New Monthly*, or even with
Napier, I care little, except so far as it might enable you
to continue in London on the outlook.   In other respects
I am nearly sure failure would even be for your good.
Periodical writing is, as I have often said, simply the worst
of all existing employments.   No mortal that had another
noble art, the noblest with but one single exception,'
(meaning " priest " or writer of the truth, *Sartor*, II, x)

[1] The editor suppresses the name.

'but would turn from it with abhorrence and cleave with his whole heart to the other.

' Incessant scribbling is inevitable death to thought. Thoughts fall on us, like seed. It is time only and silence that can ripen them. So convinced am I of the dangerous, precarious, and on the whole despicable and ungainly nature of a life by scribbling in any shape, that I am resolved to investigate again whether I am for ever doomed to it.

' I will not leave Literature ; neither should you leave it. Nay, had I but two potatoes in the world, and one true idea, I should hold it my duty to part with one potato for paper and ink, and live upon the other until I got it written. To such extremities may a *mere* man of letters be brought in Britain at present ; but no wise *you*, who have another footing, and can live in a steady genial climate till experience have evoked into purity what is in you—*then* to be spoken with authority in the ears of all.'

There was no danger of John misunderstanding what was meant by " Literature," for another letter ten days earlier had said :—

' Literature is with you another name for Wisdom, for Art, almost for Religion. Hold fast your talent that way as the most precious of your possessions : but understand ever henceforth that " Periodical writing " is the death even of this. '

A little later he gave him leave to stay a while longer in London on money Jeffrey wanted to lend him, but always for the sake of medical employment, declaring :—

' In your calculations I would have you throw out Literature altogether : indeed I rather believe it were for your good, if you quite burnt your Magazine Pen, and devoted yourself exclusively and wholly to Medicine and nothing but Medicine. Magazine work is below street-sweeping as a trade ; even I who have no other am determined to try by all methods whether it were possible to abandon it.'

He clenched the argument by quoting Jeffrey's letter at length, which showed that Jeffrey's intention was to enable John to stick to his profession. To help a

deserving young doctor over the shoals at the start was the
kind of " good action " dear to the heart of the " God-like
Ariel," and the gist of his letter (4.5.1831) was to beg
Carlyle not to hinder him :—

' I have no disposition to throw away money—especially
after having been forced to spend so much, so very unprofit-
ably, without a fair prospect of doing good by it.' (He was
referring to electioneering, which cost him £10,000 in
eighteen months.[1]) ' Trust me then my dear proud friend
in this matter—and do not fear that I will either wilfully
or thoughtlessly do anything either to injure or degrade
your brother. I will have the fear of your philosophy
before my eyes, and have little apprehension of ultimately
giving you pain by my decision.'

Carlyle stopped there in quoting this to John, but it is
worth while to read on a little.—

' And so you are writing a book—and why will you not
tell me what manner of book it is ?   And how much of it
is written, and when anybody is to see it ?   I would to God
you were not so impracticable, and arrogant.   No man
who despises and contemns educated and intelligent men,
at the rate you do, will ever have any success among them—
unless indeed a witty satirical.   I wish I could persuade
you that you are not an inspired being, and never will be
the founder of a new religion—and then your eloquence,
ingenuity and fancy might be of far more use to you and to
others.   But that solitary life and bad stomach of yours
have spoiled you to such a degree—all but the heart—that
I despair of the success even of my rough course of unspoil-
ing.   Well, God mend us all.   Good-night—write me soon
and think kindly of me.

Ever affectly yours,
F. JEFFREY. '

To finish with John, the " God-like Ariel " found time in
the midst of the political hurricane to do better than his
word.   In a month or two he questioned Dr. John and
discovered quickly that what he wanted most, and was
extra well qualified to fulfil, was " an engagement to go

---

[1] Cockburn's *Life of Jeffrey*, I, p. 307.

abroad with some rich family as a medical friend and attendant." [1] There were many such jobs then ; and in a month or two more John was attending the Countess of Clare, on a salary of £315 and all expenses, and so successful that he never was in lack of money again, and soon was repaying Jeffrey first and then his brother the money he owed them.

In May however such an issue was only hoped for ; and in reply to Jeffrey's admonitions, which were taken in good part, Carlyle could only promise to do better, and profess humility. The beauty and wisdom of being humble was one of the main themes of the book he was writing. Humility appeared to him the principle addition Christianity made to the ethics of the Stoics. Perhaps he thought it the chief of Christian virtues because he found it the hardest to practise. His effort was sincere, continual and in general successful ; but he was a borderer and a freeman by descent and a Calvinist by early creed, and as fearless as John Knox of the face of man. There was nothing of fear about his humility, which explains a great deal that puzzled observers, especially the promptitude and completeness with which he forgot all about it when off his guard, as Jeffrey noticed, even in the letter avowing humility. He seems to have written to Jeffrey to much the same effect as to his brother, about seeking another trade than letters, and perhaps without explaining that Diogenes was the title of the " hero " in his book, he declared himself ready to be another Cynic, and he made no secret to Jeffrey of the political and religious free-thinking in it. In discussing which Jeffrey was thinking of the reading public. Tho' suffering from varicose veins and drenched in business, he found time to write thus :—

EDINR.

16 *May* 1831.

' MY DEAR FRIEND,

It cannot be a greater comfort to you to receive a letter from me than it is—in itself—for me to write one. But it is a pleasure now but imperfectly at my command. I am hurried enough, as you see, and besides I have been suffering under a very painful affection of a

[1] Letter from Jeffrey to T. C.

local nature, ever since I left London. Yet I must say
something in answer to your last—a line at least, if not a
letter in return. I feel the full value of your deference
to my counsels about your brother, and hope to give you
no cause to repent it. But you alarm me about yourself.
Do not dream for mercy's sake, of the Cynic's tub, and
that unseemly romance of encountering the primitive lot
of man, with your habits of mind and body, and a young
and delicate wife, whose great heart and willing martyrdom
would only make the sacrifice more agonising to you
in the end—and it is not necessary—nor anything like
necessary. Let us draw you away from your seclusion
and inspire you with more humane thoughts. You shall
have aid—and effective aid—which you shall one day
repay, if you will, tenfold, never fear, we shall find something
for you to do, neither inglorious nor unprofitable. You are
fit for many things, and worthy of many things, and there
are more tasks and things worthy of you than, in your
Cynic moods, you are willing to believe. I made a pro-
position to you once before, which I told you, tho' rejected
at the time, was to stand waiting your acceptance for the
rest of our lives—and which you *shall* accept without more
ado, if you ever speak to me of the Cynic scheme again.
I think too that you are humanising apace, and gradually
drawing nearer to those of your own blood and lineage
to whom you should belong. I have been reading your
paper on Taylor in the last *Edinburgh*, and am more
satisfied with the patient and (*comparatively*) indulgent
tone of much of it, than with any of your former
writings. Empson mentioned it to me in London, with
great praise, and said that Macaulay and several others
(who laughed at your *Mechanical* age, and some of your
ravings about the ravings of your German novelists) were
very much struck with the force and originality of the
writing. Give yourself but fair play, and the world
around you fair play, and you will make your way in
it very well. Learn to respect and esteem men who
are your equals in intellect and honesty, tho' they
dissent entirely from your creed in taste and philosophy,
and temper your bigotry as far as to think it *possible* that
people may differ from you in all your fundamentals,
without being in a *damnable* error. Imagine it *possible*
in short that you should be wholly or partly in the wrong,
and that it may be *your* fault and not theirs, that they

laugh at some of your idolatries. I tell you again that, in all my life, I never met a good and sensible man so scornful and intolerant as you are—and it is even amusing to see how it breaks out in the middle of your professions of humility and charity. Even in this last letter, what a foolish and vainglorious diatribe about those who bore no significance but by juxtaposition !—and I know not what. Alas, alas, what is this little *significance* upon which we value ourselves ? Some trifling accident of excitability and ambition, which makes a certain fever and stir, and leaves us neither happier nor higher than our neighbours. For my part the more I see of philosophers and men of genius the more I am inclined to hold that the ordinary run of sensible, kind people, who fill the world, are after all the best specimens of humanity, and that the others are, like our cultivated flowers, but splendid monsters, and cases of showy disease. How many *significant* people do you suppose there are in the world ? Or rather in our parish, or the circle of our acquaintance ? *Unus atque alter*, (one and another), I fancy at the most, and a social, humble-minded being, who should love his brother (even tho' he does not give that endearing name to the women) is to scorn all the rest, or to keep aloof from all equal intercourse with them, and, looking with a most ridiculous supercilious pity upon the worthy reasonable people around him, who do not care about his vagaries, give himself airs of condescension when he says he wishes them well, and would be glad to assist or befriend them, but truly, as for companionship of mind or fellowship of pursuit, they are no more mates for him than the beasts of the field ! O fie on this filthy pride, and foolish straining after ideal unsocial elevation ! Pluck it from your heart my friend, and cast it from you, and you will be happier and more amiable —and not a little wiser. But I did not mean to lecture you, and will not. Let me know a little practically what scheme of life you have in view, and rely on my counsel and aid. There is scarcely anything I have more at heart than your comfort and happiness, and I think you know this. For that fair child, I have a love which is overpowering, and not the less for that *she is* a child, in some things, tho I allow her the heart of a heroine, and the courage, I doubt not, of a martyr. Heaven guard her from the fate of one ! Why does she not write to me ? My heart is athirst for kind words and words cost so little ! No matter . . . (gap in paper) . . . There is a gleam of summer to-day, and the long summer twilight spreads away so softly to the North with the dewy Venus dancing above it, that a little stream of love and softness shot into my heart as I gazed at it, thro' all the earthly influences of business and bodily pain. But now good-night ! God bless you little one. Would to God I too could be taken for a child ! And your childish womanhood is offended at it—O folly !

Ever affectly yours,

F. JEFFREY.'

Here is an example of what had offended Mrs. Carlyle.—

LONDON,

March 26th, 1831.

' Well, well, my wrangling little, earnest, kind child, you need not rail any longer at Parliament and court people, for I am done for the present, with both—my committee have unseated me.

' You really are but a better kind of great baby after all —a smart intelligent child certainly, with sweet dispositions, and a good and a *great* heart, but a little spoiled, and not quite so deeply seen in the mysteries of human nature as you fancy yourself, but if you were a little less scornful and more indulgent, I should care less about your false judgments. Why should you have so many more confident opinions than I have ? and upon matters too that depend not a little upon observation and experience ? and above all, why have you contempt for those whose tastes and opinions differ from yours ? ' (In short) 'get out of your teens.'

This way of thinking permeates Jeffrey's letters to that address and is conclusive against any supposition of flirtation. But however much she took it amiss to be treated as a child, Mrs. Carlyle was touched by the letter of 16.5.1831, and responded relentingly, for which he was effusively grateful. Yet it has to be confessed that Jeffrey, pen-caressing Mrs. Carlyle, was like a warm-hearted boy stroking a tabby which tolerates such freedom with difficulty, the affection being *all* on one side.

XII

SAINT-SIMONIANS, &c.

(1831)

THE only sad day this summer at Craigenputtock was Sunday, 8.5.1831. A week before then Larry had fallen ill of a " swelled throat," and seemed to be getting better till Friday night, when he relapsed. On Saturday night Carlyle was watching him and prescribing castor oil ; but before midnight the old horse died.—" Frightful, frightful is Death even in a brute, and pitiable and black ! " wrote Carlyle to his brother in London. " I am positively *very* sad and wae. It is almost half like a human servant's death."

He contrived this summer a birth-day present of a seal to Goethe (now 82) from " fifteen English friends," including Scott, Lockhart and Wilson, Moir, Southey and Wordsworth. The seal reminded Goethe of Cellini's description of his own work.

Still more cosmopolitan was his letter (17.5.1831) to Gustave D'Eichthal, the Saint-Simonian. It may help us to guess the gist of those he wrote to Jeffrey : for it is remarkable in Carlyle that he was as downright as Tolstoy. He practised no deceit, and little silence. He had the perfect decency of pious Scotland ; but also its outspokenness in other things, so that some of the " Silence" he was fond of preaching was like the whole of his humility, superimposed, self-conscious ; and he used his spacious vocabulary to show his thoughts without rudeness, but without disguise.

He had discovered D'Eichthal was a friend of his old pupil Charles Buller, M.P., and nephew of the D'Eichthal with whom his brother John had lived a year at Munich. He had received from him successive packets of Saint-Simonian literature, since they last exchanged letters, and this was how he answered the question—what do you think of us ? (17.5.1831) [1] :—

[1] *The New Quarterly*, April 1909, pp. 283-7.

' It were fruitless to attempt explaining myself with any precision. To write the little that I know of you, and the much that I desire to know, would fill not one but many letters.

' I may say my respect for your Brethren and Chief, personally considered, has not diminished but increased on closer survey ; that I discern in you men of clear intellectual insight, of decisive character, animated with a noble zeal, which enlightens as well as inflames ; that your speculative opinions, political, moral, philosophical, for most part carry their own evidence, and find hearty assent with me ; often, indeed I discern therein only a more decisive systematic exposition of what I had already gathered elsewhere. Especially important I reckon your delineation of our actual No-society, of the critical and the organic alternation in man's history ; your strongly emphatic precept of our duty towards the Poor, which, properly speaking, is but the old duty of Love, of mercy towards the weak, whether weak by want of pecuniary or other means ; and has been and must be the basis of all social morality. Neither can it be doubted that your motto and maxim, *to each according to his capacity, to each capacity according to its works*, is the aim of all true social arrangements. In short, were the Saint-Simonian doctrine stated as a mere scientific doctrine, or held out as the *Prophecy of an ultimate Perfection* towards which Society must more and more approximate—I could with a few reservations subscribe to it, and heartily agree with you. Nevertheless, in one quarter, lies a mighty chasm. You call yourselves a *Church*, and founders of a new *Religion*, which Religion, permit me to confess, I hitherto seek for in vain. Far be it from me to deny you a devout, *self annihilating feeling*, a recognition of God in Nature, and in all the movements of Nature, especially in man the chief object there. Neither would I lightly undertake to define what Religion is. But surely in all Religions hitherto recognised, one indispensable element was this : *Some symbol or Symbolic Representation, whereby the Divinity was sensibly manifested.* The Symbol may be the rudest, as in a Scandinavian Idol, an African Mumbo-Jumbo ; or it may be the highest, as of Jesus of Nazareth. In all cases, there must *some* symbol offer itself to the worshipper ; for hereby alone is Imagination, the true organ of the Infinite in Man, brought to harmonize with understanding, the organ of the finite.' (Note the capitals at Imagination and Infinite and the small letters at understanding and finite). ' Such Symbol, I as yet nowhere find in your doctrine. Or if our Symbol of God is henceforth to be his own great *Universe*, and our Gospel the acted *History of Man*, then to my view is such religion ill-named the Saint-Simonian ; inasmuch as it has been the Religion of all thinkers for the last half-century : of Goethe, of Schiller, of Lessing, Jacobi, Herder.'

There is self-revelation here. " The last half-century," quoth he ! In Asia it was as old as Lao Tze, the " old Philosopher," who preceded Confucius, and would not speak of the living Universe as either a He or a She. The wisest of the Greeks and Romans, Jews and Indians were of the same mind ; and doubtless it is only the imperfections of the historical records which prevent us dating the faith of all sensible people many millenniums back, in the far abysms of prehistoric time.

' I am doubtful whether you do prudently in merely *Prophesying* the blessed issue, Religious and Political, when perhaps you might forward it by other means ; why keep *pointing out* the fair Heavenly Country, which many men in all nations have already desired, when persons of such faculty as some of you exhibit, might aid in furnishing us *wings* to reach it with ?

' You would mistake widely, did you impute these strictures to wilful blindness, to unfriendly indifference, to anything but honest doubt, grounded to I know not what extent on want of information.'

(He in short invited D'Eichthal to visit Craigenputtock, and after ending ran on in a P.S.—) ' England should you visit it at present, you will find in a state of electioneering fermentation such as the oldest man has not before witnessed. Democracy has arisen, and will never lie down again, till it has got its rights ; the poor, blind monster for the present fancies that Liberty lies in the Elective franchise ; that " by knitting its chains into festoons it will be free ! " In our usual state we have three grand sects among us. First the Christians, a class still strong and even worthy,[1] far beyond what they are with you, or

---

[1] " Ever " in the *New Quarterly* seems an obvious misprint for even.

elsewhere; among these alone is there any vestige of Religion left us; secondly the Whig unbelievers whose principle is *Dilettantism* in all kinds; thirdly the Radical or Utilitarian unbelievers, for whom *soul* is synonymous with *stomach*; an *honest* class, of whom is hope.'

The Saint-Simonians included many of the brightest young men in France, and as political pioneers at this time they were much observed at home and abroad; but soon they separated in different directions. To Carlyle they were a corroboration rather than an inspiration, but even that was much. Jeffrey was soon lamenting [1] that he was being encouraged in his ultra-Radical conclusions by finding people in London to agree with him; but nobody there, not even Mill himself or Charles Buller, had so much in common with him as the bright young Frenchmen called Saint-Simonian in 1831.

In the latter half of May he answered Jeffrey, giving the gist of his book so far as finished, and saying he would try no more to live by literature, if he could find other work; to which Jeffrey responded from Edinburgh (5.6.1831) :—

' MY DEAR CARLYLE,

' You cannot overrate my will and anxiety to serve you. But I must not mislead you as to my *power*. When I said we should find work fit for you, I fear I only expressed my strong but vague and general conviction that, with a little patience and accommodation, some fitting occupation might be found or made for you. I still hold that trust and conviction, and exhort and encourage you also to hold it. But I have nothing tangible or immediate to propose, nor do I know, much more than you do, where to look or apply for practical assistance. Certainly the fittest work for you would be that which required the talents you possess, and gave scope to your ardour and enthusiasm, but *that* I fear you must *make* for yourself, at least I do not see where it is to be found—for other humbler toils, that sweat of the brow or of the brain, whereby it is man's lot (not his curse I think) to earn his bread, I cannot but think that some *might* be found, not unworthy of you, and not too irksome, and yet you are a

[1] *Correspondence of MacVey Napier*, p. 126.

P

ticklish animal to harness I fancy—and apt I should suspect not merely to kick at and break away from your yoke-fellows, but even to take an irreverent fling now and then at your driver. On the whole however you should know your own trim best—at least for a very general settlement of departments. What would you like best? (*least*, rather, I fancy I should say) some sort of *mercantile*, book-keeping arithmetical drudgery under buyers and sellers?—or official clerkships in some public office—about stamps—excise—post office or so forth?—or in dependance on the law, as keeper of records, writer in chancery engrossments?—or anything about *education* in colleges or seminaries?—or as librarian or museum keeper—arranger of manuscripts and curiosities and so forth?—or calculator for insurance companies or longitude? I do not mean any of these literally, but which of *the kinds* of thing would you least eschew and abhor? Before making any application it is really necessary to have some sort of notion, however large and loose, of your inclinings in this way. For you must feel yourself, that an application for some pleasant and profit-able employment for a man of education and good moral character—of a studious disposition—with much knowledge, and rather *too* much admiration of German philosophy—with a certain tendency to scorn the existing race of men, and all existing institutions and establishments, would not be very likely to indicate one fitted for any particular place, or to suggest any particular employment as well fitted for him.

'I daresay you do right in going to London—certainly in leaving Craigenputtock—before winter, and in going to London to look about you. I shall see you there too, and we can *talk* all things over.

'I half fear for your book, especially the radical part of it, tho' that is more likely to attract notice than the religious part—what I *most* fear is the *vilipending* of existing things and people, which I hold to be your radical error. Do not you think as much sense and genius might be shown—and in a more amiable way—in pointing out the mass of good feeling and deep sense which lies under the apparent frivolousness and selfishness of our *exterior* busy trifling life, and in explaining how that exterior is *necessary*, and by what *necessary* and inward fermentation the vital leaven of wisdom and virtue is leavening the whole lump—*all* the *elements* and aspects of which are equally necessary and useful ? Is there no chance of *this* being the *true* as well as the kind and pleasing view of our condition ? And that the despair and contempt with which you look on it, is but a narrow, peevish and shallow view, as well as an arrogant and offensive one ? Well, well, we shall settle all that when we meet—in the meantime do not think you do well to be scornful. . . .'

The reference at the end was to the prophet in scripture who maintained he did well to be angry. The reply was satisfactory. From London Jeffrey wrote (4.7.1831) :—

' MY DEAR CARLYLE,
    ' I have no tidings for you, tho' I have pressed my inquiries in all the quarters I could think of. However I have set several likely enough people to be on the lookout— and if anything occurs I shall not be forgetful of you.

Then he told what he was doing for Dr. John, and with fatherly frankness described his own health and spirits amidst the political turmoil.—

' My health I think is better than when I was here last. But the approaching campaign will try it. How often shall I envy you the cooling breezes and long evening's leisure of Craigenputtock. I can scarcely think of green fields, and the quiet listening to the thrushes, and the midnight odour of moist honeysuckle that used to soothe me at Craigcrook, without crying. I do not think I am quite made for this stirring world, tho' few people have stirred more in it, or *appeared* more satisfied with the stirring part that has fallen to them.
    ' Well, what about your book, and when are you coming up with it ? And with what hopes ? I trust your health is better. I cannot quite reconcile myself to your living buried in the smoke and stir of this huge anthill, and that fair thoughtful creature ! It does not seem a sphere for her either. But Heaven knows, and all I hope will be for the best. . .
                    Ever affectely yours,
                            F. JEFFREY.'

Two other letters followed in the same month which make his meaning plainer :—

(To Mrs. Carlyle).—' Do you remember that pathetic and deep-meaning line in an old Scottish song ? " And were not my heart light, I would die ! " I cannot tell you how often that feeling comes to me during my present life of exile and bondage. If it were not for my love of nature, I think I should die too. *It is an especial mercy of Providence, I think, that our House of bondage is placed among objects of grandeur and beauty, with the majesty of the old Abbey on the one hand, and the smooth expanse of the river on the other—with the groves and towers of Lambeth beyond. If we[1] had met near the Bank or the Royal Exchange I do not think I could have survived.*[2] —As it is, I rush out, and walk on the bridge, or place myself at a window in our calm library, and look out on the white moonlight, and the shadows of the massive trees pencilled so sharp and dark on the turf below, and then muse and start, and back to that hot, glaring, tumultuous room again, where I pass for a gay, sarcastic, patient, acute sort of person—and so I am.

'It is still beautiful weather.'

(Or to Carlyle) :—' And are you really coming to this resort and mart of all the Earth, with your manuscript in your pocket, like Parson Adams ?' There are many indications that Jeffrey saw more than one point of likeness between his friend and the hero of Fielding's *Joseph Andrews.* This letter went on to discuss at length and without reserve ' the frightful prospect of the probable proceedings of the Lords, ' and ended :—God bless you. *I see you clearly standing thoughtful at your desk, gazing on the motionless trees above you, or pacing down among the moorland muttons, listening to the larks and curlews.*[2] God bless you.'

Even a political historian would not care now for what the ministry were guessing the Peers might do ; but it is interesting to find Carlyle writing to William Graham in the course of this same Reform Bill crisis that was worrying Jeffrey :—

' By the mysterious arrangenemt of this world, it has been ordered that 200 bipeds, few of them with sense or stuff enough to make a moderate tailor, should be called *Peers*, and have the power to keep all Britain in a ferment

[1] The House of Commons.   [2] Italics added.

for months, perhaps to drive it into desperation and anarchy.
But at the same time, as old Smail the Ecclefechan
smith said : " How help it ? We must just do the best we
can for a living, Boy."[1]

" How can you help it ? " What Carlyle could do to
help was to write *Sartor*. After hearing from Jeffrey, he
wrote to his brother John (12.7.1831) :—

' In all situations there is *a Duty*, and our highest Blessedness lies in doing it. Jeffrey represents himself as on the
outlook for *me* too (as well as you) : for I told him I was
thinking of London ; felt ready to work at *any* honest
thing whatsoever ; did not see that Literature could
support an *honest* man otherwise than *à la Diogenes* ; in
which fashion too I meant to experiment if *nothing* else
could be found, which however, through all channels of
investigation, I was minded to try. He wrote back asking
what manner of Clerkship etc. . . . I do not expect that
he will be able to accomplish anything for me. I must
even get through life *without a trade*, always in poverty,
as far better men have done. Our want is the want of *Faith*.
Jesus of Nazareth was not poor tho' he had not where to
lay his head. Socrates was rich enough.—I have a deep,
irrevocable, all-comprehending Ernulphus Curse to read
upon—GIGMANITY (Snobbery) ; that is the Baal Worship
of this time ' (meaning the current idolatry).
' I shall be with you about the beginning of August.
I am struggling forward with Dreck' (with which, in
short) ' the world will nowise be enraptured. It was the
best I had in me.'

An " Ernulphus Curse " was the Roman Church's
excommunication, but the phrase was always used by
Carlyle with a humourous suggestion, here as in *Sartor*
(II and VIII), the latent quotation being *Tristram Shandy*,
(III and XI). The best thing in that book follows the reading
of the Curse. Uncle Toby would not curse the Devil himself
like that ; and being told the Devil was " damned already
to all eternity," then " I am sorry for it," quoth my Uncle
Toby. Which was often the sentiment of Carlyle, so that
even when he was cursing like Bishop Ernulphus, there was

---

[1] Letter to W. Graham, but " livelihood " corrected to "living", the
usual form, and indeed it is " living " in a later letter to Graham.

uncle Toby inside him. He had a genius for sympathy; and it is an old saying that nobody can hate a man he really knows. So Carlyle deplored the mischief being done by the Peers of England, yet rather laughed at them than hated them, perceiving they were merely stupid common men in a false position.

His next letter to his brother John (17.7.1831) shows how he felt as he was finishing.—

' I am labouring at Teufel with considerable impetuosity, and calculate that, unless accidents intervene, I may be actually ready to get under way at the end of the month.

' Courage ! Courage ! *Tapferkeit*, " deliberate valour," is God's highest gift, and comes not without trial to any. Times will mend ; or, if times never mend, then *we* will mend. I know but one true wretchedness—the want of work (want of wages is comparatively trifling), which want, however, in such a world as this planet of ours *cannot* be permanent unless we continue blind therein. I must to my Dreck, for the hours go.'

XIII

A SPEECH AT A DINNER AND A MIDNIGHT DRIVE

(FRIDAY, 22.7.1831)

WHEN *Sartor* was being finished, Editor McDiarmid came up from Dumfries with his mind in a fever of electioneering. He knew Carlyle would like to see the Reform Bill pass, because it would at least " prevent any immediate *cutting of throats.*" [1] The editor came to the moors to recreate himself and blow off steam in sympathetic company, and to announce a dinner in Dumfries in honour of Allan Cunningham, who was coming north this summer. McDiarmid was to be in the chair, and wanted Carlyle to make a speech ; to which he consented.

So on the appointed Friday, (22.7.1831), he went to Dumfries,[2] and this seems the likeliest date of an event he described in 1879 [3] :—

' I was once brought to see Mrs. Burns in her old age— she said little, nor did I (say much). I had unspeakable feelings in looking upon her, as tho' it were one of the Greek tragic heroines—Clytemnestra herself !—Bonnie Jean !— She was a quiet grave person, no good looks left.'

Then he added what shows the atmosphere in which he was to speak now (22.7.1831) :—

' Burns took his death coming late out of the " Globe," drunk, and sitting down upon a stone—a leaping-on-stone (for mounting on horseback)—which is still in the close (or yard), on a cold freezing winter's night. I remember a man in Annandale telling me that he saw Burns lying dead-drunk in the back-yard of the " King's Head," and totally unheeded, save by a passing look.'

[1] Unpublished Letter of T. C.
[2] Hogg's *Allan Cunningham*, p. 304-310.
[3] W. Allingham, *A Diary*, p. 282.

Soon after seeing " the widow Burns," if it was then he saw her, Carlyle was with the jovial company assembling at the Commercial Hotel. Allan Cunningham's first words to him when they met were about Edward Irving, pronounced a heretic by the Annan presbytery, because he said that Christ was liable to temptation. One can imagine the smiles of contempt exchanged, and the pity for Irving, as for a man who had flung himself to the dogs that were tearing him. It was hard for men of sense to avoid a sneer. Carlyle said he reflected, " They consider it more honourable to their Supreme of the World to have had his work done for him than to have done it himself : *Flunkeys* irredeemable ; carrying their *plush* into highest Heaven ! "

The Memory of Robert Burns was the toast assigned Carlyle, and he made " the speech of the evening," or rather of the afternoon, for dinners were early then.

" I don't know that I'll get it out, but I have it in me," they say he began.[1] It was the first of his public speeches and as astonishing as any. Here is the newspaper report.[2]

The Chairman (Editor McDiarmid) having called upon him as a credit to the countryside and mentioned that he had come " at some inconvenience and on the shortest possible notice," Mr Carlyle said :—

' He felt quite at a loss to express what he felt, in being thus honourably called on before a company of so many happy friends, without wandering into vague generalities, which, above all things, he was anxious to avoid. To be a credit to his native district he must do much more than he had yet done, and he considered it was still to try whether he merited that compliment. One circumstance had been stated, and he felt gratified that the chairman had done so ; he had certainly come down from his retreat in the hills to meet Allan Cunningham at a time when scarcely any other circumstance could have induced him to move from home. He conceived that a tribute could not be paid to a more deserving individual, nor did he ever know of a dinner which proceeded from a purer principle. When Allan left his native place he was poor, unknown and unfriended —nobody knew what was in him, and he himself had only a

[1] *Forty Years at the Bar*, by J. H. Balfour Brown, K.C. p. 137.
[2] *Dumfries and Galloway Courier*, 26.7.1831, reprinted in *Carlyle on Burns*, by John Muir.

slight consciousness of his own powers. He now comes back—his worth is known and appreciated, and all Britain is proud to number him among her poets; we can only say, be ye honoured, we thank you; you have gratified us much by this meeting. It has been said that a poet must do all for himself, but then he must have a something in his heart, and this Mr. Cunningham possessed; he possessed genius, and the feeling to direct it aright—he covets not our silver and gold; is sufficiently provided for within, and needs little from without. It then remains for us (continued Mr. Carlyle) to cheer him on this honourable course, and when he is told that his thoughts have dwelt in our hearts, and elevated us, and made us happy, it must inspire him with renewed feelings of ardour. Let us now recall from afar the feelings connected with the dust of Burns, and fancy with what honourable pride the lamented bard would have held out the right hand of fellowship to our honoured guest! Let us recall his worth, his manly talent, his great integrity, his misfortunes, and his sufferings, arising chiefly from neglect! Burns' works are known to every man in every clime where the English tongue has reached; at home they are sucked in by our children like their mothers' milk; from them they learn their first lessons of love, affection, independence, and from them they learn that—

> " The rank is but the guinea stamp,
>   The man's the gowd (gold) for a' that."

They are hallowed to domestic affection, and, in a word, are co-extensive with the globe itself; and I may mention a circumstance which is, perhaps, known to few in this room—namely, that within the last two months I have learned from Goethe, the greatest living German poet, that the works of our immortal bard are under translation in Berlin, so that foreign countries will speedily be as happy with them as we ourselves. His life was undoubtedly a dark tragedy; penury and cold neglect curbed the flow of his noble soul. It is plain that we possess only a tithe of what was in him, for his genius was universal; he was the first man to strike the seven-stringed lyre to ecstacy, for he was equally the minstrel, the poet and the philosopher. Alas, that such a master soul should have been crushed! Alas, that we can only reflect, while we are thus celebrating Allan Cunningham's worth, that Burns was never so honoured while in life.

' Mr. Carlyle then begged that the memory of Robert Burns should be drunk in solemn silence, as much might be thought that could not be uttered. The toast was drunk standing and in silence.'

Then in a "brief and energetic" speech Carlyle proposed the health of Francis Jeffrey, Lord Advocate, and they all made a joyful noise together, but that was matter of course in a Scotland jubilant over the new "Reform" ministry. It was the speech on Burns that amazed the meeting, or all but the few of them who knew his essay. Some of them had known Burns by sight, and nearly all had seen his widow who was still dwelling among them. They heard this serious glorification of their townsman in pleased bewilderment, a feeling that spread far beyond Dumfries, especially when Wilson as Christopher North applauded boisterously in print and corroborated. It takes an effort to realize what a novelty such respect for Burns was at that time.

The speeches over, Carlyle enjoyed himself. He must have looked like Maclise's picture then, that is to say, more like his neighbours than afterwards in most respects, but the hair not hiding his forehead so much, his face was perhaps more striking. At any rate, when once about this time he had happened to be in the house of the Dumfries Fiscal, Mr. Young, the fiscal's son George (who became a conspicuous public man, Lord Young) was bidden by his father watch the visitor,—" Take my word for it, this Mr. Carlyle will become a great man in this country. Observe his forehead," said Mr. Young; and the juvenile observer saw a "magnificent" forehead, standing out like a tower, and broad as well as high, "like a great rock of stone hewn out."

> " Nae man can tether time or tide;
> The hour approaches Tam maun ride;
> That hour, o' night's black arch the key stane, . ."

Midnight in short, found him still in the same good company; but then he had to go, resisting invitations to "sleep in Dumfries," for the reason that "the wife was expecting" him. He drove away alone in the old gig, behind a little black mare that knew the road well, which was fortunate. After so much "noise and sipping of wine," he was as well content as Tam o' Shanter, as happy as the Devil tried in vain to make Faust for a moment. The empty streets of Dumfries were bathed in the purest moonlight, as " clear as day." After two miles of the highway, he turned into the parish road, fourteen miles of which, " narrower but not to be complained of," lay between him and home, where Jane was awaiting him in pleasanter humour than the " sulky sullen dame " of the other " Tam."

He fell asleep,—he never could recall as much as the turning out of the highway. Aware of the direction of her stable the mare might have taken that turning herself, as she did all the rest for the next ten miles, abrupt turns some of them ; and whenever she came to a parting of the ways, she made no mistake at all. There were steep slopes, and dangerous roads unfenced and narrow bridges with small parapets, but nothing happened. Four miles from Craigenputtock, the sleeping passenger was jolted awake. He seized the reins astonished ; but did not for awhile realize the dangers he had passed ; and only long afterwards reflected what a lesson it was,—that tho' this wonderful world is not made for our sakes only, there is much in it to bless us unawares.

XIV

TO LONDON

(1831)

*S*ARTOR was done before the end of July, and he made ready to go to London; but first he visited Scotsbrig. His wife was to stay behind for reasons of health, his sister keeping her company; and for that very reason she now came to Scotsbrig with him, explaining, —" I want to see all of him I can."

He never saw his father again; which made him remember a trifle. At some confidential moment when they were alone, old James took two sovereigns from his drawer and pressed them upon him, and he answered,—" Surely you are fey," as if to say—" It is needless and you are too good "; the word " fey " meaning—doing something unusually good as if about to die.

His father who was always fond of him was extra kind on this visit, and openly " prouder of him than ever." When once the old man heard him say something he admired more than usual, he turned to him with sparkling eyes and exclaimed—" Man it's surely a pity that thou should sit yonder," (at Craigenputtock, he meant), " with nóthing but the eye of Omniscience to see thee; and thou with such a gift to speak."

Mrs. Thomas Carlyle was of the same opinion, announcing at once that the book that her man had just finished was " a work of genius." But parting was a wrench. On Wednesday, 3.8.1831, she did not go to bed as usual, tho' the packing was finished, but sat in the drawing-room at a table, while he was lying on his back on the sofa there. She did her best to be cheerful, but it was not easy. It was doubtful when he would return. She felt ill and thought herself pregnant. Anything might happen before they met again. He had to go at 2 a.m. His brother Alexander was to drive. It was a comfort that Alexander and his wife were to stay awhile longer there, tho' he had

EARLIEST LIKENESS OF JANE BAILLIE WELSH.

The date of this was before 1826, and it seems likely to be more flattered than usual. The familiar miniature of 1826 was never recognised by those who knew Jane Baillie Welsh in her youth. It was merely a standard type of beauty.

This is from a portrait made in Haddington by an artist nameless now, and it was hanging in Carlyle's house when he died. His niece gave it to Mrs. Chrystal, the nearest living relative of Mrs. Carlyle, a cousin on her mother's side, and it is still in Glasgow, in the house of Miss Chrystal, the cousin's daughter.

When the Carlyles were at Craigenputtock it was at Mrs. Welsh's house, near Thornhill, and she lent or gave it to Jeffrey. Mrs. Carlyle insisted on the return of it, and in a letter from London (4/7/1831), Jeffrey chaffed her about it, saying :—" My very dear child, I have that precious picture. I lent it for a week to Mrs. Montagu, and I believe they have been copying it. You do not grudge that? She says she had fancied you would look nearly so. I do not believe it—nobody ever anticipated that peculiar countenance. Those very lovely, but *too thoughtful* eyes, and that half-*obstinate*, half-capricious lip, which does not agree very well either with them or with itself. I have studied the enigma carefully, and think I half understand it."

[face p. 220

ceased to be the tenant of the farm in May. Mrs. Carlyle stood listening to the sound of the gig in the still August night till she heard no more ; then went to bed and cried herself to sleep. So at least she wrote to him, adding :— " The first thing that met my eyes on waking was your night-cap lying on my pillow ; whereupon I fell a-crying anew, and actually kissed it, I believe, tho' you know I hate red night-caps." [1]

His brother left him on his boat at Glencaple, below Dumfries, and as it moved towards England he recognised in the steerage the once exquisite Esbie, whom Galloway had brought to Kirkcaldy nearly thirteen years ago, to see Irving and Carlyle and—Margaret Gordon and others there. He was different now from what he had been in the dandy days when he used to decorate the Quadrangle of Edinburgh University, a " double-refined travelling tutor," but in private gloomily looking forward to " some Devil of a curacy." Was he a curate now ? Carlyle shared his dinner with him ; and for the " six weary hours " the boat lay at Whitehaven, it was " mysticism " he talked to Esbie as they walked about together, and that was the line of speculation least likely to offend a curate. They re-embarked at last amid a tumult of human noises and the bellowing of cattle, above which rose the sound of a fiddle, like the fire that streaked the smoke spouting from the funnel, as it used to do then.

At half-past seven on Friday morning Carlyle landed at Liverpool, and found all abed at the house of his wife's uncle, John Welsh, where he stayed till Monday. As a mason's son, he was an exacting critic of buildings, and Liverpool appeared to him " a dismembered aggregate of streets and sandpits ". Young "Alick Welsh" showed him the sights, including the Exchange and the miraculous locomotives on the new Liverpool and Manchester Railway. On the night he arrived, he " unearthed " the surgeon, George Johnston, whom he had visited in Marsden in 1825, and who was now in practice in Liverpool. John Welsh politely invited him to his house, and Esbie too. On Monday morning (8.8.1831) Carlyle departed. He had to change coaches seven times on the way, and stretching his legs at Straford-on-Avon looked again at the house

---

[1] *Nineteenth Century Mag.*, Aug. 1914, by Alexander Carlyle, p. 330. Letter of 6.8.1831.

where Shakespeare was born.   Before noon on the Tuesday
he was in the lodgings John had ready in Tavistock Square.

Next day (10.8.1831) he was "kindly received" by
Jeffrey, "looking better than I expected," and keeping
him till another caller departed.   Then they talked about
"the book."   MacVey Napier had sent Carlyle a letter of
introduction to Mr. Rees of Longman and Co., but Jeffrey
advised him now to "go to Murray rather", and gave him
a letter of introduction, the sight of which made Murray
agree at once to read it and give him a Yes or No next
Wednesday (17.8.1831). Carlyle saw or supposed that
Murray wanted "Jeffrey's interest" for some reason, and
departed feeling hopeful.

He spent the evening in the company of Badams and his
"true but girlish" young French wife, who was facing the
dreadful task of delivering her husband from drink.
Badams had been trying to "get rich quick" like the rest,
and put money into "grand mining speculations" which
turned out well enough in the long run, but led to worries
which caused headaches;   and when he sought relief in
brandy the delirium of that most dangerous of drugs was
too delightful, and was now dragging him down to death.
He and his wife were living at Enfield within reach of town,
and on hearing the news Carlyle had made his idle brother
John go there and make himself useful.   The sight of
Carlyle's letters procured for Dr. John the confidence of
Badams, and the doctor was now doing all a doctor could.

Mrs. Badams brought her husband to see Carlyle as soon
as she heard he was in London, and as often as possible.
This second day after his arrival was the second time they
had called for him.   It is written in the Buddhist scriptures,
—" None can purify another "; but on this point Carlyle
was a Christian, and resolved to do his best.

XV

SARTOR RESARTUS

THE manuscript left with Murray, *Sartor Resartus,* (The Patcher Repatched) or *The Life and Opinions of Herr Teufelsdröckh,* is one of the best books in English. In depth it is beyond Bacon as far as the Atlantic is beyond Goodwin Sands. It is as earnest as the Bible, and as full of humour as the comedies of Goldsmith. Its theme was what David Hume and Edinburgh called mysticism, a faith that was common to many freethinkers and the best of the Bible-believers—the infinity of Nature, *and* the holiness of Conscience, which has to be cultivated and obeyed. Nature makes no mistakes. What we suppose injustices and mistakes of Nature are our own misdeeds or defects of insight. This is the eternal rock foundation of all true religion, philosophy and science. So far as we see it we are right. So far as we fail to see it or forget it, we are fools ; and that is why every philosophy of the all-explaining kind is folly written large, assuredly. We can never know enough. Voltaire compared man to a mouse in a cathedral : Carlyle compared him to a minnow in a creek.

Thus at last the thought of the west as explained to the people attained the level of the east. " To know our ignorance is the best part of knowledge," said old Lao-Tze. In secret it was a very old story. There was nothing that was not common-place in Carlyle's philosophy except the candour of proclaiming it. In the life of the World a thousand years are but as yesterday when it is past ; and in the last few milleniums which alone are seen in history, while creeds succeeded creeds like passing clouds, our outlook widened to infinity in all directions of space and time, and the tales of the priests became like the fables of Aesop, negligible except for the moral lesson, if it happened to be true. Thus the " creed " of Carlyle was that of the " Independents," no creed at all, or the Quakers' " Inner Light," minus meditation on such Scripture mysteries as Heaven and the Jewish Jehovah, and plus a delight in knowledge and all the best books in the world for a Bible.

After all it is not so very odd for a man to " tell the truth and shame the sinners." The only thing odd was trying to make a living by doing so, and courting publicity. It is a very ancient maxim—" The publishers of truth do not know it—those who know it do not tell."

Of course the likeness of the stupendous chapter, Natural Supernaturalism, to the realized ideal of a Scottish sermon, is not accidental. Both Goethe and he were spokesmen of peoples delivered from Rome, and free to turn away from superstitions they saw to be untrue. As the old cock crows, the young one learns. Imitation of his fearless and outspoken father began Carlyle's enthusiasm for truth, and it was confirmed by the examples of evangelists his father honoured, living " sons of thunder," inspired by Luther and Knox. Thus Carlyle consummating the Reformation was in the right line of spiritual succession from the first Reformers.

Following Goethe, who had followed Spinoza in this, he freely used the word " God ", which made some mistake him for a kind of Coleridge, re-animating religious idols. Whereupon he talked of " The Silences " and so on, but never preserved such perfect silence on what is unspeakable as Confucius, who would never speak of " God," but only of " Heaven." " Who dare name Him ? " demanded Goethe. But it is neither a He nor a She. Perhaps nothing is so good as the common but beautiful word in Shakespeare—if only we see the idea of Shakespeare, including in Nature all mankind—and everything else.

> " *Nature* is made better by no mean,
> But *Nature* makes that mean : so. . . .
> The art itself is *Nature*."

In the words of Feuerbach,—" Not to have a religion is my religion. Not to have a Philosophy is my Philosophy. I am in dependence on Nature and not ashamed of it. Death is natural."

There is an often-quoted passage in *Sartor* :—

' On the roaring billows of Time thou art not engulfed, but borne aloft into the azure of Eternity. Love not Pleasure ; love God. This is the everlasting Yea.' . . .

Being " borne aloft into the azure of Eternity " instead of being " engulfed " in time means seeing the beauty and hearing the music of this wonderful world without a thought of oneself. Thus we may attain, by conscious effort if need be, the self-forgetting serenity to which the gifted grow with little effort, the peace within. The context makes the meaning plain; but common Christians cannot be blamed for supposing his words were intended to strengthen their hopes of eternal happiness in Heaven.

Carlyle was surprised at this and innocent in intention. He had used the word " God " loosely, but he never accepted Fichte's " Divine Idea of the World " or any other philosophy, his theory being that men could never know enough for any theory of things in general. His faith had a rudimentary simplicity. He watched the facts and distrusted formulas, with the same confidence in Nature about morals that Tyndall had about materials. Even so enlightened a Christian as John Sterling was slow to see that, and once in the fire of debate with Carlyle exclaimed triumphantly, " Flat Pantheism ! " He was confounded by the answer :—" And suppose it were Pottheism ! What does it matter if the thing is true ? "

A " peculiarity " of Carlyle esteemed a fault by some is that he saw right and wrong everywhere. This was a conviction common among practical men, tho' unusual in writers. The instinct of conscience appeared to him our true light in the darkness and the greatest wonder of the world. The use of it in *Sartor* is all the more admirable when it is remarked how little is said from hearsay. True to the methods he had early learned from Euclid and Newton and Leslie, he needed to see for himself whatever he was to believe, and did not think of teaching anything except what he believed himself. Whereby his very mistakes appeal to the reader who knows him. There is something touching in his most questionable question in the Chapter called the Everlasting No.—

' Happiness of an approving Conscience ! Did not Paul of Tarsus, whom admiring men have since named Saint, feel that *he* was " the chief of sinners " ; and Nero of Rome, jocund in spirit, spend much of his time in fiddling ? What then ? Is the heroic inspiration we name Virtue but some Passion . . . ? If Happiness be our true aim, then are we all astray. What are the terrors of the Conscience to the diseases of the Liver ! Not on Morality, but on Cookery, let us build, brandishing our frying-pan as censer.'

The Nero of history killed himself about the age of thirty-one in terror of being flogged to death, and much of his life had been as wretched as that of any of the damned in Dante's Hell. He was undersized, big-bellied and thin-legged, and the only fire in his dull eyes was lent by anger or achohol; but he had a magnificent— digestion. In fourteen years of most luxurious living, he had only three slight fits of sickness, so slight as to need no alteration in either food or drink.[1] To a chronic bilious dyspeptic, such a man would seem as enviable as an angel in Heaven.

The feeling of the contemporary Apostle Paul that he was "chief of sinners" was merely modesty, compatible with the peace within which is the best reward of virtue,—the peace which Carlyle himself achieved and found his best possession, and which is exactly what most people mean by the happiness of an approving conscience.—"The Kingdom of Heaven is within you."

The Chapter "Everlasting Yea" could be paraphrased more than once in old quotations different from any in it, yet making a cento of the same meaning. His peculiar merit is warmth of feeling. Most other writers are clammy in comparison. Their intellectual brightness is like the whiteness of snow. "We start, for soul is wanting there." Like the Winter sunshine, they lack heat. Compared to Carlyle they are often like the sophists and parasites of old compared to Epictetus, or the compliant courtiers and officials of China compared to the uncompromising Confucius and Mencius.

His wife was his first disciple, as Kadijah was Mahomet's. It would have puzzled Plutarch to find any other point of likeness except this only, that both Mahomet and Carlyle were sincere. That is a great point, however, for one sincere man can understand another. There was much more in common between Carlyle and Confucius. Their Philosophy was the same. They saw Time on the background of Eternity, and Earth on the background of infinite Heaven; but declined to discuss life after death or speak about the Gods. Their morals were the same, entire sincerity, continual work and endeavour to become better, especially by a dutiful family life and avoiding self-assertion, greed and strife. To both of them righteousness was an

[1] Suetonius' Nero, Ch. 51. See also Chs. 34, 46, 49, 50, 57, etc; and Tacitus' Annals; XV, 36, 44, 62, 67, 68; and XVI, 4, 5, 6, and 33.

Art, and not a Code, a thing to learn daily better by good example and by meditation, cultivating the conscience, discovering how to behave to another by always asking oneself how one would feel in the other's place. To Carlyle as to Confucius the business of Government was to make men do what their consciences told them was right ; but right or wrong depended little on our likes and dis-likes. No Hebrew prophet nor Greek tragedian was surer that Righteousness was eternal and unchangeable, like the laws of matter. To know better than the average what is right is the one thing needful in a leader of men ; and such knowledge is the natural reward of well-doing. The natural penalty of evil-doing is the reverse—to know less and less the right and the wrong of things, and so stumble into wickedness, not knowing it till too late. This sounds superlative moral philosophy in Europe. It is a proverb in the east, and many an illiterate man has been heard to quote it, and woman too.

It is a sublime and brotherly sentiment to forgive those who " know not what they do " ; and beautiful is forgive-ness between man and man, and possible. But Nature does not forgive, however indulgent to a first offender, and " Heaven makes no mistake." In morals as in materials, effects follow causes, and real sin brings sorrow. What hides that from us is our heedlessness, and the heaps of " laws " wherewith the domineering duffers of many complexions have overlaid society in Europe, making the Universe seem like a mass of rubbish ; and good and bad men alike are forced to study " laws " as burglars doors and gates may do—" to find how they can best get through." In nine-tenths of Europe to-day what is legal is as likely as not to be wrong, and what is illegal may be right, as the " laws " are rules that are seldom useful to anybody but the man who knows how to break them. The Legislatures everywhere too often need to learn what few Kings knew,—that the laws are settled for us by Nature. Their business is to discover what is right, and not to enact whatever is most agreeable.

With a force that would have delighted Confucius, Carlyle denounced our European wars, and never missed a chance of mocking our pet political delusion that between states there is nothing but " the law of the jungle." This is what makes us want a " League of Nations,"—as if we needed permission from some human " Government " to live in peace and behave like reasonable men instead of savages ! Considering what " Governments " are, that would make common honesty for ever impossible. Official publications are of many colours, but they are all shady, and diplomats like Jesuits are a by-word for deceit. The truth, which Carlyle seemed odd for maintaining among us tho' it had been familiar for milleniums in China, is that the eternal laws of righteousness are binding upon men under all circumstances, in families and states and all other human aggregates,—including even " companies " and " trusts,"—as unalterable as gravitation.

The penalties of disregarding them have been palpable of late, even in politics, where rascals feel unrestricted. Bad men have enjoyed too much impunity. An English Lord Chancellor was lately talking to students like the Don John of *Much Ado About Nothing,*—" Tho' I cannot be said to be a flattering honest man, it must not be denied but I am a plain-dealing villain." Too many of his colleagues feel as he did without saying so. The war now smouldering out was not " intended " by the ruck of German kings and money-men and politicians. London and Paris and Petrograd were agreed with Berlin and Vienna in wanting nothing but to go on for ever grabbing and cheating and lying, plundering Asia and Africa, and by many dodges exploiting the rest of the world. *The consciences of the whole lot were atrophied, their minds' eyes dark ; and so they stumbled into war.*

The common people who have suffered most should also blame themselves for being almost as absurd as the Egyptians, who worshipped holy he-goats and crocodiles. The war was their punishment for leaving public affairs to be the amusement of rich scamps and fools. Let them repent of that and learn what is taught, not by Carlyle and Confucius only, but also by Kant and Voltaire, Goethe and Erasmus, and all the best men in Europe and America, —that war is both wicked and absurd, a " Devilry " done by " bosses " at the cost of the people. The passage about Dumdrudge (*Sartor,* II and VIII), is perhaps the best demonstration of this in literature. Carlyle differed from contemporaries who prophesied a speedy end to war, inasmuch as he foresaw and foretold the unavoidable " blood-filled trenches and contentious centuries " between their time and the " final cessation " of it. But he shared their wishes, and even their faith in progress, so frankly that Kaiser William Hohenzollern's invocation of him in the middle of slaughter was one of the absurdities of history. He was as much a man of peace as Kant, and as utter a republican.

Such scorn for war was not the only shock to fashionable folk in *Sartor*. The social institutions they wanted people to think as unchangeable as the Atlantic were compared to clothes, to be mended or altered or replaced as needed. His disbelief in private property in land, which made Jeffrey shudder, was thus lamented by another lawyer, his friend Mr. Venables, in 1884 [1] :—

' When he wrote *Sartor Resartus*, Carlyle was a Communist, and he never thoroughly renounced his early judgment. Prof. Teufelsdröckh wishes to form an Eigenthums-conservirende (Protection of Property) Association for the protection of property in the hands, not of the owners, but of the rest of the community.'

What upset Venables was the blasphemy of doubting the excellence of the legal fiction of private property in land, which is profitable to lawyers, but has made much of Europe a desert. The reference is to part of the last chapter of the second book, wherein Teufelsdröckh proposed a society to enforce the commandment—" Thou shalt not steal," and wrote :—" Hangmen and catchpoles (bailiffs) may keep down the smaller sort of vermin ; but what, except perhaps some such Universal Association, can protect us against whole meat-devouring and man-devouring hosts of Boa-constrictors ? "

When Mr. Venables calls this communism fifty years after it was written, we may imagine what the contemporary Dogberrys would have called it, if they had understood it, when game-laws were being stiffened and the last remains of the public lands being stolen by the landowners in power, while rents were kept high by cornlaws, enforcing famine on the people. There was much more in *Sartor* revealing the rottenness of modern society ; but as his meaning has been caricatured by many to whom it was disagreeable, let us avoid debate by looking at what he was confiding to his note-book :—" No mortal cares twopence for any king or obeys any king except through compulsion : and

---

[1] *Fortnightly Review*, Nov., 1884, p. 607. See also *British and Foreign Review*, Vol. XII, (1841) pp. 305–335.

Society is *not* a Ship of War, its Government *cannot* always
be a Press-gang." This passage seems to have caught
the fancy of Mr. Froude, who quoted it aright, but by-and-
by in dwelling upon it *often forgot the nots* !

The freaks of Froude's memory are foolish indeed. The
essence of the teaching of Carlyle is that only Nature—the
great Reality in us and around us—is to be obeyed.
Against the misdeeds of slackers and sinners below and
above, the workers of the world have to protect themselves
as well as they can, by cunning and force together, as
against the snakes and the tigers. It is written in *Sartor* :—
" We must all toil or steal, (howsoever we name our stealing)." Honour and wages are due to none but workers.
While each man has to find and do his bit, the function
of Government is the better and better sharing of the
wealth wherewith Nature rewards us. The contrast in
Sartor between Dandies and Drudges is as vivid as any
picture of Rembrandt, and more convincing than anything
written in economics before. The conclusion is that the
politicians and puppets atop are to blame for the confusion,
and other men to blame for tolerating them. It is as plain
as any demonstration in Euclid. It seems almost providential that few of the politicians noticed his meaning
till the people knew it too, and the Latter-Day Prophet
was safe.

He was more " advanced " than Cromwell. Of all the
practical politicians in history, Confucius alone would have
accepted the economics of Carlyle, and few but Confucius
could match his plain dealing with men in power. Twenty-
three centuries had passed since Confucius had anticipated
Carlyle by telling Princes in China that they themselves
were misleading the people into crime by their own
excessive covetousness ; and there is hardly one of the
most " advanced " proposals for the " organization " of
labour, from " working regiments " to the public administration of land and the liquor trade, railways and mines,
which could not be supported by quotations from both the
sages.

Frederick the Great used to call himself an " advocate
of the poor." His sense of duty and sympathy with the
common people won the admiration of Carlyle ; but the
history called by his name is like Voltaire's *Essai sur les
Moeurs* in exposing the absurdity of hereditary kingship,
and the Chinese sage had also impressed that on the mind

of the east. Tho' Confucius was of royal stock he would not mention such a trifle, nor tolerate any talk confounding authority with property. He made people see so well that even dynasties dared not deny, that men in authority from top to bottom had no title to their places, except as public servants seeking the good of the public by doing what was right.

That all should work and wages be adjusted to deserts were maxims as clear as the rules of arithmetic, and indeed have seldom been questioned anywhere till lately, when the gospel of grab became the new orthodoxy, a creed not likely to continue long.

Tho' Carlyle's insistence on carrying conscience into economics made Whigs and Tories agree to keep him down as much as possible, the main difference between him and the Utilitarians and many kinds of Socialists was that he was not preoccupied about material needs. He frankly recognized them, but he did not idolize wealth. Well-doing was what mattered most, and speaking and seeing the truth. To Bentham the conscience seemed a needless appendix. It was everything to Carlyle. Thus Bentham would hand out ready-made codes for any country, while Carlyle reserved his judgment till he saw the facts in every case and as far as possible in every detail. He was dogmatic not to dogmatize, but "wait and see." It is impossible to see far away in time or space exactly, and it is a dream or delusion that we can ever know or explain everything. However hard it may seem, we must humbly submit our minds to the fact that our knowledge must ever be an infinitesimal fraction of reality. That is the truth of mysticism.

It would be too long to tell what follows out of that. The labour of the rest of the life of Carlyle was to reveal it. Take only, for brevity, the province he disliked the most and touched the least,—Jurisprudence. Recognizing reality in it means admitting that most of its patter is hocus-pocus, and that the best conceivable of codes would require continual correction, like a city Directory. This justifies some of the objections of English lawyers to "codification," at which Carlyle was one of the first of the reformers to scoff. What he most insisted upon was quick and right and cheap dispatch of business, which explains why his principles sent a shiver down the backs of Jeffrey and Venables, and made many a Lord Chief Justice and

Lord Chancellor shudder, feeling,—" The man is as rude
as Swift, and he means it all." Carlyle honoured
Frederick for what he did in law-reform more than for
his battles.

Another theme of *Sartor* is familiar in many scriptures, that
human appetites are potentially infinite, so that the
way to content is self-control, diminishing our wants.
The Stoics were never weary of saying so, but none of them
put it better than the old German proverb,—" God
Almighty can do a great deal, but He cannot please everybody." Say,—" anybody long," and there it is.

That is why selfish greed,—covetousness the Christians
used to call it,—is a crime and a blunder, and the modern
money-men who play at being monarchs of the world are
like Midas with his donkey-ears. Tho' they often have
too much, they have never enough, and the more they grab
and get, the more shabby are their greedy souls inside.

Happy are those who speedily lay to heart the truth that
we should be a-doing each his " bit," in peace as much as
in the fevered times of war. The gospel of work is far from
new. Nothing ever said for it is better than a humorous
saying in the oldest Chinese scripture :—" The day is
always too short for the man who is busy doing good ; and
for the man who is busy doing evil, it is too short too."

By precept and example Carlyle is leading us to accept
what has to be and rejoice to " do our bit " of work, and
keep from contention about wages by indifference about
them. The greatest of pleasures, the one that grows not
old, is to love the truth about the wonderful world wherein
we—pass, and pass, and disappear, like shooting-stars.
By " work " he did not mean unlimited drudgery. The
servants of Mammon are slaves. The " right way " leads
to rest as well as peace. Once more, there was nothing
new,—it is like sermons on familar texts, such as the two
old proverbs :—" Confide ye aye in Providence," and " Be
contented with little, and merry with more."

Sartor Resartus may be called the pemmican of true
philosophy. Its allusiveness has led to annotated editions [1]
so minute and perfect that nobody knowing English
need be puzzled now. Perhaps the Essays and " Heroes "
are best to begin with, but to anyone who feels called to

---

[1] In England, J. A. S. Barrett's edition is easily the best ; pub. A. and C.
Black ; and in America, Prof. McMechan's ; pub. Ginn and Co., The
Athenaeum Press, Boston.

open *Sartor* and reads it slowly, the best advice is like that of an early editor of Shakespeare—read it again and again, and again, and if at last you do not like it, you are in danger of not understanding it.

It is not merely literary, any more than the books of *Rabelais* or *Utopia*, *Gulliver's Travels* or the *Pilgrim's Progress*. It justifies righteousness, and corrects the animal's creed of grab by the brotherhood of men, which makes work and sympathy at once a duty and a pleasure. While the teaching is superlatively wise and moral, it is sincere and not sentimental but as solid as the rocks, and yet brings into sight within measurable distance the good time coming, when the world shall be a place of peace and goodwill.

In politics his method of righteous plain-dealing seems the same as that of Confucius, and in strange contrast to the ways of western politicians, preoccupied about " interests." The philosopher who fell into a well while studying the stars is a fair symbol of the best of the pilots of our ships of state. The ruck of them are rogues, leading absent-minded men into wars as abominable as those of Genghis Khan or Tamerlane. The worst collision at sea is a trifle compared to war ; yet war and war are the sure results of leaving the ships of state to be steered by noodles, who do not even understand that they must avoid collisions. We might do worse than settle that whenever a war begins, the politicians implicated, from Kings and Presidents down, should all be treated like the pilots of common ships in collision, and superseded pending enquiry,—incarcerated, perhaps, in neutral territory till the war was over. But *Sartor* did not run into such details.

It was not merely a political treatise, tho' it showed the importance of politics and the need for common honesty in public business. It held the mirror up to nature wonderfully. The very defects of Carlyle seem providential. He could not versify, and that made him put into prose like intellectual lightning the thoughts and sentiments that might have escaped in conventional conducting mediums. The best of his impassioned prose has a melody that haunts the memory and may remain among the best possessions of men for centuries, perhaps milleniums.

I

IN LONDON—WILLIAM GODWIN AND OTHERS

(1831)

THE best of the French biographers is right,— Carlyle had said his say in *Sartor*.[1] In delivering the manuscript to Murray on Wednesday, (10.8.1831),[2] he said,—" I have nothing else to do here but to get it published." Murray smiled and replied, " I'll begin it this afternoon and give you an answer next Wednesday." But Carlyle did not seem to him to be in a hurry, and really was serene as he had never been before, realizing in his western way what Buddha said :—" Better than Lordship over the Earth ; better than going to Heaven, better than ownership of all the worlds, is the happiness of the first step in holiness." And Buddha also said :—" Having made my thoughts subject to me and my attention firm, I will go from country to country, training disciples." In the same spirit had Carlyle come to town to look round. He was craving for sympathy, hoping for disciples.

The development of new clubs seemed a sign of the times ; and in the last six years much else had changed. Irving was no longer a centre of attraction except to his own big congregation ; and as he walked along Piccadilly with his long, black, grizzled hair and brown skin and broad hat might pass for Paganini the fiddler.

Carlyle thought of living at Enfield, beside Badams and Charles Lamb, in the quiet of the country and in reach of town. But soon it was plain that Badams would not long be company for anyone—he was killing himself with brandy. Carlyle did all he could to help. Mrs. Badams was nearly weeping when telling him. It had been going on for months. Badams had taken to it for an intolerable headache when worried by business, and found the stupefaction irresistible—he was drunk every day. Mrs. Montagu had " cut " Dr. John Carlyle because " he would

[1] *Carlyle*, by Louis Cazamian, pp. 120–1.
[2] *John Murray*, by Samuel Smiles, II, 349–356, where " May " is a slip for August.

not turn with her in a day from transcendental apotheosis of Badams to excommunication." To Carlyle himself, when he called on Thursday, (11.8.1831), she told a long story about Badams the cheat, and what was worse the bankrupt—she was not bothering about the brandy. What made her bitter was a bad investment for which Badams seemed to be to blame. Old Basil Montagu spoke of it gently. His wife denounced Mrs. Strachey too, for other reasons ; but Carlyle replied—" I will continue to love all parties and pity all, and hate or quarrel with none." After which it was only prudent to see a little less of her, but except this refusal to quarrel. there was never an unpleasant word between them. Two days later, Saturday, (13.8.1831), Carlyle was dining with the Stracheys at Shooter's Hill, and heard from Mrs. Strachey that Kitty Kirkpatrick was now Mrs. Phillips and a mother.

He employed his working hours reshaping part of the Literary History that missed its market, into an essay upon Early German Literature for the *Foreign Quarterly*, taking a new version of Reynard the Fox for his text, and showing through the mist of many years the old school-master of 1300, Hugo von Trimberg, who was quoted in *Sartor* for laughing at duelling.

He found himself as " hopelessly divided " from Irving on politics as on religion. Irving was against the Reform Bill and Democracy as " a thing forbidden, leading down to utter darkness," whereas Carlyle was for it, insisting that the Reform Bill was inevitable, wherever it led to : whereby he was in a minority at the divine's breakfast table one morning, when he found himself among " a strange set of ignorant conceited fanatics," the people who were soon to lead Irving into trouble by their interruption of public services. His congregation would never have turned him out if he had not suffered these persons to make a public scandal, and refused to stop them. The boldest of them, Robert Baxter, just not criminal and just not mad, was his foremost enemy in the time of trial, proclaiming then that he had been " speaking by a lying spirit, and not by the spirit of God," which was the truth for once.[1] What embittered Baxter may have happened about now. He let out a flood of noises supposed to be inspired, expecting adoration. Instead of adoring him, Irving, said he, " came up to me and said,—' Faith is very hard.' " Which

[1] *Edward Irving*, by Mrs. Oliphant, Ch. XVII.

showed the genuineness of the too-tolerant divine, who never claimed inspiration for himself, but had too much patience with fools. To a Glasgow man who told Carlyle, he spoke of the time coming—" *When* I work miracles " ; but that time never came.

So when the new sect started, he was the least Irvingite of the Irvingites, like the boss of a barricade who pointed to his rabble saying, " I must go after them as I'm their chief." Which explains why Carlyle was hoping to the end that he might deliver himself from them. Irving was like a Gulliver among the Lilliputians, and even now, amidst the hubbub of the semi-insane, he was hearing with interest all Carlyle had to tell him about the Saint-Simonians. They fixed a day to visit Coleridge again together, but it was a day of rain, and they never went.

Monday (15.8.1831).—Carlyle took breakfast with the Jeffreys in Jermyn Street. " The two Charlottes," Mrs. Jeffrey and her daughter, received him in " their choicest mood," and in the midst of the meal in came Jeffrey in a dressing-gown, and quizzed the women,—" Why, Charley, I've got the cholera, I believe." Returning to his room to dress, he soon was calling in Carlyle to talk, and telling him,—" I think it likely Murray will publish *Sartor* at some time or other." Carlyle departed with a frank in his pocket, and wrote letters home. Then he had tea with the Irvings, and went with his brother John to the house of Mrs. Kenny in Southampton Row, the mother of Mrs. Badams. There he was to meet William Godwin, now 75, the Nestor of English " philosophers " and pioneer of Political Justice, who disbelieved the current gospel of grab and saw little but evil in " Property, Property, Property."

Godwin's first wife had been Mary Wollstonecraft, the " proto-martyr of the rights of woman." He began life as a parson, but after five years had quitted the pulpit and taken to literature as a trade, because he had ceased to believe what he had to preach. He was republican by conviction too ; and tho' his novel *Caleb Williams* was his best seller, he had done good work in history, biography and politics, scoffing at both Malthus and Burke, and fearlessly uttering opinions which were " treason." George Canning said [1] that about 1792 or '93 Godwin had offered to accept him as the leader of the English Jacobins ; and Canning

[1] Lockhart's *Life of Scott*, IX, pp. 229–230.

asked " time to think " and judiciously consulted
Prime Minister Pitt, as the fittest father-confessor for an
ambitious Oxford man, and so he got into Parliament
next year and was soon an under Secretary—sublimely
aiming " higher and higher ! "—" Excelsior ! "—He never
did anything for Godwin, whose outspoken opinions made
him " impossible," but by-and-by he put Godwin's old
brother into the Charterhouse, which gave him occasion
to tell the story.

When Carlyle arrived the second Mrs. Godwin was
already there in advance of her husband, " an insignificant
old woman " now, much changed from the buxom widow
of 1801, when as Mrs. Clairmont she greeted her bereaved
neighbour so cleverly,—' Is it possible that I behold the
immortal Godwin ! " She agreed with him the marriage
laws were as bad as they could be, and married him of
course. She now sat gossiping quietly, while Carlyle
took stock of the hostess, a big and masculine French-
woman, like Aurelia in *Wilhelm Meister*.

Godwin came in a " parson's black coat," a sturdy thickset little man, with bushy white eyebrows, bald head and
bright grey eyes, a big blunt nose and chin, and well-shut
mouth. He was brisk and hearty, with a quick short
laugh that ended in a cheery chirrup. He looked with
interest at Carlyle who was hitching nearer him and trying
to " open on him," enquiring :—" What do you think
of Literary London now as compared with what it used to
be ? "

Godwin :—" Old men always prefer the bygone time,
and many of *my* friends are now gone ; but on the whole
the old time *was* the best."

Carlyle began to explain his own ideas about " co-
operation, and proselytism and so forth," which seemed to
" gratify " Godwin, but when Godwin was about to
talk he was pulled away to play whist, and Carlyle could
only look at him for the rest of the night. " There did the
philosopher sit, and a swarm of noisy children, chattering
women, noisy dilettantes round him," deafening Carlyle
as they bawled in French and English amidst the " hoarse
thunder louder than an iron forge " which two women
were " crashing " out of a piano, " under pretext of its being
music by Rossini." He suffered it for an hour and then
glided off to escape the supper, with hopes of seeing Godwin
again " under better circumstances." But he never did.

II

THE OLD COMMONS HOUSE, HENRY DRUMMOND, &c.

(1831)

ON Tuesday, 16.8.1831, Carlyle had a long interview with John Bowring, the Radical editor of Bentham's *Westminister Review*. They rejoiced together over the French Revolution of 1830 and the impending English Reform ; and parted intending and desiring better acquaintance with each each other, which was prevented only by Bowring's promotion. The victorious Whigs rewarded him by well-paid official employment which took him much abroad. As he is said to have taught book-keeping to the English Treasury, and issued the florin as a first step to decimal coinage, to say nothing of starting the wicked war on China in 1856, historians may like to know how he looked this Tuesday :—a " thin " six-footer, " bent at the middle into an angle of 150°, the back quite straight " (and the bend in part the result of having been thrown out of a gig), " with large grey eyes, a huge turn-up nose with straight nostrils to the very point, and large projecting close-shut mouth : walking restlessly about the room, frank of speech, vivid, emphatic, and verstandig" (sensible). " Such is the Radical Doctor." He gave the best advice he could about *Sartor*, in case Murray did not take it.

The next day, Wednesday, was the day that Murray had named, but he was not ready. In the evening Carlyle was admitted by " Speaker's order " to the old House of Commons, and reported to his wife :—

' It is a pretty apartment that of theirs ; far smaller than I expected, with some four ranges of benches rising high behind each other like pews in a church gallery, an oval open space in the middle, at the farthest extremity of which sits the Speaker in what seemed a kind of press— like our wardrobe, only oaken. Opposite him is the door. A very narrow gallery runs all round atop for reporters,

241

R

strangers, etc. I was seated on the ground floor below this. Althorp spoke, a thick, large, broad-whiskered, farmer-looking man ; Hume also, a powdered, clean, burly fellow ; and Wetherell, a beetle-browed, sagacious, quizzical old gentleman ; then Davies, a Roman-nosed dandy, whom I left *jannering*, (talking emptily), having left it all in some three-quarters of an hour. O'Connell came and spoke to an individual before me. You would call him a well-doing country shopkeeper, with a bottle-green frock or great coat, and brown scratch wig. I quitted them with the highest contempt.'

Meanwhile Jeffrey was reassuring Mrs. Carlyle that her husband was not neglecting appearances :—" He looks very smart and dandyish ; has got his hair cut, and a new suit, and is applying various cosmetics to his complexion," (referring to the bright red of his cheeks). " I will do what I can for the Book, but fear its extravagance and what will be called its affectation." The worshipping wife quoted this in a letter to London and went on :—" Let him not bother his dear little heart overmuch. *Dreck* is *done for* already, and no Bookseller nor body of Booksellers, no discerning public, can *undo* him—not the Devil himself can undo him. If they will not publish him, bring him back and *I* will take care of him and read him and admire him, till we are enabled to publish him on our own account." [1] To which the happy husband replied in copious caressing letters which it should never have been needful to print.

Friday, 19.8.1831, was a holy day indeed, which made Carlyle feel as if in a land of wonders where animals speak. It began with a fanatic-infested breakfast at Irving's, where they tried to make him believe in the miracles of hysterics. A letter was read from a half-witted clergyman he knew at Irongray, between Craigenputtock and Dumfries. It was written four days after the death of the wife who had kept the poor creature presentable. Left to himself he was now " speaking with tongues," babbling like a baby, " casting out a devil."

Then Irving took Carlyle to Lincoln's Inn Fields to hear a sermon from " a double of yours," said he, describing a young Alexander Scott, whom he had brought to London in 1828 to be his assistant. He was " a thin, black com-

---

[1] *More New Letters of J. W. Carlyle* by Alexander Carlyle, *Nineteenth Century Mag.*, August 1914, p. 337.

plexioned, vehement man, earnest, clear, and narrow,"
wrote Carlyle to his wife. "For a stricken hour did he
expound in the most superannuated dialect of Chroist and
so forth—the meaning of Entsagen," or self-denial, while
Irving "looked at me wistfully, for he knows I cannot
take miracles in; yet he looked so piteously, as if he im-
plored me to believe."

In the evening Irving piloted Carlyle "through the
crowd and stir of Piccadilly" to dinner in the house in
Belgrave Square of Henry Drummond, a rich banker
and saint, grandson of Henry Dundas, Lord Melville, who
used to be Boss of Scotland. Drummond was the worldly
leader of the ultra-devotees of Biblical inspiration, and
supported their organ, the quarterly *Morning Watch*.
The editor, a scribe from Wales called Tudor, was now
present to help Drummond to impress Carlyle, whom
Drummond was fond of quoting. A pious M.P. and the
delicate Mrs. Drummond completed the party. It passed
pleasantly, but disappointed Irving, whose "trismegistus"
Drummond had little glamour for the like of Carlyle. Yet
he was worth a look.

He was a man of forty-five, over six feet high and as
straight as a lamp-post, "with a high-carried, quick,
penetrating head,"—a man of fashion, saint and wit,
philosopher and dandy. Bred by his grandfather Dundas
while his mother was in India, he grew up hungering for
dominion like a cat for flesh,—a boss in search of a job,
and plenty of money to play with. He was married young
and put into the Commons, but did not flourish there, and
at 31 took to religion, and soon set out for the "Holy Land."
As when a brave dog starts on a far journey but is diverted
into a side street by the sound of a fight, so stopped he at
Geneva, where Socinians and Anti-Socinians were locked
in battle; and sorely did he worry the Church Courts
by spending money on the press as dexterously as might
have been expected of a pupil of Dundas, tho' the old man
would have shuddered at the thought of doing it to defend
the orthodox against Socinians.

By 1826 he was buzz-buzzing in London with Irving and
others over scripture prophecies, determined to see something never seen before in the old sheepskins. They
supposed the world was coming to an end, and felt sure
such news entitled them to a hearing. To such as he
"the pleasure lies in the battle, not the prize." So when

hysterical women screeching at prayer-meetings began to shock the congregation at Regent Square, and Irving moved by pastoral tenderness was rashly letting them screech away, regardless of the remonstrances of relatives and friends, including Carlyle, this modern Don Quixote sprang forward to second him,—clad in magic armour of bank paper which made him careless of bad consequences to himself at any rate. Thus bad grew worse, and hysterics which might have been easily hushed became a public nuisance ; and that may be what was meant by Carlyle saying by-and-by that " without unkindness of intention, he did my poor Irving a great deal of ill."

As, yet, however,—August, 1831,—it does not appear that Drummond had started to do any inspired screeching himself ; and much as he astonished Carlyle at dinner by discussing the self-appointed prophets seriously, he appeared without an effort what he was, a born and bred aristocrat, " well nigh cracked by pride and vanity," but pococurante—meaning " careless with artful care "—and witty as well as pious, and amply provided with that politeness which is the lightning rod of passion. So a solo of " Teufelsdröckhist Radicalism " was allowed to blend harmoniously with a chorus of ultra-pious Tory prejudice. The only detail on record is that the Swing outrages then going on—fire-raising by labourers, mainly—instead of being wholly blamed as the depravity of the men, were attributed to the " rotten social state of England," whereby the labourers were kept " half the year in raising wheat, t'other half in burning it." To this the rich banker, Henry Drummond, sincerely agreed. On his Surrey estate he was a " generous landlord, allowing allotments to his labourers as early as 1818." Tho' by-and-by an " Irvingite Apostle " and " Angel for Scotland," he went back to the Commons as Member for West Surrey, and had a " safe seat " for the last thirteen years of his life. No wonder ! He was a real " representative " of the best old-fashioned kind. While working to make dishonesty illegal in banking, he denounced the trick of selling beer adulterated and dear to pick the pockets of the poor, and proposed to abolish the taxes on it and let labourers resume their ancient freedom of malting at home. [1]

It was natural for such a man to continue a friend of

[1] *Times* report, 6.7.1850. For the other details see the *Dict. of Nat. Biography*, and books, etc., there quoted.

Carlyle. One of the last things he did was to invite Carlyle and his wife to a long visit in the country. This was all the more creditable to his politeness of the heart because of the great gulf between them in religion. Drummond could not fail to be aware that Carlyle had dropped the Christian creeds like old clothes, and spared no pains to deliver his friend Irving from fanaticism. Things were coming to a crisis now (1831). The wife of Irving was the only member of their family who went all lengths with him, and her relatives were now as earnest as his own in remonstrating against the absurdities he was tolerating. His brother, Dr. Irving, begged Carlyle to help them ; and accordingly, soon after this dinner-party, and again and again in the months that followed, Carlyle dealt faithfully with his " erring brother," in the best style of the old apostles, while Irving sat listening " with thoughtfully puckered face," nearly weeping once. He had to endure to be told that the new miracles were crazy nonsense, without warrant in scripture or common-sense. But it was too late. He was like a ship's captain who has set a wrong course, and unexpectedly beholds the breakers ahead.

He continued to call upon Carlyle. In the midst of his own distractions, the truly Christ-like divine was saddened most by the sight of the depravity around him, and was sounding the publisher, James Fraser, who was one of his congregation, about setting Carlyle as editor to remodel *Fraser's Magazine* and sweep " it clean " ; but Fraser and Carlyle merely listened with a smile to the well-meaning man.

When Heraud, who was now helping Maginn to edit for Fraser, called on Carlyle on Wednesday 24.8.1831, he stayed more than four and a half hours, perhaps to make sure of Carlyle's intentions. If so he departed happy, tho' he had bored Carlyle, who thought him " the " cheerfullest, best natured little creature extant," but did not want a *tête-à-tête* of four and a half hours. Heraud was one of the few journalists who knew German. The only authentic fragment of their talk may have been this afternoon.—

Carlyle.—" Novalis has said, the highest problem of Authorship is the writing of a Bible."

Heraud.—" That is precisely what I am doing."

He meant it too,—which enhanced the fun. He wrote

both epics and dramas, and much of his talk in the 'thirties recalls an ancient epigram :—

> You ask me if I think your epic good ?
> If I could praise your poetry, I would.

It may have been this year that he asked someone, *not* Carlyle, about his new epic,—" Have you seen my Descent into 'Ell ? "—" No, but I'd like to." Even John Mill was less patient than Carlyle, and said,—" I forgive him freely for interpreting the Universe, now when I find he cannot pronounce the h's." Like many of the best of the Cockneys, Heraud was of Huguenot descent, the most honourable lineage in England, tho' it is apt to leave one at times a little loose in the h's.

III

MILL, BROUGHAM, AND OTHERS

(1831)

BEFORE August was out, Dr. John Carlyle was engaged as attendant doctor to the Countess of Clare,[1] and as soon as their money worries were thus diminished, it was settled Mrs. Carlyle was to join her husband for the winter in London, arriving about the end of September. Her movements were carefully arranged in advance, as she was believed to be pregnant.

In the meantime William Empson, a friend of Jeffrey, whom Carlyle visited " in the solitude of the Temple," told him of Mrs. Austin and her German " Culture," and that John Mill too was reading German. " A converted Utilitarian," Empson called him, and praised young Mill so highly that Carlyle was prepared to see in him a possible disciple. He confessed—to his wife—that " almost the only comfort " he had in London was the sight of possible disciples, " ready for more light. To investigate them," he said, " will be my best work through the winter. Men united are strong ; single, the strongest is weak."

This made him urgent about *Sartor*. The world seemed to be ripe for it. It was retrieved from Murray, who had kept it ten days without reading it, and declined by Longman and Rees after two or three days' inspection. Allan Cunningham told him,—" It is almost madness to press forward a literary work now." Carlyle admitted it was not the season for reading MSS. and political excitement made it a bad year for books ; but he said that to listen to such advice would be like a rustic waiting till the river to be crossed ran dry. So he brought it to Jeffrey who had told him he would read it and see whether he should talk to Murray. William Fraser the editor of the *Foreign*

[1] Contemporary Letters correct slightly as to date etc., *Reminiscences* II, p. 201.

Review was "unspeakably willing" to help, and tried Colburn and Bentley and others, but not another publisher in London would look at *Sartor*. His own brother James Fraser, when Carlyle called upon him in his shop in Regent Street, did not offer to read it, but said he would publish it,—"if you advance me a sum not exceeding £150." Carlyle had nothing to spend on publication. "But the public will not buy books," he was told, and answered :— "The public has done the wisest thing it could, and ought never more to buy what they call books."

On Sunday, 28.8.1831, Jeffrey told him when he called, —"I have honestly read 28 pages," felt it dilatory at the start, as Carlyle admitted it was, and "very much admired the scene of the sleeping city," and will write to Murray. As for a "place under Government" which he had himself suggested for Carlyle, he said he had found there were too "many applicants" for the few places which "an economical ministry" allowed, and these were "all filled up."

Meanwhile MacVey Napier would be uneasy lest Jeffrey might be displeased at his not employing Carlyle, and wrote that he would have accepted the *Nibelungen Lied* if it had been offered to him, and Carlyle replied :—"There is no periodical now extant in Britain which I should so willingly write for, and publish *all* my essayist lucubrations in, as the *Edinburgh Review*. If you really want me to preach in your pulpit, therefore, you have only to say so," [1] and he suggested an essay on Johnson ; but Macaulay had forestalled him, and he had to think of something else. Consulting Jeffrey, he told his wife,—"I found my own idea confirmed that Napier was anxious enough to have me write, but afraid less I committed him ; so that 'agreeing about subjects' would be the difficulty."

Jeffrey did as he promised on Sunday (28.8.1831). He wrote to Murray about *Sartor* that very day ; and as a result of an interview with him, Murray soon agreed to print a first edition of 750, on "half profits," that is without getting or giving anything, but leaving the author the copyright thereafter. On these terms the printing started.

Before this news reached Mrs. Carlyle she had written to him (29.8.1831) :—"I must smile at the idea of Jeffrey recommending your manuscript to Murray. He will not, Dearest, dare not. Trust only in yourself, and there trust

[1] *Correspondence of MacVey Napier*, pp. 112–114.

to *all lengths.*" [1] In another long letter three days later (1.9.1831), she incidentally alludes to what Jeffrey had said :—" Jeffrey admires the sleeping city. Thank him for nothing. He would have been the dullest of mortals if he had not. My beloved Dreck ! My jewel of great price ! The builders despise thee ; but thou will yet be *brought out with shouting*, and I shall live to see thee in thy place. All these discouragements do but increase my confidence, as a candle burns brighter for being snuffed ; for *Dreck* is imperishable, indestructible as the substance of the four elements ; and all Bookseller-dom, all Devildom, cannot prevail against him ! "[2]

Immediately after reading his wife's letter agreeing to come to London, Carlyle walked to Mrs. Austin's at Hampstead. He received an enthusiastic welcome, and was invited to return on Friday to meet Mill.

On Friday, (2.9.1831), he stepped into the House of Lords, and watched Jeffrey arguing an appeal.—" The fat Rutherford sate also within the ring, with Dr. Lushington, the divorcer ", and some clerks, and outside it a " handful of listeners and loiterers." The centre of interest to Carlyle was Chancellor Brougham. He had a couple of colleagues, one of them " the ugliest man extant, " and was anything but a beauty himself.—" very particularly ignoble-looking," a " stony " face with restless, dangerous eyes,—" nothing but business " there, " no ray of genius, and even a considerable tincture of insincerity. He was yawning awfully, with an occasional twitching up of the corners of the upper lip and point of the nose. A politician truly and *nothing* more."

To listen to cases was always Purgatory to Brougham. He used to write letters while the lawyers gabbled by the day. On this occasion, in compliment to Jeffrey perhaps, he was affecting to listen ; but as soon as Carlyle heard that Jeffrey would be talking two hours longer, he departed.

In the evening he was listening to the " timid-eyed, painful " Law-professor John Austin pouring out his special blend of Utilitarianism and metaphysics, in a clanging metallic voice, while his wife poured out green tea. Carlyle was taking neither ; and it was a relief to walk away with John Stuart Mill, with whom he had

---

[1] *More New Letters of J. W. Carlyle*, by Alexander Carlyle, *Nineteenth Century Mag.*, August, 1914, p. 341.
[2] *Ditto*, p. 344.

" almost four hours of the best talk I have mingled in for
long." Mill came with him almost to his door. " You will
like Mill," he assured his wife, describing him :—" Slender,
tall and elegant, with small clear Roman-nosed face, a
fair complexion and earnest eyes." It may have been now
that he told Mill that on sight of his papers in the *Examiner*
he had said to himself,—" Here is a new Mystic." [1] They
were both to breakfast with Empson on the Tuesday, and
on the intervening Sunday he wrote to his wife with
reference to Mill and Empson :—" These rudiments of a
Mystic school are by far the most cheering phenomenon I
see in London," while Mill wrote to Sterling that the
acquaintance of Carlyle was " the only substantial good
I have yet derived from writing those papers." " He is
a great hunter out of acquaintances," said Mill. They
soon saw much of each other, and the more they saw, the
better were they pleased. [2] Charles Buller wrote (12.9.1831),
" I rejoice that you think so highly of John Mill. I have
just heard from him. He understands and esteems you, as
you do him. That is as it should be. In names and professed doctrines you and John Mill differ as widely as the
poles ; but you may well meet on the love of truth."

Buller was right ; and seldom had any teacher as worthy
a disciple as John Stuart Mill. It was now more than two
years since Mill (aged 22 in 1828) became acquainted with
D'Eichthal (aged 24), and began corresponding on politics
and religion with him,—the same apostle of religion according to Saint-Simon who wrote to Carlyle last year. [3]

[1] Autobiography of J. S. Mill, p. 174.
[2] *Letters of J. S. Mill*, I, pp. 16 and 25–6 ; and Carlyle's journals.
[3] See J. S. Mill, *Corr. Inédit. avec G. D'Eichthal* (1898).

IV

A LATTER-DAY LUTHER AT LARGE

(1831)

ONE Friday, (8.9.1831), Carlyle was walking to Jeffrey's for a frank when he was stopped for five or ten minutes by the coronation procession, William and Adelaide on the way to Westminster. He told his wife the sight was not worth a few yards' walk. After many " caps and feathers " came the royal carriage, all " glass and gilding, like a huge glass lantern, and there (were) the poor old King and poor ugly Queen, dimly seen sitting like two foolish wax dolls—which they were—letting themselves be trailed in their lantern go-cart." Then an odd thing happened, he confessed.—" What took me I know not : but I burst into the heartiest fit of laughter I have had for some time : and perhaps one ought rather to have cried ; for it was the ghost of the past, perhaps taking leave. Poor King ! They will be consecrating him now. What avails it ? *Ex nihilo nihil fit* " (nothing is made from nothing).

As Jeffrey had to be at the show, there was no frank for Carlyle, who wrote without it ; and his wife replying (11.9.1831) said she had been frightened on seeing the letter had not a " frank " on the address.—" Was Jeffrey ill, as the newspapers are reporting ? Or were you quarrelled with him, as you seemed in the road to be ? Neither, thank God ! Only the poor old Wax-doll getting its crown put on." [1]

The first and best of the Charles Dilkes was then making the *Athenaeum* newspaper prosperous ; and reporting to his wife a private talk with him, Carlyle said :—" The man is very tolerant, hospitable ; not without a sense for the good, but with little power to follow it, and defy the evil. That is the temper in which I find many here : they

---

[1] *More Letters of J. W. Carlyle* by Alexander Carlyle, *Nineteenth Century Mag.*, August 1914, p. 346.

deplore the prevalence of dishonesty, quackery and stupidity; many do it—like Dilke—with apparent heartiness and sorrow: but to believe that it can be *resisted*, that it will and shall be resisted, herein poor *Teufelsdreck* is well-nigh singular." In his journal he noted:—

'Colburn and Bentley the Booksellers are known to expend ten thousand pounds annually—I had this from Dilke, who had it from their man of business—on what they call "advertising," more commonly called *puffing*.

'Puffing flourishes in all countries; but London is the true scene of it; (partly owing to its size). It is rich also, stupid and ignorant, beyond example; thus in all respects the true Goshen (or happy land) of Quacks.

'Every man I meet with mourns over this state of matters; no one thinks it remediable; you must do as the others do, or they will get the start of you, or tread you under foot. "All true, Mr. Carlyle; BUT—" I say:—"All true, Mr. Carlyle, AND—" The first beginning of a remedy is that some *one* believe a remedy possible; believe that if he cannot *live* by truth, then he can die by it. Dost *thou* believe it? Then is the new Era begun!'

By this time Carlyle was looking beyond Goethe, taking a line of his own. His favourite hero now was Luther. If he had had a little more money, if politics had not interfered with literature and William Fraser been able to accept and pay for the Literary History he commissioned, Carlyle would have been compiling a Life of Luther in Germany, instead of doing *Sartor* and coming to London to enquire of editors what they wanted that he could supply. When Napier did not take *Dr. Johnson* Carlyle proposed "an essay on Luther, which has lain in my head for several years"; and when 36 pages were offered, pleaded for more:—"the thing I had in view was some picture of Martin Luther and of his environment—*what* he was, and *how* he was; a matter requiring perhaps to be re-interpreted,"—which did not tempt Napier to stretch his limits. Supposing metaphysics safer, he suggested a review of a three-volume essay on Man by a Mr. Hope. Carlyle admitted that the philosophy of life was a current topic, mentioning similar books by Godwin, Coleridge and Schlegel; and promised to have "something" ready by

December, which the cautious editor might refuse if he liked. [1] " I trust to you for a striking paper," wrote Napier in reply.

The printing of *Sartor* had not gone far when Murray repented, and in the beginning of October he returned the manuscript with the reader's opinion which is often printed in an Appendix and was attributed to Lockhart. [2] So the hope of publishing *Sartor* was deferred. John Mill read it in manuscript, and after him Charles Buller, Dilke and others.

On Luther at present Carlyle had to be silent, another disappointment ; but that did not make Luther the less precious to him as an example. He was feeling himself " rather wicked," and confessed to his wife that he " absolutely felt ashamed " as he read the Table Talk of his hero. " What have I suffered ? What did he suffer ? One should actually, as Irving advises, ' pray to the Lord,' did one but know how to do it. The *best* worship, however, is stout working. *Frisch zu* ! (Cheer up !) " Reporting to his brother John (21.10.1831) the indefinite postpone- ment of *Sartor*, he added : —" I am perfectly contented. What I have written I have written : The reading of it is another party's concern." He continued to watch events without any decrease of self-confidence. In Macaulay's revered Sir James Macintosh, whom he saw at Jeffrey's, he detected the " business mouth and chin " and " sensible official air, not without a due spicing of hypocrisy and pedantry—no doubt involuntary." Macaulay himself was hit off to him by Mill as " set in there," in the Commons, " to make flash speeches, and he makes them."

" The best of the Fourth Estate now extant in Britain " seemed to Carlyle to be Fonblanque of the *Examiner*, who received him cordially,—" a long thin man " of " wrinkly, baggy face " and keen eyes, with " far more in him " than usual, and really intent on mending the condition of the poor, whose pockets were being picked by tobacco taxes and other indirect dodges of politicians. In short, sincerity in what to " public men " is seldom more than a way of talking, real sympathy with the people, was Carlyle's test of political worth. He wrote to his mother this winter :

[1] *Correspondence of MacVey Napier*, pp. 115–119. MacVey Napier's own letter is quoted in T. C. *Letters*, I. p. 356.
[2] *Conversations with Carlyle*, by Sir C. Gavan Duffy, p. 90. For other details see Froude, and S. Smiles' *Memoir of John Murray*, II, pp. 349–356.

" It is painful to walk these streets, and see so many cold
and hungry and naked and ignorant beings, and have
so little power to help them ; " and he jotted in his note-
book what he saw as he looked around in his daily walks,
with fellow feeling in plenty, and also the free detachment
as of a visitor from another planet.—

' How men are hurried here into double quick speed ;
so that in self-defence they *must not* stay to look at one
another ! Miserable is the scandal mongery and evil
idle speaking of the country population : more frightful
still the total ignorance and mutual heedlessness of these
poor souls in populous city pent. " Each passes on, quick
transient ; regarding not the other or his woes." Each
must button himself together, and take no thought—not
even for *evil*—of his neighbour. There in their little cells
divided by partitions of brick or board, they sit strangers,
unknowing, unknown ; like Passengers in some huge Ship,
each within his little cabin : Alas ! and the Ship is Life,
and the voyage is from Eternity to Eternity !
' Everywhere there is the most crying want of GOVERN-
MENT, a true all-ruining anarchy : no one has any *knowledge*
of London in which he lives ; it is a huge aggregate of little
systems, each of which is again a small Anarchy, the
members of which do not *work* together but *scramble*
against each other.
' The Soul lies dead in the bosom of man ; starting out
only in mad ghastly Nightwalkings—*e.g.* " the gift of
tongues "—(in Irving's church): Ignorance eclipses all things
with its owlet wings ; man walks he knows not whither ;
walks and wanders till he walks into the jaws of Death,
and is there devoured.—Nevertheless, God is in it : here,
even here, is the Revelation of the Infinite in the Finite :
a majestic poem,—tragic, comic or epic—couldst thou
but read it and recite it ! Watch it then ; study it, catch
the secret of it, and proclaim the same in such accent as
is given thee Alas ! the spirit is willing, but the flesh is
weak.
' (At Jeffrey's) Macintosh was talking mysteriously
with other " Hon. members " about " what was to be done."
—Something à la Dogberry the thing looked to me ; tho'
I deny not that it is a serious conjuncture ; only believe
that *any* change has some chance to be for the better, and
so see it all with composure.

'Meanwhile *what* were the true duty of a man ; were it to stand utterly aloof from Politics—not ephemeral only, for that of course, but generally from all speculation about so called systems, etc., etc.—or is not perhaps the very want of this time, an infinite want of Governors, of Knowledge how to govern itself ? Canst *thou* in any measure spread abroad Reverence over the hearts of men ? That were a far higher task than *any* other. Is it to be done by Art ; or are men's minds as yet shut to Art, and open only at best to oratory ; not fit for a *Meister*, but only for a better and better Teufelsdroeck? *Denk' und schweig.*' (Think and be silent).

The political excitement made lecturing as unprofitable as writing books ; and tho' Dr. John Carlyle's success removed immediate stringency, Carlyle had to earn one or two hundred pounds a year for self and wife, and his only way to do it then was by writing what editors wanted.

He did not count on any official employment, and none was ever offered him. But Jeffrey was calling often, twice a week when in London and well, and Basil Montagu repeatedly urged,—" Apply to the Lord Advocate for the Registrarship in one of the six new Bankruptcy Courts." A letter from Mrs. Montagu containing her husband's suggestion Carlyle did at last pass on to Jeffrey, and Montagu had the pleasure of testifying to Carlyle's abundant fitness Jeffrey engaged to speak of it, and did so ; tho' as Carlyle wrote to John in October,—" he seemed to think with my-self that there was hardly any hope in it." Assuredly if fitness were the test, Carlyle was an ideal candidate ; but nothing happened. Brougham was as little drawn to him as he to Brougham. For which we may be thankful.

V

JEFFREY SUFFERING

(1831)

MRS. Carlyle soon discovered the newspapers had been right, Jeffrey was ill, undergoing a painful operation about the time she arrived.[1] She offered to help, being handy at nursing; but Mrs. Jeffrey did not want to be bothered with her; and as soon as he could, Jeffrey himself wrote (11.10.1831) :—

'MY DEAR CHILD,
'How ill I must be when I had rather not see you ? Most of my forenoons are spent in *agonies* which it would grieve you to witness, and which your presence would rather aggravate than relieve. If I have an hour's lulling of the pain before dark I must spend it in dictating *necessary* letters, and in the evening, I am stupified with *laudanum*, and so worn out that I am not fit for conversation. So we must wait a little. I shall send to you as soon as I can talk to you. My heart feels the kindness of your offer to come to me—and the truth. *Violent* pain annihilates everything but itself, but in its remissions it is sweet to think of those we love. May you never be incapable of thinking of them ! There is no evil whatever to be compared to long continued violent pain. You and C. think this a sad heresy, and God grant you may never be forced to adopt it. I have had a dreadful day. But by dint of opium, my state is now bearable. It is a miserable existence. But either the pain or I must soon wear out now. Heaven bless and protect you.

Ever affectly yours,
F. JEFFREY.'

It was the pain that wore out first. He called at their lodgings, 4, Ampton Street, Gray's Inn Road, as soon and

[1] Cockburn's *Life of Lord Jeffrey*, I, pp. 323-4.

as often as he could, and corresponded diligently with
Mrs. Carlyle, tho' everything he wrote was plainly meant
for both, and once indeed he said so,—" Does not Carlyle
know yet that *you* is a *plural* pronoun ? Or *dual* at all
events ? " This was from Wimbledon and may have
referred to an invitation to spend there " a day or two
with us." He poked fun occasionally, as on 31.10.1831 :—
" How do you like London ? I am afraid you live too much
with crazy or half crazy people."

On   Thursday,   17.11.1831,   he   concluded :—" With
kindest love to Carlyle, for whom alas, I have no tidings,
from Chancellors (about a post) or booksellers (about
Sartor)." This letter was to announce a call on Saturday.—

' Have we indeed been two months within reach of each
other, and met only two or three times ? Shame, and why
has this been ? You will say it has not been your fault.
But let us talk not of faults. I told you not to come when
I was in agonies, and you never came at all, and I was three
times at your door, and never found it open, and you live
and are occupied with people I cannot care about, and
I feel, or fancy, that you are cold or scornful to me, and
the things to which I am devoted—and this brings ice
about my heart, and you do not care that it should be melted!
Oh, the folly of these repulsions in such a world as this !
But I will think no more of them, and I am coming to
see you.'

He discovered in time it was the same " repulsion "
which kept Mrs. Jeffrey out of Mrs. Carlyle's house and
Mrs. Carlyle out of Mrs. Jeffrey's. " It is the pillow that
sunders families," say the Muslims. But in this instance,
as Mrs. Jeffrey always liked and welcomed Carlyle, and
Mrs. Carlyle always liked and welcomed Jeffrey, the men
had the rare good fortune of being able to continue friends
in spite of the armed neutrality of their wives.[1]

When he paid the promised call, she was down with
influenza and he could not see her. So on Monday,
21.11.1831, sending a tempting description of Wimbledon,
to which they were both invited, he recanted the blame in

---

[1] See Footnote 1, p. 53. Such sentiments are generally reciprocal. Both
ladies deserve praise for self-control.

his last letter with a perfection of politeness worthy of such a " God-like Ariel."—

' I hope you are better, my dear child. I cannot tell you how my heart sank, when I found' (you were ill, in short). ' I wrote you a foolish, pettish, unreasonable note the other day. I suppose I am not quite recovered, when I write in that way. Will you—*haud ignara mali*—allow me this unhappy privilege of infirmity ? I daresay I do not deserve it. But we shall settle this, with our other scores, when I can have one half hour's quiet talk with you. When shall this be ?' (Then came the invitation.) ' But at all events I shall call again about 2 on Thursday . . .'

" *Haud ignara mali*," not unacquainted with suffering, was a pretty touch. The use of Latin tags was then the freemasons' slang of " educated " men in England,—he was treating her as an intellectual equal, which was what she liked the best.

VI

BADAMS AND LAMB AT HOME

(1831)

IT is likely to have been when the Carlyles were at Enfield, that Jeffrey called three times running and found them not at home. They stayed three or four days with Badams and his wife, and saw as much as they wanted of Charles Lamb, who came daily with his sister in honour of such a visitor, and did not seem the best company one could have wished for Badams when he was drowning himself in brandy. Unlimited gin and good listeners exhilarated Lamb, and as long as he could keep his head above the flood he amiably tried to amuse.

" There are just two things I regret in English history," said he. " First, that Guy Fawkes's plot did not take effect. There would have been so glorious an explosion. Secondly, that the Royalists did not hang Milton. Then we might have laughed at them," and so on, and so on. The poor fellow was trying to be funny.

Carlyle was curious about Hazlitt, recently dead and long a friend of Lamb ; but the old joker could not or would not tell anything worth hearing,—would do nothing but be witty by denying truisms and abjuring good manners. One evening, when Mrs. Carlyle's porridge was placed before her on the supper table, " Let us taste the stuff anyhow ! " cried Lamb, and dipped his spoon into her bowl.

" Your astonishment at my porridge," said she, " cannot exceed my surprise at your manners," and she had her bowl removed ; but happily for his own comfort, Lamb was too drunk to be much distressed at the snub, and maybe never knew it, and came again with his sister, " daily or oftener." He was " Cockney to the marrow," and applause had turned his head : " He was the *leanest* of mankind, tiny black breeches buttoned to the kneecap and no further, surmounting spindle legs also in black, face and

head fineish, black, bony, lean, and of a Jew type rather ;
in the eyes a kind of *smoky* brightness or confused sharpness;
spoke with a stutter ; in walking tottered and shuffled :
emblem of imbecility bodily and spiritual, and yet something too of humane, ingenuous, pathetic, sportfully
much-enduring."

Mr. Lucas canonizing him declares he " cannot say
where Carlyle gathered his information as to Lamb's
hopeless drunkenness," and he puts it down to " tattlers "
and " gossip," which is absurd, and talks of Carlyle making
an " attack " [1] when in truth he never wrote or spoke about
the man in public, [2] criticised him only in private, and never
said anything that was doubtful or ill-natured. Drunkenness was fashionable then, and Lamb never dreamed of
concealing such an amiable weakness. Walking with Dr.
John Carlyle in London, he dived into one pub after another
for a pot of porter till he could carry no more. [3] At Badams's
and other houses, he clamoured for more gin till he was
happy, as Lucas might ask for another cup of tea. Mrs.
Procter wrote to Mrs. Jameson that he dined at her house
at five o'clock, and by seven was so drunk that he could
not stand, so that he had to be taken to the drawing-room
on the back of Martin Burney like a sack of coals, while
he amused the company by singing :—

> " Diddle, diddle, dumpty, my son John
> Went to bed with his trousers on,
> One shoe off and another shoe on,—
> Diddle, diddle, dumpty, my son John."

He slept till ten o'clock, and awakened " more tipsy
than before," and between his fits of beating Martin Burney
he kept saying, " Please God, I never enter this cursed
house again." He wrote a note the next day begging
pardon, and asking when he may come again. [4] But that
was because he cursed the house. It never occurred to
him to apologize for being fuddled. O these biographers !

[1] *Life of Charles Lamb*, by E. V. Lucas, pp. 638–641.

[2] It was Froude and not T. C. who *published* it.

[3] Told with many similar details by Dr. John C. to David Masson, who
told D. A. W.

[4] See for both this letter and the porridge incident, a footnote, pp. 218
and 219 of the Grolier Club's (1898) edition of Carlyle's *Two Note Books*,
edited by C. E. Norton.

VII

D'EICHTHAL AND OTHERS

(1831)

THO' Enfield disappointed them, London was a continual treat. There were callers at their lodgings in Ampton Street nearly every day, which comforted Mrs. Carlyle for what she suffered from the detestable climate. Early in November, Charles Buller dropped in, "a great tower of a fellow, six feet three in height, a yard in breadth," and full of talent and goodness likely to be turned to "notable account." His friend John Mill came in an hour after, and they sat talking oblivious of time, making what Mrs. Carlyle said was "a pleasant forenoon call of seven hours and a half."

It was by Mill's contrivance that, on 10.11.1831, Henry Taylor of the Colonial Office gave a breakfast in honour of Carlyle to some friendly "parliamentary, diplomatic young men, of pleasant easy manners." It was Mill too that satisfied Carlyle's curiosity about Ebenezer Elliott of the Corn-Law Rhymes, and in curious contrast to the men at Taylor's, brought to his lodgings Detrosier, a "Manchester lecturer to the working classes." Still more uncommon were "the most interesting acquaintances we have made," according to Mrs. Carlyle,—two of the Saint Simonians. "Fancy how my heart beat," she wrote to her sister-in-law, Jane the lesser, "when a card bearing the name of Gustave D'Eichthal was sent up. I happened to be alone." She gave him and his companion a cordial welcome, and they talked at large with pleasure till Carlyle arrived. She said,—"He is a creature to love at first sight, so gentle and trustful and earnest-looking, ready to do and suffer all for his faith." His friend Duverrier seemed a stronger man, "prepossessing and commanding," tho' unluckily "pitted with the small-pox."

In 1921 Saint-Simon is reported to be a favourite author—in translations—in China! At any rate the bright young

" martyr " souls, whom his teaching and example kindled, embodied the best of the humane enthusiasm of the French, which the wars of Napoleon had almost obliterated from German and English minds. After all, our own George and the German kings had begun the killing, and Napoleon was their making. The endeavours of Goethe to make literary material of the French Revolution had all failed as they deserved, for fiction is the art of showing types, and the one thing sure about the French Revolution of 1789 was that it was peculiar, and needed to be studied before it could be explained. Carlyle was at the right distance from it, just as far as Herodotus from the Persian War, and more than any other event in history, it had made the world intelligible to him, confirming his faith in the justice of Heaven. However, he was now about to discover that a living faith of that sort was not of much use to one who wanted to live by writing for the *Edinburgh Review*.

VIII

CHARACTERISTICS

(1831)

THE essay on Mr. Hope's three volumes Carlyle called " Characteristics," and dispatched on 17.12. 1831 with leave to Napier to refuse it, but not to alter a word. The editor pleaded in vain for another title,—and said, " I do not understand it, but it has the stamp of genius." Byron himself was never more " devil-may-care " than this contributor, who wrote to his brother in correcting the proofs :—" Napier receives it with respect, yet finds it ' inscrutable ' on a first persual : my own fear was that it might be too *scrutable* ; for it indicates decisively enough that Society—in my view—is utterly condemned to destruction, and even now beginning its long travail throes of Newbirth."

Tho' much in it has been assimilated and seems common-place now, it is easy to see why the Whig contributors to the *Review* were shocked at the editor's obtuseness in passing it. He had hoped metaphysics was a subject on which Carlyle would be harmless ; and the essay is a masterpiece on Metaphysics, but it was too downright for the Whigs.

Philosophically its purport is the use and abuse of self-consciousness, the necessary limits of knowledge and thought, and the morbid condition of Society.

Carlyle rebuking self-consciousness is like Satan rebuking sin. He had been too self-conscious, himself, from sick-ness and juvenile religion, and was all the more earnest now in denouncing such a bad habit, exactly as St. Augustine had noticed himself extra emphatic against sins like his own, and the drunkard reformed makes the strong teetotaller.—

' The healthy know not of their health, but only the sick ; this holds no less in moral, intellectual, political, poeti-cal, than in merely corporeal therapeutics. The sign of health

is Unconsciousness.   The healthy Understanding is not the
Logical, argumentative, but the Intuitive ; for the end of
Understanding is not to prove and find reasons, but to
know and believe.   Thus the Irrefragable Doctor is often
futile, while by some winged word of a Luther, a Napoleon,
a Goethe, shall we see the difficulty split asunder.

' Let the free, reasonable Will, which dwells in us, as in
our Holy of Holies, be indeed free, and obeyed.'

There was some excuse for a suspicion of cant in his
insistence on " faith " being what keeps " the heart within
peaceable and resolved."   He shrank as if by instinct
from anything that might unsettle simple Christians,
but clearly enough implied what he did not say plainly,—
that the " faith " required was not any kind of orthodoxy,
but sincerity and what might or might not be contained
in orthodoxy,—the courage to do right without counting
costs, the feeling that the Soul of the World is just.

What shocked the politicians was his plain-dealing in
politics and economics, for he roundly wrote :—" In
the highest stage of civilisation, nine-tenths of mankind
have to struggle in the lowest battle of savage or even
animal man, the battle against famine."   A sentence
like that in a fashionable quarterly seemed out of place,
like dirty rags in the drawing room.

What horrified them delighted Leigh Hunt, who sent
Carlyle one of his books and came to see him and became
his friend for life [1] ; but Macaulay wrote to Napier :—[2]

' As for Carlyle, he might as well write in Irving's unknown
tongue at once.   The *Sun* newspaper, with delicious
absurdity, attributes his articles to Lord Brougham.'

Which may be why Brougham was cursing both
Carlyle and the *Sun*, to say nothing of editor Napier, to
whom Jeffrey was moved to write in sorrow more than
in anger, on sight of this essay, (7.2.1832) :—[3]

' *I fear Carlyle will not do*,[4] that is, if you do not take
the liberties and the pains with him that I did, by

---

[1] *Correspondence of Leigh Hunt*, I, p. 321 etc., and *Autobiography* chap.
XXIV, and the Carlyle *Letters*, etc.

[2] *Correspondence of MacVey Napier*, p. 122.

[3] *Ditto*, p. 126.

[4] Italics added.

striking out freely and writing in occasionally. The misfortune is that he is very obstinate and, I am afraid, conceited, and unluckily in a place like this, he finds people enough to abet and applaud him, to intercept the operation of the otherwise infallible remedy of general avoidance and neglect. It is a great pity, for he is a man of genius and industry, and with the capacity of being an elegant and impressive writer.'

As Napier was not allowed to take any " liberties," he saw his way now clear, and the *Edinburgh Review* printed no more for Carlyle except an article on Corn Law Rhymes already arranged. Carlyle does not appear to have suspected that long-nosed " Naso " had any other reason than natural stinginess or lack of cash for paying him badly, and never solicited him. He thought as little as possible about money and was stand-off with editors. Thus when Procter now let him know that Bulwer Lytton had " some disposition " to employ him in the *New Monthly*, and that it would be advisable to call, he answered nothing and did not call until, as he told his brother, " the mystagogue of the dandiacal body wrote to me a most bland and euphuistically flattering note, soliciting an interview as my ' admirer '."

IX

HAYWARD THE MOCKER NOT MOCKING

(1831–32)

DINING out this winter Carlyle met Abraham Hayward, the editor of a successful quarterly *Law Magazine*, who had learned in Germany to appreciate " Faust " and was now putting finishing touches to his own version of it. His translation pleased Carlyle so well that it saved him from making another, and the " vivacious " Hayward took to Carlyle " by a strange impetus," as he had never taken to anybody before. On hearing of the *History of German Literature* which had missed its market, he hurried of his own motion to the prosperous editor and Professor, Lardner, who had two interviews with Carlyle and all but settled to pay £300 for a two-volume History, to appear in his Cyclopaedia or Cabinet Library. Carlyle was calculating that he would only need to add about 170 pages to what he had done, and " thereby get my hands washed of German, and my whole say about it honourably said ". Tho' Lardner dropped the business, the spontaneous kindness of Hayward was not forgotten. The friendly acquaintance thus begun continued forty years.

Carlyle was twice at least in his rooms this winter. " A set of Oxonian Templars " were dining there on the first occasion, " stupid in part, limited wholly, conceited, obscene," tho' likely to be above the average of Oxford, were it only because they were Hayward's friends. The Rhadamanthine journal goes on.—" A dirty evening ; I at last sank utterly silent," or turned to Mr. Bernays (Professor of German in King's College). He " could *say* little tho' in many words." Which makes one feel as if one knew him,—a common type.

Another evening was more prosperous, the fellow guest being Sir Alexander Johnston, who had worked long and well in Ceylon, and when a student in Germany had been acquainted with Schiller.

On Friday, 6.1.1832, the *Athenaeum* had the name of Carlyle in large letters. Carlyle saw it in the Strand, and wrote in his journal a week afterwards that on sight of it, he " hurried on with downcast eyes, as if I had seen myself in the Pillory. Dilke (had) asked me for a scrap of writing with my *name* : I could not quite clearly see my way through the business—for he had twice or thrice been civil to me. I gave him *Faust's Curse,* which hung printed there. Incline now to believe that I did wrong ; at least imprudently. Why yield even a hair's-breadth to Puffing ? Abhor it, utterly divorce it, and kick it to the Devil ! This little adventure, however, *hat nichts zu bedeuten* " (is of no consequence).

X

DR. JOHNSON, &c.

(1831–32)

"I SHALL meddle with nothing more till I have a better *workshop*," he wrote to his brother in December, when finishing *Characteristics* ; but Fraser then sent him Croker's *Boswell's Johnson*, and where could he find a better place than London for writing on the great Londoner ? As " plenty of magazine editors " were applying to him, and any of them would be glad to get a review of the work of Croker, a conspicuous politician, Carlyle asked himself,—" Am I bound to give Fraser the article ? " He gave Fraser the benefit of the doubt.

He had long felt ready to write on Johnson, and nothing could stop him now ; but before he began he received from Bulwer Lytton (11.1.1832) a curious proposal which was new to him.— [1]

' If you are disposed to undertake for the March number of the N.M. (New Monthly) Mag., the life of Frederick the Great—I beg to say that I would in no way tie you down as to quantity.—But you can make it the same length that you would in a quarterly review.—It is a fine subject.'

One Sunday this winter, Rogers asked Jeffrey what manner of man Carlyle could be, who wrote so good a Life of Schiller, and Jeffrey in reply " praised him very much," and reported to Mrs. Carlyle he had done so.

One morning about the turn of the year,—for reading Croker and the many books mentioned by Croker was work for weeks,— Carlyle went searching for Johnson's places of abode, in the company of one Glen, a " disciple "—a young man " reading law "—and found the house off Fleet Street, where the dictionary was composed. A man

---

[1] Unpublished letter addressed to T. C., 4, Ampton St., Gray's Inn Road.

they questioned, just scraping his feet at the door, was the landlord and invited them in.—" Here, you see, this bedroom was the doctor's study, and that was the garden where he walked for exercise," a little backyard ! " These three garret bedrooms were the place he kept his pupils in," said the landlord, supposing Dr. Johnson a school-master, and the dictionary copyists his pupils. " I have spent many a pound and penny on it since then. I let it all in lodgings to respectable gentlemen ; by the quarter or the month ; it's all one to me."

London did not suit antiquarian research as well as Annandale. The answer " Don't know " was commoner in London than anywhere ; but " old Smith of the Museum " was helpful ; and groping after vestiges of the past Carlyle discovered the very room wherein Johnson's friend Savage was born, " one of the horridest holes in London." As he read about days that were gone and went about looking at their relics, he noted :—" The World grows to me ever more as a Magic Picture, a true Supernatural Revelation, stern but grand. Shall I ever succeed in copying a little therefrom ? "

ACQUAINTANCES OLD AND NEW

(1832)

BY Friday, (20.1.1832), he had started writing and felt lonely, falling back, as if at Craigenputtock, upon the "Communion of Saints" he found in books. Yet they had " company enough." On that Friday afternoon came Jeffrey, " very lively," and glad to hear Carlyle's remarks on Cholera, presumably the same as he had been sending to his mother.—" It is a disease of no such terrific quality, only that its effect is sudden, and the people have heard so much about it. Scarcely a year but there is a *typhus fever* in Glasgow or Edinburgh that kills far *more* than the Cholera does." And again :—" When was Death not here ? This Cholera is little else, if one look at it, than an opening of men's eyes to behold what their usual blindness prevents them from observing ; that their Life hangs by a single hair ; that Death is *great*, and forever *close* at their hand."

As usual he escorted Jeffrey most of the way home. Some of their " hurried assiduous talk on this occasion " is interesting.

Jeffrey :—" Sheil was once *convicted of a lie* : it was some story he told of police tortures or such like, in the Catholic Association ; (after) having been that very day *convinced* that it was not true." (How could Jeffrey or any other know he was "convinced " ?)

Carlyle :—" O'Connell is a real specimen of the almost obsolete species, *Demagogue*. His cunning is the sign, as cunning ever is, of a *weak* intellect, as of a weak character."

He asked why more appeals came to the " Lords " from Scotland than from Ireland, and Jeffrey said :—" The Irish Courts are identical (in rules and law) with the English. (So) their decisions are little apt to be reversed. (Whereas) in any Scotch case, from the Chancellor's ignorance, there is a *chance*—like the throwing of dice—that he may decide either way. Eldon often decided palpably wrong." Which is a very good reason for Home Rule for Scotland.

Then Jeffrey went on to curse " the whole system of English Law," as not only worse than the Scotch, but also so bad as to justify " a fixed spirit of revolt in the minds of all men.—It must be totally new-made. In my younger days, it was said if you had a contention about £30, let it go either way, do not enter Court at all : *now* the £30 has become £80, and the advice is repeated with that variation. Very bad." There have been reforms enough since then, but Brougham as a law-reformer was not equal to Frederick, and our " laws" are still too like a hereditary disease.

When Carlyle came home, Gustave D'Eichthal the Saint-Simonian was awaiting him. They had a long talk in French and English. D'Eichthal's ideas were narrow, but he seemed to be a new-fashioned " pure martyr and apostle."

He was not long away before Arthur Buller arrived— the younger of the two ex-pupils and now a " promising " and " handsome " fellow. He brought a companion, " my best friend," and Carlyle being booked for a dinner-party at Fraser's in Regent Street, they walked with him to the door of the shop, " and there took leave with stipulation of speedy re-meeting."

William Fraser and Allan Cunningham were the only two already known to Carlyle, of those he found in the back-room where they dined. The poet Hogg was in the easy chair of honour, enduring by not heeding the " not very malicious " banter of Lockhart and the rest, and singing his own songs after dinner with feeling. Novelist Galt had the sedate air of a " Greenock burgher, mouth indicating sly humour and self-satisfaction." He was somewhat deaf. He and Fraser kept Carlyle company in holding back from the smut that emerged when whisky punch began to loosen the tongues of the others, who did not notice them.

Next Sunday (22.1.1832), a letter arrived from John in Italy, and tho' Carlyle was loath to " waste " his working time on letters, he started in the forenoon to write one to his mother to accompany John's, which had to be sent on at once. But Sunday was more than week-days liable to interruption ; and while he was writing, in came various callers, followed by John Mill and Detrosier ; and then

Gustave D'Eichthal.   When they departed it was time for dinner, after which he hastened to add as much as possible to the home letter before tea.   It was not finished till Monday, for after tea, off went Carlyle and his wife together to hear Robert Owen of Lanark lecturing—" preaching " he called it in writing to his mother.

What he intended to be the beginning of his *Dr. Johnson* was cut off and published in advance as an essay on Biography,—an argument that biographies were the essence of history and of " all Art too."   In the style of *Sartor*, he assigned to an imaginary Professor Sauerteig (sour dough or leaven), a declaration that nothing mattered but reality, and that the right sort of man should say and write nothing but what he believed.

It was an old story in China ; but it sounded strange and new in western literary circles.   The usual defence of fiction, that it sets forth typical characters, was ignored. Sauertieg insists that even Homer was " hollow and false " so far as he did not believe his story, and classes Shakespeare himself among the fictioneers, tho' at the top, while he puts the fashionable novelists at the bottom.

Such were the thoughts Carlyle had been articulating amidst interruptions, when he went on Sunday evening for a rest to listen to Owen's plans for renovating society. He was calculating on going home soon and having many more talks with his father, to whose strongest conviction he was now returning,—there is nothing fine but fact, and fiction's fudge ;—but his father had died that morning.

XII

DEATH OF HIS FATHER

(1832)

IN the Ampton Street lodgings Carlyle had no back-yard to smoke in, and his wife did not allow the pipe in their rooms. So he used to go to the top of the cistern behind the house and sit smoking there " like the emblem over a tobacconist's door." [1] While thus engaged on Tuesday, 24.1.1832, he heard the postman's knock and hastened in, supposing it might be a letter from Scotsbrig. It was from his sister Jean. He found it open in his wife's hands, and she was weeping :—

Sunday, 22.1.1832.

' Father took a severe cold last Monday, got only one right night's sleep since he turned ill, sometimes insensible. The doctor durst do nothing.

' Last night he fell into a sort of stupor about ten o'clock, breathing higher and with greater difficulty. He spoke little to any of us. Seemingly unconscious of what he did, he came over the bedside, and offered up a prayer. He departed almost without a struggle this morning at half-past six. The funeral is to be on Friday ; but my mother says she cannot expect you to be here. Write to her directly.'

" When the news first reached me," wrote Carlyle to his brother John in Rome three weeks later, " I sat silent some minutes, the word ' telos ' (the end) pealing mournfully through my heart till tears and sobs gave me relief." He laid his work aside and wrote to his mother at once, confessing to her, he got " little relief from tears," and copiously saying whatever he could think of as likely to comfort her, and adding :—" I have given orders that

---

[1] *Early Letters of Jane Welsh Carlyle*, by D. G. Ritchie, pp. 202-3.

T

no one is to be admitted here till after the funeral on Friday. After Friday I return, as you too must, to my wordly work ; for that, also, is work appointed us by the heavenly Taskmaster."

After finishing letters, Carlyle began to write reminiscences of his father, which may have been suggested by what appears in Boswell's book, the advice which Dr. Johnson gave his friend John Elphinstone in June, 1750 :—

' You have lost an excellent mother. . . .

' There is one expedient by which you may, in some degree, continue her presence. If you write down minutely what you remember of her from your earliest years, you will read it with great pleasure, and receive from it many hints of soothing recollection, when time shall remove her yet farther from you, and your grief shall be matured to veneration. To this, however painful for the present, I cannot but advise you, as a source of comfort and satisfaction in the time to come.'

In some such spirit Carlyle wrote the memoir of his father. In leaving by his will his papers to his brother John, he mentioned it as the only one " of moment," saying it was " most likely *un*fit for printing ; but to be taken charge of and preserved in the Family." It is the best bit of the *Reminiscences*, and a " permanent addition to literature," say the critics, and if they are right it illustrates the doctrine of *Characteristics*, for it was not intended to be printed at all.

He told his mother the only interruption of the seclusion in which he and his wife were living.—

' Since I wrote last I have been in Scotsbrig more than in London. . . . Edward Irving on sending up his name was admitted to me on Friday afternoon. His wife was with him. He prayed with us I think about the time they would be in the churchyard. I felt that he meant kindly ; yet cannot say that either his prayer or his conversation worked otherwise on me than disturbingly. His whole mind is getting miserably crippled and weakened ; his insane babble about the tongues and the like were for me like froth to the hungry and thirsty. My father was a *Man*, and should be mourned for like a man. We had to forget our well-meaning visitors, and again take counsel with ourselves, and I trust with the God that dwells in us in *silence*.

' Jane faithfully bore and suffered with me. We spoke much. I trust that she, too, is one day to " become perfect through suffering," and even on this earth to struggle unweariedly towards perfection as towards the one thing needful. In our two fathers we found a great similarity. Both were *true* men.

' God hath done all things well. Let us rest here ; it is the anchor of the soul.'

About this time Carlyle and his wife walked along Holborn into the city, arm-in-arm, as was the fashion then, and came upon two boys fighting, with a ring of grinning blackguards round them. He rushed through and tore the fighters asunder, with some passionate rebuke, whereof we hear only,—" in this world full of death," and everybody silently complied. This was like him. Fighting was the besetting sin of the Borderers, and the hatred of it, which made him so sincere and pugnaceous a peacemaker all his life, was learned from his father's example more than anything else. The writings of Voltaire and Goethe merely corroborated.

The same might be said of the earnestness which inspired his own conduct. He wrote a letter about this time to a young man, who seems to have asked advice on " entering the career of letters."

' Remember now and always that life is no idle dream, but a solemn reality, based upon Eternity, and encompassed by Eternity. Find out your task : stand to it : the night cometh when no man can work.'[1]

In his first letter to his mother after his father's death, he wrote :—" Could I write my books as he built his houses, and walk my way so manfully through this shadow world, and leave it with so little blame, it were more than all my hopes."

In the Memoir he said the same.

' The Force that had been lent my Father he honourably

[1] *Edinburgh Review*, 1881, pp. 469-470. " Some fifty years ago " is the time mentioned.

expended in manful well doing. Nothing that he undertook but he did it faithfully. I shall look on the Houses
he built with a certain proud interest : they stand
sound to the heart, all over his little district : no one that
comes after him will ever say, Here was the finger of a
hollow Eye-servant. They are little texts, for me, of the
Gospel of man's Free-will. I owe him a noble inspiring
example.'

Which recalls the maxim in the Chinese Bible :—

" Remember aye your good forebears—
Behave like worthy sons of theirs."

XIII

CARLYLE AND MACAULAY ON JOHNSON, &c.

(1832)

THE interrupted work was resumed and quickly done. In the midst of it he breakfasted several times with H. Crabb Robinson, from whose diary we learn that he said at table (11.2.1832).—" Edward Irving is quite mad on the subject of the unknown tongues and therefore incurable. He has so connected this with Christianity that he cannot separate the one from the other."

Crabb Robinson describes Carlyle (12.2.1832) :—

' I had an interesting morning with him. He is a deep-thinking German scholar, a character, and a singular compound. His voice and manner, and even the style of his conversation, are those of a religious zealot, and he keeps up that character in his declamations against the anti-religious. And yet, if not the god of his idolatry, at least he has a priest and prophet of his church in Goethe, of whose profound wisdom he speaks like an enthusiast. *But for him, Carlyle says, he should not now be alive.*[1] He owes everything to him ! But in strange union with such idolatry in his admiration of Buonaparte. Another object of his eulogy is—Cobbett, whom he praises for his humanity and love of the poor ! Singular, and even whimsical, combinations of love and reverence these.' [2]

A day or two after this James Fraser called and persuaded him to write a short essay to introduce a portrait of Goethe in the magazine. He coupled Goethe with Napoleon as the " two great men " of the time. By the help of Mrs. Carlyle, Fraser also induced him to " stand for his picture,"

---

[1] Italics added.
[2] H. Crabb Robinson's *Diary, etc.*, III., p. 2, and the *London Mercury Mag.*, October, 1922, pp. 609–610.

and the clever Maclise " in about twenty minutes," [1] produced the best likeness of Carlyle in his prime.

The article on Dr. Johnson was finished about 8.3.1832 and sent to press at once, in time to be published in *Fraser's Magazine* little later than Macaulay's in the *Edinburgh Review*. A new edition of Boswell's Johnson had been hailed as an event because Mr. Croker, the editor, was a conspicuous Tory politician, and the critics were all in full cry then on one side or the other.

Macaulay's biographer, comparing his essay with Carlyle's, is careful to note :—" The two critics seem to have arrived at much the same conclusion as to the merits of the work ;" which is true. They agreed that Croker's edition was the worst in the market. But even in dealing with the unfortunate politician, and still more about Boswell and then Johnson, the difference between Carlyle and Macaulay is like that between an impartial judge and a partisan advocate. " The right kind of man," said Confucius, " is instinctively impartial,—he looks to principles and not to persons, whereas the common man is the reverse, —he is for ever taking sides."

Macaulay maintained that Boswell wrote the best biography in English by dint of his defects, his shamelessness and other weaknesses. " If he had not been a great fool, he would never have been a great writer." Carlyle's case was that Boswell succeeded in spite of his defects, because he " had an ' open sense,' an open loving heart, which so few have : " and a reverence for real worth which mastered his vanity and the prejudices of his education and position. A plainer issue was never joined, and time has settled it. The imitators of Boswell, thick as the motes that people the sunbeam, have mimicked all his faults and follies, but none of them has made a book like his ; whereas Carlyle, whose failings were entirely different, has more than equalled Boswell's achievement by genius, truthfulness and reverence for worth. It is true that neither Sterling nor Cromwell nor Frederick was in himself so interesting as Johnson ; and a biographer is like a portrait painter,—a great subject is needed for a great picture ; but compared to Carlyle, Boswell is like a painter who has done only one great portrait, while

---

[1] W. Allingham, *A Diary*, p. 203 ; and contemporary letters. See Frontispiece to *Carlyle Till Marriage*.

Carlyle is a Rembrandt whose work is like a mirror of the living world.

Macaulay missed the meaning of Dr. Johnson too, caricaturing the outside of the man, and leaving as much a mystery as ever the reason why he had long been an oracle of the English. Carlyle revealed what justified the national regard for such a typical John Bull, his truthfulness, earnest righteousness, and kindness of heart. His superstition and old-fashioned piety were genuine too, not make-believe,—the natural result of " the best intellect in England " being nursed " in the idol-cavern of a poor Tradesman's house in the Cathedral city of Lichfield." His prejudices lessened little the value of his moral wisdom. Carlyle's guess that Johnson steadied England against revolution was a novelty then, but is a commonplace to-day.

To belittle Johnson was the cue of the Whigs. Macaulay was " the man for their money." But a sincere reformer like John Mill was able to gratify Carlyle by declaring " the paper on Biography and on Johnson " better than anything " else that I have read for years past, more precious to me than I know well how to state. I have read it over and over till I could almost repeat it by heart." [1]

The *Johnson* finished, Carlyle had only to wind up his affairs in London, preparing for a summer's work at Craigenputtock. On Saturday, 17.3.1832, he saw Irishmen with shillelahs and heard it was St. Patrick's Day, as he went to the British Museum to explore what it could tell him on Diderot, about whom he was to write. Another day he was in the Commons lobby with William Fraser, when Macaulay came out from the " house " and bought two oranges.

" That is a sign," said Fraser, " that he is going to speak." They tried to get admittance in vain. Here is Carlyle's note :—

' Macaulay is a short squat thickset man of vulgar but resolute energetic appearance. Fair-complexioned, keen gray eyes, a large cylindrical head close down between two strong round shoulders ; the brow broad and fast receding, the crown flat. Inclines already to corpulence, tho' not five-and-thirty. The globular will one day be his shape, if he continue. I likened him to a managing ironmaster with vigorous talent for business (and) little look of talent

[1] *Letters of J. S. Mill*, I, pp. 26–32.

for anything else. He is the young man of most force at present before the world. Successful he may be to great lengths, or not at all, according as the times turn : meanwhile the limits of his worth are discernible enough. Great things lie not in him, intrinsically common. He is the only young man of any gift, at this period, who is a whig ; another characteristic. He may be heard of, and loudly ; but what is being heard of ? Whosoever beats a drum is heard of. Let us hope too that M. will gain better insight, a clear, manly foundation, and be what he might be : " a man among clothes-screens." ' (Which he did—as well as he could.)

He was now culminating in politics, a champion on the winning side, to be rewarded soon by a share in the " spoils." At the dinner-table old Talleyrand, who had come over to reconcile the London politicians to Louis Phillippe, and did not enjoy harangues, said Macaulay disappointed him,—" They said he was a great man, and he's only a big book." Perhaps he was remembering the description of Boileau by the mother of Voltaire,—" a clever book, but a silly man." Sydney Smith translated it and called Macaulay " a book in breeches," while Mrs. Carlyle's uncle John Welsh of Liverpool applied the phrase to Thomas Carlyle.

XIV

PARTINGS

(1832)

FOR reasons of health Carlyle and his wife were both looking forwad to a summer at Craigenputtock, and to
show how much she had suffered from continual
coughing etc., Mrs. Carlyle was fond of quoting what her
husband's old acquaintance Dr. Allen said now,—she "has
the remains of a fine woman."[1]

In the last weeks, Carlyle was more than ever in Fraser's
back-parlour in Regent Street, becoming familiar there
with William Maginn, the Rabelais from Cork who inspired
the *Magazine* and was its " Oliver Yorke,"—" a shortish,
thickset man, with a fine gray eye," who looked over forty,
but was only 39. He also had quitted teaching long ago
to pursue the " career " of letters, but by this time he was
sure of nothing but,—" punch is punch." As Lockhart
was to write,—

" Barring drinks and the girls, I ne'er heard of a sin :
Many worse, better few, than bright, broken Maginn."

He was drowning disappointments which he scarcely
articulated even to himself, for a soul of such a quality
is disinterested by instinct, and is absent-minded about
money. The tragedy of his life was typical, which explains
the earnestness of Carlyle in warning young men against
the " career " of writing for wages.

Brewster whom he also saw at Fraser's (15.3.1832) was
luckier,—" Sir David " now, " still full of projects and
purveyor activity," talking of Brougham as " *this* Chancellor," and the one that mattered, and sociably letting
Carlyle know that the great one's eye was on him.

When Irving called to bid adieu, he was in the crisis
of his fate. The managers of his church were reluctantly

---

[1] *Early Letters of Jane Welsh Carlyle*, by D. G. Ritchie, p. 199.

taking steps to turn him out, because he would not stop the
interruptions of public worship. He only needed to
promise to let them be stopped ! If ejected he would
have to depend on the fanatics for a living, and his belief
in their " tongues " was hardly more than that of Dr.
Arnold of Rugby, who thought them possibly a real miracle,
and " a sign of the coming of the day of the Lord." [1] So
Carlyle was plain-spoken, Irving sitting silent in the middle
of the floor, with downcast head and painful attentive face.
Carlyle was facing him, and Mrs. Carlyle on Irving's
right. It was not the first time they had debated the
miraculous tongues, but it was the last.

Carlyle :—" You must permit me a few words for relief
of my conscience, before leaving you for we know not what
length of time, on a course which I cannot but regard as
full of danger to you. The ' 13th of the Corinthians '
to which you always appeal is surely too narrow a basis
for so high a tower as you are building on it ;—a high lean
tower, or quasi-mast, piece added to piece, till it soars
far above all human science and experience, and flatly
contradicts all that,—founded solely on a little text of
ancient writing in an ancient book ! No sound judgment,
on such warranty, can venture on such an enterprise.
Authentic ' writings ' of the Most High, are they found in
old Books only ? They are in the stars and on the rocks,
and in the brain and heart of every mortal, — not
dubious there, to any person, as this ' 13th of the
Corinthians ' very greatly is. It does not beseem you,
Edward Irving, to be hanging on the rearward of mankind,
struggling still to chain them to old notions not now well
tenable ; but to be foremost in the van, leading on by the
light of the eternal stars, across this hideous delirious
wilderness where we all are, towards Promised Lands that
lie ahead. Bethink you, my friend, is not that your plainly
commanded duty ; more plain than any ' 13th of the
Corinthians ' can be ? I bid you pause and consider.
That verily is my solemn advice to you.

" You know very well it is in the name of old friendship
I am saying all this. I do not expect you will at once, or
soon, renounce your fixed vows, connections and methods,
for any words of mine ; but perhaps at some future time

[1] See letter of 25.10.1831 to Rev. F. C. Blackstone, pp. 174-5, of Life of
Dr. Arnold, by Dean Stanley.

of crisis and questioning dubiety in your own mind you may remember these words of a well-affected soul, and they may then be of help to you."

In the " mildest " low tone and with a " face full of kindness and composed distress," Irving began,—" Dear Friend," and stated his defence in a modest and magnanimous way Carlyle admired ; and then departed, " with kindest farewells."

Another sad parting was with Badams. When he called to say " Good-bye," he burst into tears, bemoaning the brandy that was killing him. " Pressed down like *putty* under feet," he said, " and no strength more in me to rise." " Come to Craigenputtock for the Summer," was their reply, and they used their " best temptations." He was to leave Enfield at any rate soon ; but he *would not* be persuaded. And before long he died; and Carlyle said,— he " was among the men I loved most in the world."

A. W. Schlegel, a Bonn Professor, who had translated Shakespeare, and felt *himself* " the genius of the age," was now enjoying a little lionizing in London. Carlyle left a card upon the " old fool," but thought him a snob and was glad to miss him. " He paints his face," wrote Carlyle in his diary, correctly. Heine describes him lecturing to his class in kid gloves, diffusing many fragrances around, and never naming an English Lord of the Treasury without calling him " my friend." He was now sixty-four. He received a public dinner from a Literary Union, which meant Hayward and Professor Lardner mainly ; but Carlyle escaped.

His wife and he left London on 25.3.1832, returning as they had come, by Liverpool, and in passing through Shrewsbury he chuckled to hear the coachman adjuring a dilatory person,—" Be alive ! " He was fond of quoting that coachman afterwards. No wonder ! The phrase puts the right way of thinking into a nutshell,—" Be alive ! "

XV

GOETHE, CORN-LAW RHYMES AND SMELFUNGUS

(1832)

THEY spent the first week or two with relatives. It was on 14.4.1832 that in passing through Dumfries he received the news that Goethe was dead and told a brother,—" I feel as if I had a second time lost a Father." He returned to the moors with the feeling,—" Thank Heaven, I know my trade : it is to *write truth* while I can be kept alive by so doing, and to die writing it when I can no longer be kept alive. So feeling, I look upon all mortals with the friendliest humour ; let Kings and Chancellors fight their own battles. Let the Devil go his way, and I will go mine."

A letter from Hayward in London (6.4.1832) [1] decided what he should do first.—

' Dear Carlyle, I write to beg you to exert yourself to get some degree of justice done to Göthe. Bulwer wants a paper about him—a sort of amplified necrology, giving the general features of his character and indicating the nature of his influence on the mind of Germany and indeed of Europe, would be exactly the thing ; and I told him at once that there was no living Englishman but you who could do it as it ought to be done, and Schlegel says the same. I hope therefore that the same motive that induced you to give the sketch to Fraser may induce you to take up the pen for Göthe again, for if not well done, it will be badly done by somebody, and thus the sum total of erroneous notions concerning him will be increased. It is true he is sure of righting himself with posterity, but why should his contemporaries be left unabused ? *All of us— I mean your friends and admirers here—want you to drive Blackwood (in the last No.) to his ships, or to the devil, if*

---

[1] Printed here from MS.

you like, for the wretched shallow ignorance of that last Noctes was really startling : yet it has its influence. . . . '

Carlyle was willing and sat down to write, but found it difficult to start, and moralized :—

' The whole thing I want to write seems lying in my mind ; but I *cannot get my eye on it.*   The machine is lazy, languid ; the motive principle cannot conquer the inertia.

' A question arises, whether there ought to be, in a perfect society, *any* class of purely speculative men ?   Whether all men should not be of active employment and habitude ; their speculation only growing out of their activity and incidental thereto ?

' The Grand Pulpit is now the Press ; the true Church is the Guild of Authors.

' Every man that writes is writing a new Bible ; or a new Apocrypha ; to last for a week, or for a thousand years : he that convinces a man and sets him working is the doer of a *miracle*.

' *Ought* any writing to be transacted with such intense difficulty ?   Does not the True always flow *lightly* ?

' One thing is plain : Take not *too* much care about thy writing, or aught else.   It is *trivial*, as thyself art, and will *soon* perish,—let vanity whisper what she may. Quick, then, Do it *honestly* ; *perfectly* thou wilt never do it.   Time flies ; while thou balancest a sentence, thou art nearer the *final* Period.—Cast thy thought forth with some fearlessness.

' This I must say for myself : It is seldom or never the Phraseology, but always the Insight, that fails me, and retards me.   On then ; on ! why stand describing how thou shouldst move ? Forward, and move, in *any* way.'

This was on Sunday, 22.4.1832 ; and by Thursday, 26th, he had finished a fine essay which gave satisfaction ; but what is now remarkable is what is not in it,—there was no reference to what had been in *Blackwood*.   To that extent Hayward and Bulwer would be disappointed. Tabooing strife as wrong in itself was so regularly the practice of Carlyle, however, that they would not be surprised, tho' a biographer has to confess that in this instance it did not cost Carlyle an effort to keep the peace, so great was his liking for John Wilson, the

" bully " of Blackwood's *Noctes* and the champion of
" No Change." There was a gulf between him and Carlyle,
impassable like that between Satan and St. Michael in
Byron's Vision of Judgment,—

> " Yet still, between his Darkness and his Brightness,
>   There passed a mutual glance of great politeness."

That the liking was mutual appeared in the sequel to
what Carlyle wrote next, an article on Ebenezer Elliot's
Corn Law Rhymes for Napier, who " may well be excused
for rejecting it," Carlyle confessed, " so intensely ' specu-
lative-radical ' is the whole strain of it."

" Smelfungus " appears as an alias for the writer in this
essay, a modest alias, used for forty years, and familiar
in 1832 as the name under which Smollett was ridiculed
in Sterne's *Sentimental Journey.*—

' The learned Smelfungus travelled from Boulogne to
Paris,—from Paris to Rome—and so on :—but he set out
with the spleen and jaundice ; and every object he passed
by was discoloured or distorted.—He wrote an account of
them ; but 'twas nothing but the account of his miserable
feelings.

' I met Smelfungus in the grand portico of the Pantheon :
—he was just coming out of it.—" 'Tis nothing but a huge
cock-pit," said he. " I wish you had said nothing worse
of the Venus of Medicis," replied I ; —for in passing through
Florence, I had heard he had fallen foul upon the goddess,
and used her worse than a common strumpet, without the
least provocation in nature.

' I popped upon Smelfungus again at Turin, in his return
home ; and a sad tale of sorrowful adventure he had to
tell. He had been flayed alive and bedevilled at every
stage.

' " I'll tell it," cried Smelfungus, " to the world." " You
had better tell it," said I, " to your physician." '

Goethe had felt like that at Venice in 1790, and in
writing to his employer compared himself to Smelfungus,
which may be why Carlyle assumed the nickname. It often
fitted him only too well, and there is something humble and
humane in the humour of it on many occasions.

There was no humour visible to respectable Whig readers

of this essay in 1832. It seemed shocking. There was no patronizing palaver such as befitted an Edinburgh Reviewer dealing with a working-man. On the contrary, Carlyle was mocking at Respectability and drawing attention to Elliot's advantages in having had to work, and even showing how much the rich and great might learn from him. Scoffing at 'universities in a time when Books have come into the world,' he declared ' the first principle of human culture to be that men must, before every other thing, be trained to *do* ' some useful work, and attributed much of the prevailing confusion to the neglect of this, which made "educated " people stupid. He agreed in blaming the Corn Laws, but intimated that even when ' the " Bread-tax," with various other taxes,' were abrogated, ' the diseases of a world lying in wickedness ' could not be so simply cured, but needed in politics ' a long, painful course of medicine and regimen, surgery and physic.' He insisted on the 'mournful' fact that the workers were worried about food and lodging and kept in fear of beggary, and roundly declared that ' Tools ' should now be glorified instead of ' Arms,' and preaching patience in plain words he congratulated the Corn-Law Rhymer on the spiritual achievement he had already made, in having become a ' king of his own mind and faculty. Not one in the thousand, even among sceptred kings, is king of so much.' . . .

The *Edinburgh Review* was a Whig Periodical and its Editor Napier a common conventional Whig. He passed such stuff with a groan ; but for reasons already explained was able to comfort himself that it would be the last of his afflictions of that sort. He did not want an essay on Authors which was offered next [1]; and tho' shy of saying so, he wanted nothing more from Carlyle.

In Boston the *Edinburgh Review* with this thing in it was better appreciated than at home. The Rev. R. W. Emerson of that city soliloquized in his journal on sight of it, that he was "cheered and instructed by my Germanic new-light writer, whoever he be. He gives us confidence in our principles. He assures the truth-lover everywhere of sympathy." So Emerson enquired the name of the writer before going to Europe next year.[2]

Before very long John Wilson also dealt with Elliott's

[1] *Correspondence of MacVey Napier*, pp. 129, 130.
[2] *Memoir of R. W. Emerson*, by J. E. Cabot, I, p. 193.

poetry, and disappointed Blackwood as much as Carlyle had disappointed Hayward by tabooing vituperation. Wilson did not omit to say he differed from his author about the Corn Laws, but he did so in a perfunctory way, and the little pious patter he put in was like a curate's reading prayers, while he expatiated on the literary merits of the " Rhymer," whom he classed with Cowper and Crabbe, Wordsworth and Burns, and described as " the sole and great poet of his own order, the mechanics and artisans of England." There was abundance of solid sense and eloquence in what he wrote, but nothing more eloquent than his silence towards that audacious Radical, Carlyle, as if signalling from afar,—" Whatever we differ about, we can agree about Poetry, you see, and both praise Ebenezer Elliot."

XVI

BUSINESS AND POLITICS

(1832)

THE next article commissioned was for the *Foreign Quarterly*, but before beginning it he went to Scotsbrig, to give effect to his father's will (10.5.1832). Some houses in Ecclefechan, yielding between twenty and thirty pounds a year, were left in life-rent to his mother ; and these when she died, and all other things at once, were equally divided among the five sons and daughters, Alexander and James, Mary, Jane and Janet. It was only on reading the will that Carlyle knew his father had done as he had advised,—" Leave John and me out as *our* share is already received, I having been *educated*, and John through me," while the others on the farm " helped by their toil to earn " what he had.

In a day or two everything was amicably settled. The youngest brother James was to carry on the father's farm, and his mother and unmarried sisters to stay there in the meantime. They were working women, not encumbrances. The mother herself worked both in the house and in the fields, and set a good example by being cheery. Once she had been out hoeing turnips all day, and in the evening the other workers gave her a start, and there was a merry race home to the farm-house.[1] Before long James was to take a wife and his sisters to get married, but their mother lived at Scotsbrig for the rest of her life. On the Sunday the brothers visited their aunt Mrs. Brown, whose husband had taught the mason's trade to their father and uncles. She was now in her eightieth year. She used to go about in a red cloak, and the children called her a witch.[2] She was garrulous " to endless copiousness " at sight of an audience ; but tho' " her memory seemed excellent, she

[1] Told D. A. W., July 1896, by Matthew Murray of Ecclefechan who saw and heard her.
[2] Told in 1896 by Mr. Wells of Waterbeck.

289

U

would not talk to questions." Why should she ? She enjoyed the visit, and would not make a toil of a pleasure.

Political rumours floated to Scotsbrig. The country was in confusion because the King was refusing to make new Peers enough to carry the Reform Bill, which made the ministry resign. A butcher at Annan had been sent to jail for beheading an effigy of King William. The people burned it. At Dumfries on Monday, 14.5.1832, Carlyle found Editor McDiarmid bubbling with fury at "King Arthur," meaning Wellington, who was preparing the army for civil war. He will " pass a bill, perhaps very like the other, perhaps better," said Carlyle to McDiarmid, and curiously enough that was what Peel wrote to Croker on 12th May that he would need to do, which was Peel's sufficient reason for holding back. But as yet the public did not know he was doing so, and the fright and fury of McDiarmid were common. Everybody was discussing whether the soldiers would fire on the people.

It was as sordid as anything in Tacitus. The Dizzy-Machiavelli of the day was ex-Chancellor Lyndhurst, leading King William and Wellington and the whole pack of peers. When the reformers came into power, he had jockeyed them into giving him a life-job as a judge on £7,000, because, as his biographer Lord Chancellor Campbell has explained with tender sympathy,[1] " he was exceedingly poor " as " the retired allowance for a Chancellor was then only £4,000 a year,—an income quite inadequate to support Lady Lyndhurst's fashionable establishment, so that Lyndhurst could hardly make ends meet, or " contrive to prevent executions being put into his house." He was therefore hungry to be Chancellor again, and would not have minded the slaughter of other people. But Peel would not follow him, and he had to wait, for the Peers took fright. In all directions men were resolving to desist from paying taxes, the Common Council of London petitioning Parliament to refuse supplies. The populace which had been lately cheering the King as a " Patriot " was ready to hang him now. Carlyle as usual would not be stampeded, soliloquizing in his diary :—

' Granting the King to be an Imbecile and Nonentity, has he changed so much for the worse ? Poor " Patriot

[1] *Lives of Lord Lyndhurst and Lord Brougham*, by John Lord Campbell, pp. 70–89 (1869 edn.).

King ! " The wisest man in the world might pause in that situation : what shall the foolishest do ?

'The only reform is in *thyself*. Know this, O Politician, and be moderately political. For me, I have never yet done any one political act ; not so much as the signing of a petition. My case is this : I comport myself wholly like an alien ; like a man who is not in his own country ; whose own country lies perhaps a century or two distant. When the time comes, should it ever come, that I can do *any good* in such coming forward, then let me not hang back. Meanwhile pay thy taxes to his Majesty and the rest, so long as they can force thee ; the instant they can*not* force thee, that instant cease to pay. This has been my political principle for many a year. The passing or the failing of innumerable Reform Bills might not alter it much : money is paid to him who does a service worth money ; obedience is due to him who governs : to him who wears the governor's *mask*, the *mask* of obedience,— as to the ass in lion's skin (who in any case could kick)— while you are near him.'

He did not reflect that his refusal to sign the anti-Catholic petition in 1829 was as much a political act as signing it would have been. As for never voting, he had never had a vote, and when the new Act made him eligible he paid the needful half-crown for registration. The soliloquy was not meant for any eye but his own, and shows his inmost thoughts. The crisis was passing as he was writing (16.5.1832). Wellington gave up the job, and Grey got leave to make as many peers as needful. The Reform Bill was an Act by June ; and Lyndhurst had to watch Brougham have another innings, like a dog with teeth watering, as he eyes another with a bone. How the two Woolsackers wrangled, and dropping into the truth for once, imputed bad motives and gave each other the lie, till it suited them to combine to worry common enemies, may be read in many histories, but not in this.

All there is room for is what Lyndhurst said not very long after he had missed the great place in history he had played for on this occasion, and after his expensive wife had died and been buried. Here is Mrs. Carlyle's report of what passed current in Society for many decades, and was better known than any other speech of his.[1]—

[1] Unpublished Letter.

'When Lord Lyndhurst's first wife died, old Croker,' the admirer of Chesterfield's Letters, 'put on a long face and a black coat and went to condole with his Lordship. His Lordship received his condolence with due solemnity and said in a heart-struck tone :—" My dear Croker, be kind to your wife while she is with you ! Oh, my dear fellow, love her and cherish her while she lives ! But, when she dies, don't bury her *in the country*—it has cost me fifty pounds for turnpikes, By God ! " '

XVII

HOME AGAIN

(1832)

IN craving for disciples Carlyle was more like Buddha or Confucius than a modern man of letters " on the make," as may be seen from his note-book, early in June.—

' Very kind letter from Mill, whose zealous and quite credible approbation and appropriation of *Johnson* gratifies me, I doubt, more than it should. Unspeakable is the importance of man to man. A tailor at Thornhill, who had vehemently laid to heart the *Characteristics*, was also a glad phenomenon to me. Let a million voices cry out, " How clever ! " it is still nothing ; let one voice cry out, " How true ! " it lends us quite a new force and encouragement.'

The reference is to Robert Shankland, who did tailoring for Mrs. Carlyle and her mother's family.[1] Carlyle used to " look in " upon him at Thornhill when visiting Mrs. Welsh there.

His wife's " earthquake " or spurt of housework on reaching Craigenputtock after many months in London was longer than usual ; but in June she had time to invite Eliza Miles, a daughter of the family they lodged with in Ampton Street, to visit them (16.6.1832).—

' My dear Eliza . . . I never forget my gentle Ariel in Ampton Street—it were positive sin to forget her, so helpful she was, so beautiful, so kind and good ! Besides, this is the place of all others for thinking of absent friends, where one has so seldom any present to think of. If a little while ago I was near being swept away, in the hubbub,

---

[1] *Thornhill and its Worthies*, by J. L. Waugh, p. 94.

so now I find myself in a dead calm.   All is again in order
about us, and I fold my hands and ask, What is to be
done next?   "The duty nearest hand, and the next will
show itself in course."   So my Goethe teaches.   No one
who lays the precept to heart can ever be at a stand.
Impress it on your " twenty children " (that I think was
the number you had fixed upon), impress it on the whole
twenty from the cradle upwards, and you will spare
your sons the vexation of many a wild-goose chase,
and render your daughters for ever impracticable to '
(meaning safe from) ' *ennui*.   Shame that such a malady
should exist in a Christian land ; should not only exist,
but be almost general throughout the whole female
population that is placed above the necessity of working for
daily bread.   If I have an antipathy for any class of people
it is for *fine ladies*.   I almost match my Husband's
detestation of partridge-shooting *gentlemen*.   Woe to the
fine lady who should find herself set down at Craigenputtock
for the first time in her life, left alone with her thoughts,
no " *fancy bazaar* " in the same kingdom with her ; no
place of amusement within a day's journey ;   the very
church, her last imaginable resource, seven miles off.   I
can fancy with what horror she would look on the ridge of
mountains that seemed to enclose her from all earthly
bliss ! With what despair in her accents she would inquire
if there was not even a " charity sale " within reach.   Alas,
no ! No outlet whatever for " lady's work," not even a
Book for a fine lady's understanding !   It is plain she would
have nothing for it but to die as speedily as possible, and
so relieve the world of the expense of her maintenance.
   ' For my part I am very content.   I have everything
here my heart desires, that I could have anywhere else,
except society, and even that deprivation is not to be considered wholly an evil : if people we like and take pleasure
in do not come about us here as in London, it is thankfully
to be remembered that here the "wicked cease from troubling
and the weary are at rest."   If the knocker make no sound
for weeks together, it is so much the better for my nerves.
My Husband is as good company as reasonable mortal
could desire.   Every fair morning we ride on horse-back
for an hour before breakfast (my precious horse knew me
again, and neighed loud and long when he found himself
in his old place).   Then we eat such a surprising breakfast
of home-baked bread and eggs, etc., etc., as might incite

anyone that had breakfasted so long in London to write a pastoral. Then Carlyle takes to his writing, while I, like Eve, " studious of household good," inspect my home, my garden, my live stock, gather flowers for my drawing-room, and lapfuls of eggs ; and finally take myself also to writing, or reading, or making or mending, or whatever work seems fittest.   After dinner, and only then, I lie on the sofa and (to my shame be it spoken), sometimes *sleep*, but oftenest dream waking.   In the evening I walk on the moor (how different from Holborn and the Strand !) and read anything that does nor exact much attention.   Such is my life,— agreeable as yet from its novelty, if for nothing else.   Now would you not like to share it ?   I am sure you would be happy beside us for a while, and healthy ;   for I would keep all drugs from your lips, and pour warm milk into you. Could you not find an escort, and come and try ?   At all rates, write and tell me how you are, what doing and what intending.   I shall always be interested in all that concerns you.   My health is slowly mending.   Yours affectionately, JANE CARLYLE.'

It was from this Eliza Miles, a member of Irving's church and running home once " in a tremor of tears," that Carlyle received the best report of the miracles of hysterics.   She never came to the moors,—travelling was difficult then, especially for women, and the young Mr. Snowden, who became the father of her large and prosperous family, was sufficient counter-attraction ; but she welcomed them when they returned to London and remained a friend for life.

On the same day (16.6.1832), Carlyle was writing to Mill, having recognised as his an article in the *Examiner* on Bentham, who had just died (6.6.1832) at 84, bequeathing his body to be dissected.   " Brave Bentham," wrote Carlyle now to Mill,—" All week I have thought of that Dissecting Table, with a feeling of solemnity.   A Character is a completely fashioned Will."

Which shows how Carlyle would be sincere in 1840 in the lecture-room when he exposed the nakedness of Utilitarianism, but said he intended no " offence against the man Jeremy Bentham," who was " comparatively worthy of praise." [1]

[1] Vol. III, Book XI, Chapter XXVIII ; of this *Life of Carlyle*.

BOOK X
WRITING HISTORY
1832–37

I

LANDOWNERS, AUTHORS, &c.

(1832)

THE moral murk of politics and the law has to be remembered in fairness to Jeffrey, who could not altogther escape being tainted by it, as even Shakespeare lamented he himself was by the stage. Mingling fun and earnest in a letter to Mrs. Carlyle, he alluded to her husband's rash downrightness about the legal fiction of private property in land. He was never weary of remonstrating about that, as Erasmus might have remonstrated with Luther before he blurted out the truth.

' Give my love to Carlyle. I think he liked London better than you did, and yet he profited little and probably still holds that the great . . .[1] sufferings of society are owing to . . .[1] the great . . .[1] of the nation, and to a depraved taste for preserves of pheasants and partridges among the rural proprietors, which is about as near being true as the visions of the astronomer in Rasselas. *O Caecae hominum mentes* (O the blindness of men's minds !). It always provokes me to see him throwing away great talents In about five years after my death he will come to think more as I do.'

Jeffrey was aware the *Edinburgh Review* would now taboo him and anticipated the sight of *Sartor* might make other editors do ditto. To Jeffrey as a townsman and a lawyer the land laws with all their iniquities were things to be taken for granted, like gravitation,—current conventions to be accepted, like the streets.

Carlyle had the free outlook of a villager in fresh contact with Nature, and equipped with prodigious knowledge, he was heedless of everything but seeing what was what. Far from balancing how to make Adam Smith palatable to men in power, he was noting in July :—

---

[1] Omission due to gap in paper and illegible words in MS.

' Was there ever a more merry-andrew-looking thing
—if we consider it—than for a wretched creature named
man, or gigman ' (meaning snob or " gent "), ' alighting for
one instant on this " everlasting earth " to say, it is mine !
It ! . . .

' The greatest of all past or present anti-gigmen was
Jesus Christ. This age is quite especially wrecked and
sunk in gigmanism ' (snobbery).

Then come remarks on Authors. He was contemplating an
essay upon them which was never written, because it was not
wanted. ' Homer's " Iliad " would have brought the
author, had he offered it to Mr. Murray, on the half-profit
system, say five and twenty guineas. The *Prophecies* of
Isaiah could have (been) remunerated with a five pound
note. To speak of *paying* the writer of a true Book is, on
the whole, delirium. The thing is unpayable ; the whole
world could not buy it ; could the whole world
induce him, by fee or reward, to write it *otherwise,*
opposite wise ? Then is he no writer, only a deplorable
despicable scribbler, waiting till the besom of destruction
sweep him away.

' Authors are martyrs, witnesses for the truth ; or else
nothing. Money cannot make or unmake them ; they are
made or unmade, commanded and held back by God
Almighty alone, whose inspiration it is that giveth them
understanding : yet for the world whom they address, for the
fitness of their language towards it, their clearness of insight
into its interests ; the ear *it* shall give them ; for all in
short that respects their revelation *of* themselves (not
their existence *in* themselves), money, as the epitome and
magic talisman of all Mechanical Endeavour whatsoever,
is of incalculable importance. Money cannot hire the
writing of a Book ; but it can the printing of it : the
existence of a Public Library, or non-existence thereof,
in the circle where a Thinker is born, will forward his
thinking, or obstruct and prevent it ; when the Thinker
has discovered truth, it depends on money whether the
world shall participate in such discovery, or not participate.
In how many other ways (as when your nascent wise man
is poor, solitary, uneducated, etc.), can the " Talisman of
Power " cut away impediments and open out the path !
Many a fallen *spark* too is quenched, or lives only as a
spark, which could have been fanned into a cheerful Light

and Fire, profitable for guidance, for spiritual solace. (No end to all this, which is to go into the essay on *Authors*).'

The fine air and quiet made Craigenputtock ideal for his wife's health and his own ; but the loneliness was too great, and the lack of books a continual obstruction to his work. As he wrote to John this summer,—" Why is there not a Majesty's library in every county town ? There is a Majesty's jail and gallows in every one." His appetite for books was like that of fire for fuel.

He needed no library but his own for *Goethe's Works*, which occupied him from May to July, and is now remarkable mainly for proclaiming the significance of Hero-Worship ; but when he began to work upon an essay on *Diderot*, the first preliminary was the reading of twenty-five octavo volumes. He was returning to the French, having said his say about the Germans. The French Revolution, he often said, had done more than anything else to reconcile him to reality. He was writing now on Diderot because the *Foreign Quarterly* had commissioned an article upon him ; but the attraction was that Diderot helped to cause the Revolution.

II

A MAID'S MISFORTUNE

(1832)

MEANWHILE his wife had more excitement than usual. Her maid had had almost as much leisure as herself and less to read about, and so came more into touch with neighbours, and now had to hurry home suddenly to give birth to a baby. Mrs. Carlyle had to bestir herself for a week or two, till a successor was found, and when at last at leisure for a letter to Jeffrey, which he had been begging for months past, she could not be as explicit to him as to her women friends. She seems to have copied some verses of her mother's, and whatever vague words she used in self-depreciation might be attributable—tho' he never suspected it—to a natural misgiving that she might have contributed by her negligence to her maid's " misfortune." It seemed to him she was taking too seriously her usual pose of her husband's first disciple, the dutiful wife or female saint, the perfect woman ever in distress because she is no better. So he responded in a gush of words a few of which may suffice (22.7.1832).—

' MY DEAR, DEAR FRIEND,
            ' Why is there this " numbing spell " upon our spirits ? I live indeed in another element and another sphere, and it is a strange and tantalising, and almost a fearful thing, to catch these glimpses of your strange and enchanted solitude.
    ' My life has been very much as it was. Tell me of that lone and melancholy upland, and tell me of your health and spirits. I like to think of your gallopings, but not of your musings at home. You must allow me to regret that you are not more cheerful and more social, that you are not more satisfied with what you do, and are obliged to seek pardon and indulgence for not performing more adequately a task which has never been laid upon you

but in fancy. O my dear Friend, be happy ; and believe
that all opinions *must* be false which tend to depress an
innocent spirit, and to impose upon a conscience void of
offence a conviction that it is chargeable with blameful
want of exertion.

' I called the other day on Mrs. Austin. Is not she
imaginative and mystical enough for you ? Yet she wears
her mind open to the enjoyments and even to the *vanities*
of the world you despise. Come to Craigcrook. Kind
love to Carlyle.'

Carlyle was soliloquizing (8.8.1832) :—

' I cannot understand *Morals*. Our current Moral Law
(even that of philosophers) affronts me with all manner of
perplexities. *Punishment* neither is nor can be in proportion to the fault ; for the commonest of all examples, take
the case of an erring woman. Ought there to *be* any
unpardonable offence ? Ought the judge in any case to
say irrevocably, *Be Thou Outcast* (as proud fathers have
done to erring daughters for instance) ? The World has
declared, Yes. Neither is there wanting some ground for
it. Necessity rules our existence : Man should step in
and be as stern as Necessity, and *take the word out of its mouth*.
Perhaps ; yet not with clear certainty. This is the " Place
of Hope." Should man's mind have sudden boundless
transitions of that sort ; have *vaporific points*, and *freezing
points*, or should it not ? *Weiss nicht* (don't know). It
is all confused to me : seems to be all refounding itself.
Happily the practical is nowise dubious.

' Toleration, too, is miserably mistaken ; means for most
part only indifference and contempt. What is bad *is*
a thing to be the sooner the better *abolished*.

' *Great* is self-denial ! Practise it where thou needest it.
Life goes all to ravels and tatters where that enters not.
The old monks meant very wisely : hit thou the just
medium.'

Which was wise but too widely worded—there were monks
and monks.

III

"DIDEROT", &c.

(1832)

HE remarked in a letter to John in August :—" I need not trouble you with the Reform Bill rejoicings— and then, alas ! with the electioneerings. *It is here that the Reform Bill comes to the test. Set the angel Gabriel to elect a Parliament : how shall he succeed when there is none to elect ?* "[1] Or, as he soon wrote to Mill :—" O for a few members *worth* electing ! But patience ; these are coming." Here is a new clue to English history. The representation of course remained a sham. The " Reform " was deliberately arranged to keep the electors from choosing any but rich men or their like. But even when representation is perfect, there must be good men available before such can be elected. Thus it was easy for such as Carlyle to keep cool, while welcoming the signs of change, tho' most of the younger men caught the public excitement and shared the public hopes. Thackeray who was not yet twenty-one was delighted to oblige his friend Charles Buller, and go down to Liskeard and plunge into electioneering, which is much pleasanter at any time than reading law. He had written to his mother (18.7.1832) :—" I wish to God I could take advantage of my time and opportunities as C. Buller has done. To be sure, he has had greater advantages than most men. Not the least of them that Carlyle was his tutor."

Liskeard elected Buller, and was lucky. He was one of the Radicals, who were so few in the Commons that they hardly counted, but voiced the needs of the bulk of the nation. Dumfries was not so fortunate. One day Carlyle happened to be down there he saw at the west end of the " mid-steeple " in the market-place the " hustings " as they called it, what seemed " a monstrous-looking joiner's

[1] Italics added.

304

shed," wherein General Sharpe was the Whig candidate
perorating against the Tory Hannay. " The pot calls the
kettle black," was all Carlyle could think of such a sham
of "representative" government, and he declared it as
dull as a dog-fight.

On Monday 13.8.1832 he went riding in Galloway for
a few days to escape the company of his wife's uncles,
John Welsh of Liverpool and Robert, an Edinburgh
lawyer, coming with a " tag-raggery " of lawyers and dogs
to slaughter the grouse. By 21.8.1832 he was home and
writing to his mother mentioned he was letting the shooting,
to make sure of having no such trouble again. He told her
he had still over twenty volumes to read before he could
" put pen to paper," and he said :—

' I have sat these two days, in the solitary moors,
reading from nine in the morning till ten at night, with
hardly intermission for my meals and my pipes : so that
my head is quite filled with foreign matters, and I could
almost forget that beyond these heaths there is a wide Earth,
and I myself *am not out* of the world, but still in it.'

A few days later in thanking Mill for appreciating the
essay on Dr. Johnson, and accepting his offer to lend French
books, he modestly said he was " not an artist but an
honest artisan," and described the loneliness of Craigenputtock. " Were I of the Spasmodic School, I could gnash
my teeth," he wrote ; but instead of that he rejoiced in " the
first and last blessedness of man : honest work to toil at. . .
It is only in idleness that I am unhappy."

Reporting progress in reading Diderot to Dr. John
Carlyle (31.8.1832), he said :—

' A very large mass of magazines, reviews and such like,
I have consumed like smoke within the last month, gaining,
I think, no knowledge except of the *no*-knowledge of the
writing world. Books produce a strange effect on me here ;
I swallow them with such unpausing impetuosity from early
morning to late night, and get altogether filled and intoxi-
cated with them. A little talk were wholesome dissipation
for me, but it is not to be had, and one can do without it.
My Janekin, if not a great speaker, is the best of listeners,
and what she does say is in general real speech and not
clatter.'

x

In the same letter there is an odd remark about the Churches, a farmer's family he had lately seen in Galloway. Church had had a farm near Annan in 1814 and Carlyle became acquainted with him when visiting James Johnstone there.

'The Churches were in high spirits to see me ; I remembered with a shudder that it was nine years since my last visit. The old people were hardly changed, healthy and prosperous. Great change in the younger parties : two female infants become rather interesting young ladies ; John, whom I remember in bib and tucker, shot up to six feet and more, a talking, prompt, rather promising young man, intended for the factor line. I could not but reflect, as I have done more than once of late, how small a proportion of mere *intellect* will serve a man's turn if all the rest be right. John Church, as I said, promises well ; James, of Calcutta, is doing admirably well ; and their heads are both of the smallest. Church was full of Herculaneum, and will question you strictly when he gets you.'

The letter ended with a flood of questions about men and things round Naples. His " ruling passion " was like Goethe's,—" more light." At the time of writing Carlyle was in his element, plunged in Diderot's volumes, with no more serious affliction in prospect than that when he had finished them, he would want more books than Dumfries libraries could supply. Four days later he soliloquized with the pen (3.9.1832) :—

' I thank Heaven I have still a boundless appetite for reading. I have thoughts of lying buried alive here for many years, forgetting all stuff about " reputation," success and so forth, and *resolutely setting myself to gain insight, by the only method not shut out from me—that of books*.[1] Two articles (of fifty pages) in the year will keep me living ; employment in that kind is open enough. For the rest, I really find almost that I do *best* when *forgotten* of men, and nothing above or around me but the imperishable Heaven. It never wholly seems to me that I am to die in this wilderness : a feeling is always dimly with me that I am to be called out of it, and have work fit for me before I depart, the rather as I can do *either way*. *Let*

[1] Italics added.

*not solitude, let not silence . . . and isolation make a savage of
thee—these, too, have their advantages.'* [1]

Carlyle is " going mad for speech," wrote his wife this
month, September, announcing they might go to town in
Winter. His own way of putting it to Mill was :—" I
long for the sound of human voices, were they only those
of Edinburgh *Dilettanti* and *Philosophes*. Radicalism
enough I can utter for myself, whenever I open my mouth ;
enough and to spare."

He now repaid Jeffrey the loans to John and himself,[2]
and was even receiving an offer of money from John, who
was eager to repay, if he needed it, the advances made to
him long ago ; but by dint of thrift, Carlyle contrived to
need it not, tho' he had to consider and count his cash with
care. Thus on Wednesday, 5.9.1832, his mare kicked
her harness to pieces ; and as there was " no superfluity of
money going just now," he contrived to delay till the spring
the need of spending five pounds on a new set of harness
by mending the old set himself, getting an awl and thread
from Dumfries.

By the middle of September he was writing Diderot, and
finished in a month an essay which has mainly shaped our
English thoughts on Diderot ever since, for tho' much has
been written little has been added. On the day after
finishing it (16.10.1832), Carlyle wrote to Mill and in
discussing the Utilitarians and others quoted his favourite
maxim,—" We must just do the best we can for a living,"—
and told about the man he had first heard saying that, the
Ecclefechan blacksmith, Smeal (or Smale):—" He toiled
faithfully with hammer and anvil, till past ninety, that he
might keep free, that he might not *beg*: *he* did so; and
we— ? Shame on us !—" Then applying the maxim to
his own case, he said he had learned last winter in London
that " he need not hope to get out of periodicals."—

' My Editors are my Booksellers, a monstrous method :
yet still a method. " Allah is great " as the Arabs say :
there is ever some resource left ; and *meditation, like murder,
will out.*' [1] Which is an excellent saying. He went on :
' A question often suggests itself, whether we shall never
have *our own* Periodical Pulpit, and exclude the Philistine
therefrom, above all keep the Pew-opener (or Bibliopolist)

---

[1] Italics added.

[2] Jeffrey's letter of acknowledgement is dated, Loch Long, 22 September,
1832.

in his place ; and so preach nothing but the sound word ?
The Answer, however, comes not. Meanwhile : Speak !
Preach ! The Night cometh. Where men are, there is
an audience.'

They did not intend to go to Edinburgh till December,
and now, as usual after a spell of writing, Carlyle and
his wife drove about visiting relatives, not avoiding Dumfries
tho' the Cholera was causing a panic there. " Every
ball has its billet," said Carlyle to his uncle Aitken in
Dumfries, meaning " every bullet," and spoiling the jingle,
as usual.

Then his sister Jane and his mother came to keep him
company at Craigenputtock some weeks, and he did another
bit of work there, which seems to have been the essay
" On History Again," like an offshoot from the Diderot
article, and interesting as showing the spirit in which he
was approaching the French Revolution. History was
declared to be " the most profitable of all studies,"
the " universal Divine Scripture," whose " plenary
inspiration " was beyond a question. Which was more
edifying than amusing, and printed by Fraser ruefully. He
had asked and would have liked better an obituary notice of
Sir Walter Scott ; but Carlyle would not do it.

His wife was much at Templand this fall. Her mother
was ailing or supposed she was, till suddenly the women
noticed that old Walter Welsh, the " grandfather," was
ill ; and then they bestirred themselves. Mrs. Welsh
loved her father. She was good at nursing. So was her
daughter. For several weeks they were so busy that tho'
working together they had not a single quarrel : which was
well, for old Walter " had numbered fourscore years " and
this was his last illness.

IV

A SCENE AT A FUNERAL

(1832)

IN November the old man died and was buried among his kindred at Crawford on the upper Clyde. After he had been laid in the ground there, his prosperous son John from Liverpool was sitting at the head of the dinner table in Crawford hotel. The day was short and many were in haste, with a long way to go. " There was a big crowd and the resources of the hotel were overtaxed," said a bright girl in her teens who was waiting table.[1]

Carlyle was asking for something, trying in vain to make himself heard by her in the midst of the talk going on, when suddenly John Welsh bawled,—" Carlyle, the next time you come here fetch your own butler."

There was a sudden, painful hush. To the surprise of everybody and the admiration of the bright girl attending, Carlyle alone of all the crowd seemed not to hear what had been said, tho' he had ears of the quickest, as they whispered to each other. The loud talk suspended was resumed by degrees, and nobody openly discussed what nobody present was ever likely to forget.

Mrs. Carlyle never heard of it ; and in the *Reminiscences* it is finely forgotten.

[1] To D. A. W. at Crawford, in August 1902. She is the authority for what follows. She had been landlady of the Inn for many years and often told the story. She was Mrs. McQueen, born Cranstoun, and then very old. She was more wideawake than an average person in the prime of life. The Rev. C. McKune who introduced D. A. W., said to him in private that she was sure not to romance.

V

FASHIONABLE AND OTHER NEWS

(1832)

CARLYLE and his wife stayed only a day or two at Templand after the funeral, and then hastened to relieve his mother who was alone at Craigenputtock. The farm at Templand was given up, and Mrs. Welsh got a long lease of the house. If Carlyle and his wife could have lived with her, the rent of Craigenputtock, which her daughter had assigned to her, was enough to keep them all in their usual way. But that easy solution of the economic problem was impossible, because Mrs. Carlyle could not live in the same house with her mother without quarrelling. In the opinion of sensible women who knew them, it would have been all right if she had been bearing children and needed nursing ; but while both were in health and the only work needed was light for one, they were sure to bicker. The blame was not so much Mrs. Welsh's as Carlyle supposed. His mother was not so blind as he was to his wife's weak points, and even when in charge at Craigenputtock, as she had now been, she kept perfect peace by doing as near to nothing as possible and saying nothing—whatever she saw—in a way that women admired but men could never understand, least of all her wife-worshipping son. As a lady who often lived with young Mrs. Carlyle said,[1]—" She had no system and did her housework in spurts, and of course she was never wrong and had a nasty tongue."

For the sake of books and work and company Carlyle was feeling he should live near Edinburgh or London ; and this winter's visit to Edinburgh was to help them to determine which. Mrs. Austin, whom Jeffrey called "the bearded beauty", was one of the attractions of London ; and a letter from her (25.12.1832) was one of the last the

---

[1] To D. A. W.

Mrs. Welsh, from a miniature belonging to Miss Chrystal, Glasgow, grand-daughter of Mrs. Welsh's brother.

[face p. 310

Carlyles received before leaving home. She told of her latest translations, and how Mrs. Jeffrey considered her a monster made up " of all we Whigs hate," a Radical and an Absolutist. In a womanly way she confessed a hunger for praise from Carlyle, saying Goethe had been " just about to write " to her when he died, and she dwelt upon the budding beauty, etc., of her daughter.—

' Lucy grows a tall, fair girl. At least, people call her handsome. She is, at any rate, intelligent and simple, and strong, and not like the children of the " *upper classes*." Mrs. Bulwer told me that her little girl of four said, in answer to some question about her little cousins,—" I suppose they have seen by the papers that I go to school." '

As the year was ending Carlyle was reading the *French Revolution* of Thiers, which Mill had lent him, and writing many pages of notes from it in his journal, including something significant (28.12.1832) :—

' French Revolution well worth study. It was a stripping bare of the human soul : a fearful bursting out of the Infinite thro' the thin rinds of Habit. How do men act in these surprising circumstances ? This is a question well worth asking. Should like to study it farther, far farther ; and will try some day.'

VI

EDINBURGH AND JEFFREY

(1833)

ON New-Years-Day Carlyle rode to Scotsbrig to give to his mother the pleasant surprise of a day more of his company before he went to Edinburgh. By the first Monday of the year (7.1.1833), his wife and he were in a hired flat and not far from their first home, Comely Bank. He was almost daily in the Advocates' Library, rejoicing in the books and saying to himself, as if admonishing Andrew Carnegies of the future, that it was futile to found universities now.—" The only university " worth having to-day was " a public library."

The first month was brightened by Jeffrey. Safely elected and "sick of electioneering," he was resting at home, and chafed at their delay in coming to Edinburgh till he heard what caused it. He came often and stayed long, " brisk and in good humour, talking like a pop-gun," and sure to tell of old Talleyrand, whom he had studied at Holland House last year, and heard describing Voltaire and Malesherbes, Louis XVI and Turgot.[1] Himself in his sixtieth year, Jeffrey played battledore assiduously with Mrs. Carlyle. She had a flirtatious style of playing which could not be expected to please Mrs. Jeffrey, but was little more than old habit, due to playing the game for years with Dr. Fyffe.

The librarian of the Advocates' Library was a Dumfriesshire man, David Irving, whose career had been not unlike Carlyle's, tho' a few years earlier. He had been a student when Carlyle " was sucking." He now told Carlyle an Astronomy Professorship would soon be vacant in Glasgow and " in the gift " of the Government, which meant Jeffrey. " Apply at once," was his advice. Carlyle reflected that however he might be " careless about all that time can give," he " could undertake to teach astronomy, as

[1] Cockburn's *Life of Jeffrey*, I, 327–8.

soon as most things, by way of honest day-labour : not otherwise, for I have no zeal now that way." He mentioned it to Jeffrey, but in his shy and consciously modest way said nothing of his own qualifications, which Jeffrey forebore to ask about, as Irving was premature. The chair was not to fall vacant for a year or two. Thus it happened that Jeffrey knew less than almost any of Carlyle's acquaintances about his knowledge of astronomy and mathematics.

The chief remaining political task for Jeffrey before retiring to the bench was " Burgh Reform," replacing the privileged town councils of Scotland by elected bodies. The last political act of the old council of Edinburgh was defying public opinion and electing M.P. a Tory Dundas in 1831 in preference to Jeffrey. In the closing months of its existence it was now threatening a more cynical " job." It seemed about to appoint as successor to Leslie in the chair of Natural Philosophy, one of the "College prizes " in its gift, a youth who had the best " Tory pull." The Whig candidate was Brewster, whom Carlyle met canvassing councillors on the day he arrived in town. It was confided to Carlyle that if Brewster failed, as seemed likely, he would need to go into the Church of England and get a " living " from Brougham. Whereupon Carlyle soliloquized upon him :—" 'Once a noble soap bell, now a drop of sour suds.' Such is the history of many men." But the most striking fact about the election in the eyes of Jeffrey and Carlyle was that the non-party candidate, Thomas Galloway, who had no chance with the council, was as far above Brewster in qualifications as Brewster above the Tory, being " the best living writer on mixed mathematics " and distinguished in science, and with ten years' experience in teaching it at the military college, Sandhurst. For these reasons he was recommended by the best men of science and mathematics from Woolwich (Gregory) to Glasgow (Thomson) ; but the council did not care. However, the pressure of public opinion [1] turned a vote or two, and Brewster was elected.

Before then, by the beginning of February, Jeffrey was in London, with wife and daughter and pet parrot, and

---

[1] *Scotsman*, Wednesday, 6.12.1832, etc. The private papers of Thomas Galloway came to D.A.W. as a residuary legatee and nearest relative in Scotland ; and he made notes from them before destroying them ; but did not see the connection with T. C. till later.

bestirring himself successfully to put a final end to town councils of that sort. Handicapped by sickness tho' he was, he was soon thanking Carlyle for " putting me on seeing " Leigh Hunt, whom he visited and liked and helped to extricate from debts and other worries. Wherever he passed, the " dainty little spirit " seemed to sweeten the air, like another St. Ives, reputed the only lawyer saint in the Church. Let him be called our Protestant lawyer saint,—he can bear the comparison. Mrs. Carlyle was down with influenza when he left and Jeffrey became sick on reaching London, and wrote from there (14.8.1833) :—

' MY DEAR CARLYLE,

         ' Thank you for your kind letter.' (Then, after talk about Mrs. Austin and Mrs. Carlyle's health and his own, and the Irish policy of the ministry :—)' We have got a more airy and spacious house than we had before and I hope you will come to see us in it. I left home this last time, more sadly and reluctantly than last year, partly perhaps because I had settled more down to my old habits and occupations, and partly because I feel more sensibly how fast Life is ebbing away with me, and how little I can reckon upon any long period of enjoyment, after another return (to Edinburgh). Oh, this strange dream of life and this starting at the sleep—or the waking rather—in which it is to end. God bless you.

                         Ever Yours,
                                 F. JEFFREY.'

VII

IN EDINBURGH

(1833)

WHEN Jeffrey had gone, Sir William Hamilton was the chief intimate remaining, an " earnest " man and " genuine," and as fond of social walks as Carlyle himself ; but the season did not favour country outings, and Carlyle discovered again that dining and supping in company " did him mischief." He did not always restrict himself to a potato on such occasions, and many a time he wished he had done so, when it was too late.

George Moir he found shrivelled into a Tory, and uncomfortable in his company, as if fearing such association might damage his prospects.

Robert Mitchell who had been like an elder brother to Carlyle was now a prosperous Edinburgh teacher, but " in very poor health " and close to an early grave, tho' happily he did not know it. He insisted on giving a dinner-party in Carlyle's honour, and was rewarded by the amusing astonishment of the " didactic " guests at Carlyle's exposition of belief and Radicalism as compared with (Edinburgh) " opinion and Whiggism." The guests were not all " didactic "—there was Dr. Brown among them, a " logic-chopper good to behold," and an advocate, Semple, " an overflowing Kantist," good-natured and lively, compared to a " bottle of champagne or soda-water uncorked." It was a pleasant party.

It may have been Mitchell, but also may have been a college lecturer, with whom Carlyle had sundry conferences this winter on Logic, which he mentioned to Mill to show he could have patience to discuss it with him also. The Edinburgh man he described as " the strangest old school-master in a new body only forty years old. . . . He thought Logic was to be the salvation of the World." Whereas in the opinion of Carlyle, " the grand difficulty is to *see* somewhat, to *believe* somewhat ; a quite mystic operation, to which Logic helps little ; to which, proclaim what laws of vision you will, nothing but an eye will be of service." [1]

In balancing Edinburgh against London, Carlyle thought first of John Wilson and John Mill, and it helped to incline him to London that in correspondence with Mill he enjoyed the " profitable communion ", which is only possible between sincere and earnest men who trust each other. Speech on such conditions Carlyle called "cheerfuller than light," and five or six years ago, when politics seemed negligible, John Wilson had given him a taste of that ; but now John Wilson disappointed him, and seemed almost as afraid of being compromised by contact with him as " little Geordie Moir." He called on Wilson, who did not return his call. One day they met in the street and " exchanged civilities " as of yore, and Wilson said in separating,—' I will come and have a talk at home with you, if you will allow me, the very first day I have leisure." This was satisfactory, but nothing happened. So the genial Gordon once more asked Wilson to supper and begged Carlyle to come for another ambrosial night ; but perhaps at his wife's instigation Carlyle decided Wilson was " not worth an indigestion," and did not go. Supposing Wilson wanted to evade him, he failed to notice him the next time they met, " cut him " in short,—Carlyle was prone to pride when off his guard. He had been strongly attracted and felt repelled. Wherein he was mistaken. Wilson did not mean to repel him, but only to be circumspect, and even after " the cut" avoided quarrel. In a letter to Mill at the time there are Carlylean lamentations over the backslider of genius conforming to conventionalities :—' The Conservatives here, I think, are wholly in a very fretful, tremulous condition : Wilson himself, tho' he loves me, would evidently rather not meet me ; I have seen him only once, and perhaps we shall hardly meet again. There is no man in the Island who has so wasted himself : a mass of Power standing on *no* basis ; drifted about by every

---

[1] *Letters of J. S. Mill* by Hugh Elliot, I, 26–102 ; and W. L. Courtney's *J. S. Mill*, and *Letters of T. Carlyle to J. S. Mill and J. Sterling and R. Browning*, pp. 23–80, edited by Alexander Carlyle, 1923.

breath ; turned [1] into the despicablest weakness. Pity enough ! Yet Nature is *infinitely* rich : the two eggs one eats at breakfast could have filled the whole world with winged creatures ; and they are swallowed at one meal and no damage done. So with *geniuses* ; a thousand can be spent ephemerally [1]; if one gets to maturity we shall be content.'

Maybe to please his mother Carlyle was making the most of the goodwill manifested towards him by a leading divine, McCrie, the same who wrote a good life of John Knox and discredited Scott, when he showed a bias against the Covenanters. McCrie was a big, "stiff-backed, stalking kind of man, intelligent and honest, but heavy." He "rather pressingly invited " Carlyle to call, and said all he could to confirm him in the inclination to write about the Reformation and the Church in Scotland, about which Carlyle was for some time " reading violently " this winter. Opinions such as he expressed in letters to Mill would delight the heart of old McCrie :—Howie's *Scots Worthies* and *Cloud of Witnesses*, once popular in Scotland, were " a pair of true People's Books ; and truly worth more for the People than all the Diffusion Societies will promulgate for a generation or two. It is not ten years since I, an enlightened Sceptic, first deigned to look in them ; but my reward was great : they are in fact most notable Books . . . The Scotch Presbyterian Church, alone of all Protestant Churches, for some time was a real church. . . John Knox is one of those unmanageable fellows who once for all have taken in hand to act and speak not respectably but honestly ; and have no manner of notion that God's Truth should alter its attitude for men's pleasure." Another thing that made " John Knox and the Scottish Kirk peculiarly significant " for Carlyle was that they showed how " Ideals do and ought to adjust themselves with the Actual." They made " a *genuine* Ideal, that did subsist with life in it for a hundred and fifty years ! " [2] And so on.

McCrie was not long in discovering that Carlyle was not " one of us," tho' he was friendly to the pious, and tho' there was a good deal in the tone of his talk in intellectual circles to justify the hopes of the religious set as well as of the Tories that he might be a champion on the side of

[1] In the *Letters of T. Carlyle to J. S. Mill*, etc., by Alexander Carlyle, p. 49, there is " lamed " instead of " turned " and " apparently " instead of " ephemerally," different readings of the same MS. D.A.W. copied from the MS. before Alexander Carlyle's book was published.

[2] See footnote 1, p. 316.

things as they are. For example, in some house this winter he was denouncing the then fashionable style of mockery, and a serious person entitled to speak with authority, one hopes it was not Jeffrey, defended the fashion, saying :— " Belief has done immense evil, witness Knipperdolling," a German contemporary of Luther, and his followers " the Anabaptists, etc.," to say nothing of French Revolutionaries and Puritans.

To which Carlyle replied more warmly than he found it pleasant to recall :—" True, Belief has done some evil in the world ; but it has done all the good that was ever done in it ; from the time when Moses saw the burning bush and believed it to be God appointing him deliverer of his people, down to the last act of belief that you and I executed. Good never came from aught else."

Carlyle did not suspect in time how exasperating this rejoinder must have seemed to men of sense, because it put them in a dilemma, either to leave him a victory he did not deserve, or expose themselves to be called infidels. He used " belief " with a double meaning. The belief in question was religious belief ; and he defended it by taking the word in its widest sense, believing whatever you see to be true. Nobody doubted the use of that kind of belief ! The reference to Moses was worse, for it implied that one should take the truth of the Bible for granted. Along with this he was so downright that even his big vocabulary did not always enable him to be courteous. He had his full share of the common love of contradiction too. So it is not strange that he discovered people were saying :— " Carlyle is wasting his considerable talent on impossibilities and can never do any good."

He began to feel he had lost the art of conversation and become in Craigenputtock like a John the Baptist, which strengthened his conviction that he should live somewhere else. Jeffrey comforted him (15.3.1833), when he complained :—

' Do not fancy that people repel you. I can see that you are improving, and have good hope that in time you may become almost as tolerant of your fellow sinners as the Sinless Being who made them.'

His private journal shows Carlyle fumbling after sincerity and a firmer grip on his Faith in the justice of Nature.

The belief he craved and valued was not in a possibility or in a working hypothesis, but the sort of belief one acts upon instinctively. The fanatics seemed to have a monopoly of it in Edinburgh, and his aim was to reach " Faith," that is to say, conviction and sincerity, as genuine as theirs but without delusion. He admitted to himself that they were right in calling it a " God announcing miracle," tho' he no more believed in Jehovah than in Jupiter ; for he felt that the right sort of Faith was not to be got by argument, and he did not yet quite realize that a man cannot believe whatever he wills. He soliloquized with the pen :—

' All is Whiggery here, which means " I will believe whatsoever I shall be forced to believe." Know the worth of Belief. Alas ! Can'st thou acquire none ?

' That the Supernatural differs not from the Natural is a great Truth. The Philosophers went far wrong, however, in this, that instead of raising the Natural to the Supernatural, they strove to sink the Supernatural to the Natural. The gist of my whole way of thought is to do not the latter but the *former*. I feel it to be the epitome of much good for this and following generations.'

Tho' now aware that the *Edinburgh Review* would yield him no more wages, he was not worrying about that, feeling sure that unreason within himself was the only enemy. Once his " inward light " was clear again, the world would " lie under his feet " and a way would open. A fellow-feeling makes us understand. He was walking Edinburgh streets one day this winter when the words of Jesus passed through his mind and almost brought tears to his eyes,—" Be of good cheer, I have *overcome* the world." He asked himself,—" What was his overcoming ? Poverty, despite, forsakenness, and the near prospect of an accursed Cross." In other moods, perplexed between the choice of Edinburgh or London, he felt that the ' one thing needful ' was best put in the proverb,—" With all thy getting, get understanding."

This was in a letter to John Mill, with whom he was carrying on a curious and intimate correspondence this year,[1] the most peculiar part of it perhaps his exhortation to Mill to read the Bible, to help him over the long fits of

[1] See Footnote on p. 316,

depression from which he said he was suffering, and which Carlyle confessed " are a thing too well known to myself ; indeed, with me they have stretched themselves into long continuous years, and but for happy accidents, kind orderings of Providence, would have brought me to desperation." Mill took the advice and soon was told,—" There is still no Book where I find the Spiritual Warfare of Men tenth-part so faithfully delineated, so cheeringly too, and instructively," as in the Bible, in short, which Carlyle described as the " Book of Books " for " *heartiness* " and " *sincerity*." They particularly agreed about the first of the Gospels, Carlyle declaring,—" Great, soul-inspiring is that poor artless Biography by St. Matthew." It was maybe in part to cheer up Mill that he expatiated on how much he was himself the better of Mill's friendship, which made him feel he was not alone.—" It is a most solitary world ; from Dan to Beersheba you walk, and find nothing but *Masks*, a real Man is now almost as rare as a God has always been."

When once he told Mill that he wondered at " the boundless capacity man has of loving," Mill answered (9.3.1833), that what he wondered at was rather the " narrowness of that capacity," which narrowness appeared to him " the eternal barrier between man and man," and he went on, with a trace of Cockney complacency percolating into his philosophy :—

' Your picture of Edinburgh is *triste* ' (or dismal) ' enough, and might serve for all other provincial towns ; there is an *odour* of literature and intellect about Edinburgh ; at Glasgow, Liverpool and the like, there is little else than the *stench* of trade. London is better, tho' bad. There are here some *true* believers, among whom your thoughts would not fall like hand-grenades and put them to flight. If you determine to leave Craigenputtock, there is surely no place so good as this, at least in the most important of all good things which locality can bring—kindred companionship.

' I have no news to tell ; the Reformed Parliament has not disappointed me any more than you ; it is (as Miss Martineau, I understand, says of Brougham) so ridiculously like what I expected. . . .'

Mrs. Carlyle's vote was for London too. She assured her " dear Eliza " Miles of Ampton Street that her winter in Edinburgh was "fully more unhealthy" than the previous one in London.

The minds of men, to say nothing of women, are more mysterious than the stars,—their mutual influences cannot be measured ; but certainly Mill contributed more than advice to the decision in favour of London. He was himself an attraction, and the French books he plentifully supplied were making the French Revolution more palpable, and drawing Carlyle away from the Reformation of religion led by Luther and Knox. His letters to Mill show his thoughts were drifting in that way. The French Revolution seemed to him to make the world more intelligible.

He read Thiers "with great avidity," but found him "rather uncommunicative" as to the "private biographic" details of life. It is curious that his opinion of Thiers which Froude has quoted was as true of Froude himself as of any Frenchman,—"Dig where you will you come to water." There was nothing odd in that. Carlyle was well aware how little historians had yet troubled to make their statements fit the facts. Goethe as well as Dr. Johnson agreed with Walpole that histories were sure to be false, and Rabelais had scoffed at those who believed them, saying,—"An honest man and of good judgment is always believing what is told him and he finds written."

From the letters to Mill it appears that what seemed to Carlyle the worst in Thiers was the "pagan" creed that Might is Right, as if the power to do a thing gave the right to do it. "He will prove to you every hero of his throughout to be perfectly justified in doing whatsoever— he has succeeded in doing." Thiers appeared to him to be "like the modern French School generally" a man of "hard, mechanical, all-for-politics disposition." French authors, "even of genius," Carlyle told Mill, "seem to get along comfortably without any *conscience*, or ever feeling the want of one." In advising Mill to write upon the French Revolution he said it was "the grand *work* of our era" and still not understood. "In France itself Knowledge (of it) seems only just beginning," and elsewhere there was Error which he declared to be "infinitely worse than Ignorance."

Writing now in Edinburgh his *Cagliostro* for Fraser, Carlyle made good use of Goethe's description of Cagliostro's mother and sister at Palermo, but never mentioned Goethe's play about him or Schiller's fiction, which shows where

Y

Carlyle had now arrived and prepares us for new opinions. The change was disconcerting to a "windy disciple of myself and other men," whom he discovered this year in Edinburgh, John Stuart Blackie, fresh back from Germany and full of faith in *Faust* as a new Apocalypse. Blackie was to be well-known as a Professor of Greek, etc., but now as a young man of twenty-four preparing for the bar, he was making a metrical version of *Faust*. Carlyle confessed he once had thought as Blackie did, but changed his mind ; and when the new translation was sent to him, he attributed the vogue of *Faust* " to the sorrow-struck, sceptical feeling of these times." [1]

Reporting to Mill his success in seeking materials for French history in Edinburgh, he mentioned,—"A series of Revolution Portraits (engravings) gave me great satisfaction," Danton and others, a Paris folio of 1810. " Tell me if these heads are reckoned genuine." He explained to Mill, " as my book-provider ", that he was interested in any human experience but apt to be bored by speculation. Thus he said the recent report of the trial of the Saint-Simonians " was better than any drama I had read for years."

He lamented to Mill the " hollow jargon " he had to hear instead of "sincere speech ", and exhorted him,—" Go on boldly whithersoever you have light to go. To all men there is one thing possible ; to speak and act God's truth. . . . You have chosen this ' better part.' " And after he had been several months in Edinburgh he was writing,—" There is still nothing here resembling you which I can fall in with," and anticipating their talk when next they met, he wrote:—" Glory to God ! There are still here and there on the earth some articulate-speaking mortals ; the highest, mysterious gift, that of language (for ' man is properly an *incarnated Word*') has not yet utterly dissipated itself into inane chattering and cawing ; there is still Communion for men with men."

" I once loved Edinburgh," he told Mill, " and still do not hate it. I hope some day you and I shall see it together." But he could not deny it made him feel himself a "stranger," more so than London, while the like of Mill was there. There were a few like Henry Inglis who read the MS. of *Sartor* with enthusiasm, but no publisher would look at it, and John Gordon, nestled safely in some college

[1] *John Stuart Blackie*, by A. M. Stoddart, I, pp. 148–9.

clerkship on £300 a year, was cynically candid, saying,—
" All men are quite taken up with making a livelihood."

He tried not to blame them, but confessed to his brother,
—" The things they are running the race for are no prizes
to me." He was too interested in the world as a whole
to be pre-occupied about his own little part. It was a
time of quick change in Scotland. Landowners were
rackrenting and sweeping the people off the land where
their forebears had dwelt for centuries, and manufacturers
exploiting the steam-engine were sweating them when
huddled in the towns. "We have two blustering Turkey-
cocks lecturing here at present on the negroes," wrote
Carlyle to Mill. "While we, under softer names, have not
only slavery but the fiercest Maroon war going on under
our very noses, it seems to me Philanthropy and Eleuther-
omany might find work nearer home. But names do change
things."

A few days later (26.3.1833) he was writing to his un-
successful-farmer brother Alick :—

' Millions of mortals are toiling this day, in our British
Isles, without prospect of rest, save in speedy death, to
whom for their utmost toiling, food and shelter are too
high a blessing. When one reads of the Lancashire
Factories and little children labouring for sixteen hours
a day, inhaling at every breath a quantity of cotton *fuzz*,
falling asleep over their wheels, and roused again by the
lash of thongs over their backs, or the slap of " billy-rollers "
over their little crowns ; and then again of Irish Whitefeet,
driven out of their potato-patches and mud-hovels, and
obliged to take the hillside as broken men,—one pauses
with a kind of amazed horror, to ask if this be Earth, the
place of Hope, or Tophet' (meaning Hell), ' where hope never
comes ! A good practical inference too, every one of us
may draw from it : to be thankful that with him it is *not*
yet so, to be content under many griefs, and patiently
struggle on towards a better day ; which, even in this
world, cannot fail to dawn for the afflicted children of men.
One grand remedy against the worst still lies partly open :
America and its forests, where you have only the wild
beasts to strive against. I understand there never was
such emigration from these parts, at least from Edinburgh,
as this year. People of all sorts are going : labourers,
shopkeepers, even Writers to the Signet, and country

Lairds. They are right. But, in the meantime go on tilling : surely the Government will apply itself in earnest to Emigration, as the sole remedy for all that most immediately presses on us.'

A few days later (31.3.1833) he was confessing to himself that there was " *no* encouragement " for him in Edinburgh :—
' It is taken for granted, I find, that of me nothing can be made—that I am, economically speaking, but a lost man. No great error there, perhaps ; but if it is added by my friends themselves that therefore I am spiritually lost ? One's ears are bewildered by the inane chatter of the people ; one's heart is for hours and days overcast by the sad feeling : " There is none then, not one, that will believe in me ! " Great in this life is the communion of man with man. Meanwhile continue to believe in *thyself*. Let the chattering of innumerable gigmen (or snobs) pass by thee as what it is. Wait thou on the bounties of thy unseen Taskmaster, on the hests of thy inward *Daemon*. Sow the seed-field of Time. What if thou see no fruit of it ? Another will. Be not weak
' Neither fear thou that this thy great message of the Natural *being* the Supernatural will wholly perish unuttered. One way or other it will and shall be uttered—write it down on paper any way ; speak it from thee—so shall thy painful, destitute existence not have been in vain. Oh, in vain ? Hadst thou, even thou, a message from the Eternal, and thou grudgest the travail of thy embassy ? O thou of little faith ! '

Thus, like Milton, Carlyle was sometimes conscious of his calling—" more than enough." He was meditating on the French Revolution, and wanted Mill to write on it. When consulted by Mill as to whether Alison's new *History of Europe* was worth reviewing, he said it was, admitting that Alison could " not understand the French Revolution " because he was " an Ultra-Tory," but saying his notes gave evidence of wide enquiry.
Mill did the review suggested but returned the advice, exhorting Carlyle himself to do the history. Carlyle felt he must be doing something,—" I seldom write," he had explained to Mill, " from any cause but the terrors of an evil conscience." As he found the multitudinous French

memoirs more attractive than any documents discoverable about Knox and the Church of Scotland, he decided to try his hand at narrative instead of preaching on paper as hitherto, and start with the scandalous chronicle of the Diamond Necklace trial of 1786. He thought of beginning at once in Edinburgh ; but after finishing *Cagliostro* he was bilious and rested, that is to say he merely read at large, " manuring " his mind, or as he expressed it to Leigh Hunt,[1] he was " not idle, yet fallow." This lasted long after their return to the country in May ; so that when Mill took his vacation this year in October and went to Paris, instead of taking it earlier as Carlyle had hoped he would be doing and coming to Craigenputtock, he was to be making enquiries in Paris for Carlyle to elucidate the Diamond Necklace, and buying books and maps to satisfy his curiosity about the French Revolution.

Shortly before leaving Edinburgh, Carlyle wrote to Mill what illustrates the impatience of contradiction which has been attributed to his family.—' On the whole I have learned nothing this winter ' ; nor in short heard a word worth hearing : ' however, there was contradiction in abundance ; and contradiction itself is a kind of instruction. *This* was the world thou hadst to work in : kick not against the pricks.'

[1] *Cornhill Magazine*, 1892, p. 493 ; an anon. article consisting mainly of letters of Leigh Hunt.

VIII

RETURN TO THE COUNTRY

(1833)

IN April a Haddington boy, Bob Skirving, who knew
Mrs. Carlyle as an old friend of his mother, was sparrow-
nesting in the ruined church, and saw her enter
it. She did not seem to see him. He hid in a corner, and
watched her sit upon the flat stone which covered her
father's grave; and after what seemed a very long time
she went away.[1] She had been ill in Edinburgh. Her
mother nursed her. In April her cousin Helen Welsh
from Liverpool was also with them.

On the first Tuesday in May (7.5.1833), Carlyle and his
wife, having sent off their baggage the week before, walked
to the " North Bridge " to catch the Thornhill Coach at half-
past six in the morning, and arrived three minutes after
it had gone. About which she told Bess Stodart [2]:—
" You know *my* way of being always too early—perhaps
you do not know that my husband always puts off till the
last moment : this, almost the only, discrepancy in our
habits has produced many little argumentations betwixt
us which on that ill-fated morning I for the *first time*
determined to evade . . . tho' up in good time." So she
let him " trifle away *five minutes* " too much.

There was nothing for it but to wait two days longer,
which she said she spent " in bed with the dreadfullest
headache." He had two swims in the sea, and read some
writings of Sir George Mackenzie, an elegant moralist
interesting as the judicial murderer of Covenanters, the
" bloody Mackenzie " of Scotch history. But the staple
reading of these two days was the Life of the Scottish-
American Paul Jones, which gave the materials of two of
the best paragraphs in his *French Revolution*.

On Thursday (9.5.1833) they caught their coach, and

---

[1] *Early Letters of Jane Walsh Carlyle*, by D. G. Ritchie, pp. 303-4.
[2] *Ditto*, p. 234.

" after a stifling stew of nine dusty hours " arrived at Thornhill, Mrs. Carlyle in a fever of Influenza. She was too weak, she said, to sit in the gig to be driven the half mile of distance to her mother's house, preferred to " go or stagger, hanging on his arm, and instantly took to bed." In a few days he went to Scotsbrig. It was not till the second Monday, (20.5.1833), that they reached home, and on the third, (27.5.1833) he was proposing to Fraser to publish *Sartor* serially in his magazine, which was agreed to at a reduced rate. Instead of the £200 he had hoped for, he received £82, and 58 copies made from sheets. Yet even this was better than spending £60 for printing it ; and all the more welcome because nobody was asking him this summer for an article, and last year's forecast of indefinite study at Craigenputtock, supported by two articles a year, seemed likely not to work.

He did not worry, but went on reading without writing all summer, and while turning his intellectual telescope upon the French Revolution as the great event of his time, his note-book shows him cross-examining himself, as if clearing his mind like an astronomer his glasses. He asked himself whether he was not too " intolerant," too contemptuously indifferent " to those who were not forwarding him," and too emphatic ? He feared he was " the very vainest" of men, with the same sincerity as a Paul might feel himself the chief of sinners, and never a saint was more sincere in prayer than when he wrote :— " God deliver me from vanity, from self-conceit, the first sin of this universe, and the last, for I think it will *never* leave us." Nobody can deny that he knew his weakness !

It might be called an answer to the prayer that he began to recognise he had no " Poetic Talent,"—a phrase of many-coloured meanings. He had not the knack of rhythm and rhyme, or of fictioneering, tho' he had imagination and intellect. The humility he was struggling after did not hinder him from feeling glad that he had no hack-work, for he said to himself :—

' The thing I want to write is quite other than an article. Happily the chief desire of my mind has again become to *write* a masterpiece, let it be acknowledged or not. The Idea of the Universe struggles dark and painful in me, which I must deliver out of me or be wretched.

'In *all* times there is a word which, spoken to men, would thrill their souls. But the way to find . . . (and) speak it ?

'It is good to be humbled. Life is a school : we are perverse scholars to the last and require the rod.'

There is more in his concluding sentiment than the prejudice of a teacher by trade. He put his thoughts in plainer shape to Mill :—

'A multitude of things require adjustment in me : it was a great kindness in my destiny too that precisely at this period I could pause without economical inconvenience ; the first time I have had any inward wish to pause. I feel sometimes that I am not idle, tho unemployed to the eye. We shall see what will come of it. In some week or two however, I shall probably be again at my Desk ; according to my old maxim that one should not puzzle, should not speculate ; but having got even a little light, go instantly to *work* with it, that it may become *more*. I have a general feeling growing of late years that " I am all in the wrong " ; and shall always have it, for we live in a Dualistic world. Strange how in ourselves, as in all earthly things, a little nucleus of Truth and Good rolls itself on in a huge comet-like environment of Error and Delusion ; and yet at length in some degree the Error and Delusion evaporate and vanish (as Nonentities, mere Negations) and the fraction of Good is *found* to be a reality ! '

While thus Carlyle was peering into the mysteries of Nature, his easy-going brother Dr. John had come to Craigenputtock in June and stayed two months with them, prescribing for Mrs. Carlyle with success. She wrote to Eliza Miles in July to coax her to come to Craigenputtock and warned her against doctors in general, declaring them " of no value," but saying :—

'My brother-in-law is a paragon of the class, but he is so by—in as much as possible—undoctoring himself. He told me yesterday, " Could I give you some agreeable occupation to fill your whole mind, it would do more for you than all the medicines in existence." '

This continued his opinion all her life, that work was

MRS. CARLYLE.

From a painting in 1843 by Gambardella, made for Jeannie Welsh, a young cousin from Liverpool who had been staying with Mrs. Carlyle after her mother died. Jeannie Welsh became afterwards Mrs. Chrystal. In a letter to her (4/4/1843) Mrs. Carlyle reported: 'Your picture is finished. . . As for the *likeness*, it looks *simple* enough. Carlyle thinks too simple "*for anything*!" (as you say in Lancashire). The eyes, he says, "want expression," the mouth "wants character"—but for one person that finds it less *inspired-looking* than the original there will be twenty finding it excessively flattered. Gambardella's own criticism was (with a look of ineffable complacency), "it looks too young! I must put in some wrinkles!" Which, of course, he never did, so that seventy years later it looked younger than a picture of her as a girl.

[face p. 328

what she needed to make her well. Her mother seems to have agreed with him, and so did she for the present. At any rate upon his treatment she "improved to a wonder." [1]

It was on this visit that he pointed to a wayside bush of rushes and said,—" It stands there because the whole world could not prevent its standing," which reminds one of the " survival of the fittest." It was a clever summary of the Edinburgh Science of his student days made popular by Darwin by-and-by. John left in August, escorted by his brother across the Solway.

The next visitor was Emerson from America. John Mill had intended to come, but could not get leave of absence in time ; and sent a description of Emerson, who had got a letter of introduction from him as well as from Gustave D'Eichthal, in Paris. " From one or two conversations I have had with him," wrote Mill, " I do not think him a very hopeful subject." [2]

[1] Besides unpublished letters, see e.g. *Early Letters of Jane Welsh Carlyle,* by D. G. Ritchie, pp. 204–5.
[2] *Letters of J. S. Mill,* by Hugh Elliot, I, pp. 60–1.

IX

EMERSON AT CRAIGENPUTTOCK

(25 AND 26.8.1833)

THE American stranger was a man of thirty, who had lately been the minister of a fashionable Unitarian church in Boston. Watching the current of European corruption in a detached way from that pinnacle, he had discovered in 1832 that Carlyle was "the latest and strongest contributor to the critical journals," and wondered whether even such a one would not feel stronger if told that someone in Boston was watching him.[1] "If Carlyle knew what an interest I have in his persistent goodness, would it not be worth one effort more, one prayer, one meditation ? But will he resist the Deluge of bad example in England ? " It seemed almost too much to hope for. However, in February of that year, Emerson lost his wife, who left him money enough to make him feel independent, and before the year was out he parted amicably from his congregation, pleading scruples about communion services and saying little about doubts more fundamental.[2] He came globe-trotting to Europe to divert his mind, and in going about was seeking a glimpse of those already familiar to him by name. He was just too late to see Goethe or Scott. In Italy he saw Landor. In London he watched Wellington at the funeral of Wilberforce, and enjoyed for an hour the talk of Coleridge at Highgate. In Edinburgh on Sunday, 18th August, he preached in a Unitarian Church in Young Street, to the admiration of Alexander Ireland and some others ; but none in that circle could direct him to his next objective. Mr. Ireland had to report [3] :—" There was almost insuperable difficulty in ascertaining where Mr. Carlyle then lived, and I well remember the pains Mr. Emerson took."

[1] For quotations from *Emerson's Diary* in this chapter, see Vol. III, pp. 180–6, 199, and 573 : and see the *Memoirs of R. W. Emerson*, by J. E. Cabot, I, 194–7.

[2] Ireland's *Emerson*, p. 147.

[3] *Ditto*, p. 320.

330

But " at last the Secretary to the University "—John Gordon, belike—directed him and seems to have notified Carlyle, who confessed,—" I was much surprised, as I did not know my name was known in America," [1]

So next Sunday, (25.8.1833),—" He descended on us out of the clouds as it were," wrote Mrs. Carlyle. " He came from Dumfries in an old rusty gig," said Carlyle,[2] who insisted on sending it back to return the next day. He was warmly welcomed, and told them soon of the bereavement that had set him roving. The day was fine. He and Carlyle went for a walk while dinner was being prepared.

The next " four-and-twenty hours " were " very happy." They talked and heard talk to their heart's content, and Emerson used to declare the talk of Carlyle there one of the " three things which had struck him most in his visit to Europe." [3]

' Carlyle,' he wrote,[4] ' was as absolute a man of the world on that hill-farm, as if holding on his own terms what is best in London. He was tall and gaunt, with a cliff-like brow, self-possessed, and clinging to his northern accent with evident relish ; " in London yonder," " I liked well," " aboot it," " ay, ay," etc. ; full of lively anecdote, and with a streaming humour, which floated everything he looked upon. His talk playfully exalted familiar objects.

' " Blackwood's " was the " sand magazine " ; Fraser s nearer approach to life was the " mud magazine " ; a piece of road near by that marked some failed enterprise was " the grave of the last sixpence." When too much praise of any genius annoyed him, he professed hugely to admire the talent shown by his pig. He had spent much time and contrivance in confining the poor beast to one enclosure in his pen, but pig, by great strokes of judgment, had found out how to let a board down, and had foiled him.'

Besides Wordsworth and Coleridge, they discussed the Earl of Lonsdale, the town of Whitehaven, a Liverpool duellist, Allan Cunningham, Hazlitt, Walter Scott, and the

---

[1] To various persons. These actual words are from the note-book of Mrs. Anstruther, as spoken in her house at Ballikinrain to her on 26.7.1876.

[2] To Moncure Conway. See Moncure Conway's *Thomas Carlyle*, pp. 40–42.

[3] *Reminiscences of Thomas Carlyle*, by A. J. Symington, p. 28.

[4] For anything of this mosaic of Emerson's writings which is not in his journal and letters, see Chapter I of his *English Traits*.

coronation of King William, Carlyle remarking that he had
" made up his mind to pay his taxes to William and
Adelaide Guelph with great cheerfulness as long as William
is able to compel the payment," but not " a moment "
longer.

" Landor's principle is mere rebellion," he remarked,
when Emerson spoke about Landor, and he feared that
that was the American principle also. ' Carlyle deprecated
the state of a man's " living in rebellion " as he termed
it, with no worship, no reverence for anybody.   Himself,
he said, "would worship anyone who showed him more
truth." '

In a letter of 1834 there is a slight mistake of Emerson's.[1]
" He expressed some impatience of his total solitude, and
talked of Paris as a residence.   I told him I hoped not ;
for I should always remember him with respect meditating
in the mountains of Nithsdale."   Carlyle intended only
a visit to Paris.   As he wrote to his brother John now,—
" The French Revolution engages me.   My chief errand to
Paris were freer enquiry into this."

As Emerson discovered before he wrote *English Traits :*—

' He was already turning his eyes towards London.
" London is the heart of the world," he said, " wonderful
(were it) only from the mass of human beings." (He) liked
the huge machine.   Each keeps its own round.   The
baker's boy brings muffins to the window at a fixed hour
every day, and that is all the Londoner knows or wishes to
know on the subject.   But it turned out good men.'
(Meaning,—Good men sometimes prospered there.   David
Masson thought he might be thinking of the like of G. L.
Craik or it might be Fonblanque or Bowring, Lockhart or
Dilke.)

" As a place to live in," Carlyle told Emerson, " I prefer
London to any other. (In Craigenputtock) my only
companion to speak to is the minister of Dunscore kirk.
I used to go sometimes to the kirk, and envy the poor
parishioners their good faith.   But I seldom go, and
the minister has grown suspicious of us, and does not
(now) come to see me."[2]

He said John Mill " is the best mind I know ;   more

---

[1] Letter in O. W. Holmes's *Emerson*, p. 78.
[2] *Memoir of R. W. Emerson*, by J. E. Cabot, I, p. 195.

purity, more force (than any other) ; has worked himself clear from Benthamism." [1]

' He had read in a current book that when the writer enquired in a New York Hotel for the Boots, he had been shown across the street, and had found Mungo in his own house, dining on roast turkey. He thought this " the best thing " in the book, as it showed that " a man can have meat for his labour."

' He still returned to English pauperism, the crowded country, the selfish abdication by public men of all that public persons should perform. " Government should direct poor men what to do. Poor Irish folk come wandering over these moors. My dame makes it a rule to give to every son of Adam bread to eat, and supplies his wants to the next house. But here are thousands of acres which might give them all meat, and nobody to bid these poor Irish go to the moor and till it. They burned the stacks, and so found a way to force the rich people to attend to them."

' " The Duchess of Queensberry was appointed to possess this estate," said he.—" By God Almighty," added the the lady.

' Carlyle does not pretend to have solved the great problems,' (arising from the discovery that the current religion was untrue, apparently), ' but rather to be an observer of their solution as it goes forward in the world. I asked him at what religious development the concluding passage in his piece upon German Literature and Characteristics pointed. He replied that he was not competent to state even to himself,—he waited rather to see. He is the most catholic of philosophers ; he forgives and loves everybody, and wishes each to struggle on in his own place and arrive at his own ends. But his scale of eminence is about the reverse of the popular scale, Scott, Mackintosh, Jeffrey, Gibbon,—even Bacon, are no heroes of his. Burns, and Samuel Johnson, and Mirabeau, he said, interested him, and I suppose whoever else has given himself with all his heart to a leading instinct, and has not *calculated* too much.

' Plato he does not read, and he disparaged Socrates ; and, when pressed, persisted in making Mirabeau a hero.

[1] *Memoir of R. W. Emerson,* by J. E. Cabot, I, p. 195.

Gibbon he called the splendid bridge from the old world to the new. He liked Nero's death, " *Qualis artifex pereo !* " (What an artist is dying in me !) better than most history.

' *Tristram Shandy* was one of his first books after *Robinson Crusoe*, and Robertson's *America* an early favourite.

' He took despairing or satirical views of literature at this moment ; recounted the incredible sums paid in one year by the great booksellers for puffing. Hence it comes that no newspaper is trusted now, no books are bought, and the booksellers are on the verge of bankruptcy.'

That books were not selling then was true. According to the *Author*, for example, (May, 1898) :—" The most dead, dull and dejected time in the whole history of English Literature was the early 'thirties. In the autumn of 1832 there were hardly any books published at all." The relative importance of puffing as one of the causes of this was exaggerated at the time. Politics did most.

When Emerson told Carlyle how cordially his essay on Burns had been appreciated in America, his wife said,— " That is always the way ; whatever he has writ that he thinks has fallen dead, he hears of two or three years afterwards." [1]

' Mrs. Carlyle told of the disappointment when they had determined to go to Weimar, and could not go. The first thing Goethe sent was the chain she wore round her neck, and how she capered when it came ! But since that time he had sent many things.'

Only on one topic was Emerson disappointed. " Carlyle's talent," he remarked to himself, " lies more in seizing the idea of the man or the time, than in original speculation. He seems merely to work with a foreign thought, not to live in it himself."

We have to recall that Emerson had recently lost his wife and had just been preaching in an Edinburgh pulpit. Bereavements revive the hope of life after death, and among many the conscience itself is entangled with it, so that from Confucius to Carlyle the men of sense have agreed to taboo the topic. Where nothing can be known, nothing

---

[1] Letter in O. W. Holmes's *Emerson*, p. 78,

should be said. Here is Emerson's report of how his questions were parried.

' We went out for a walk over long hills, and looked at Criffel, then without his cap, and down into Wordsworth's country. Then we sat down, and talked of the immortality of the soul. It was not Carlyle's fault that we talked on that topic, for he had the natural disinclination of every nimble spirit to bruise itself against walls, and did not like to place himself where no step could be taken. But he was honest and true, and cognisant of the subtle links that bind ages together, and saw how every event affects all the future. "Christ died on the tree; that built Dunscore Kirk yonder; that brought you and me together. Time has only a relative existence." '

So the sunny-faced Emerson departed happy next day, (26.8.1833). "I saw him go up the hill," said Carlyle afterwards.[1] "I didn't go with him to see him descend. I preferred to watch him mount and vanish like an angel."

In Carlisle that night the " merry " traveller wrote what he remembered. Then he waited upon Wordsworth, and on Sunday (1.9.1833), when about to embark at Liverpool, he thanked God in his diary for having shown him Landor and Coleridge, Carlyle and Wordsworth, tho' all the four of them were " deficient in insight into religious truth."

" The comfort of meeting men of genius such as these," he wrote, "is that they talk sincerely, they feel themselves to be so rich that they are above the meanness of pretending to knowledge which they have not, and they frankly tell you what puzzles them. But Carlyle—Carlyle is so amiable that I love him."

The liking was mutual. Carlyle confessed to Mill (10.9.1833), that he had learned from the visitor that some Unitarians might be " limited " at worst and " not hollow. . . . Emerson, your presentee, rolled up hither, one of the pleasantest interruptions to our solitude. He staid with us four and twenty hours, and was thro' the whole Enyclopedia with me in that time. What I loved in the man was his health, his unity with himself, all seemed to

---

[1] To Lord Houghton : see *Memoir of R. W. Emerson*, by J. E. Cabot, I, p. 197.

find adjustment with him, spontaneous, peaceable, even humble."

The last word was very like him. Before long he was expatiating on it to Mill in a way that explains what he meant by praising Emerson for being humble.—' It is long years since I first saw the meaning of Humility (Entsagen), and it came on me like water on the dying of thirst, and I felt it and still feel it to be the beginning of moral life. Unhappy that I am ! Could I keep that always in my eye, I too had "overcome the world." '

It always cost him an effort to be humble, but he did his best with much success,—which is surely a good example. Pride is our besetting sin and never needs teaching,—it keeps us stupid and often leads to strife, sometimes to ruin.

X

"THE DIAMOND NECKLACE"

(1833)

BOTH Mill and Emerson were mature before they met Carlyle and so were rather friends than disciples. They were influenced by him, and he was influenced by them in turn. It might appear unseemly in Mill to obtrude advice about writing ; yet he " dealt faithfully " with his friend, remarking of the *Cagliostro* this August,[1]— " I know not why you should call it ' half-mad ' ; it is merely like much of your writing—half-ironical, half-earnest ; it may be of use to some people. If human beings would but do thoroughly all they do, I believe with you that Good would be much more forwarded than Evil : *halfness* is the great enemy of spiritual worth ; whatever shames any human being out of that, is of unspeakable value."

Before there was any written reply to this, Mill wrote again (5.9.1833), and mentioning *Sartor* as well as *Cagliostro* he frankly enquired,—" Whether that mode of writing between sarcasm or irony and earnest be really deserving of so much honour as you give it by making use of it so frequently. Are there many things worth saying in that manner which cannot be said in a more direct way ? Much of your phraseology fails to bring home your meaning so well as would perhaps be done by commoner and more familiar phrases." [1]

Replying on 24.9.1833, Carlyle said all he could to persuade Mill to write more about the French Revolution. He praised the review of Alison's History, which Mill had already written on his advice. He subscribed to every word of that, he said, including the emphasis.—

' Emphasis in uttering, what is it but the natural result of entireness in believing ; the *first* condition of all worth

[1] *Letters of J. S. Mill,* by H. Elliot, I, pp. 61–69.

in words spoken ? Give me a man that has legs to stand on.
I set little store by tolerance (perceiving what is so called
to be) Indifferentism. . . . How different is that honey-
mouthed, tear-stained, soup-kitchen Jesus Christ of our
poor shovel-hatted modern Christians from the stern-
visaged Christ of the Gospels, proclaiming aloud in the
Market-place (with such a total contempt of the respecta-
bilities) : " *Woe* unto you, Scribes and Pharisees,
hypocrites ! "

'About my style, your interrogatory is right. I think
often of the matter myself ; and *see* only that I cannot yet
see. Irony is a sharp instrument ; but ill to handle without cutting *yourself*. I cannot justify, yet can too well
explain what sets me so often on it of late : it is my
singularly anomalous position to the world,—and if you
will, my own singularly unreasonable temper. I never know
or can even guess what or who my audience is, or whether
I have any audience : thus too naturally I adjust myself
on the Devil-may-care principle. Besides I have under
all my gloom a genuine feeling of the ludicrous ; and could
have been the merriest of men, *had I not* been the sickest
and saddest. Thus stands it : but I tell you I will mend ;
and what more can man do ? Now I beg of you write with
all abandonment.'

" Doubt not but that I shall do so, more and more,"
was Mill's reply, on 5.10.1833, when he was about to
leave for Paris, and in later letters and many a talk he
let himself go ; but he could not change his nature. A
man's character is his fate, and he lacked what Carlyle had
abundantly, a sense of humour, the happiest of all human
endowments. It may be doubted whether he ever realized
the force of what Carlyle was soon telling him in discussing
a projected new Radical periodical, and explaining the
success of Blackwood's and Fraser's Tory Magazines.—
'The Radicals as yet have almost no genius . . . *There is
a kind of Fiction which is not Falsehood*,[1] and has more
effect in addressing men than many a Radical is aware of.
. . The Radicals appear *naked*,' whereas Blackwood's
and Fraser's men have 'theatrical costume with orchestra
and stage lights, and thereby alone a wonderful advantage.'
Mill acknowledged at once (5.10.1833) the force of
Carlyle's suggestion that he should write,—' something

[1] Italics added.

more elaborate than I have yet written on the French Revolution : it is highly probable I shall do it sometime if you do not, but besides the difficulty of doing it tolerably, there is the far greater difficulty of doing it so as to be read in England, until the time comes when one can speak of Christianity as it may be spoken of in France—as gone, never to return, only what was best in it to reappear (Heaven knows when). Without *saying out* one's whole belief on that point, it is impossible to write about the French Revolution in any way professing to tell the whole truth. I have been reading the New Testament. As far as I know your impressions about Christ, *mine* are exactly the same. How strikingly just, for instance, is your contrast in your last letter between the Christ of the Gospels, and the namby-pamby Christ of the poor modern Christians. Since you were so much pleased with Emerson, I feel encouraged to try you with almost any person whatever who has any sort of good in him ; I should have thought *he* was about the last person who would have interested you so much as he seems to have done.'

When Dr. John had departed and Mrs. Welsh found her daughter well, she took her to Moffat to drink the waters, which only did harm by reviving the bile. Mrs. Carlyle came home sick before the end of September.[1] The motive of the Moffat expedition was palpable. Her mother was shuddering at the thought of London, and felt what others saw that pregnancy was the one way to make her daughter be docile and willing to live within easy reach at Edinburgh ; and a course of Moffat waters was one of the fashionable ways of predisposing married women to pregnancy.[2]

Meanwhile Mill had gone to Paris on holiday, and was there getting books for Carlyle and noting down for his benefit from Comte's lips the cash details of house-keeping in London and Paris.

Before the month was out, the Rev. John Hunter of the Tron Church, Edinburgh, procured from his brother, who lived at Barjarg, within ten miles of Craigenputtock, access for Carlyle to a fine private library there, with plenty of the French Revolution books he wanted,—a welcome

---

[1] *Early Letters of Jane Welsh Carlyle*, by D. G. Ritchie, p. 247. Date *fixed* by *Letters of T. C.*, II, p. 117.

[2] From a lady who knew Mrs. Welsh, reported by her daughter. Many married women similarly situated resorted to Moffat ; and an Edinburgh specialist in women's diseases told D. A. W. they used to be advised by doctors to do so.

addition to those he was getting from Edinburgh, London and Paris. In a letter to Dr. John on 1st October he said :—

‘ The *thing* I want to do is precisely the thing I cannot do. My mind would so fain deliver itself adequately of that “ Divine Idea of the World ” ; and only in quite *ina*dequate approximations is such deliverance possible. I want to write what Teufelsdröckh calls the story of the *Time-Hat* ; to show forth to the men of these days that they also live in an Age of Miracle ! We shall see. Meanwhile, one of the subjects that engages me most is the French Revolution. My chief errand to Paris were freer enquiry into this.’

Then after telling how he would write a “ History of the Diamond Necklace ” to try his hand at narrative, *whether editors wanted it or not*, he mentioned the safe arrival of books sent, and added :—‘ Finally, yesterday, I drove over to Barjarg to get *the keys of the Library* most handsomely left for me by the Hunters ; so that I could seize the Catalogue and some half-dozen volumes and hasten off with them, to return at discretion ! It is really a very great favour ; there are various important works there ; reading which I am far better than at any University. For the first time in my life I have free access to some kind of Book-collection ; I a Book-man. One way and other, we look forward to a cheerfullish kind of winter here.’

In a long letter to Leigh Hunt four weeks later (29.10.1833) he said :—[1]

‘ This winter, at all events, and who knows how much more, we mean to spend here. London I liked much, but the fogs and smoke were pestiferous ; Edinburgh I find has left but a sad impression of hollowness and dullness on me : however, both might yield profit ; and now a solitary winter, filled to overflowing with books (for I have discovered a Library here), may be the profitablest of all. You, as a determined Book-moth, will appreciate my felicity, when you hear that I read some ten hours often at a sitting, divided by *one*, for a walk, which I take like physic. My head grows a perfect “ Revolt of Paris ” ; nothing occurring to divert me ; only the little Table-clock (poor

little fellow) suggesting now and then that I am still in the
world of time. I fall asleep at last towards midnight,
amid the Cannon volleys, shrieks and legislative debates,
the laughter and tears, of whole generations ;—for it is
mainly History and Memoirs that I am reading. Now
and then I shall perhaps write something, were it only for
Prince Posterity. Thus you see us with winter at our
door ; but with huge stacks of fuel for the body's warmth,
and for the mind's.

' A benevolent artist rehabilitated the Piano : a little
music is invaluable to me ; better than sermons ; winnows
all the bitter dust out of me, and for moments makes me a
good man.'

His wife was more explicit to Bess Stodart (9.11.1833).
Here is something she wrote, sandwiched between
personalities and needlework.[1]

' A great Godsend has befallen my Husband this autumn,
in which, as in all his other Godsends and Devilsends, I
heartily participate. John Hunter (who never saw him)
has been induced to confide to him the keys of the Barjarg
Library (an extensive and valuable collection), with leave
to borrow therefrom at discretion. You cannot figure what
an inestimable benefit it is, in our situation, or what
exhalations of gratitude rise from my Husband's soul
towards the minister of the Tron. I verily believe if he
were in Edinburgh, he would even go and hear him preach,
to show his sense of the kindness. Two gig-boxfulls of excellent books have already been brought over and consumed by
one party like reek, while I have selected therefrom *Memoirs
of Marie Antionette* (by Mme. Campan), *Œuvres de Mme.
Roland* (the very best woman I ever scraped acquaintance
with), *Mémoires de Mme. de Staël*, a clever, spirited, little
creature, quite superior to the sentimental de Stael-Holstein
that I used to make such work about in my "*wee existence*",
and finally a Life of Cooke the Actor, as a warning against
drunkenness.'

It may be only a coincidence that two weeks sooner
Carlyle in writing to Mill had said he preferred Madame
Roland to de Staël, as Madame Roland " utterly divests

[1] *Early Letters of Jane Welsh Carlyle*, by D. G. Ritchie, pp. 250-1.

herself of *Cant*," which de Staël " never could even resolutely try to do."

Like his wife's music in the evening was the effect on Carlyle of reading Homer at regular intervals, which he was doing this winter in the company of an unfortunate Mr. Glen, a young gentleman he had met in London, now lodging near him for the sake of his health. The head of Glen was stuffed with old Greek vocables. It was expected his health would benefit by the occupation, and Carlyle was rewarded for his kindness by a better insight into " Homer." He had books about it by Heine, Voss and others sent from Edinburgh by Inglis, and wrote to his brother, Dr. John :—

' Nothing I have read for long years so interests and nourishes me : I am quite surprised at the interest I take in it. All the *Antiquity* I have ever known becomes *alive* in my head : there is a whole gallery of Apelleses and Phidiases that I not only look upon but *make*. Never before had I any so distinct glimpse of Antique Art ; those Pompeii Engravings of yours, and all of the sort I have seen, first get their significance.'

In returning Voss, etc., he told Henry Inglis who had sent them that he loved Homer " better than any other Book except the Bible."

Like Venus from the sea in the ancient story, like mist from the water in the morning, so *The Diamond Necklace* rose from all this reading, finished with an effort (17.12. 1833),—for it needed an effort to write anything after he had access to the Barjarg Library. Assuredly *The Diamond Necklace* is better narrative than anything he had done yet, more Homeric indeed. But it need not be supposed there was any conscious imitation. Carlyle was returning to Nature and to the contempt for fiction which is natural to an earnest adult mind. He was a born teller of true stories, recovering now from the bad effects of " education," from which his docility had made him suffer more than usual. In artistic perfection and fidelity to fact *The Diamond Necklace* was the fitting Prelude to the French Revolution. It was the last thing he wrote at Craigenputtock.

XI

JOHN MILL AT PARIS

(1833)

CARLYLE could not afford to visit Paris next year, and benefited all the more by Mill's inspection of it now. His journal shows him balancing (1.11.1833) :— " Shall I write a Life of Bonaparte ? A French Revolution ? " Mill not only hunted for books, he explored the ways of thinking of contemporary Parisians, and reported at length to Carlyle when he came home (25.11. 1833) about some of the best of them, and Godefroi Cavaignac in particular.—[1]

' One must be at Paris to know how profoundly irreligious the French are. Our friends the Saint-Simonians have done much good. The Père (Father) having been let out of prison has gone with others of the set to persuade the Pacha of Egypt to let them cut a canal across the Isthmus of Suez. What has become of those who went to Constantinople in search of *la femme libre* (the woman at large) I do not know. One or two have become disciples of Fourier. Some have become Catholics ; but none of the considerable men. The great majority have retained of St. Simonianism about as much as is good and true, dropping the rest.

' Among the individuals of another kind two made a particular impression upon me, republican leaders of different sorts, Carrel the editor, a Conservative Republican,' with such views of the French Revolution as Mill had never ' met in any book,' and ' Cavaignac, President of the active stirring revolutionary party, who look up to Robespierre, and aim at *l'égalité absolue*. He is for taking the first opportunity for overthrowing the Government by force, in six months, or a year at farthest ; a man whose name

---

[1] *Letters of J. S. Mill*, by H. Elliot, I, pp. 74–80, and published letters of T.C.

is energy, who cannot ask you the commonest question but in so decided a manner that he makes you start ; a man of irresistible power and indomitable will. Intense in everything, he is the intensest of atheists, and says, " I don't like those who believe in God," because " it is generally a reason for doing nothing for man." His notion of duty is that of a Stoic—he conceives it as something quite infinite, and having nothing whatever to do with happiness, something immeasurably above it. According to him man's life consists of one perennial struggle against evil, which but for that struggle would overwhelm him : generation after generation carries on this battle, with little success as yet : he believes in progress ; that the only satisfaction man can realise is in battling with evil ; that there sometimes comes one great clearing off on one day of reckoning called a revolution ; that it is only on such rare occasions, very rarely indeed on any others, that good men get into power, and then they ought to seize the opportunity for doing all they can ; that any government which is boldly attacked by ever so small a minority may be overthrown, and that is his hope with regard to the present government.

' His notion of *égalité absolue* is rather speculative than practical : he says he does not know whether it should be by an equal division of the *means* of production (land and capital), or by an equal division of the produce. When I stated to him the difficulties of both, he felt and acknowledged them ; all he had to propose were but a variety of measures *tending towards* an equalisation of property, and he seems to have a strange reliance on events, thinking that, when the end is clearly conceived, the circumstances of the case would, when power is in the right hands, suggest the most appropriate means. Cavaignac is the son of a conventionalist and regicide. He is a much more accomplished man than most of the political men I saw there ; has a wider range of ideas, converses on art and most subjects of general interest, always throwing all he has to say into a few brief energetic sentences, as if it was contrary to his nature to expend one superfluous word.

' I am to correspond with Cavaignac and Carrel. . . . I think you will go to Paris next summer, and I probably pay my visit to you there instead of Craigenputtock.'

Replying in December Carlyle announced the completion

of the *Diamond Necklace* and said that only the lack of
money to spare prevented them going to Paris. Unable
to see the Parisians again at home, he discussed the
details Mill had sent him, remarking how 'everybody' there was 'in the most indignant Opposition
to Providence. They eat their victuals cursing the cookery
and live uselessly, and die as a fool dieth.' Carrel and
Cavaignac 'were at least a more emphatic species . . .
Cavaignac's very Atheism is better Theism than that of
Shovel-hat-dom ; the wretchedest dish-washings at present
in the world.' And yet the Atheism was a counter-perver-
sity.—' Whoever recognises the infinite nature of Duty
believes in a God, against his own consciousness,' that is to
say, altho' he supposes he does not !—Which is not so
absurd as it seems. In common with many contemporaries,
Carlyle was meaning by " God " no ancient Hebrew idol
but the Soul of the World, the "All-creating Nature" which
inspires the souls of men.

The strange hubbub about " the good of the species "
so noticeable at Paris did not appeal to Carlyle, who said,—
' No real benefactor of Mankind ' went to work in that way,
but ' rather worked out what was best and purest *in
himself*,' and left the " good of the species " to God, believing ' no good thing ' ever is lost. That was how
Christ himself had lived, said Carlyle, congratulating Mill
on his reading the New Testament and understanding it.

Dragged into discussion of creeds, he was soon admitting
there was no difference between them except that Mill
as yet was ' consciously nothing of a mystic,' meaning
he did not realize the limits of human knowledge. The
argument from ' marks of design ' was absurd, and so on.
' And so I live in a kind of Christian *Islam*,' meaning
submission to what has to be, ' and say at all turns of
Fortune, " God is Great," and also " God is Good," and
know not aught else that I could say. " Walk humbly
in well-doing," there is no other road for one,' and in short
he identified " Entsagen " with " Humility " ; and soon
afterwards *excused himself from further discussion* on ' those
beliefs of yours ', as it ' might rather unsettle and perplex
than forward and strengthen you,' and to be growing
healthily and ' not closed in, which I trust you will never be,
is all that any kind of world theory can do for any man.'

Suffice it here to add that according to Mill, Carrel

" would certainly be President of the Republic if there were a republic within five years, and the extreme party did not get the upper hand " ; but in a year or two he perished miserably in a duel, the news of which was brought to Carlyle by Godefroi Cavaignac then in London.

In the 1830 Revolution, this Godefroi Cavaignac had demanded a Republic, in an interview with Louis Philippe, in a " big, gloomy room of the Palais Royal." Louis Philippe wanted a throne for himself and spoke of his father, " Egalité Orleans." " Altesse," (Highness), said Cavaignac to him, " vous finirez comme lui," (you'll end as *he* did), meaning—on the guillotine ! Carlyle was fond of telling this, and it now helps to explain the panic flight of Louis Philippe in 1848. But in 1833 he seemed secure on the throne, and Cavaignac had soon to go into exile in London. Becoming a friend of Carlyle there, Cavaignac was a living book of reference at his elbow while he was finishing his Revolution history. Carlyle who ' loved him much ' described him to Mill as ' the best Frenchman by many degrees whom I have met with. A courageous and energetic man, with much free Nature and bonhomie in his composition ; really a son of Nature, tho' French and in this time.'

It was a brother of his, General Cavaignac, who became military dictator and kept order in Paris in 1848, and would have been elected President, if the rabble had not run after Napoleon the Little.

[1] *Literary Recollections*, by F. Espinasse, p. 239.

XII

THE BREAK WITH JEFFREY

(1833–34)

WHILE *The French Revolution* of Carlyle was thus growing mysteriously as living things do, there was a break with Jeffrey this winter which has been misreported, and was never quite understood by either Jeffrey or himself.

The last of Jeffrey's political battles had been won. He was wintering at home, aware he would soon be there for good as he was about to retire to the bench, and writing long and friendly letters to both the Carlyles. He tried to coax them to winter again in Edinburgh. Thus to Mrs. Carlyle :—

(On 14.11.1833.)

' MY DEAR INFANT,

'Am I forgotten yet ? The *affairé* (or busy) official of Whitehall has a heart as mindful as the recluse of Craigenputtock—and if the recluse objects to this, her creed is the paltrier. The imposed tasks of life have little to do with its voluntary movements, and the treadmill is the same distraction (or degradation) whether it grinds out fine sifted speculations on Diderot and Goethe, or responses to pragmatical Town Clerks on the working of the Burgh Reform Act.

' I heard of you last from my cheerful friend the Dr. (John Carlyle) recently before leaving London, and he spoke favourably of your health. Best love to Carlyle. I hope his dyspepsy and misanthropy are milder.'

(On 4.12.1833)

' MY DEAR INFANT,

' I thank you a thousand times for your letter. It is very kind, very reasonable, and above all, very *tolerant* and very *cheerful*. God bless you, my large hearted, high minded child—for you are but a child you know after all—

with your pretty bits of lessons and exercises—and your magnanimous purpose of fighting for your pet fancies— or convictions, as you call them. *Fighting is about the worst kind of child's play—and of such is* NOT *the kingdom of Heaven.*[1] But you do not mean to fight anybody—not even me.—It is but a way of speaking.'

This was one of the vivacities he afterwards begged pardon for, " if " she was vexed ; and with humorous inconsistency in this very letter, as if to make offence impossible, he wrote :—' I am determined to learn German, and give battle to that race of canting muddy-headed pretenders. I want Macaulay to clapperclaw Niebuhr in the meantime, and Palgrave to demolish Goethe.

' And now it is dark December, and the roaring blasts must be dismal in your upland solitude. Come down and shelter among human habitations. It is not good for either of you to be so much alone. Let us put away all tone of wrangling. I know I offend in that sort, but I will not again, and so Heaven bless you. Ever affectly yours,

F. JEFFREY.

'I shall write to Carlyle one day soon.'

Accordingly four days later he wrote (8.12.1833) :—

' MY DEAR CARLYLE,

' You are very good, and very reasonable, and I value your love for me very highly. Why I do not write— (or have not written, for we shall put that in the past tense, if you please) I cannot well answer, to myself, and therefore not to you.' (The letters to Mrs. Carlyle had told of his being " a good deal damaged in health " before leaving London in August. He now runs on.)—' Only writing or not, never doubt that I shall always have a great affection for you—with some provocation—and some admiration—and a most sincere desire for your happiness— —or if that word offends you—your well-being—right-mindedness — strong workingness — or whatever else is your favourite synonym for a desirable condition of being.

' Let nothing shake this faith in you, and I think I shall never do anything to shake it. You say much changes within you—let me hope that some of the changes may bring our views more near to each other. For my part I

---

[1] Italics added. Jeffrey underlined only *not*.

do not change much. I think zeal for creeds more and
more ludicrous—and that all discussion, which aims at
much more than exercising our faculties, and exposing
intolerance, is very tiresome and foolish. Do any of your
mutations tend *this way*? I fear not. What do you do
up in the mountains, all winter? Or why will you not
come down' (and so on)? 'And what do you read in your
treasure trove of a library? *My passion is for historical
collections, I mean contemporary documents, and full length
samples of the ages that are past. Your speculative history
I hold very cheap—unless indeed it be of my own making—
and therefore I utterly loathe and contemn the dogmatical
dreams of Niebuhr, which is not bricks without straw but
bricks without clay. Poetry is the best, but it exhausts and
excites too much, and for working days I prefer Rushworth
and old Chronicles, or even a well printed chartulary or record
of authentic charters. It is a fine thing that same authenticity
and a rare.'* [1]

Such love of " authenticity " is a sample of the love
of fact or reality for itself, which pervaded all sensible
people in Scotland then more than now. The love of
poetry Jeffrey avowed was not so usual. Shakespeare
was less esteemed than he is to-day, and in him Carlyle
and Jeffrey had a favourite author in common. A little
while ago (16.8.1833) Jeffrey was telling Cockburn :— [2]
" I would willingly give up half my fortune, and some little
of the fragments of health and bodily enjoyment that
remain to me, rather than that Shakespeare should not
have lived before me."

To return to the letter, there followed personal news
(about Empson, Macaulay, etc.) and enquiries about
" your brother," and chaff,—" Why are you not as sociable
and cheerful as he is? It would be a fine thing now, if it
should turn out that your lofty self-tasking philanthropy was
merely the result of a bad secretion of bile, even if you did not
go the length of exhilarating the ordinary at Cheltenham,
with parodies of Goethe and epigrams on Edward Irving."
Then after telling about his own brother and hinting he
might retire himself very soon from politics, which in fact
he did within six months,[3] he wrote :—

[1] Italics added.
[2] Cockburn's *Life of Lord Jeffrey*, I, p. 350.
[3] *Ditto*, p. 352.

' God bless you. Write to me when you are minded. I shall answer, better at least than in the year 1833. *But at all events let me know whenever you think I can do you, or anybody you care about, any good.*[1] My Charlottes send their love to you ' (and so-on).

It should be explained that the heaviest work of the Lord Advocate in those days was making appointments. As Jeffrey complained to Cockburn this year,[2] he found it infinitely irksome to have to deal with " applications for places and offices, from a common exciseman up to a supreme judge, through all the variations of ministers, schoolmasters, professors, justices of the peace, lords-lieutenants, staff surgeons, colonels, consuls, King's confectioners, etc., etc." In short the patronage and power of his post were merely trouble to the God-like Ariel, who was an uncommon kind of politician. He was among the politicians, but not of them. " He only, in a general honest thought, and common good to all, made one of them." He really wished to appoint the fittest men, and so set a good example to the new town councillors, about to be elected in place of the old gangs, of whom even the Tories used to say that they would be harder to mend than Hell.

In December 1833 the newspapers were mentioning a vacancy difficult to fill at Edinburgh. An " Observer " fit to be professor of Astronomy was needed for the fine new Observatory, on a moderate salary, and there was no likely man in sight.

Meanwhile Carlyle was finding he might be frozen out of periodical writing. The *Foreign Quarterly* had declined the *Diamond Necklace* in advance. Nothing he had done lately was succeeding. *Sartor* was giving offence. In 1867 he recalled how at this time, and for years before and after now, his heart's desire was " *any* honest employment by which one might regularly gain one's daily bread."

' (I) *could*,' he used to think, ' learn to do honestly so many things, nearly all the things I have ever seen done, from the making of shoes, up to the engineering of canals, architecture of mansions as palatial as you liked, and perhaps to still higher things of the physical or spiritual

[1] Italics added.
[2] Cockburn's *Life of Lord Jeffrey*, pp. 347–8.

kind ; *would*, moreover, toil so loyally to do my task right, not wrong ; —and am forbidden to try any of them ; see the practical world closed against me as with brazen doors ; and must stand here, and perish idle ! '

A proof that he was right in feeling himself all-round efficient is that he invented this winter (1833–34) the "screw-cogs"[1] for roughening horses' shoes in frosty weather, which came into general use. The " model shoe " he had made at Dunscore smithy can still be seen at " Carlyle's House." [2] When Benjamin Franklin invented the " open stove," he declined to patent it, thinking patents wrong, and " having no desire of profiting by " them. He published for the public use an account of his stoves, " their construction and manner of operation." [3] In the same way and perhaps imitating Franklin, Carlyle this winter published full details of his invention, describing how with his horse thus shod he could " ride over a Swiss glacier."

He now ceased to oppose so firmly his brother Alick's " day-dreams " of America and declared to John (24.12. 1833) :—

' I often enough think,—what if I should go to America myself ! Thousands and millions must yet go ; it is properly but another section of our own country, tho' they rebelled very justly against George Guelph, and beat him, as they ought. We shall determine nothing rashly,—nothing presses.'

The need for an Observer at Edinburgh seemed a fair opportunity. He was strong in Mathematics and Astronomy, and felt sure he would soon be at home in such work. His old enthusiasms were not dead, but only asleep. The more he thought of it, the better he liked the prospect of " interrogating the eternal Stars in the silent midnight." So on 11.1.1834 he wrote to Jeffrey a letter [4] he thus described to John :—" I thought what an *honest* kind of work it was ; how honestly I would work at it for my bread, and harmonise it with what tended infinitely higher than bread, and so wrote with great heartiness, telling him all

[1] Called "Cogs ", " Frost Studs " and " Frost Nails " in adverts., January, 1921.
[2] Carlyle's House, The Back Dining-Room, 1923 Cat., item 180.
[3] *Autobiography of B. F.*, end of Chap. VIII.
[4] Letter lost.

this," but at the same time " with modesty and brevity "[1], which left Jeffrey in the dark about his qualifications.

Jeffrey was bent on setting an example how to select a man for such an appointment, and had been making it known in every way he could " that no testimonials would *be looked at*, except from persons of weight and authority in this particular branch of science," and that " Government " (which meant Jeffrey) would give the place " according to the recommendations of Herschell, Airy, Babbage and some six or seven other " such men, including Brewster and Napier.

Accordingly it had been offered to Thomas Galloway,[2] who had been a candidate for the Natural Philosophy chair last winter, and was one of the best of living astronomers. But he declined, accepting instead the better paid employment of Actuary to the Amicable Life Assurance Co. His greatest achievement was to prove the movement of the Sun, that it sweeps through space with all its planets like a huge steamer with a few small boats in tow ; and observations at the Cape of Good Hope were used by Galloway in showing this. Now the Cape Observer was Thomas Henderson, an Edinburgh man, once Jeffrey's clerk and secretary. So Henderson applied for the Edinburgh place, as Galloway did not want it.

It seemed an ideal solution, agreeable and right. Then came the letter from Carlyle, which Jeffrey answered by return of post, tho' wearied and unwell(14.1.1834). *As he had no inkling of Carlyle's special qualifications*, and never knew that Galloway, Brewster and Co. would have preferred Carlyle to Henderson, he must have supposed he was being requested to be partial, and may have been pleased to show how he could select a professor more fairly and sensibly than the Town Councillors last winter.—

' MY DEAR FRIEND,

     ' It is best to tell you at once that I do not think there is the least chance of your getting the chair of astronomy, and that it would be idle to make any application.'

---

[1] The last four words are from *Reminiscences*, Norton's Ed., II, 266.

[2] Grand uncle of D. A. W., who knew his widow, and inherited his papers : but what it is needful to tell here has long been in print. See *Dict. Nat. Biog., Encyc. Brit*, 11th Ed., and see the *Memoir of Augustus de Morgan*, by his wife, pp. 60, 155, 180–2, etc., etc.

Omitting mention of the offer to Galloway, which Carlyle never knew, he explained how he was leaving the appointment to the experts. The work was rather observing than teaching. The instruments were expensive and easily damaged. So Henderson was " the most hopeful of the candidates now in the field, my clerk or secretary before going to the Cape as Observer." Which naturally led Carlyle to conclude the thing was settled and the " experts " a mere pretence, and to resent more than usual what followed in the letter, a very fierce statement of what Jeffrey felt about his recent writings. *Characteristics* had shocked him, and *Corn Law Rhymes* and *Diderot* ; and in the December *Fraser*, the second instalment of *Sartor* had let him see in print more than he had read in the manuscript.—

' I am very sorry. I have always felt deep regret at your not having some regular profession. That of a Teacher is no doubt a most useful and noble one. But you cannot actually exercise it, unless you offer to teach what is thought worth learning, and in a way that is thought agreeable, and I am afraid you have not fulfilled either of these conditions. No man ever did more to obstruct the success of his doctrines by the tone in which he promulgated them. It is arrogant, vituperative, obscure, anti-national, and inconclusive. As you begin to experience the effects, you may perhaps give more credit to my testimony than you used to do. You will never find (or make) the world friendly to your doctrines, while you insist upon dragooning it into them in so hyperbolical a manner. Forgive me all this. I am sick, and scrawl, tired of my own compelled activity, and look forward, with more recoiling of heart than I like to own, to the contentious scene which lies before me.'

Then after kind personalities and saying he was glad " my fair cousin," meaning Mrs. C., was well, he concluded : —' We shall move (to London) I think about the 28th. Write before that time. God bless you. Ever Yours.
FR. JEFFREY.'

" He canna hinder thee of God's Providence," said old Mrs. Carlyle, who was on a visit at Craigenputtock when this letter arrived. Her daughter, " Jane the Lesser," had lately married a cousin Aitken, a house painter in Dumfries, and her youngest son, James, was about to

2 A

marry. She wanted to see as much as possible of Tom, while he was still at Craigenputtock, and promised in effect to come and live with him wherever he was, if she was not happy at Scotsbrig with the wife of James.

Carlyle replied to Jeffrey " good humouredly, by the first post, in the old light style," and thanked him for the swift dispatch. To his brother John he reported :—" I have written suppressing all indignation. I can see him even in this letter to be miserable, and am bound to help him, not aggravate him. His censures, too, have something flattering even in their violence—otherwise impertinent, he cannot tolerate me, but also he cannot despise me. On the whole, dear Jack, I feel it very wholesome to have my vanity humbled from time to time. Would it were rooted out for ever and a day ! "

On the evening before departing for London, (4.2.1834), Jeffrey wrote again, revealing what had been in his mind when writing three weeks before. The Rhetoric and English Literature chair in Edinburgh was soon to be vacant and so to speak in his gift. It was better paid than Astronomy, and the purport of his letter was to let Carlyle know beforehand not to apply. He protested :— " If I were the Patron of the Rhetoric chair, I should venture to appoint you, tho' with some consciousness of responsiblilty." But he had to consider his colleagues. He might have said that as an Ultra-Radical Carlyle was as hateful to the Whigs as to the Tories. What he did say was that " Govt." had all but decided to abolish the chair. The " Poet Campbell " might be appointed to it, but assuredly nobody " less generally accredited, or with a name less generally attractive."

" The best laid schemes of mice and men gang aft a-gley " or asquint. The " Govt." went out in December, and in 1835 the desirable professorship went to " little Geordie Moir," the " respectable Tory " advocate, who sketched Craigenputtock. To return to Jeffery's letter of 4.2.1834 :—

' You are very good natured to me,' he said, ' and set down my vivacities to the right account. I am afraid they do no good, but God knows they are not meant to hurt or offend you. But is it not a melancholy and rather provoking thing, to feel (and again on an occasion like this) that what I cannot but consider as perverse views and absurdities, should thus be accumulating obstacles to your ever attaining either the public position or the general respect to which your talents and diligence might otherwise have entitled you ?

' While things are as they certainly will be all my life, I do not think there is the least chance of your being admitted into any regular Seminary, as a Teacher, with such doctrines, and such a tone of inculcation, on record against you, as must be referred to, even in proof of your qualifications.

' I do not yet know where I shall be in London. But you may address to me at the House of C.

' God bless you—Ever Affectly. Yours,

FR. JEFFREY.

' I have (word omitted = indulged in) vivacities with my fair cousin too, for which, if they vex her, I beg her pardon. *But who would not be provoked to see Titania in love with Bottom.'* [1]

Here ended the "friendly or effusive" correspondence between Jeffrey and Carlyle. The last sentence of the postscript, which Froude supposed the key to the break, was perhaps the pleasantest reading in it. To flatter the wife was always a safe way to please Carlyle, and his *Reminiscences* and letters show he rightly understood *this* letter as an attempt to make amends for the one before it. The misunderstanding about the Astronomy chair was never cleared; yet " deep ineffaceable resentment " existed only in the fancy of the foolish Froude. Carlyle and Jeffrey never quarrelled or missed a chance of coming together as long as Jeffrey lived ; and even strangers who happened to witness their reunions used to remark how much they liked each other.[2]

In old age Carlyle reflected :—

' What a finger of Providence was this of the Edinburgh Observatory ; to which, had Jeffrey assented, I should certainly have gone rejoicing ! These things really strike one's heart. The good Lord Advocate, who really was pitiable, and miserably ill off, in his eminent position, showed visible embarrassment at sight of me, come to settle

---

[1] Italics added. See *Thomas Carlyle* by J. A. Froude, II, p. 401.
[2] David Masson and others to D. A. W., verbally.

in London, without furtherance asked or given ; and on other occasions seemed to recollect the Astronomical catastrophe, in a way which touched me, and was generous. He was returning home,' (retiring to the bench in Edinburgh, in short), ' a solidly wise resolution.'

It was May, 1834, when he was leaving London and Carlyle coming to settle there.

XIII

TO LONDON

(1834)

CARLYLE confessed to himself at once that he had been depending a little upon Jeffrey. Before the end of February and soon after he discovered Jeffrey was not going to do anything for him, he decided to come to London. "Burn our ships!" cried his wife, rejoicing at the prospect of seeing the last of Craigenputtock. They both were in the best of health; but the regular employment he counted on in 1832 was threatening to fail. Besides, man cannot live on fresh air alone, "nor woman either." They wanted company. They wrote at once to Mrs. Austin, Hunt and others to help them by looking out for a London house for Whitsunday, and till then the Barjarg Library kept him happy with "whole heaps of books." As he had told Mrs. Austin :—

'I think I have arrived at a kind of pause in my history. I have written very little for a year; less than for any of the last seven. I stand as if earnestly looking out, in the most labyrinthic country, till I catch the right track again. We shall do our best.'

From Mill he was hearing of a new Radical quarterly, the *London Review*. Mill had the refusal of the editorship, and said he hoped Carlyle would find it "more congenial than *Fraser's Magazine*. Such an article as 'Corn Law Rhymes' would have suited perfectly. The plan is to drop every kind of lying, (including) the lie of pretending that all the articles are reviews. There is to be no *we*, but each writer is to have a signature."

Charles Buller was to be a contributor. Sir William Molesworth had advanced enough to keep it going awhile.

357

" How much will your Review take to launch it then ? " he had asked. " Say £4,000," answered Mill. " Here then," said Molesworth, writing a cheque. Carlyle agreed to write for it when it started, and hoped they might think of him as editor, deciding to accept any offer of that sort on tolerable terms. He said to himself he could not write for nothing. He had rather less than £300 " to front London with." But he felt he had " plenty of Radicalism," and told his brother so whenever he heard of the projected Review. Indeed he was far in front of the Radicals of his day, and aware of it, but liked them well because they were free from hypocrisy and falsehood,—" no poison " in them, he used to say, tho' " barren." Mill and he agreed that Buller in Parliament and Fonblanque out of it were the only two Radicals " of genius."

At the same time Fraser was reporting that *Sartor* was being received with " the most unqualified disapproval." As Jeffrey had anticipated, such stuff was frightening editors. A magazine is as conventional as a church or a shop, and *Sartor* in *Fraser* was like a John the Baptist in a cathedral pulpit. Yet Carlyle was so far from repenting the outspokenness which was making him " impossible " that he was now (18.2.1834) telling his brother Alexander to train his little daughter " to this as the corner-stone of all morality : *to stand by the truth ; to abhor a lie as one does Hell-fire*," which was " taking " the name of Hell " in vain " or " in a Pickwickian sense." He was not thinking of the Bible, but paraphrasing the speech in Homer assigned to Achilles :—" Hateful to me, even as the gates of Hades, is he that hideth one thing in his heart and uttereth another."

As soon as the " winter deluges " abated, (5.3.1834), Carlyle went to Scotsbrig to break the impending change to his mother, who took it quietly and piously. She had been anticipating it, whereas poor Mrs. Welsh had been hoping against hope to the last and broke into tears.

He was to go in advance of his wife to hunt for a house. " The life of an author," he wrote to Henry Inglis in returning books, (28.4.1834), " is now mine without remedy, and among the most difficult and painfullest ; nevertheless pray for me only, that I do not become a scoundrel ;—in the highest garret, I have no other prayer."

On Friday, (9.5.1834), he breakfasted in his sister's house in Annan, and in taking leave promised to his mother, —" You *shall* see me once yearly, and regularly hear from

me, while we live." Then his brothers went with him to
the steamer for Liverpool. Somewhere on the road to
London, his coach met a Trades'-Union procession.
Carlyle from the coach box saluted it "gravely," and the
leader of it gravely responded. By Tuesday, 13.5.1834,
he was in his old lodgings, 4 Ampton Street, Gray's Inn
Road.

He went to see Mrs. Austin that evening at Bayswater,
and was welcomed with a kiss and a " Niagara of gossip."
The most important item was that a young Mrs. Taylor,
tho' encumbered with husband and children, had ogled John
Mill successfully, so that he was " desperately in love."
There was nothing to confirm this in Mill's demeanour
when they met, but on Friday Charles Buller corroborated
hilariously,—the news was true.

Carlyle walked about inspecting houses in Brompton
and Kensington, which he liked best for the sake of " the
glorious Kensington Gardens," and north to Camden
Town, and Primrose Hill and Hampstead, and south to
Chelsea, near Leigh Hunt. Chelsea was the least fashionable locality, but had once been fashionable, and a good
house vacant there, 5 [1] Great Cheyne Row, appeared
"nearly *twice* as good as any other we could get at the money,"
—the rent was £35 ; and that was the one his wife selected.
They entered on 10th June, and the very first thing he
wrote in the house was a letter to tell his mother all about
it (12.6.1834).—

' We lie safe down in a little bend of the river, away
from all the great roads ; have air and quiet hardly inferior
to Craigenputtock, an outlook from the back windows
into mere leafy regions, with here and there a red high-
peaked old roof looking through ; and see nothing of
London, except by day the summits of St. Paul's Cathedral
and Westminster Abbey, and by night the gleam of the
great Babylon affronting the peaceful skies. Yet in *half
an hour* we can be, with a pair of stout legs, in the most
crowded part of the whole habitable Earth ; and every
quarter of an hour a Coach will take you for sixpence.
We are south-west *from* the smoke ; so during great part
of the year we shall have no more to do with it than you.
Nay even in East winds, we are near *five* miles from the
old, manufacturing part of London, and the smoke is all

[1] Now 24.

but gone before it reaches us.—As for the House itself, it is probably the best we ever lived in : a right old strong roomy brick house, built near one hundred and thirty years ago, and likely to see *three* races of their modern fashionables fall before it come down : all in perfect repair. Our furniture suits it well ; being all of a strong *weighty* sort.   In addition I should have mentioned a little garden behind, where all is as yet barren or weedy, except a cherry tree with almost *ripe* cherries on it, and two miserable rose-bushes : however, I have got a new set of Garden-tools (for six shillings), and will soon give it at least a clean face.   It is of admirable comfort to me in the *smoking* way : I can wander about in dressing-gown and straw-hat in it, as of old, and take my pipe in peace.   I think, were the Railways done, you must see it all with your own eyes, my dear Mother ; that were the shortest way.

' The Literary craft is hardly *so* bad as I expected. I find I shall get my Book (on the French Revolution) *printed* without cost ; but probably nothing more.   In the meantime I have some Magazine things in my eye' (for current expenses, in short) ; ' and then if my Book were *well* written, and out, I shall have a better name to start Lecturing, etc., with.

' My friends here continue all very kind, and do more for me than I had right to expect.   Hunt who lives close by, is not only the kindest but the politest of men ; has never yet been near us (which we reckon very civil), but always delighted when I go and rouse *him* for a walk ; and indeed a sprightly sensible talker he is, and very pleasant company for a stroll.   Jane greatly preferred his " poetical Tinkerdom " ' (his " hugger-mugger " household) ' to any of the unpoetical Gigmandoms (even Mrs. Austin's) which I showed her.'

By the end of June they were fairly installed and friends were calling freely, Leigh Hunt the oftenest, three or four times a week ; and thirty-seven years afterwards (28.6. 1871), recrossing Battersea Bridge with Allingham, Carlyle said :—" Leigh Hunt used to walk with me in the first years after I came to Chelsea.   He was sweet and dignified, and his talk like the song of a nightingale."[1]

In Hunt's own room there were but two chairs, which was awkward when two callers came ; but " the noble

[1] William Allingham, *A Diary*, p. 204.

Hunt receives you," Carlyle wrote to his brother (27.6.1834), " in the spirit of a king, apologises for nothing, places you in the best seat, takes a window-sill himself, and folding closer his loose-flowing ' muslin cloud ' of a printed night-gown in which he always writes, commences the liveliest dialogue on philosophy and the prospects of man (who is to be beyond measure ' happy ' yet) ; which again he will courteously terminate the moment you are bound to go."

A flood of happy children made the home of Hunt alive, and even Mrs. Hunt's continual borrowings, which some- times went the length of a " fender," did not quite exhaust the patience of Mrs. Carlyle, whatever she said about it. One of the things she would not have lent even to Mrs. Hunt was a picture Dr. John had brought from Italy last year. Carlyle liked it and she hung it now in the drawing- room, which was his work-room for the first half of every day : —a common-looking coloured lithograph of a ragged old man sitting behind a trestle-board, with a quill-pen in his hand, another behind his ear and a third in his ink- bottle,—a peripatetic letter-writer for the illiterate. " He is a delightful old fellow," said Carlyle on the first sight of him,—" shows you Literature in its simplest, below which it *cannot* sink." Describing to John how they were arrang- ing things, he did not fail to mention where they put " my beloved *Segretario Ambulante*," (itinerant secretary).

XIV

THE "HISTORY" IS BEGUN

(1834)

CARLYLE was more uneasy than he let his mother suppose. It was a bad time for "Literature." The Editor of the *Foreign Quarterly* was still willing to take his essays but unable to pay for them. "Nothing seems to thrive but Penny Journals."

The last instalment of *Sartor* was to appear in August; and James Fraser was a man of his word and sure to finish it as bargained; but when Carlyle called upon him at his shop in Regent Street, Fraser let him know he saw more profit in Maginn and Co.'s blarney of the Tory type. He said one of his oldest subscribers had come in to him to curse *Sartor*, saying,—" If there is any more of that damned stuff I will, etc., etc." Many felt like him; but an American order had come for a copy of the magazine " so long as there is anything of Carlyle's in it." The honest business man was candidly perplexed.

Carlyle proposing "articles on French Revolution matters," translations mainly, Fraser would not take them. He seems to have wanted the *Diamond Necklace* as a serial, but would not produce it as a book, and said that if Carlyle offered him the Book he was projecting on the French Revolution, he would print it for half-profits, which meant no profits to the author for the first edition, but also no risk and immediate publication. Carlyle agreed. So *Fraser's Magazine* got the *Diamond Necklace* and it was to be printed when the *French Revolution* was about to appear, which was expected to be about March, 1835, and in one volume. By the end of June Carlyle was at work upon the history. He went to the British Museum more than once a week, walking " through the palaces of Belgrave Square, through the squalid dens of St. Giles—the extremes of life ",[1] and thereby hangs a tale.

He discovered what few suspected to be in the British

---

[1] Unpublished letter to W. Graham.

Museum, a great collection of contemporary printed matter about the Revolution, " inaccessible for want of a proper catalogue," and he mentioned [1] the labours of " the respectable sublibrarian " on it in a way that seemed little amiss, but Panizzi never forgave. Assuredly as " Keeper of the Printed Books " (1837), and " Chief Librarian " (1856), Panizzi spitefully did all he could to prevent Carlyle utilizing the Museum for research on the Commonwealth and on Frederick.[2] Why ? Nobody knew ; and Lords and Ladies, etc., remonstrated with Panizzi in vain. Carlyle wrote a conciliatory letter to mollify him, to which he sent a reply so insolent that even a biographer was ashamed to print it.[2] A subordinate of Panizzi has revealed the secret.[3] The unpardonable offence " was in all probability the designation of ' respectable Sub-Librarian ' applied to the high and mighty Keeper of the Printed Books in the British Museum, a man who, etc. . . ." Carlyle got most of what he wanted quietly ; and abstained with an effort from appealing to the public, as he was aware he might have done in the *Times* with success. He called the fellow nothing worse than a " fat pedant." Panizzi had come into exile in England, and been patronised by Roscoe, and put into the Museum by Brougham, and is only worth mention for the sake of explaining that the words which gave such a mortal sting to him were innocently used and no offence was intended. He *was* the Sub or Assistant-Librarian when the words were written, and promoted to " Keeper " about the time they were printed. Carlyle was probably not aware of his promotion when correcting the proofs, tho poor Panizzi supposed the world was applauding and watching him. This experience of the result of letting politicians " job " into a librarian's salary an Italian lawyer who came here as a political exile may have weighed with Carlyle by-and-by, when he decided to fight Gladstone attempting a similar " job " at the expense of the London Library. But that was still in the distant future.

The British Museum Library was merely a place of reference. When he sat down to work upon the French

[1] Footnote to the *Parliamentary History of the French Revolution*, in Thomas Carlyle's *Essays*.
[2] Fagan's *Life of Panizzi*, I, pp. 335–337.
[3] *Literary Recollections* by F. Espinasse, pp. 71–3, and 190–2.

Revolution, he had nearly two hundred books about it, not counting many already read and returned ; and early in July John Mill sent him his collection, and continued to buy and send him more, the *Memoirs* of Mirabeau, for example. At last there were about 150 books lent to him by Mill, who came to walk with him every Sunday afternoon, as regular as "the Sabbath bells,"[1] and on many details of the history was able to help him.

What he could not do was to make Carlyle the editor of the new *London Review*. His father and Sir William Molesworth had to be considered, and they would not hear of such a thing. Carlyle was not long in London before he discovered with surprise how much he was understood and hated by the "ruling classes" and their apologists. It was rash to be associated with him. His fellow-feeling for workers in general put him too far in the front for the most advanced of Radical periodicals. When he now distributed some copies of *Sartor* made by stitching magazine sheets together, he sent six to distinguished literary gentlemen in Edinburgh, and *not one acknowledged receipt*. His brother John afterwards said to Espinasse,[2] — "These London men tried to keep my brother down, but they couldn't." The truth was that the men who tried to keep him down were the conventional leaders in Church and State, both Whigs and Tories.

Sir William Molesworth, Bart., M.P., an eloquent and rich young landowner of long descent, and good repute and connections, was called "a Radical in politics and an Infidel in religion" for such atrocities as these.—He championed in the Commons six Dorset labourers sentenced in March, 1834, to seven years' transportation for trying to start a Trades' Union ; and he advocated national education and the commutation of tithes ! And one of the writers in his Review did not believe in Hell-fire ! That was his crowning crime. The periodical exposed him to his enemies, tho' there was nothing stronger in it than his own and Mill's mild blend of humanity and common sense. All the gentlemen of his county combined against him. He had to seek another seat, and twice over was hindered from marrying a young woman he wanted. Whereat he was more surprised than others were. If he had let the author of *Sartor* be the editor of his quarterly, he might have met

[1] *Conversations with Carlyle*, by Sir C. Gavan Duffy, p. 170.
[2] *Literary Recollections*, by F. Espinasse, p. 112.

a social catastrophe, all the worse if such an editor made it pay, as he might have done, by putting in less argument and more narrative, and by tabooing theology.[1]

When the Macedonian Alexander, with the usual arrogance of the wholesale killer by trade, remonstrated with his old tutor Aristotle for publishing his " books of oral doctrine " which laid his teaching " open to all," the tutor answered that he had both " published and not published," as he had " written in a style instructive only as memoranda to those already conversant in that sort of learning." No such excuse was possible to Carlyle. He was downright, and tho handicapped by an education which set him thinking in several languages and stifled simple utterance, he struggled for clearness above everything and was sincere, reflecting :—

' Saturday night (sunset), July 26, 1834.—Nothing can exceed the *gravity* of my situation here. " Do or die " seems the word ; and alas ! what to do ? I have no confidant. For five days together I sit without so much as speaking to anyone except my wife. Mood tragical, gloomy, as of one forsaken, who had nothing left him *but to get through his task and die.* No periodical editor wants me : no man will give me money for my work. Bad health, too, (at least, singularly changed health), brings dispiritment. Fears of beggary, etc., besiege me. On brighter days I cast these off into the dim distance, and see a world fearful, indeed, but grand : a task to do in it which no poverty shall hinder.

' Can friends do much for one ? Conversing here I find that I get almost nothing. Alone ! alone ! " May we say " (my good father used to pray) " may we say we are not alone, for the Lord is with us." True ! true ! Keep thy heart resolute and still ; take advantage of what time and chance *will* offer (to thee as to all) ; toil along and fear nothing. Oh thou of little faith ! Weak of faith indeed ! God help me !

' For about a month past I have been resolute about writing. Subject, " The French Revolution." Whole boxes of books about me. Gloomy, huge, of almost boundless meaning ; but obscure, dubious—all too deep for me ; will and must *do my best.* Alas ! gleams, too, of a work

[1] *Life of Sir William Molesworth,* by Mrs. Fawcett, pp. 57-9, 85, 108-113, etc.

of art hover past me ; as if this should be a *work of art*.
Poor me ! '

Fraser had just read to him (without revealing names
but he soon was told it was from Father O'Shea of Cork
to another Irishman in London, likely to be Maginn) a letter
which contained " a *true* and one of the friendliest possible
recognitions of me " ; and at the same time he received
his first letter from Emerson, exalting *Sartor*. Which was
all " comfortable," he confessed to himself, saying,—
" Precious is man to man." To Henry Inglis, another
admirer of *Sartor*, he wrote (8.7.1834) that " the critical
world of London " were like bugs, blind, stinking,
poisonous, etc.[1]

In answering as Emerson had begged him to do, he made
a quotation which has been misunderstood (12.8.1834) :—

' My dear Sir,—Some two weeks ago I received your kind
gift (of books) from Fraser. To say that it was welcome
would be saying little : is it not as a voice of affectionate
remembrance, coming from beyond the ocean waters, first
decisively announcing for me that a whole New Continent
exists,—that I too have part and lot there ! " Not till
we can think that here and there one is thinking of us,
one is loving us, does this waste Earth become a peopled
Garden." '

When this was published, John Ruskin declared it
" disputable, blameable and pitiable that the rest of the
world was waste to him unless he had admirers in it."[2]
It was a correct quotation from Goethe's *Wilhelm Meister*,[3]
and Ruskin requoting wrongly mistook the point. Goethe
did not make Theresa say that " the rest of the world was
waste " to one unless one had " *admirers* in it," but that
" this waste Earth becomes a peopled Garden " whenever
" we can think that here and there one is thinking of us,
one is loving us." There was no itch for admiration, but
a craving for affection. Theresa was not an artist in
anything but housewifery,—the right kind of " lady."

Carlyle confessed to Emerson,—" I came to London for
the best of all reasons,—to seek bread and work." Far from

[1] Unpublished letter.
[2] *Praeterita*, I, 192.
[3] Book VII, Chapter V.

defending the defects of *Sartor*, he answered,—" If you dislike it, say that I (as Fritz the Only said) ' will do better another time.'"   "Fritz the Only" was a German phrase for Frederick the Great.

His brother John consoled him for not getting the editorship, saying, " Disappointment on disappointment only simplifies one's course."   Carlyle agreed, declaring :—

' The only thing certain would have been difficulty, pain and contradiction, which I should probably have undertaken ; which I am far from breaking my heart that I have missed.   In general I abate no jot of confidence in myself and in my cause.   Nay, it often seems to me as if the extremity of suffering, if such were appointed me, might bring out an extremity of energy yet unknown to myself.   God grant me faith, clearness, and peaceableness of heart.   I make no other prayer.'

Which is only correct if he meant " No other prayer for himself."   A letter he had written (29.7.1834), to Bess Stodart's uncle, Mr. Bradfute, has a " prayer " for Edinburgh [1] :—

' I get hardly any news from Edinburgh, well as I love and shall always love that old stone Town.   It is hard, but clear and strong, in spirit as in outward form ; built on rocks, looking out upon the everlasting sea.   May it flourish, and evil never[2] gain dominion over it.'

He wrote to John in the middle of August (15.8.1834) :—

' The London street tumult has become a kind of marching music to me ; ' (in another letter he compared it to Niagara.)   ' I walk along following my own meditations without thinking of it.   Company comes, and there is talk enough.

' Allan Cunningham was here two nights ago : very friendly, full of Nithsdale, a pleasant *Naturmensch*' (or natural man, as distinguished from the others next described, Mill and Hunt), ' Mrs. (Platonica) Taylor and the Unitarian Fox.

---

[1] *Early Letters of Jane Welsh Carlyle*, by D. G. Ritchie, p. 260.
[2] The words—" evil never "— are conjectured, as a fold in the paper made a gap.

' The French Revolution perplexes me much. More books on it, I find, are but a repetition of those before read ; I learn nothing, or almost nothing, further by books, yet am I as far as possible from understanding it.'

On Monday, 1.9.1834, he began to write it, the most enjoyable of all his writings, and enjoyed by the writer, in spite of accidents which kept him at it till 1837. As he said in 1866 of himself and his wife,—" We were not at all unhappy during those three years of French Revolution." This was his way of saying they were happy, as well as they might be. The double negative is a favourite way of talking in the north. There was a countryman of his whose highest praise for anything was,— " Not bad." " You wouldn't say more of Heaven itself," he was told, and answered,—" It's all I ask of Heaven itself,—to say the same of me."

EDWARD IRVING AND JOHN STERLING

(1834–5)

WHEN Carlyle was beginning his history, Edward Irving visited him at Cheyne Row for the first time, and the last. Since ever Carlyle came to London three or four months ago, he had been anxious about him. On the day of arrival he was walking in Kensington Gardens when " a black figure " rose from a side seat and with both hands clutched his hand,—it was Irving, whose thick black hair had become gray in the last two years. His face was flabby and pale, and dashed with a hectic flush ; and he admitted he was in lodgings at Bayswater for better air ; but spoke of his weak health as " temporary " and " of small account "—the summer " would soon set him up again." In the short talk which was all they had time for, as neither was alone, " a short peal of his old Annandale laugh " contrasted painfully with his haggard look, which haunted Carlyle, who called often at his lodgings and then at his house, but seldom saw him.

He might not have seen him at all, but that he appealed to William Hamilton, an " excellent city Scotsman," who had married Mrs. Irving's sister and now intervened successfully. Mrs. Irving had misgivings about Carlyle's influence. Besides, she had been engrossed by a little son who died, and was almost as slow as her husband to believe he was dangerously ill. From the first Carlyle's opinion was what every competent person would now approve, that Irving who was preaching many times a week in his synagogue in Newman Street, should go at once to Italy or Switzerland for the winter and have perfect rest. But Irving would not hear of such a thing. He had little experience of sickness in himself. Throughout his life he had enjoyed " a giant's strength," and for two years he had been preaching to his flock in curious anticipation of Christian Science " the idea that disease itself was sin

369

and that no man with faith in his Lord ought to be over-powered by it." [1] It was consumption that had gripped his lungs, and the hopefulness of consumptive patients strengthened his delusion.

From Scotland his old friend William Graham appealed to Carlyle to deliver him from "these agents of Hell," [2] to wit, "the four and twenty elders" of his "synagogue in Newman Street," who called themselves "prophets" and "apostles" etc. Carlyle explained that these un-fortunates were rather above than below the Christian average "in this city; which however is no superhuman praise"; and he insisted the present danger was physical disease. "If Irving live, he will, as I keep prophesying, kick it (the new sect) to the Devil (who is mostly the father of it), and be himself again. But his life is no sure possession." And again :—" I can never forget the man he was; one of the largest-souled, truest, most genial men it was ever in my blessedness to meet in this world. I say with Uncle Toby : He *shall* not lie there and die ; ' he shall march, he shall, by— ! ' "

In desperation Carlyle appealed to all relatives and friends of Irving within reach. At William Hamilton's in Cheapside one evening, the old father-in-law, Mr Martin from Kirkcaldy, listened to him earnestly but unconvinced, yet saying,—" He grows weaker and weaker, and no Doctor can find the least disease in him. So weak now, he cannot lift his little baby to his neck ! "

The doctor attending him at last declared " a milder climate " would be " the only safe thing for him " this winter. But he was no more heeded than Carlyle. The Newman Street " prophets " had bidden him go to Scotland and " do a great work in his native land," and now they " yielded to his own wish to wander slowly through the country, wending his way by degrees to Scotland, with the hope of gaining strength, as well as doing the Lord's work, by the way." [3] And then it was that he called at Cheyne Row. It was in the late afternoon that he came on horseback to their door, and stayed " a friendly hour " with them. [4]

" Weak " as he was, he was like his old self. " It seemed

---

[1] Mrs. Oliphant's *Edward Irving*, Chapter XVII.
[2] Unpublished letters.
[3] Mrs. Oliphant's *Edward Irving*, Ch. XIX.
[4] Unpublished letters.

to us," wrote Carlyle to Graham [1] (14.9.1834), " his faith in the Tongue-work was getting thinner." He congratulated Carlyle on taking to " writing History," which would bring him closer to reality, he seemed to intimate, and glancing at the room decorations, said of Mrs. Carlyle,—" She has always a little bower of elegance round her, be where she will "; and told her,—" You are like an Eve, and make a little Paradise wherever you are." This was a clerical commonplace, and pleased Carlyle as praise of his wife. He never noticed the absurdity,— for Eve did not " make " Paradise, she only caused her husband and self to be put out of it. But nothing absurd was meant by Irving, whose manner was sincere and affectionate, " yet with a great suppressed sadness in it."

" I told him," Carlyle wrote to Graham, " that for all his wild errors, wide as the Poles from my way of thinking, I prayed for no other medicine but *continuance of life* to him ; if he lived, my faith was he would clear his own way. But *life*, as I affectionately urged, was a thing we *could* not dispense with. I earnestly, even solemnly, called on him to think of this ; to fly, whatever might befall, out of London, which was a Mill of Death to him. He admitted it was true ; said, he was himself intending to ' ride off ' somewhither into quietness and rest till he saw how it proved."

In a simple loving way he rose and said farewell, and Carlyle held his bridle while he mounted, and stood on the steps watching him till he turned the corner.

At last the good Irving was beginning to have misgivings. It is likely to have been soon after this visit that he said to Henry Drummond :—" I should have kept Thomas Carlyle closer to me : his counsel, blame or praise, was always faithful ; and few have such eyes ! " He left London about the beginning of September, and travelled gently west and then north ; but the change to purer air had come too late. He was gaunt and " ghastly " when George Gilfillan was watching him preaching for the last time in Edinburgh in a small chapel in Carruther's Close to an audience of twenty.[2] He died in Glasgow on Sunday night, 7.12.1834 ; and James Fraser brought the news to Carlyle, and obtained for his Magazine the short essay

---

[1] Unpublished letters.
[2] *The History of a Man*, by the Rev. Geo. Gilfillan, p. 185.

now enshrined in the *Miscellanies*. It tells how the good
strong man had been led astray by popular applause, but
never was insincere.

Nearly everybody of sense was surprised to hear it, the
clergymen who had been assailing him, from Henry Duncan
down, the most of all. But it was true, and corroborated
by evidence discovered afterwards. The dying Irving had
" sent from Glasgow a curious *Letter* to his *Gift of Tongues*
Congregation ; full of questionings, dubieties upon the
Tongues and such points ; full of wanderings in deep waters
with one light fixed on high,—' Humble ourselves before
God, and he will show us ! '—Letter indicating a sincerity
as of very death ; which these New Church people (Henry
Drummond and Co.) first printed for useful private
circulation, and then afterwards zealously suppressed and
destroyed." But Carlyle preserved his copy, and after
many years it was given to Irving's nephew, who printed
it in an edition of his uncle's *Select Works*.

While his essay on Irving was still fresh in the hands of
the readers of *Fraser's Magazine*, Carlyle dropped into the
India House for a chat with John Mill, and was introduced
to John Sterling who had done the same. It was nearly
a year since Mill had told Carlyle of Sterling as a " disciple
of yours " ; and now they departed together and walked
by the quietest roads as far as Knightsbridge, conversing
copiously, " but *except* in opinion, not disagreeing."
When at last they came to where their roads separated,
they had made up their minds to see more of each other,
and soon were intimates, old Sterling and his wife taking
cordially to their son's new acquaintance.

Thus friend succeeds to friend mysteriously, as life
to life.—

' Between two worlds life hovers like a star,
    'Twixt night and morn, upon the horizon's verge.
How little do we know that which we are !
    How less what we may be ! The eternal surge
Of time and tide rolls on, and bears afar
    Our bubbles ; as the old burst, new emerge,
Lashed from the foam of ages ; while the graves
Of empires heave but like some passing waves."

XVI

CURRENT EVENTS

(1834-5)

"YOU are too indignant against Destiny," wrote Carlyle to a farmer brother (28.8.1834); "It is a fault of my own too"; and arises from "Pride. Humility is the lesson we *are to be taught*. Happy for us if we can learn it; and so with wise submissiveness 'bear our cross,' and skirt many an obstacle which we cannot *mount* over, and would fain destroy. Call on God to guide you in the way, for it is not in man to guide himself; and so with your eye on fixed heavenly loadstars, walk forward fearing nothing."

In old-fashioned dialect, — as it had to be, for their mother was sure to read it many times,—this was what he was doing himself. If he had been able to linger over his history, he might have said his say as hitherto in long, loose essays, sprinkled with scanty anecdotes,—transfigured sermons. He was prone to preach on paper, like other people. But he had less than £300 in hand, and felt bound to do what he could to have a readable volume ready for Fraser to publish as soon as possible. So his journal and letters show him adjusting himself to facts, and feeling like and occasionally comparing himself to a pious Muslim who can truly say,—" I am one who accepts what has to be,—kismet."

In September he said to a woman praising *Sartor*,— " Madam, it is a work born in darkness, destined for oblivion and not worth wasting a word on." This was what he might have said of any book, and was conscious modesty, which did not hinder him from comparing *Sartor* by-and-by to " a stone thrown into a sheet of water. I see the circle of its influence widening every day." [1]

He warmed to his work when he started writing, and quoted to his mother his wife's verdict, that what he was writing was " more readable " than *Sartor*. " Once fairly

---

[1] *Literary Recollections* by F. Espinasse, pp. 70 and 209.

afloat," he told her, he cared for nothing. To himself he said,—"except when writing, I never feel myself that I am alive." His routine was breakfast at nine, work till two, dinner and then walk till tea, and seldom anything after then but reading for the next day's writing.

The book rather grew than was shaped. Without any theory into which to fit his facts, intent on telling well and pleasantly whatever he could be sure was true and interesting, he soon saw something new and beautiful arising under his hands and was happy. To his brother John he announced his style was altering, adding (21.9. 1834) :—" It shall be *such* a book : quite an epic poem of the Revolution ; an apotheosis of Sansculottism ! Seriously, when in good spirits I feel as if there were the matter of a very considerable work within me." And a few weeks later he wrote again.—" I feel at every sentence that the work will be strange ; that it either must be so, or be nothing but another of the thousand-and-one ' Histories,' which are so many ' dead thistles for Pedant-chaffinches to peck at and fill their crops with ' ; a kind of thing I for one wish to have no hand in. Jane rather thinks it will do.' "

One afternoon towards the end of September he saw in the back garden " a huge spider " kill a fly. He watched it till it killed a second. Then he angrily lifted something and killed the spider, and began reconsidering how many and unfathomable are the " forces at work in Nature." About the same time, going into the city to cash a remittance from John for his mother, he went into the Stock Exchange, and saw enough to remind him of " Trade's contentious Hell,"—" about a hundred men jumping and jigging about in a dingy contracted apartment, and yelling out all manner of sounds, which seemed to be auctioneer's offers, amid laughter and tumult." A red-necked official came up to him and said this place was " private, sir," and he departed with " a thousand pardons," glad he had seen it.

One Thursday night (16.10.1834) the glare of fire in the sky was noticed from the top back windows, and he went and watched the burning of the two Houses of Parliament, meeting in the crowd the Dr. Matthew Allen whom he visited at York long ago and had not seen since he left London in 1832. What interested Carlyle most was the demeanour of the crowd, enjoying the sight and complain-

ing of nothing but that the low confused mass of buildings
" did not make a good fire ! " They whistled to encourage
the breeze, applauding it when it came as if it had come to
their whistle, and crying as the flames shot up,—" Come,
now, that's not so bad ! "—" There's a *flare-up* for the
House of Lords ! "—" A judgment for the Poor-Law
Bill ! "—" There go their *hacts* ! "

One morning this same October he recollected sadly
that if he had taken Leslie's advice long ago and become
an engineer, that would have given him a livelihood and
brought him into touch with men,—" my two grand wants
and prayers," he now confessed to himself. As he faced
the possibility his book might never pay and lecturing fail
him like periodical writing, he wondered whether it was
still too late to take to engineering. It seemed so.

He always felt that teaching of some kind was his trade,
and wrote hopefully to an " Educational Association "
advertising for a man to organize a " Normal School " in
Glasgow, after going over England and into Germany to
study foreign methods ; but nothing happened. Before
long a Mr. Weir, who was editing a Radical paper in
Glasgow, called and told him the " Association " was a
" miserable kirk-session affair," with too narrow an outlook
to employ a man like him.

He had thoughts of imitating Leigh Hunt's London
Journal ; but said " No " at once to an offer of regular
work on the *Times*, which he received from the editor,
Edward Sterling, the father of his friend John. He would
not write against his convictions, as a man of his opinions
would have to do if on the staff of the organ of the rich and
conservative. Besides, he was not seeking immediate
employment, but considering how to make a living after the
history was finished. His friends were chaffing him
about " living upon nothing." But he went quietly and
steadily on his way, and applied to himself a phrase in a
Sansculotte Deputy's letter,—" All right here, only the
food is lacking."

In November when he was busy over the " Taking of
the Bastille," the political pot in England seemed like
boiling over, when the King dismissed the Reformers and
put Wellingtom, Peel and Co. into power, in contempt
of the Commons. Carlyle attended a meeting in town
(21.11.1834), where Charles Buller was in the chair. He
told his mother that his old pulpil was " one of the sensiblest

people I see " and " going to make himself notable as the most decisive of Radicals." There were about two thousand men at the meeting, " mostly the better kind of operatives ; many under thirty. The murmur of their assent or dissent, above all the kind of *bark* coming from two thousand voices, at any sound or mention of Toryism and its insults, was grand to hear. It was bitter earnest with them. In Wellington's shoes I would not willingly be : he thinks to rule Britain like a drill-sergeant ; but will find it not answer."

Before the year was out Carlyle was aware his history would fill all the winter and need to be in two volumes at least. He completed the first in the middle of January, and paused then to look round. He felt, he told Emerson afterwards, " as if my head were fairly above water," and decided to make the history three volumes, not two. He hoped to be finished by the end of May. " I am about *half-done,*" he said at the time (28.1.35), " for a good deal of the stuff is laid in."

He found comfort in saying to himself when beginning the second volume (7.2.1835),—" No honestly exerted force can be utterly lost, the seed thou sowest will spring. Food and raiment thou hast never lacked, and shalt not." But he had serious thoughts of quitting Literature as a trade, remarking,—" It is now some three and twenty months since I earned one penny by my craft. I have been ready to work, abler than ever. To *ask* able Editors to employ you will not improve but worsen the matter. When want is approaching one must have done with whims." But for the immediate present, he had only to " keep one's own self in right balance, free and clear."

He was anxious to be " perfectly accurate," which cost him " great searching and trouble," all the more because his " forerunners " had neglected it. But he was " full of his task " and " saw it getting on," and assured his mother, (17.2.1835) :—" In my mind, I feel quite young yet ; and *growing,* as when I was eighteen : this is the greatest blessing. Hurry is of no use ; one does nothing of any weight by *hurrying.* Many a time I think of my good father's method of working ' without haste, without rest.' I am not so wise in my trade ; which, indeed, is more difficult to manage wisely."

In *Fraser's Magazine* for March the history was advertised as " getting ready " ; and Carlyle was working

then at the Feast of Pikes, the first book of volume two,
He felt he was doing a work of " considerable significance,"
delineating a " Fact " of world-wide importance, in a
state of serene indifference to economic and all other
personal considerations. " I know not how it was," he
told a brother, describing the time that ended on 6.3.1835,
—" I had not felt so clear and independent, sure of myself
and of my task, for many long years."

XVII

HOW VOLUME ONE WAS BURNED

(1835)

BESIDES his wife the only reader of his manuscript was John Mill, who took finished sheets home to read at leisure. His praise grew stronger as the work went on, and " he began to think there never had been such a book written in the history of the world." [1] When Carlyle was absorbed in " The Feast of Pikes," Book I of Volume II, the first volume was taken away by Mill to read it all again and " make notes on it, which he was well qualified to do," Carlyle told Emerson.

Unfortunately by this time the home of Mill for all but working days was a house on the riverside at Kingston occupied by Mrs. Taylor, whom Cavaignac named " The Armida of the *London and Westminster*." Carlyle told Norton,—" She was the daughter of a flourishing London Unitarian tradesman, and her husband was the son of another, and the two families made the match." Her grand-daughter said Mrs. Taylor's father was a landowner whose land was sold for debt, and at eighteen she was married to a wholesale druggist. Carlyle's talks to Norton and Gavan Duffy tell the rest. [1]—

' Taylor was a very respectable man, but his wife found him dull ; she had dark, black, hard eyes, and an inquisitive nature, and was pondering on many questions that worried her, and could get no answers to them.' Or as Carlyle told John Morley, " She was full of unwise intellect, asking and re-asking stupid questions."

' That Unitarian Clergyman William Fox who patronised Peter and Paul as ignorant but well-intentioned persons, and delivered prayers which some one ' (mimicked by Carlyle) ' described as the most eloquent prayers that ever

---

[1] *Letters of C. E. Norton*, I, pp. 496–498, and Sir C. Gavan Duffy's *Conversations with Carlyle*, pp. 166–170, and the *Letters of J. S. Mill*, edited by Hugh Elliot, and the *Lives* of him, by Bain and Courtney are used here to supplement the letters, etc., edited by Froude, Norton and A. Carlyle.

were addressed to a British audience, had probably the Taylors among his congregation ; at any rate he told Mrs. Taylor that John Mill was the man among the human race to relieve in a competent manner her dubieties. With great difficulty he brought Mill to see her ' (in 1831). ' And Mill who, up to that time, had never so much as looked at a female creature, not even a cow, in the face, found himself opposite those great dark eyes, that were flashing unutterable things while he was discoursing the utterable concerning all sorts of high topics.

' Mill was spell-bound. She wrapped him up like a cocoon. He used to go to her in all his troubles to be comforted, and in all his difficulties to be guided, and probably to be flattered a little besides.

' From that time all Mill's enjoyments in life centred in her.

' Officious friends suggested to Mr. Taylor that he was letting things go too far. (So he) remonstrated with her. She told him he might blow up the house if it seemed good to him, but she could not give up this friendship. There were children to be considered, and he thought he had better endure than make a clamour. The result was that Mr. and Mrs. Taylor determined to separate, and she took a small house at Kingston-on-Thames, where Mill was in the habit of going on Saturdays to spend the next day.'

This interrupted Mill's Sunday walks in Chelsea neighbourhood. He came in the evenings once or twice a week ; and for the sake of a leisurely perusal, he left the manuscript of the French Revolution volume at Kingston from one week-end to another. Of course Mrs. Taylor had to read it also ; and she was sitting up over it one night (Thursday, 5.3.1835, it is likely), and was suddenly " surprised at the flight of time ", and laid it " carelessly upon the table " [1] and went to bed. In the morning the maid who was kindling the fire mistook it for waste-paper and put it in the grate, and in a few minutes only " three or four tatters " were left unburned.

On Friday, (6.3.1835), Carlyle and his wife at tea together recognised the sound of Mill's " short rap " at the front

[1] *Thomas Carlyle*, by A. H. Guernsey, pp. 86–89, quoting the Rev. Mr Milburn's report of T. C.'s talk. The report is substantially accurate, as contemporary letters etc. show, altho it needs correction in details. Mr. Milburn was handicapped as a reporter by being blind ; but that very fact had led him to cultivate the memory.

door, and Mrs. Carlyle rose to welcome him as he entered,—
pale, unresponsive, " the very picture of despair," "distraction in his aspect," so like a ghost that she cried,—
" Gracious Providence, he has gone off with Mrs. Taylor ! "
Perhaps she had heard the wheels of a cab, and looking out
had noticed a lady inside it. Mill begged her "half-
inarticulately gasping," to go down and speak to Mrs.
Taylor. Carlyle took hold of Mill and led him to a seat
rather looking than asking questions. He waited till Mill
could speak, and then was told that the first volume was
annihilated. With touching gallantry, Mill said that *he*
had left it lying about, and laid no blame on the woman,
who took none to herself and drove away alone without
entering. It was only long afterwards that the truth was
known.

Like Newton's dog Diamond, she could not realize
what she had done ; but as for Mill, " I could not complain,"
wrote Carlyle to Emerson, " or the poor man seemed as if
he would have shot himself." He stayed " three hours,"
Carlyle and his wife both comforting and speaking peace
to him, and talking with an effort about indifferent matters
to restore his equanimity.

Poor Mill insisted,—"Such a thing never happened
before."

" Yes, though," answered Carlyle, " Newton and his
dog Diamond."

" True, but Newton went mad over it."

" Well, well, we shall hardly be so bad as that," said
Carlyle, and turned the talk to something pleasant till
he went away, and said to his wife as the door closed after
him :—" Mill, poor fellow, is terriby cut up. We must
endeavour to hide from him how very serious this business
is to us."

She answered with a burst of sympathy, flinging her
arms about his neck, and lamenting aloud, condoling
and encouraging him. They sat talking till late, and his
" fixed word " to her in the end was,—" It *shall* be written
again."

The night was " full of emotion," with occasional sharp
pain, as if something were cutting him or grasping him hard
round the heart. He longed for " some psalm or prayer "
that he could have uttered and his loved ones joined in ;
but there was none. " Walk humbly with thy God,"
he said to himself, and was thankful he could keep his

composure. At last he slept, and dreamed of his dead
father and sister Margaret, as if " alive, yet all defaced with
the sleepy stagnancy, swollen hebetude of the grave,—and
again dying in some strange country : a horrid dream ! "

Yet it was a painful wakening, as he faced the facts.
He felt in general as if he had been like a schoolboy who
had laboriously written out his copy and was showing it
proudly to his Master, who suddenly tore it and said,—
" No, boy ! Thou must go and write it better."

" What can I do but obey ? " he asked himself in his
journal next day (7.3.1835) ; " obey and think it the best ?
To work again ; and Oh ! may God be with me, for this
earth is not friendly. On in His name ! "

Sitting down to his desk in this spirit, he wrote a letter
(7.3.1835).—

' MY DEAR MILL,
' How are you ? You left me last night with a look
which I shall not soon forget. Is there anything that I
could do or suffer or say to alleviate you ? For I feel that
your sorrow must be far sharper than mine ; yours bound
to be a *passive* one. How true is this of Richter : " All
evil is like a nightmare ; the instant you begin to stir
under it, it is gone."

' I have ordered a *Biographie Universelle* this morning ;
and a better sort of paper. Thus, far from giving up the
game, you see, I am risking another £10 on it. Courage
my friend ! ' He went on to show how worse might have
befallen him, namely, physical disease. He was still able
to write the Book and would do it. " As a kind of solace "
to Mill, he set him searching for a French book he much
needed, and did not forget to send thanks " to Mrs. Taylor
for her kind sympathies."

He thought of writing to his brother John at once ;
but his wife said,—" It will only grieve him," and he took
her advice not to let any of his relatives know until he
" was under way again " and able to " speak peace to them
with the sorrow." To others also he said as little as possible,
and did not name Mill even to Fraser, who had to be told
at once (7.3.1835),[1] but was entreated :—" *Do not mention*
the mischance to anyone : it would give great pain to some

---

[1] Unpublished letter. A copy made in 1896 is dated 17, but its contents
and references to it in other letters show that the date was 7.

whom I love were it talked about." In the same letter
Fraser was re-assured :—

' *That* first volume (which pleased me better than anything I had ever done) *cannot* be written anew, for the spirit
that animated it is past, but *another* first volume I will
try, and shall make it, if not better or equal, *all* that I can.
This only is clear to me : that I *can* write a book on the
French Revolution ; and that, if I am spared long enough
alive, I will do it. Tooth and nail. I am advancing
daily as fast as it is in me,' (and in short hope to be ready
for next spring, which shows how hopeful he was.)

Mill sent a cheque for two hundred pounds as compensa-
tion, but Carlyle would only take one hundred, the actual
cost of living while he was writing what had been burned ;
and Mill had to be content with presenting to him a
complete copy of the *Biographie Universelle*, which Carlyle
had just commissioned Fraser to buy. Another luxury
Carlyle allowed himself was shelves to hold the books with
which his house was overflowing.

The " Feast of Pikes," Book I of Volume II, was
continued as if nothing had happened, and completed
within a week of the catastrophe, and a perusal of it was
offered to Mill, " provided you durst take it. . . . Of
all men living you are henceforth the least likely to commit
such an oversight again." Surpassing Don Quixote in
gallantry and make-believe, poor Mill replied :—" Another
bit of manuscript I will not take. I would bear the badge
of my unworthiness. If however you would give me the
pleasure of reading it, give it to Mrs. Taylor." ! ! ! Carlyle
was not so simple as he looked and did not risk that, deciding
to desist from lending manuscripts. So the lady was not
tempted farther, and " as for her," said Carlyle to Norton
afterwards, discussing the destruction of volume I,—" I
never heard that it very much diminished her content in
life."

Before the end of the month, he had rewritten the
" Death of Louis XV," the first book of volume I, and
then felt free to send the news of the accident to his
relatives, assuring his mother that the new beginning was
" certainly no worse " than the first version, " a thing
that gives me great comfort, for I now find that I *can* do
it ; of which, before trial (so *irksome* was the business)

I had no certainty. You cannot think what a comfort the feeling that I am doing an honest work gives me : I have not been as contented for many years."

He told Emerson :—

' This *French Revolution* is the dreadfulest labor ; all is so inaccurate, superficial, vague in the numberless books I consult ; and without accuracy at least, what other good is possible ? Add to this that I have no hope but at *best* to be scolded and reproached. The Bookseller may lose his printing. Yet if life is lent me, I shall be *done with* the business, I will write this " History of Sansculottism," the notablest phenomenon I meet with since the time of the Crusades or earlier ; after which my part is played. I must seek another craft than literature. I suffer also terribly from the solitary existence I have all along had ; it is becoming a kind of passion with me, to feel myself among my brothers.

' As for America and lecturing, it is a thing I do some-times turn over. Lecturing is a thing I have always had some hankering after ; it seems to me I could really *swim* in that element, once I were thrown into it.'

So while Carlyle was writing again the first volume of his history, Emerson found time, tho courting a second wife, to collect the facts and figures needed to let him see how good his prospects would be as a popular lecturer in America,—which made him feel he always had that in reserve. Meanwhile he went on steadily, doing daily about two folio pages, equal to four or five of print, before going out for his walk about two o'clock. " Beautiful," he wrote to John (30.4.1835), " is that of brave old Voss, and often comes in my mind : ' As the Earth, now in azure sunshine seen of all the stars, now in dark tempests hidden, *holds* her journey round the sun,' " so he was " letting it thunder round him " and going his way. It was a time of great political excitement in England, but he felt like a looker-on. He thought King William should go home to Hanover and wished well to the Radicals, but he did not share the delusion he found current even among them. " The condition of the poor people is improving daily," he heard with astonishment at " routs " and dinners ; and once at least he answered grimly,—" Well, gentlemen, the Poor, I think, will get up some day, and *tell* you how improved their condition is."

On 21.4.1835 he wrote inviting Mill and another for to-morrow if he cared for the company he would find, namely Allan Cunningham and his brother and wife and a " Scotch-Teutonic " Dr. Willis, " with the beautifullest English wife, who plays and sings like a seraph." Or Mill could come the next day and find them alone.

Mill was eager to pay him for articles in his new Radical *London Review* ; but Carlyle would let nothing interfere with the rewriting of the volume which had been burned. At last he began to feel himself like a man trying to swim without water ; and doing nothing. " I filled page after page," he said afterwards,[1] " but ran the pen over every line as the page was finished."

This was early in May, before he had reached the middle of the volume. Looking out of the window, " half-hearted and dejected," he noticed a bricklayer building a wall.—" With his trowel he'd lay a great splash of mortar upon the last layer, and then brick after brick upon this, striking each with the butt of his trowel, as if to give it his benediction and farewell ; and all the while singing or whistling as blithe as a lark. And in my spleen," continued Carlyle historically, " I said within myself, ' Poor fool ! How canst thou be so merry ? ' And then I bethought me, and I said to myself,—' Poor fool *thou*, rather, that sittest here by the window, whining and complaining ! What if thy house of cards falls ? Is the Universe wrecked for that ? The man yonder builds a house that shall be a home perhaps for generations. Up then at thy work, and be cheerful ! ' "

What he used to say he learned from watching the brick layers and masons was that a wall need not be mathematically perpendicular, but only perpendicular enough to be strong. He had to learn to get done once and for all. " The bricklayer does not insist on all being smooth as *marble*, but only on having a certain *degree* of smoothness and straightness ; and so he gets a wall done." This was a thing he dwelt upon when he resumed his work. The immediate lesson—to cheer up—required him to take a rest. As he often said, the unrested horse or writer *cannot* work. So he paused on 10.5.1835, and two days later sending to

[1] See Footnote on p. 381.

cheer his mother the latest letter from Emerson with good news of *Sartor*, he reported to her thus :—

' You will learn without regret that I am *idling* for these last two days. A man must not only be able to work, but to give over working. This is the first time I ever deliberately laid work down without finishing it. In fact it is the strangest thing I ever tried, that of rewriting my first Volume ; one must vary his methods according to the task he has : take it gently, take it fiercely, you cannot tickle trouts in the way you spear whales. On the whole, it has given me very great trouble this poor Book. I still trust to get it written and if thou even *canst* not write it (as I have said to myself in late days), why then be content with that too : God's Creation will get along as it should without it. At all events my head shall settle itself, and my face clear itself in the pure May air of these days : I shall then be readier for this work, or for whatever else.'

In the same strain he wrote to Emerson next day (13.5.1835) :—

' I have digested the whole misery : I say (to myself), if thou canst *never* write this thing, why then never do write it : God's Universe will go along better without it. My Belief in a special Providence grows yearly stronger, unsubduable, impregnable. Bodily exhaustion I will at least try to exclude from the controversy. By God's blessing, perhaps, the Book shall yet be written ; but I find it will not do, by sheer direct force ; only by gentler side-methods. I have much else to write too : I feel often as if with one year of health and peace I could write something considerable ;—the image of which sails dim and great through my head. Which year of health and peace, God, if He see meet, will give me yet ; or withhold from me, as shall be for the best.'

2 C

XVIII

VOLUME ONE IS FINISHED AGAIN

(1835)

HE tried to resume work after a week or two but could not. He had to wait. He read with relish Dante's *Inferno*, and much other " light literature " such as novels in various languages, including the first five of Marryat, *Peter Simple* and the rest ; and he took much exercise.

Already at Henry Taylor's, whose laugh was like Irving's, he had met old Southey," like a lean pair of tongs," excitable but good, and the " robust veteran " Wordsworth. In May and June when the London season was at its height, he found much to look at, " running about amongst people and things," as for example, (4.6.1835), to a " rout " at Mrs. Buller's, where he saw Dan O'Connell, Peninsular Napier, and many another celebrated then. One bright sunset in June he was sitting on the stump of an old oak in Hyde Park, beholding the glory of the world " rolling and curvetting past on the Serpentine Drive," a " very superb " show, and " given gratis," while he reflected as he looked.—

' This, then, is the last efflorescence of the Tree of Being. Hengst and Horsa were bearded, but ye gentlemen have got razors and breeches ; and oh, my fair ones, how are ye changed since Boadicea wore her own hair unfrizzled hanging down as low as her hips ! The Queen Anne hats and heads have dissolved into air, and behold you here and me, prismatic light-streaks on the bosom of the sacred night. And so it goes on.'

In the middle of June he noted that he was now under-standing better than when he translated it the verse of Goethe :—

386

" There in others' looks discover
What thy own life's course has been,
And thy deeds of years past over
In thy fellow-men be seen."

At private teas and dinners, he was described as
unobtrusive but downright, and strong in his language
when it was his cue to speak. It was at Mrs. Austin's
in those weeks that he first met Sydney Smith and heard
him " guffawing " amid his admirers, " shaking his great
belly "—a fellow of infinite fun (if not much humour) and
of a fine digestion and some sense, " piercing hazel eyes "
above his " massive Roman nose."

Composed and quiet in the crowd, Carlyle may have
appeared to Smith a typical Scot. He needed no effort
to be still and stern. He noted in his diary that he saw
" Death and Eternity " glaring " through these thin
cobwebs " of the drawing-rooms.

Coming home from Mrs. Austin's on this occasion " along
Regent Street," he encountered the " street walkers "
there, which made it sometimes seem " hideous, almost
infernal " ; but now unspeakable pity swallowed up
unspeakable abhorrence.

" Accidentally " Carlyle heard from Sir William Molesworth of possible employment on an Education Commission
and wrote to Mill for information (1.6.1835), saying that
Buller had undertaken to recommend him to Lord John
Russell :—" You are not ignorant of my individual views
. . . it is almost the only business I could with perfect
heartiness employ myself on here," feeling equal to the
work, in short, and in need of some regular occupation
for an income. Nothing happened.

He was writing letters in many directions at this time,
and honouring with pleasure letters of introduction
Emerson had given to Dr. Barnard and Professor Longfellow, the poet.[1] They were the forerunners of a host
that continued coming from America all his life, and
were nearly always welcome. Even before a brother and
sister of his own had crossed the water, America appeared
to Carlyle an improved and much enlarged edition of his
native country. "It is really a great blessing of Heaven",
he now told his brother Alick, " that there *is* land where

---

[1] *T. C.'s Letters*, etc., and *Life of H. W. Longfellow*, by S. Longfellow, I.,
pp. 204–5.

the husbandman's hand will bring him corn for his ploughing and where man's perversion has not stepped in to say,—
' Thou that tillest, let another reap ! ' "

With John Sterling he frankly discussed the objections
to the " style " of *Sartor*, but remarked to himself by way
of conclusion that style was like a man's skin, and not like
a coat which could be cast off, and that he should simply
do his best. When told that his style was " too full of
meaning," he wished it had no other fault ! The fact
was that he was now writing naturally, as if speaking, and
not conventionally. The enthusiasm of even a Wordsworth for the " pure wells of English undefiled " appeared
frivolous to a man as earnest as Paul or Socrates or
Confucius. The method of Mencius was never better
practised throughout the two millenniums since it was first
explained :—" The meaning is what matters : so do
not let a word mislead as to the sentence, or a sentence as to
the paragraph, or a paragraph as to the whole :—the right
meaning is everything." Carlyle was so intent on making
the meaning right that he was prone to dispense with polish.
As he told John Sterling this June :—

' A man has but a certain strength ; imperfections
cling to him, which if he wait till he have brushed off
entirely, he will spin for ever on his axis, advancing no-
whither.' (The best way is.—) ' Know thy thought—
believe it—front Heaven and Earth with it, in whatsoever
words Nature and Art have made readiest for thee. Do
you reckon this really a time for purism of style ? I do
not. With the structure of our Johnsonian English
breaking up from its foundations, revolution *there* is visible
as everywhere else.'

It was in this letter that Carlyle comforted Sterling,
who had resigned his curacy but not altogether ceased
to think as a curate, and had been complaining that the
author of *Sartor* did not believe in a " Personal God." He
was told in effect that that was not the kind of thing to
talk about. One has to see what is what as well as one
can and do one's best.—' Assure yourself, I am neither
Pagan nor Turk, nor circumcised Jew, but an unfortunate
Christian individual resident at Chelsea ; neither Pantheist
nor Pottheist, nor any Theist or *Ist* whatsoever, *having the
most decided contempt for all manner of Systembuilders and*

Sectfounders, feeling well beforehand—taught by experience— that all such are and even must be WRONG.' [1] By God's blessing, one has got two eyes to look with ; and also a mind capable of knowing, of believing : that is all the creed I insist on.'

As one idle week followed another his strength returned, and in the beginning of July the history gripped him again, and swept him on as if " enchanted." By rigorous regimen, he kept his balance, and there was no more interruption. One afternoon about the end of August, his errand was to meet his mother-in-law at St. Katherine's Dock, and he had a " pleasant " trip up the river with her in a wherry, doubly pleasant in the hot dry weather then prevailing, which made the London pavements like an oven. Walking on them a man felt baked, with " the spine all gone, as if one were a serpent trying to stand on its tail." In the parks, the trees were dingy and the fields were brown and "bare as an old scratch wig." The ground was rent in cracks and the dust rose if you stamped upon it. So when there was no errand down the river, he had to take his exercise mainly in the evenings roaming over the Parks, " a beautiful region " he much liked ; but rain came down at last, and nothing stopped his work till a wet afternoon, Monday, (21.9.1835), when he finished the new Volume One as well as he could, and wrapped it up. His wife thought it better than the first version. His own opinion to his brother John, (23.9.1835), was that it was—" not *very* much worse ; worse in expression, but better compacted in the thought." However, it was the best he could do, and he joyfully added,—" The rest of the Book shall go on like child's play in comparison."

---

[1] Italics added. The only word underlined was *wrong*.

XIX

THE SECOND VOLUME RESUMED

(1835)

MRS. Welsh had found her daughter sick in August, and had been happy nursing her. Mrs. Carlyle was now well, and did not need or want a rest and change as her husband did, and her mother was to stay till the latter end of November. So the only question was, whither should he go ? John was expecting him at Munich, where Schelling, the " Pantheist of the Spirit " and celebrated then, was ready to welcome him ; but he excused himself and went to Scotland for October, not to disappoint his mother, who counted on seeing him every year.

Besides the usual farmhouse supplies, he was bringing home to London a new Scotch servant. Mrs. Carlyle was never long without worry about servants, wherein she was very different from her mother, who may have been more reasonable in some of her fault-finding than Carlyle supposed. Dr. John incurred the displeasure of Mrs. Carlyle by saying plainly that her main affliction was want of occupation, and she would stand less from her mother than from her doctor. This autumn she filled some of her idle time with Italian lessons, and she had callers nearly every day. She reported to her husband the purchase of a spacious old sofa, which he referred to in a letter to her from Scotsbrig (2.11.1835).—

He confessed in it how in Chinese phrase he was " making his thoughts sincere," for the sake of his own peace of mind, or what used to be called " the happiness of an approving conscience."—

' One thing I can more and more determine to adhere to —it is now almost my sole rule of life—to clear myself of cants and formulas as of poisonous Nessus shirts ; to strip them off me, by what name soever called, and follow, were it down to Hades, what I myself know and see. Pray God only that sight be given me, freedom of eyes to see with. I fear nothing then, nay, hope infinite things. It is a great misery for a man to lie, even unconsciously, even to himself. Also I feel at this time as if I should never laugh more, or rather say never sniff and whiffle and *pretend* to laugh more. The despicable titter of a " Duke," for example, seems to me quite criminally small.' (" Duke " was John Wilson's nickname for Francis Jeffrey.) ' Life is no frivolity, or hypothetical coquetry or whiffery. It is a great " world of truth," that we are alive, that I am alive ; that I saw the " Sweet Milk well " yesterday, flowing for the last four thousand years, from its three sources on the hill-side, the origin of Middlebie Burn ' (which runs through Scotsbrig farm), ' and noted the little dell it had hollowed out all the way, and the huts of Adam's posterity built sluttishly along its course, and a sun shining overhead ninety millions of miles off, and ' eternity all round, and life a vision, dream and yet fact woven with uproar on the loom of time.

' What you say of the sofa is interesting, more than I like to confess. May it be good for us ! I feel as if an immeasurable everlasting sofa was precisely the thing I wanted even now. Oh dear ! I wish I was there, on the simple greatness of that one, such as it is, and Goody might be as near as she liked. *Hadere nicht mit deiner Mutter, Liebste. Trage, trage ; es wird bald enden.* (Don't quarrel with your mother, dearest. Be patient ; be patient. It will soon end).'

Before coming home he discovered a blacksmith he could trust, who was glad to buy his old horse Harry cheap, and give him an easy old age. Returning about the first week in November with Ann Cook, the newly discovered maid, Carlyle took pains to make her comfortable, coaxing her to eat and giving her the inside place in the coach as the night was cold and wet.

A letter he had sent to his brother John after he returned to London reveals his feelings on this holiday.[1]

' That village of Ecclefechan, which I passed through once or twice, gave me the strangest unearthly feeling ;

[1] Copied from MS. 1896.

very sad, very ugly, yet not without a grandeur even a sacredness in the middle of such squalor. What is Eternal Rome, Jerusalem or Nazareth itself but a *temporary* set of huts and habitations, where Being begins, and is, and then is not—under God's *un*changing Heaven? Alas, I often feel as if Hades itself were slight change to me, from this fearful and wonderful mystery of a world; surely no greater miracle it were,—past finding out. Let us bow down in the dust; and in silence (since for the present one has no words) feel with the old wise, " tho *He* slay me, yet will I trust him." *Hier steh' ich; kann nichts anders; Gott hilf mir.'* (The words of Luther at Worms,—" Here I stand, and can do nothing else; God help me." The letter continues.—)

' On the whole, I often meditate on Christian things; but find as good as no profit in talking of them here. Most so-called Christians (I believe I should except the worthy Mr. Dunn) treat me instead with jargon of metaphysic formulas, or perhaps shovel-hatted Coleridgian moonshine. I admire greatly that of old Marquis Mirabeau '(what he said of his son in blame and Carlyle often quoted in praise of the Mirabeau of the Revolution):—'" *Il a humé toutes les formules!"* (He has swallowed all the formulas.) A man *should* " swallow " innumerable " formulas " in these days; and endeavour above all things to look with eyes. But whither this all? Unfortunately almost no-whither.—

' If I tell you that my poor scribble is again under way you must not grow weary of me and it: I have next to nothing else at present that seems to belong to me in this world.'

He was not long home before the history was advancing steadily. He made no secret to wife and relatives, however, that he reckoned on no profit from it when done, and expected to have to seek another trade. To this he was reconciling himself as he explained to his sister (4.12.1835): —" I am fast growing wearied of sickliness," etc. " I believe myself to have at bottom a very *healthy* frame of body, and soon or never, I ought to think of getting in possession of that. Let the whole world say or sing what it will, the course that has led a man into continual *ill*-health is a *wrong* course, and Nature herself surely warns him aloud to quit it." This would please his mother, whom he re-assured (24.12.1835) by a promise to keep

America " as the last shift," and stay " on this side of the water " as long as possible.

By this time Sterling had come to live in London and " work " with the pen. He was almost as frequently as Mill a companion of Carlyle in afternoon walks, but could not interest him in " Schleiermacher and others of that stamp." Another favourite was Mill's Paris acquaintance, Godefroi Cavaignac, who was now an exile in London. The high-minded Detrosier was dead and D'Eichthal gone to Greece. So it was a great blessing to have another living link with the best traditions of French politics. Perhaps the best help that Mill gave Carlyle was the acquaintance of such a friend. Carlyle declared Cavaignac " a Repub-lican to the bone," a " Bayard " or ideal knight, a man of natural politeness, punctilious yet sincere, and even better than a " Bayard " for he had " wit and fancy at command. We had many dialogues while *French Revolution* struggled through its last two volumes ; Cavaignac freely discussing with me, accepting kindly my innumerable dissents from him, and on the whole elucidating many little points to me."

He pleased Mrs. Carlyle by telling her,—" *Vous n'êtes pas Écossaise, Madame, désormais vous serez Française* ! " (You aren't a Scotchwoman, you'll be French in future !) She was soon writing :—

' We have another foreigner who beats all the rest to sticks, a French Republican of the right thorough-going sort, an " *accusé d'Avril* " ' (April criminal, presumably one of the press-prosecution victims,) ' who has had the glory of meriting to be imprisoned and nearly losing his head ; a man with that sort of dark half-savage beauty with which one paints a fallen angel, who fears neither heaven nor earth, for aught one can see, who fights and writes with the same passionate intrepidity, who is ready to dare or suffer, to live or to die without disturbing himself much about the matter ; who defies all men, and honours all women, and whose name is Cavaignac.'

He may be remembered by one of his best stories, which both Carlyle and his wife quoted often. Some boys were teasing a drunken Frenchman, who adjured them as gravely as any Quixote : " *Vous êtes des injustes. Je m'en appelle a la postérité* ! " (You are unfair in this. I appeal from you to posterity !)

XX

WRITING THE "HISTORY", "MIRABEAU", &c.

(1836)

THE history went on without further interruption to the end of the second volume, the intellectual electricity passing to its object quietly as if through a sufficient cable. There was a kind of spark in a letter to his brother John (26.1.1836).—

'Basil Montagu had a life benefaction all cut out and dried for me—No : it depended on the measure of gratitude whether it was to be ready for me or for another. A clerkship under him at the rate of £200 a year, whereby a man lecturing in mechanics' institutes in the evening, and doing etceteras, might live. I listened with grave fixed eyes to the sovereign of quacks, as he mewed out all the fine sentimentalities he had stuffed into this beggarly account of empty boxes—for which too I had been sent trotting many miles of pavements, though I knew from the beginning it could be only moonshine—and, with grave thanks for this potentiality of a clerkship, took my leave that night ; and next morning, . . . sent an indicative threepenny (a letter by post). My wish and expectation partly is that Montagudom generally would be kind enough to keep its own side of the pavement. Not very expressible is the kind of feeling the whole thing now raises in me—madness varnished over by lies which you see through and through. One other thing I could not but remark—the *faith* of Montagu wishing *me* for his clerk ; thinking the polar bear, reduced to a state of dyspeptic dejection, might safely be trusted tending rabbits. Greater faith I have not found in Israel. Let us leave these people. They shall hardly again cost me even an exchange of threepennies.'

A few weeks later the offer of an editorship at Lichfield was received through Mill apparently, and was treated more respectfully. He answered Mill :—' I can do nothing ' with it, ' least of all at present ' ; but he recommended

To Mill he was equally plain-spoken soon afterwards.—
" I am sick of the Girondins. To confess a truth, I find them
extremely like our present set of respectable Radical
Members. There is the same cold clean-washed patronising
talk about ' the masses,' a word, expressive of a thing,
which I greatly hate ; the same Formalism ; hidebound
Pedantry, Superficiality, narrowness, barrenness. I find
that the Mountain was perfectly under the necessity of
flinging such a lot of men to the Devil ; whither also I
doubt not *our* set will go, tho I hope in a milder manner,
our motion not being of that so extremely rapid kind."

When John went north, Carlyle resumed his place at
his desk, tho' far from rested enough. He could not afford
a longer holiday, and had to confess to himself (1.6.1836):—

' My dispiritment, my sorrow and pain are great, but I
strive to keep silent. Silence is the only method. I am
weary and heavy-laden, wearied of all things, almost of
life itself—yet not altogether. It is fearful and wonderful
to me. Often it seems as if the only grand and beautiful
and desirable thing in this dusty fuliginous chaos were to
die. Death ! The unknown sea of rest ! Who knows
what hidden harmonies lie there to wrap us in softness,
in eternal peace, where perhaps, and not sooner or elsewhere,
all the hot longings of the soul are to be satisfied and
stilled ?

' An eternity of life were not endurable to any mortal.
To me the thought of it were madness even for one day.
Oh! I am far astray, wandering, lost, " dyeing the thirsty
desert with blood in every footprint." Perhaps God and
His providence will be better to me than I hope. Peace,
peace ! words are idler than idle.'

He began by writing an essay on Mirabeau, which
Emerson called a Colossus by a Michael Angelo. " It
inspires self-trust," he wrote to Carlyle, " by teaching the
immense resources that are in human nature ; so I sent it
to be read by a brave man who is poor and decried. The
doctrine is indeed true and grand which you preach as by
cannonade, that God made a man, and it were well to stand
by and see what is in him."

In another interval of rest soon afterwards, Carlyle
wrote an article on the 23 volumes of the Parliamentary
History of the French Revolution by Buchez and Roux,
wherein he criticised both Mignet and Thiers with candour.

Mill was editing the Review in which these essays appeared
and remonstrating against some strokes of humour was
answered :—" It is burlesque ; but ought it not to be so ?
The Jacobins' Society and their doings are not sublime. . .
They are a mixture of truculence, audacity and absurdity,
not *without* something of sublimity, which, if the English
are ever to get at it, this . . . banter and bluster may be
the means of conveying to them."

Mill had not ventured to accept the *Diamond Necklace*,
but Fraser was taking that, and for these three papers
Carlyle was receiving over a hundred pounds, which made
him feel economically safe for another year,—long enough
to finish the Revolution history. " If I persist in this
wretched scribbling craft," he wrote to Mill on 2.5.1836,
in bidding him " cut and clip at discretion " in these essays,
—" I purpose rather to write more things in the currente
calamo manner " (running-pen way) ; " and to gain the
habit of doing it." In the meantine, however, he soon
added :—

> ' As to my quarrel with the Nominative-and-verb, I
> do assure you it is one that I daily reflect on with great
> sorrow ; but it is not a quarrel of my seeking. I mean
> that the common English mode of writing has to do with
> what I call *hearsays* of things ; and the great business for
> me, in which alone I feel any comfort, is recording the
> *presence*, bodily concrete coloured presence of things ;—
> for which the Nominative-and-verb, as I find it Here and
> Now, refuses to stand me in good stead. Hence our quarrel ;
> and separation, really an unblessed one ! I do believe,
> however, that I have not taken all I could have got from
> this poor Nominative-and-verb ; but I *will do it*—more
> and more as I grow wiser.'

There was no such pliability about the substance of his
doctrines, and he soon was telling Mill about his " Review,"
that tho' he noticed " nothing absolutely false or bad "
in it,—

> ' This is not *right* Radicalism yet . . . There is no right
> Radical in the Company if it be not yourself, and perhaps
> still more *my*self. " *Je ne trouve personne que moi qui a
> toujours raison; faut avouer, ma chère,*" said the Duchess
> de la Ferté, "*personne que moi !* " ' (" There's nobody but
> myself always right, I see," said the Duchess de la Ferté,
> " I must confess it, dear—nobody but myself ! ")

XXI

DOMESTIC EVENTS

(1836)

IN June he heard an Italian Improvisatore performing ; and receiving a ticket from Cavaignac saw Figaro at the French theatre, and thought the chief performer " the best comic actor " he ever saw. The chief news of the month, however, apart from the writing done, was a rare event, an instance of friction between him and his wife which a biographer can tell without fictioneering. In 1824 she had presented to him a " jemmy hat " of fashionable style, and he had begun dressing up to it, and fain would she have kept him doing so for ever. But Dr. John this summer being fresh from Italy had taught him how to be happy in hot weather, and soon after John went north, our hero reported to him (June, 1836) :—

‘ I have got my white hat ! A most noble broad-brim ; price 6/6 : of great comfort to me ; and this not by the brim alone, I find, but also by the size, which lets in the air about me, and prevents the intrusion of headache : I find my last three or four hats have been far too little. Jane shrieked, nay almost literally grat (or wept), when she first saw me in such headgear : however I persisted (resolute against headache) ; and she ’ compromised in short. On 6.6.1836 he was telling Mill he had promised not to wear it ‘ in her sight.’ But ‘ Cockneydom happily does not seem to mind me at all,’ he told his brother, and in a few days the afflicted wife condescended to say of the hat, " You do very well in it."

A few weeks later the tailor at Thornhill who appreciated *Characteristics*, Shankland, was making trousers for Carlyle, and the cockney tailors had lost a customer. The free and easy hat was having the effect foreseen by the woman who shrieked and almost wept at the sight of it. He was going to dress in future as cheaply as he comfortably could.

The Edinburgh teacher Robert Mitchell died this summer. "It gave me a very sorrowful emotion," Carlyle told his mother. "He was the oldest friend I had ; one of the most innocently, gently industrious, well-doing, persevering men, just one year older than I am." It had been Mitchell who set him thinking freely more than twenty years ago by lending him Hume's essays, and refusing to scoff with him at sceptical shoemakers, or continue a ' Divinity ' and go to Edinburgh to preach as an apprentice for the sake of appearances.

Another who died this summer was the philosopher of the Radicals, old James Mill, the father of John. On his deathbed he had longed for the food of his childhood when he had a mother to love him, and the Carlyles had supplied oatmeal and taught the women how to make porridge. He had not failed to remonstrate roundly with his son about "Mrs. Platonica Taylor," bidding him not "be in love with another man's wife," to which John answered with strange simplicity,—"I have no other feeling for her than I would have for an equally able man." The old man dead, there was no other to take Mr. Taylor's part. The woman returned to her husband's house occasionally, but played the invalid and neglected her duties. It was doubtful whether he could have divorced her, even if willing to undergo the indecent exposure of law-courts. Mill would have fought like a wild cat in a corner. Taylor did not try. If he had shot Mill, he would have been treated as a criminal. "There were children to be considered," as by-and-by Carlyle explained to Gavan Duffy enquiring. So Taylor left the couple to their fate. Carlyle was sorry for him as an innocent good man, "the pink of social hospitality." It was he who one evening this year [1] brought in a very "bright young man" called Mazzini to see Carlyle,—the best of the Italians who came to Cheyne Row, as Cavaignac was the best of the French.

The sea may be ignored, but not sex, which is everywhere. They who ignore it suffer. Mill had a bad breakdown this summer,—what a biographer has called " an obstinate derangement of the brain, accompanied by nervous twitchings in the face, and great mental depres-

[1] Dated by T. C., in W. Allingham, A Diary, p. 208.

sion." [1] Doctors might agree he should marry or take a
mistress and quit Mrs. Taylor ; but who was to tell him
that, after his father died ? He cut the Austins and the
Grotes, Miss Martineau and Roebuck, for dropping hints,
and the fear of some such offence seems to have made him
starchy when Carlyle spent a week-end with him at Dorking.
Mill continued talking, talking, talking, in an unnatural
way that sorely perplexed the visitor, who saw he was
ill and was anxious to help him but could not see what
to do, except of course to be scrupulously silent. Mill
got leave of absence. His brothers convoyed him to
Lausanne, where Mrs. Taylor took charge of him, and they
went to Italy together unattended. He was back to duty
in about three months.

Early in July Carlyle had started work on the third and
last volume, and the torrent of utterance was again like
spiritual electricity passing through a sufficient cable ;
but now he was himself becoming tired of it. Wherein
he was far from being a freak or even odd,—he was like
other people.

Thus he confessed to Emerson last June (27.6.1836) :—

' Of the whole mountain of miseries one grumbles at in
this life, the central and parent one is that you cannot utter
yourself. The poor soul sits struggling, impatient, longing
vehemently out towards all corners of the Universe, and
cannot get its hest delivered, not even so far as the voice
might do it. Imprisoned, enchanted, like the Arabian
Prince with half his body marble : it is really bad work.
Then comes bodily sickness. . . . Till at last one does rise,
like Eliphaz the Temanite ' (a friend of Job) ; ' states
that his inner man is bursting (as if filled with carbonic
acid and new wine), that by the favour of heaven he *will*
speak a word or two. Would it were come so far,—if it
be ever to come ! '

He often felt like that, as if " bursting with meaning that
would and must get out, a most indescribable uneasy
feeling, were it not for the hope," he said once. And now,
when he was in the very act of fully and freely uttering
himself, interpreting the greatest event for a thousand
years, like an inspired prophet whom humanity had to

[1] *J. S. Mill*, by Samuel Wellington in the *Westminster Review*, 1905,
pp. 11–30.

heed,—behold !—the only happiness he can see in front of him is to " get done with " it and be silent. In short, he was like other men. He confessed he had always plenty of " desperate hope," like his favourite Cervantes, and in the manner of Cervantes he defined " this world " as the " place of hope," which was reasonable enough for a definition. Man seldom is blest, but often about to be so.

The same is true of woman. Early in July his wife went off to Scotland, forwarded by her Liverpool uncle, who gave her a warm shawl as a birthday present. She was welcomed by her mother in the hotel at Dumfries, she reported, (19.7.1836), with " such an embracing and such a crying " that " the very Boots was affected with it, and spoke in a plaintive voice all morning after. Mother looks well ;—and is making a perfect fool of me with kindness. I was scarce home when she presented me with a purse she had worked for me,—filled with sovereigns ! So that I shall not be the poorer for my journey."

From London she got nothing but good news, to encourage her to stay as long as possible. In a bright long letter her husband mentioned he had completed the first section (September) of the third volume, and said :—

' A hundred pages more,' (= two hundred of print), ' and this cursed book is flung out from me. I mean to write with force of fire till that consummation ;—above all with the speed of fire ; still taking *intervals*, of course, and rest-ing. . . . For two or three days I have the most perfect rest now. Then Louis is to be tried and guillotined. Then the Gironde, etc., etc. : it all stands pretty fair in my head, nor do I mean to *investigate* much more about it, but to splash down what I know in large masses of colours ; that it may look like a smoke-and-flame conflagration in the distance, —which it is.'

The forecast any reader can now see was realized. Perhaps the most amusing bit of the letter is a glimpse of a fashionable reception of the period, (13.7.1836), a political one. The crush as a whole must be left to the imagination. There were "seven Persian princes with scimitars, turbans and long greenish gowns " for every-body to see ; and here is what maybe nobody but Carlyle saw,—what the actors themselves would hardly notice or remember.—

' I must tell you a thing I *saw* at Mrs. Buller's rout. Charles Buller led Cavaignac up to introduce him to a large lady, Mrs. Grote : Cavaignac went without struggling, tho' verily like a sheep led to the slaughter ; the presentation performed, he made I think *five* successive low bows to Mrs. Grote (a very shower of rapid bows) ; then, without uttering a word, reeled back, like a sheep *from* the slaughter (or a *calf*, for you know how he goes), and landing in a very elegant attitude, stood, five paces off, with his hat behind his back, looking out into space, and the general movement of the rout,—*this* whole Introduction, Acquaintance, Friendship being begun, carried on, finished and abolished with such incredible brevity.'

Here is a sparkle of the wit of Charles Buller himself.— " Destroy the Church of England ! " he cried. " You must be mad—it is the only thing between us and real religion." [1] But this cannot be dated.

In calling for Cavaignac, who was to be under " his escort," Carlyle had met Cavaignac's mother and sister, who had come to keep him company in exile, and remarked that the sister was " beautiful with courage and intelligence," tho' her features were plain and the mouth showed " temper." He may have been mistaken about the mouth, for tho' she played the piano incredibly well, she was continually suffering, and died before long. Her mother was half distracted, weeping and weeping and crying once what goes to one's heart still, like a shriek of sorrow and despair, —" *Ah, monsieur, c'est un màuvais esprit qui régit ce monde !* " (Oh Sir, it's an evil spirit which rules this world !)

Mrs. Welsh had the same infinite love for her daughter as Madame Cavaignac ; but this summer she seems to have thought as Dr. John did, that her daughter's main affliction was having too little to do, so that what she needed now was not nursing but occupation, exercise, and fresh air. Carlyle himself was writing to his wife,—" Be not solitary, be not idle." He recommended work she did easily, the translating of some papers for Cavaignac. Her cup of bitterness foamed over when her cousins from Liverpool came to fill the house and divide with her her

---

[1] *Life and Letters of B. Jowett*, by R. and L. Campbell : quoted in *Studies of a Biographer*, by L. Stephen, II, p. 140.

mother's attentions. A fortnight after the letter quoted last she wrote again (2.8.1836) :—

' It will not be long that there will be any need of Letters passing between us. Nothing could make living here at all expedient for me, except the conviction that I was thereby gaining physical good ; and such hope fades every day. I shall get better in London, or not get better, as may please the Upper Powers. In any case, " there is no use rebelling against Providence ",' (a quotation of a favourite expression of Dr. John) : ' but the rain it raineth every day ; there is no *victualling* to be had till ten,—at least not without an almost superhuman effort,' (meaning, not without asking for it), ' and I wake quite regularly at four ! There is no quiet to be had, except in your own bedroom, with the door locked ; for the children are in perpetual movement, seeking whom they may devour ; there is no bread to be had ' (of the kind I like, she implies). ' You know my mother's way : she will give you every-thing on earth, except the thing you *want* ; will do anything for you, except what you *ask* her to do. As for new milk, you may have it in any quantity ; but . . .'

But, in short, at the wrong time, and ditto the sip of brandy needed to make it wholesome, it cannot be got at the exact moment wanted without asking for it ! Was ever a woman so afflicted before ? She would have hurried home at once but that Dr. John, who should, she thought, have stayed in the north to attend to her, was now at Cheyne Row. Her husband in reply, (8.8.1836), adjured her to pray for the same " meekness, submission to the will of Heaven, which we so often laugh at in poor Jack," and to shake off " that Edinburgh style of mockery ! Me too with its hard withering influence, its momentary solacement, fataller than any pain, it had wellnigh " killed, in short, " but I flung it off, and am alive. Oh that my poor much-suffering Jane had done so too from the heart and recognised necessity was just ; that the thing stronger than we, was also the better (and the) wiser."

The letter was written in haste and not for publication, —it was not philosophically worded. He bade his wife look out " from those Templand windows. The earth is green, jewelled with many a flower. The sky (is) beautiful, over-head Come back again by easy stages. Be peaceable.

Harden not thy heart, but soften it. Open it to hope and me. Say all that is kind to your mother for me. Forgive her ' ways of doing.' They are *her* ways, tho' very torment-ing. God be with thee, my wee Goody." He resumed his sermon sixteen days later (24.8.1836), saying :—" Be not faithless, but believing. Do not fling life away as insupportable, despicable, but let us work it out and rest it out together, like a true two " ; and in his news of his brother he gives a glimpse of the interior at Cheyne Row.—

One Saturday, (20.8.1836), Dr. John said,—" Here is a ticket Lady Clare has sent me. Will you not go and see the King prorogue Parliament ? " " Sir," answered Carlyle, " if he were going to blow up Parliament with gunpowder, I would hardly go, being busy elsewhere."

John departed on a Monday, (29.8.1836), and on the Thursday following, (1.9.1836), Carlyle was walking fast to meet the coach by which his wife was travelling. It had arrived before its appointed hour, however, and with sudden surprise he recognised her trunk on the top of a Chelsea bus " in the rolling torrent of Fleet Street." She saw his face at the door. " No room, Sir, can't get in," said the Conductor. But he kept up with the bus till somebody went out, and then he got in. He had been writing " Regicide," Book II of Volume Three, that day ; and finished it on the Saturday week following, (10.9.1836) ; but the intellectual electricity was unseen, unheard. What he boasted about for weeks to come was recognising that trunk.

XXII

FINISHING

(1836–7)

IN October a painter from Scotland named Lewis, whom
Carlyle had met at Dumfries, called to say he had come
to settle in London and wanted to paint his portrait
" that it may do me good by exhibiting it next summer.
The picture after that will be yours," he added. " Do,"
said his wife earnestly, " before you grow quite old." So
on 23.10.1836 and other days he was giving Lewis sittings,
and getting " considerable amusement," he reported to
his mother, " from rugged Glasgow stories he kept telling
me all the while. One I have laughed at twenty times
since :—An old coal-miner was bragging of the great depths
he had been to in the heart of the earth ; a neighbour
wished to know, *how* deep specially ? The other said
"he could not tell how deep it might be, but he had ' many
a time heard the Deevil hoastin' " (or coughing). The
picture was finished in less than a month, and was
" glaringly recognisable." It was sent to his mother
by-and-by.

A picture shows the outside form and colour. Something more of Carlyle than that was seen in these months
by Harriet Martineau, who was brought to their house
about the middle of November by Miss Wilson of Eccleston
Street. Harriet was then only thirty-four, but four years
ago she had had the luck of Byron, and wakened to find herself famous, because of her stories illustrating Political
Economy. She had just returned to London from a two
years' visit to America, and had much to tell about it
likely to be useful to one thinking of lecturing there,—to
say nothing of Carlyle being the biographer of Schiller, the
" supreme idol " of her early days.[1]

She was so much run after that she saw enough company
without paying calls ; but by way of exception went to

---

[1] *Life of E. B., Lord Lytton*, by his grandson, II, p. 57.

see Carlyle, and liked him so much that as long as she lived in London she and Miss Wilson used to drive down together about once a fortnight. It was friendship at first sight on both sides. " She pleased us far beyond expectation," wrote Carlyle to his mother, (20.11.1836). " She is very intelligent-looking ; really of pleasant countenance ; was full of talk, tho' unhappily deaf almost as a post, so that you have to speak to her through an ear-trumpet." She asked him to dinner, and he decided to " cultivate the acquaintance a little."

By this time the third volume was far advanced ; but the effort required to finish it was almost beyond his strength.

' When I first knew him,' (wrote Harriet by-and-by),[1] ' he rarely slept, was woefully dyspeptic, and as variable as possible in mood. When my friend and I entered the little parlour our host was usually miserable. Till he got his coffee, he asked a lot of questions, without waiting for answers, and looked as if he was on the rack. After tea, he brightened and softened, and sent us home full of admiration and friendship, and sometimes with a hope that he would some day be happy.' Perhaps he was then getting coffee at the tea-table as a special favour. He liked it very hot. When once he was complaining it was cold, his wife said,—" Put a red-hot cinder in your mouth, that'll content you." Harriet goes on.—

' His manuscript is beautifully neat, when finished ; and a page holds a vast quantity of his small upright writing. But his own account of his toil in authorship is melancholy. He cannot sleep for the sense of the burden on his mind of what he has to say ; rises weary, and is wretched till he has had his coffee. No mode of expression pleases him ; and, by the time his work is out, his faculties are over-wearied. It is a great object in his case to have the evenings amused, that his work may not take possession of his mind before bedtime.' (Much of this resembles Mrs. Carlyle's talk and may be repetition of it ; but Miss Martineau was doubtless speaking her own opinion when she added :—) ' His excessive slowness is a perfect mystery to me,—considering that the work is burdensome. If he dwelt lovingly on its details, and on his researches, I could

---

[1] *Autobiography of H. Martineau*, I., pp. 377-378, and 432-3.

understand it. But perhaps he does, more than he is aware of.'

Which was a happy guess. He enjoyed his work so much that he was in continual danger of over-strain. At this time he was not only exhausted utterly, but worried as well, for he was facing the need of finding another means of livelihood, a serious thing for any man after forty. He could not go on much longer without an income, and knew better than to expect to get money soon from the history, tho' hopeful of its success. " Once or twice," as he remembered afterwards, when taking his constitutional and passing " among the flood of equipages at Hyde-Park Corner," and seeing the governing class in its glory, " I recollect sternly thinking : ' Yes ; and perhaps none of *you* could do what I am at ! ' But generally my feeling was, ' I will finish this Book, throw it at your feet ; buy a rifle and spade, and withdraw to the Transatlantic Wilder-nesses,—far from human beggaries and basenesses ! ' This had a kind of comfort to me ; yet I always knew too, in the background, that this would not practically do." It was too late for him to be a farmer. If he went to America now, it would be to live by lecturing.

In the last weeks of 1836 Cavaignac was resorting to his house more than usual, because he was afflicted by his sister's death. " It is a wild matter Death, to a man of his Credo," wrote Carlyle on 9.12.1836 to Mill, whom he was then persuading to employ Leigh Hunt, who was more hard-up than usual. Carlyle declared,—" I know not what Hunt would deliberately undertake that he would not render worth reading," and when Hunt was in haste to be paid before the article was written, Carlyle reassured Mill saying Hunt had " read for it."

Before the year ended the printers had started on the *French Revolution,* and on Thursday, (12.1.1837), Carlyle was so close to the end of writing it that he did not go out after early dinner as usual, but resumed the pen. Before the short winter's day was dark, he read the concluding sentences to his wife and said,—" Thank God it is done, Jeannie."

It was a damp tepid evening, but his walk was overdue. Leaving her to read the last sheet, for she had been reading steadily behind him, he remarked,—" What they will do with this book, none knows, my Jeannie, lass ; but they have not had, for a two hundred years, any book that came more truly from a man's very heart : and so let them trample it under foot and hoof as they see best ! "

" Pooh, pooh ! They cannot trample that," was her cheery answer ; and out he went up Gloucester Road towards the Parks, and rambled there at random as he was fond of doing till he came home for supper, and before going to bed he tied up the papers for the printer.

XXIII

PROOFS, &c.

(1837)

NEXT day (13.1.1837) he had walked far and wide, "about twenty miles," before dinner, and was treated by his wife to a bread pudding, which he told his mother he enjoyed, and he added to comfort her :—" My health is really better than anybody could expect. The foundations of this lean frame of mine must be as tough as wire."

Before the first set of proofs came to hand, he began writing letters that were overdue, as for example to John Sterling (17.1.1837).—

' This Book is disgusting to me by the faults of it ; the merits will not be seen for a long time. It is a wild savage Book, itself a kind of French Revolution ;—which perhaps, if Providence have so ordered it, the world had better *not* accept when offered it. With all my heart ! What I do know of it is that it has come hot out of my own soul ; born in blackness, whirlwind and sorrow ; that no man, for a long while, has stood speaking so completely alone under the Eternal Azure, in the character of man only, or is likely for a long while so to stand. It has come near to choking the life out of me.'

He enquired about Sterling himself who was living near Bordeaux for his health, and tactfully comforted the invalid for having to live abroad instead of in London by describing the London fog at the time of writing. Apropos an announcement that Sterling was 'rather *quitting* Philosophy and Theology,' he went on :—' I predict that you will quit them more and more. I will give it you as my decided prognosis that the two Provinces in question are become Theorem, Brain-web and Shadow ; wherein no earnest soul can find solidity for itself. Shadow, I say ; yet the shadow *projected* from an everlasting

Reality that is within ourselves :—quit the Shadow, seek the Reality.

' Mill is in better health, still not in good. He has influenza and I see little of him. *The set of people he is in, is one that I have to keep out of. No class of mortals ever profited me less. There is a vociferous platitude in them, a mangy hungry discontent ; their very joy like that of a thing scratching itself under disease of the itch.*[1] Mill was infinitely too good for them ; but he would have it, and his fate would. I love him much as a friend *frozen within ice* for me.'

Nevertheless Mill was soliciting a spare set of proofs, that he might have an essay upon the history ready before it was published, and this, he said, " not for the Book's sake, but for his Review's." The proof-correcting beginning 18.1.1837 continued to the end of April, with many pleasant intervals of rest, as Carlyle explained to his mother (18.2.1837).—

' Sometimes (the printers) keep me busy, tumbling among all sorts of rubbish, broken pieces of paper, books, slips, ink and confusion,—really like a man dighting (or sifting) chaffy corn in a barn, for the whole blessed day ; then they will give me a holiday for two days. The Book comes out like *dighted* (sifted) corn. I never knew till now on looking at it this second time what a thing it was,— a perfect oak-clog. Many a man will find it a hard nut to crack.'

His meaning was more fully expressed to his brother John in Rome (17.2.1837). After explaining how much work he was giving the printers, making each Chapter a Book, subdivided into many chapters with epigrammatic headings, cutting out and adding and in short " incredibly " improving it, were it only by " letting in a great deal of daylight into it," he said :—

' I find " on a general view " that the Book is one of the *savagest* written for several centuries ; it is a Book written by a *wild man*, a man disunited from the fellowship of the world he lives in ; looking King and beggar in the face

---

[1] Italics added.

with an indifference of brotherhood, an indifference of contempt,—that is really very extraordinary in a respectable country.   The critic of a respectable nature cannot but be loud.   There is no word in his belly harder than the words *it* utters, by implication or directly, about him and his. A wild man ;—pray God only that it be *à man !*   And then buff away, smite and spare not : the thing you can kill, I say always, deserves not to live.'

The weather was worse than usual in the beginning of the year, " mud and fog and drizzle " causing more than the usual sickness, so that " week after week " the " funeral bell never ceased."   Mrs. Carlyle had influenza three times in a few months, and lay coughing in a room adjoining her husband's workroom on the first floor, while clever Dr. Morrah, fearing consumption, looked grave and kept her in bed as much as possible, adjuring her to be careful and send for her mother, which at last she did.   But on Friday (17.2.1837), long before her mother came, the sky was blue again, " inexpressibly cheering " to Carlyle, who told his mother he was walking about all that day, " blessing Heaven that a new year was born out of the winter's blackness," and concluded his letter next day, (18.2.1837) :—

' But I must close this up : the sun is getting out in spite of a showery morning, and I ought to fare forth and take the good of it.   Blessed sun ! it is sent to all living ; and the whole wealth of the Bank of England is not equal to a beam of it.   We hope it will get the length of Annan too. These hideous wet-blankets of cloud-vapours must get away, and summer come back to us.   The printer's devil (so they call the little boy that comes and goes) will be here to-night with work, work! I ought to be aired and fresh.'

Mrs. Carlyle wrote to Sterling in February :—

' The tag-raggery of printers' devils drives one from pillar to post.   *Quelle vie !* (What a life !) Let no woman who values peace of soul ever dream of marrying an author. But this I observe to you in confidence ; should I state such a sentiment openly, I might happen to get myself torn in pieces by the host of my husband's lady admirers, who already, I suspect, think me too happy in not knowing my happiness. You cannot fancy what way he is making with the fair intellects here ! There is Harriet Martineau presents him with her ear-trumpet with a pretty blushing air of coquetry, which would almost convince me out of belief in her identity ! And Mrs. Pierce Butler bolts in upon his studies, out of the atmosphere as it were, in riding habit, cap and whip, my Scotch domestic remaining entirely in a nonplus whether she had let in " a leddy or a gentleman ! " And then there is a young American beauty ! " Snow and rose-bloom " throughout, not as to clothes merely, but complexion also ; large and soft, and without one idea, you would say, to rub upon another! And this charming creature publicly declares herself his " ardent admirer," and I heard her with my own ears call out quite passionately at parting with him,—" Oh, Mr. Carlyle, I want to see you to talk a long time about— *Sartor* " ! SARTOR, of all things in the world ! What could such a young lady have got to say about SARTOR, can you imagine ? '

The girl may have meant to tell how popular it already was as a book in America.

The American news was exciting curiosity in London, and there were many and various expectations, such as had brought the painter Lewis to their house. Harriet Martineau lamenting how Carlyle had to suffer was comforted by the solid Allan Cunningham, " who knew and loved him well," she said. He told her :—" Carlyle will be very well and happy enough, if he gets a little more fame."

" Are you in earnest ? " she asked.

" I am," he answered, " and sure I'm right. You'll see that I am." [1]

She did not think so. She felt sure Carlyle was not writing for fame, declaring her mature opinion in her Autobiography :—

' He seemed to me just the man to write because he needed to utter himself, without ulterior considerations. One day I was dining there alone. I had brought over from America twenty-five copies of his SARTOR RESARTUS as re-printed there ; and, having sold them at the English price, I had some money to put into his hand. I did put

[1] *Autobiography of H. Martineau*, I. p. 384, etc.

it into his hand the first time : but it made him uncomfortable, and he spent it in a pair of signet rings for his wife
and me.   This would never do ; so, having imported and
sold a second parcel, the difficulty was what to do with the
money.   My friend (Miss Wilson) and I found that Carlyle
was ordered weak brandy and water instead of wine ; and
we spent our few sovereigns on French brandy of the best
quality, which we carried over one evening, when going
to tea.   Carlyle's amusement and delight at first, and all
the evening after, whenever he turned his eye towards the
long-necked bottles, showed us that we had made a good
choice.   He declared that he had got a reward for his
labours at last : and his wife asked me to dinner, all by
myself, to taste the brandy.

' We three sat round the fire after dinner, and Carlyle
mixed the toddy while Mrs. Carlyle and I discussed some
literary matters, and speculated on fame and the love of
it.'   (It was the fashion then to make a fuss about fame
and think it fine to labour to win it, as simple-minded
persons still suppose.)   ' Then Carlyle held out a glass of
his mixture to me with,—
' " Here, take this,—It is worth all the fame in England." '

Perhaps this talk was what made him remark in a
letter to his brother John at Rome, (21.3.1837) :—" The
longer I live ' fame' seems to me a more wretched Kimmera "
(The Frenchman Detrosier's version of Chimera) ; " really
and truly a thing to be shied (at), if it came ; I think of
Rousseau's case sometimes ; and pray God I may be
enabled to break whinstones rather, or cut peats, and
maintain an *un*fevered heart.   God keep us all, I pray again,
from the madness of Popularity !   I never knew one it
did not *injure* ; I have known strong men whom it killed."

XXIV

THE FRENCH REVOLUTION

(1837)

THE *French Revolution* by Carlyle is as good a history as any yet written, and the publication of it was a more important event than Jena or Waterloo. It showed that righteousness was a law of nature, like gravitation, and that the evolution of society in Europe was inevitable and right. The feudal fighters, like Kilkenny cats, were giving place or changing to commercial scramblers, the money grabbers of to-day, who must in turn give place to their betters, communities of workers. In the good time coming surely like the movement of the stars, but slowly, as the flowers come and the trees, we shall be ashamed of riches without work, and only the right sort of people shall be held in honour. The glimpses science gives of the long abysms of time behind us should teach us patience and hope. The more clearly the truth of things is seen, the less is the danger of confusion and war.

Whatever happens this history is like Gibbon's *Roman Empire*, or Thucydides, not likely to be superseded soon. What makes a book of history good or bad? If it is not a good story, it is not really history, and if it is not true, it is second-rate fictioneering. It must carry conviction. But truth is not confined to details, as pedants suppose. For a historian to be truthful, he must be wise as well as impartial, not only willing but able to comprehend great men and sympathize with all kinds, and that is why good histories are so few, and joint-stock histories inevitably failures. Heaps of facts can no more make a history than paints make a picture.

Once more as often of old when light came into the world, it was not welcomed. It is not merely that men love darkness rather than the light, because their deeds are evil. That is not always true; but the light of the mind is like the body's,—it must come gradually to be pleasant, without any sudden change. For more than forty years the English had believed the bosh their rulers told them about the Revolution. The truth was sure to shock them.

The " University taboo " of Carlyle is like the long " taboo " of Shakespeare there, like a bank of clouds that veils the rising sun. The modern pedants serving money-grabbers are sometimes stupid enough to be sincere, or at least as sincere as the shabby scholastics who served the church in the same way in the middle ages. But they can no more supersede Carlyle than Shakespeare, and the ugly gods of the money-bags shall follow the gods of bullets and knives and the other mumbo-jumbos of the past into oblivion. " The earth hath bubbles as the water has, and these are of them."

The review that Mill wrote was a ' courageous article,' Carlyle told him, (18.7.1837). It ' said openly of my poor Book what I durst not myself dream of it, but should have liked to dream, had I dared '. Undoubtedly it " accelerated " the success of the history, as Mill boasted all his life, correctly.[1]

' This is not so much a history, as an epic poem,' said he, ' and notwithstanding this, the truest of histories. His characters are realities, like those of Shakespeare's plays. An ordinary historian sets before us mainly his *opinions*. Mr. Carlyle brings the thing before us in the concrete, and in short brings us *acquainted* with persons, things, and events, before he suggests to us what to think of them. This is the very process by which he arrives at his own thoughts.

' Differing partially from some of Mr. Carlyle's views, we hold his theory of the Revolution to be true,—it was the breaking down of a great Imposture. The King and Feudal Nobility and the Clergy' had in short become insincere and good for nothing.

' Sympathy with human nature looks out from every page. You meet passages of grave drollery unsought for, arising from the simple statement of fact and true natural feeling, and soon after comes a soft note as of dirge music, or solemn choral song of old Greek tragedy, which makes the heart too full for utterance, and forces you to close the book

---

[1] *Autobiography of J. S. Mill*, 1873, p. 217,—see the *Early Essays of J. S. Mill*, edited, 1897, by J. W. M. Gibbs, pp. 271–323.

and rest for a while. Again there are aphorisms which deserve to live for ever; characters drawn with a few touches, much genuine philosophy. A most original book in its complete sincerity. When we consider that Wordsworth, Coleridge and others, whose deviation from the beaten track was but a stone's throw compared with Mr. Carlyle's, were ignominiously hooted out of court, and had to wait for a second generation, we might well imagine that the same or a worse fate awaits Mr. Carlyle.'

The quotations were well-chosen and copious. He leaves modern critics little to say but ditto. Surely it was a great feat to write a criticism in which there is nothing out of date after eighty years except perhaps the " Mr."

Carlyle was as scrupulous about accuracy as Newton, and refers to his authorities in footnotes whereby his statements can be checked. His essay on the sinking of the Vengeur correcting on new evidence a thrilling episode in his history, after it had been published, is a fine example of loyalty to fact.

Perhaps the most important correction in detail is that Varennes was distant from Paris not 69 miles but 150, so that in 1791 the fugitive king had been going between six and seven miles an hour, and not between three and four. There are several places called Varennes.

The greatest of French Historians, Michelet, spent over eight years on the period covered by Carlyle's work. The archives were open to him and he was on the spot, and his history is three times as long. Yet the differences between the historians are so trifling as to justify the French critics who call Carlyle the " English Michelet,"—only let them remember that it was from 1845 to 1853 that Michelet was writing on the Revolution. He followed Carlyle—in more than time.

Carlyle and Michelet agreed in blaming the men in power and not the people. Perhaps the chief correction which Michelet's greater command of documents enabled him to make on Carlyle's facts concerns the episode of the Diamond Necklace, rather than the French Revolution itself. The alterations needed are important.[1] The best documentary evidence was destroyed, which made falsification easy,

---

[1] *Histoire de France*, by Michelet, Vol. XIX and Chapters XVI, XVII, and XVIII, as well as his *History of the French Revolution*.

and the judges winked at the tricks of Abbé Georgel.
La Valois was a mistress of Rohan, and before she heard
of the Necklace she was being maintained so sumptu-
ously from public money he embezzled, that she
lived in a large house with fourteen servants. Neither
she nor Lamotte her husband needed to steal; and
the Diamond Necklace was taken to the Cardinal's
house. Lamotte was sent to London at the Cardinal's
expense to sell small diamonds detached from it. He
rendered proper accounts, was allowed a commission,
and returned in due course. But Rohan was the head
of the church; and to save the face of church and court,
the trial " behind closed doors " was staged as much as
possible to make scapegoats of La Valois and her husband.
She was controlled at the trial by terror of torture and
hope of impunity; and anything she did blab was not
written down. "Abbé Georgel himself admits that special
care was taken not to write anything indiscreet."

The cunning of the Court overreached itself. The priest
was whitewashed, but the Queen's good name was spoiled,
as both the historians have described. What is characteristic of Carlyle is that where he had to guess and mistook
or was misled, it was by thinking too well of sundry.

The unfortunate Queen, Marie Antoinette, " the widow
Capet," seemed loathesome to the French reformers, like
a Goddess Kali revelling in blood; while the ecstatic Burke,
like a well-paid showman, proclaimed her an outraged
divinity, a beautiful blend of lady-love and Mother of
God, which Tories ever since have tried to believe, dis-
sembling dutifully their inevitable doubts. But now when
the essential facts are sure, the only question is between
Michelet's interpretation and Carlyle's, and the remarkable
thing is that her condemnation is based on conservative
principles.

Michelet was like Burke in judging her as a Queen.
She was guilty of senseless extravagance and many other
mistakes, such as partiality to her native Austria. She
was foolishly susceptible to the selfish pressure of courtiers,
and her faults helped on the catastrophe. No doubt
there is evidence to support these findings,—Michelet is
right and Burke is wrong, to that extent; but Carlyle,
who laughed at hereditary kingship, saw the woman inside
the queen, and judged her accordingly. *She was a woman
put in a false position by no fault of her own.* Her

mistakes were the natural result of her simplicity. She meant well, stood by her husband and children, and did her duty bravely as well as she saw how, and suffered so much that it is stupid not to pity her, a good woman in affliction. There is a touch of humane genius in the allusion to her son's fate.—" The boy, once named Dauphin, was taken from his mother while she yet lived ; and given to one Simon, a cordwainer. Simon taught him to drink, to swear, to sing the *carmagnole*. Simon is now gone, the poor boy lies perishing, ' his shirt not changed for six months' ; amid squalor and darkness, lamentably,—*so as none but poor Factory Children and the like are wont to perish, and NOT be lamented !* "[1]

This was typical. Here was Shakespeare's ideal imported into history, and the mirror held up to nature. The English " ruling classes " were bewildered. Their scribes have been trying ever since to belittle the book in vain. The bubbles of Burke were burst and bothered nobody any more. He was blasted incidentally, without an effort, and only mentioned when needed as a witness.—

' Great Burke has raised his great voice long ago ; eloquently demonstrating that the end of an epoch is come, to all appearance the end of Civilised Time. Him many answer ; but the great Burke remains unanswerable ; " the Age of Chivalry *is* gone," and could not but go, having now produced the still more indomitable Age of Hunger.

' A set of mortals has risen, who believe that Truth is not a printed Speculation, but a Practical Fact ; that Freedom and Brotherhood are possible in this Earth, supposed always to be Belial's, which " the Supreme Quack " was to inherit ! Who will say that Church, State, Throne, Altar are not in danger ; (and) the sacred Strongbox itself ?

' A Glorious Revolution, oversetting State-Prisons and Feudalism ; publishing, with outburst of Federative Cannon, in face of all the Earth, that Appearance is not Reality, how shall it subsist among Governments which, if Appearance is *not* Reality, are—one knows not what ? In death feud, and internecine wrestle and battle, it shall subsist with them ; not otherwise.

' Rights of Man are jabbered of in China and Japan. Where will it stop ? Not the remotest Dalai-Lama shall

---

[1] Italics added.

now knead his dough-pills in peace.—Hateful to us, as is the Night ! Bestir yourselves, ye Defenders of Order ! They do bestir themselves : all Kings and Kinglets.

' High Potentates with Emigrants publish (from) Pilnitz their hope and their threatenings, their Declaration that it was " the common cause of Kings."

' Where a will to quarrel is, there is a way. Might one not *partition* France, as we have done Poland, and so pacify it ?

' Look where you will, immeasurable Obscurantism is girdling this fair France, which, again, will not be girdled by it.' (And so the result was) ' WAR.'

In the same way as he hardly mentions Burke, so he says little of Paine, " the Rebellious Needleman," who was in Paris and a " Deputy ", but in the background. The controversy between Paine and Burke was important to English-speakers, but there was no room for it in this history. On the morrow after Louis XVI decamped from the Tuileries, however, there is a welcome glimpse of Paine. Robespierre was shivering at the thought of " a Saint-Bartholomew of Patriots " ; but bold Tom Paine, along with " fervent Achille de Châtelet," plastered Paris with placards that there " *must be a republic*." Madame Roland tried to encourage Robespierre by the sight of them, and spoke of ' preparing men's minds for a Republic. " A Republic ? " said the Seagreen, with one of his dry husky *un*sportful laughs, " What is that ? " O seagreen Incorruptible, thou shalt see ! '

Many a time some strange opinion which the facts had led Carlyle to form appears plainly ; but always the reader feels free to form his own and can be sure there is a minimum of mistake and no humbug at all. The excitement culminates in the third volume with the clash of the common people of Europe against the German kings and other killers by trade. Like Homer's epic or a bas-relief sculpture, the history does not conclude but merely ceases. The Napoleonic wars were one sequel ; and another was the Willie-and-Nicky war of 1914.

Battles are a bore, and like bodily diseases only worth a look to see how to minimize the mischief they do and the risk of recurrence. The *gabble about glory* is out of date. But the French Revolution marks a stage in the social evolution of mankind.

Some suppose Carlyle was thinking of this or that in
current politics when writing, but it is easy to guess
too much, like those who spell out mysteries in Shakespeare. When Carlyle intended an allusion, he generally
left no room for doubt about it, as when he quoted the
1836 Report of the Irish Poor Law Commission, and said
the " Sans-potato " Irishman was more miserable than the
French Sansculotte, who had at least a hope of deliverance.
—" Starvation is starvation.—Such things go on in silence
peaceably :—and Sansculottisms follow them." What
most rejoiced Carlyle in the Revolution was the setback it
gave to Snobbery and Imposture. He told the moral
of his tale like an old-fashioned Scotch preacher, as downright and dogmatic as if he had been giving a lesson in
mathematics.—

' That there be no second Sansculottism in our Earth
for a thousand years, let us understand well what the first
was ; and let rich and poor of us go and do *otherwise*.

' Aristocracy of Feudal Parchment has passed away with
a mighty rushing ; and now, by a natural course, we arrive
at Aristocracy of the Moneybag. It is the course through
which all European Societies are, at this hour, travelling.
Apparently a still baser sort of Aristocracy ? An infinitely
baser ; the basest yet known.

' In which, however, there is this advantage, that, like
Anarchy itself, it cannot continue. Thought is stronger
than Artillery-parks. The Heavens send us generous
hearts into every generation. And now what generous heart
can pretend to itself, or be hoodwinked into believing, that
Loyalty to the Moneybag is a noble Loyalty ? Mammon,
cries the generous heart out of all ages and countries, is
the basest of known Gods, even of known Devils. In him
what glory is there, that ye should worship him ? No
glory discernible ; not even terror : at best, detestability,
ill-matched with despicability ! Generous hearts, discerning, on this hand, wide-spread Wretchedness, dark
without and within, moistening its ounce-and-half of
bread with tears ; and, on that hand, mere Balls in
flesh-coloured drawers, and inane or foul glitter of such sort,
—cannot but ejaculate, cannot but announce : Too much,
O divine Mammon, somewhat too much !—The voice of
these, once announcing itself, carries *fiat* (let it be !) and

pereat (let it cease to be !) in it, for all things here below. Meanwhile we will hate Anarchy as Death, which it is ; and the things worse than Anarchy shall be hated *more*. Surely Peace alone is fruitful. Anarchy leaves vacancy behind. Know this also, that out of a world of Unwise nothing but an Unwisdom can be made. Arrange it as thou wilt, it remains the new prey of new quacks and unclean things, the latter end of it slightly better than the beginning. Who can bring a wise thing out of men unwise ? Not one."

" Slightly better " be it noted. Carlyle as a historian is matter-of-fact, and also optimist and ever-hopeful. It may be his purity of soul. It is an old saying that— " Corruption and Pessimism are twins." There is no warrant in history for despair. But there is no lesson plainer than the burden of the books of Carlyle,—behold the truth. We must never blink reality or look for anything but evil results from evil-doing. In short, we must learn sense somehow. Like other laws of Nature, Justice must be studied and obeyed—our world can never be a paradise for fools. Events have confirmed his grim conclusion. The puppets in " power " continue trying to keep earth as horrible as it was in the " middle ages," stinking like a slaughter-house for the pleasure and profit of the idle. Mammon is as bad as Mars. But still Humanity is moving upwards as surely as the earth swings round the sun, and the sun keeps shining, whether we see it or not.

What Carlyle wrote was no more meant for eloquence than a demonstration in Euclid, and it is equally plain. It was a great comfort to the politicians that few of the " rabble " could read, and that not many readers were likely to heed Carlyle. Which is also a reason why so many who know better pretend that he is hard to understand, altho in truth it is only needful to read his history slowly to find it as plain and palpable as the daily papers, and infinitely more trustworthy. Indeed it may be said that the fashion of epigrammatic headings which began in the American newspapers was suggested by this history ; and perhaps the best thing ever said of his style was Emerson's remark that it was conversational. It was not of style but substance that Milnes was thinking when he wrote in his note-book :—" Carlyle's writings make on me the impression of the sound of a single

hatchet in the aboriginal forests of North America." [1]
He seems less of a pioneer to us because he was so often
both original and right, and much that appeared to be
strange and doubtful in 1837 is commonplace to-day ;
which only enables us to enjoy the more the wonderful
story told so well that we feel as if living at the time and
looking on. [2]   He said himself by and-by, when the " French
Revolution " was mentioned, [3]—" I put more of my life
into that than into any of my books."

[1] *R. M. Milnes* (*Lord Houghton*), by Wemyss Reid, I, 193.
[2] The best edited edition is the illustrated edition by John Holland Rose
(*Bell*).
[3] *Literary Recollections* by F. Espinasse, p. 55.

INDEX